In Search of
New Social Democracy

"*In Search of New Social* Democracy is an extremely timely and helpful book. It is hard to imagine solving the world's problems without an effective and powerful democratic left. Unlike most treatments that attempt to understand developments on the contemporary left, Törnquist examines social democratic movements in the global North and South, generating insights and lessons that should be of interest to scholars, practitioners and concerned citizens across the globe."
    Sheri Berman, Professor of Political Science, Bernard College, Columbia University

"What defines Social Democracy, how has it changed over generations of struggles, what does it look like in the Global South and what are the challenges it faces going forward? These are the ambitious questions that Törnquist, building on a lifetime of fieldwork and critical reflection, tackles in this sophisticated and highly readable and engaging book. Drawing on a sweeping comparative and historical analysis as well as a grounded understanding of the contextual and political complexities of making Social Democracy work, this book is a must-read for all those who care about the contemporary crisis of global capitalism."
    Patrick Heller, Professor of Sociology and International
    and Public Affairs, Brown University

"This is the best book I know to connect the post-World War 2 democratization in Europe and the former colonies with that of the third wave. It is a very rare for one person to have such a long and intensive engagement with grassroots democratization movements, in such a variety of countries, driven by such a combination of passion and intellectual rigour. The many sketches of dedicated activists the author has met over the years are delightful. (…) His highly analytical book is at the same time a personal memoir. (…) A lifetime dedicated to fieldwork has given the book a historical depth that no library study or fly-in-fly-out consultancy have ever had."
    Gerry van Klinken, Professor of Southeast Asian Social and Economic History,
    University of Amsterdam and Royal Netherlands Institute
    of Southeast Asian and Caribbean Studies

"In this engaging book Törnquist draws on a lifetime of research on progressive democratic politics in Indonesia, the Philippines and the Indian state of Kerala, together with his experience of activism at home in Sweden, to reflect on the prospects now for Social Democracy. Törnquist's call, finally, for broad alliances in support of rights and welfare reforms, as the basis for the renewal of Social Democracy, has a particular resonance in the context of recovery from the Covid pandemic."
    John Harriss, Professor of International Studies, Simon Fraser University
    and Centre for Modern Indian Studies, University of Göttingen

"Olle has taken on a massive project, comparing the attempts at progressive social democratic reform in four separate countries. He succeeds, combining detailed historical accounts with sweeping conclusions. He succeeds not just with exacting scholarship, but because he shares the hopes and goals of the parties he studies."
    Dr. Joel Rocamora, former President Akbayan party, current Executive Director,
    Institute for Popular Democracy, Quezon City

"This is an absolutely remarkable book by one of our most incisive analysts of Social Democracy's limits and possibilities. The current volume is anchored in rigorous analytics, extensive and careful empirics, and animated by a comparative imagination (...) Based on an extensive career's worth of work, it is part global survey of the state of Social Democracy today, part personal reflection and narrative on a career well-spent, part rich portrait of the people and collectives who seek change, and part impassioned plea that we not abandon the promise of Social Democracy. (...) I am thankful he has written it as honestly as he has, for it is not a book about endings. As he shows, Social Democracy can – and must – be reinvented to reverse setbacks of recent years and face the global challenges of the ones ahead."

Gianpaolo Baiocchi, Professor, Global and Latin American Social Movements, Gallatin School, New York University

"*In Search of New Social Democracy* is a must-read for all wanting to understand the global crisis of Social Democracy and why adjustment to current globalization is insufficient for the rebirth of a strong progressive movement. Törnquist convincingly argues that despite the root causes of the crisis stemming from an untamed market driven globalization, the answers of Social Democracy far too often set aside the global dimensions. Only through an internationalist restart – based on broad alliances, North-South partnerships and transformative strategies fighting elitist democracy – can trust and support in Social Democracy be restored. Holding important keys to the reinvention of Social Democracy I am hopeful that Törnquist's "end-book" is not an end but rather a new beginning."

Anna Sundström, Secretary General, Olof Palme International Center, Stockholm

"Törnquist draws on insights accrued over a lifetime of research to explain why reformist social movements have not made more of a difference in India, Indonesia and the Philippines. Part personal memoir, part intellectual musing, this very accessible book delves into an eclectic selection of 'moments' across time in each of these settings, searching for hints that a social democratic vision for a new world order could yet prevail."

Michele Ford, Professor of Southeast Asian Studies, University of Sydney

In Search of
New Social Democracy

Insights from the South – Implications
for the North

Olle Törnquist

ZED

LONDON · NEW YORK · OXFORD · NEW DELHI · SYDNEY

Zed Books
Bloomsbury Publishing Plc
50 Bedford Square, London, WC1B 3DP, UK
1385 Broadway, New York, NY 10018, USA
29 Earlsfort Terrace, Dublin 2, Ireland

First published in Great Britain 2022

Library of Congress Cataloging-in-Publication Data
Names: Törnquist, Olle, author.
Title: In search of new social democracy : insights from the South – implications
for the North / Olle Törnquist.
Description: London ; New York : Zed Books, 2021. | Includes bibliographical
references and index.
Identifiers: LCCN 2021009042 (print) | LCCN 2021009043 (ebook) | ISBN 9780755639762
(hardback) | ISBN 9780755639779 (paperback) | ISBN 9780755639786 (epub) | ISBN
9780755639793 (pdf) | ISBN 9780755639809 (ebook other)
Subjects: LCSH: Democracy–Developing countries. | Social justice–Developing countries. |
North and south. | Political development. | Developing countries–Politics and government.
Classification: LCC JF60.T669 2021 (print) | LCC JF60 (ebook) | DDC 321.8–dc23
LC record available at https://lccn.loc.gov/2021009042
LC ebook record available at https://lccn.loc.gov/2021009043

ISBN: HB: 978-0-7556-3976-2
         PB: 978-0-7556-3977-9
         ePDF: 978-0-7556-3979-3
         eBook: 978-0-7556-3978-6

Typeset by Integra Software Services Pvt Ltd.,
Printed and bound in Great Britain

To find out more about our authors and books visit www.bloomsbury.com
and sign up for our newsletters.

Contents

Illustrations

Figure

Maps

Pictures

Timeline

Preface

This is my 'endbook', for all who contributed their insights, and for those who wish to benefit from them when moving on.

In retrospect, I have tried to distil the conclusions from the studies I engaged in during half a century, of why it was so difficult to renew broadly framed Social Democracy in the Global South before and during the third wave of democracy, how this matters in the North too, and if a new Social Democracy is feasible.

To this end, I have re-read, of course, my main books and articles within which there is a detailed substantiation of the arguments and conclusions in this book. (There is a guide in the list of references, which also includes additional references.) But to bring alive how I arrived at my conclusions, I have also returned to the notes from interviews as well as to logbooks, conversations and photographs. When much of it heaped up on the floor of my studio, I tried at one point to count the number of transcribed in-depth interviews, arriving at some 1,635, but failed to quantify the logbook-notes from visits, meetings, focus group discussions and seminars. There were also some 1,800 structured six to eight hour-long interviews by assistants, for our participatory assessment of Indonesia's democratization.

The exact numbers do not matter, but they indicate that the work has been a collective effort. Most of those who contributed are mentioned in the basic reports, listed in the references. They also include details of the selected conversations cited in this book. Here and now, however, I cannot but thank you all for sharing insights and analyses, for good and sometimes intense discussions and for investing your time in the idea of probing the challenges of Social Democracy from a sympathetic but critical point of view as well as for your trust, which I hope I have not abused.

With your permission, I wish to mention my *initial* mentors anyway. 'At home', Lars Rudebeck and the late Björn Beckman; in Indonesia, the late Arief Budiman, the late Joesoef Isak and my first assistant Wiratmo Probo; in the Philippines, Randy and the late Karina Constantino David; in Kerala, P. K. Michael Tharakan and Thomas Isaac; in West Bengal, Nripen Bandyopadhyay and the late Boudhayan Chattopadhyay; in New Delhi, Neera Chandhoke.

I started to work on this book in 2009. It took many scrapped outlines and draft manuscripts to find how to prioritize and make sense of the insights, stories and conclusions. And as the years passed, there had to be updates too. I also wished to widen the perspectives to Scandinavia, and to some extent South Africa and Brazil. During this period, I benefitted immensely from joint work and generous comments and advice from, in particular, in Indonesia, Lena Avonius, Teresa Birks, Luky Djani, M. Nur Djuli, Vedi Hadiz, Eric Hiariej, Gerry van Klinken, Max Lane, the late Cornelis Lay, Shadia Marhaban, Stanley Adi Prasetyo, the late A.E. Priyono, Willy P. Samadhi, Purwo Santoso, Amalinda Savirani, Osmar Tanjung, Surya Tjandra and the assistance of Nusya Kuswantin and Debbie Prabawati; in the Philippines, from Marie Chris Cabreros, Joel Rocamora, Teresa and Ed Tadem, and Nathan Quimpo; in Kerala, from K. K. George, P. K. Michael Tharakan and T. M. Thomas Isaac; in New Delhi, from Neera Chandhoke, Niraja Gopal Jayal and the assistance of Radhika Chatterjee; about Brazil, from Einar Braathen and Gianpaolo Baiocchi; about South Africa, from Jeremy Seekings and Chris Tapscott's and Tor Halvorsen's workshops; and, more generally, from Øivind Bratberg, Vegard Bye, Fredrik Engelstad (along with the other contributors to our *Reinventing Social Democracy* book), Bernt Hagtvet, Eva Hansson, Lars Rudebeck, Kristian Stokke, and, especially, always, from John Harriss, a staunch sailor at that.

Research is usually also indebted to teaching and loved ones. In this case, many thanks to the students in Uppsala, Oslo and Jogjakarta, and the crew at the Olof Palme Center in Stockholm, who as participants in my courses encouraged and discussed initial summaries of arguments that shaped this book; to Patrik and Felix for sympathies; and to Birgitta for asking crucial questions I never thought of.

Finally, I want to acknowledge economic support over the years from the universities of Uppsala and Oslo, the Swedish and Norwegian research councils and international development authorities. I also wish to express my appreciation to Mathew Little, who patiently and carefully edited my Pidgin English, with great understanding for the substance, to forever mate Jonas who handled the pictures, and to architect son Patrik who drew the maps.

Part One

Introduction

The mystery – and how to solve it

In a world on the brink, one might have thought that Social Democracy would carry increasing conviction by the 2020s to boost democracy and rights in the face of growing inequalities and conservative movements, climate change, forced migration and pandemics. But the established parties dwindle, and their losses are rarely compensated by radical offshoots. Social democratic ideas are gaining ground in the United States, but Trump lost only by a thin margin. The right-wing groups are still there, and neo-conservatism remains strong among those who feel betrayed by liberalism. Counter-movements have multiplied and protests increased, but organizations are often scattered, alternative programmes incomplete and the pathways rare. Why is the classical Social Democratic vision of development based on social justice by democratic means losing ground? Why does the field lie so open to politicians such as America's Trump, Europe's right-wing nationalists, India's Modi, the Philippines' Duterte, Brazil's Bolsonaro and many others? This, perhaps, is the mystery of our time.

This book maintains that the crisis of Social Democracy is global. In the North, historically, its successful models were nationally confined. Today they have been weakened by neoliberal governance, market-driven globalization and conservative reaction. And efforts to rethink the roadmaps have not been convincing, even in the Nordic strongholds. In the South, social democratic-oriented leaders attracted much praise in the context of the third wave of democracy for combining global markets, welfare and popular participation. Yet, there have been serious backlashes, even in showcases like South Africa, the Philippines and Brazil.

Nonetheless, in view of this book, the South is where Social Democracy is most urgently needed, both for common people and because this is where the key to renewal may be found. Economic growth in the South by way of reckless exploitation of people and resources assuaged some of the absolute poverty, until Covid-19, but worsened inequality and remains the supreme global threat to both society and the climate. Similarly, it is the source of forced migration and streams of refugees. There is certainly a need for change in the North as well, but transformation in the South is the lynchpin. Is it feasible? Many analysts say the old conditions in the North that shaped the first generation of Social Democracy are missing in the South. But actually, as this book shows, if one gets to know the problems better, new options appear on the horizon.

WHAT IS SOCIAL DEMOCRACY?

There is a tendency, among radicals in particular, to disassociate themselves from Social Democracy by confining it to the designated mainstream parties. This makes me recall the late 1960s and 1970s, when it was common to avoid problems of political Marxism by defining the 'eastern regimes' as inauthentically socialist. That solved nothing. In Chapter 2, this book argues that fruitful analyses call for impartial definitions that are inclusive of several tendencies. The aims and means of classical Social Democracy serve as a point of departure. They boil down to development based on social justice – and by now, environmental justice too – plus the popular engagement and liberal democratic politics required to get there. This book is about different attempts in this direction, irrespective of what the adhering parties and movements call themselves.

Roots of crisis

History is the crucial point of departure. The roots of the crisis of Social Democracy are often neglected. They must be identified and considered in search of a better roadmap. In the North, the challenges occurred with the deregulation of the international exchange rate regime in 1971, which opened up the field for the market fundamentalists. Meanwhile competition from export-driven industrialization in southern Europe and East Asia, as well as the steep rise in oil prices, resulted in insufficient demand for imports in these countries to offset the amalgam of stagnation and inflation in the North. Hence, nationally confined Keynesianism was unviable, and neoliberalism gained ground.

Progressives like Olof Palme and Willy Brandt tried to go beyond 'Social Democracy in one country', envisaging a 'New International Economic Order' and a 'North-South Programme for Survival' in cooperation with the non-aligned movement in the South. But whatever their efforts, the non-aligned partners were not strong enough. Even successful liberation movements did not have much economic clout. The attempts at democratic developmental states in countries such as Indonesia, India and Tanzania had failed or were backsliding. In 1973, another US-nurtured 'middle class coup' ousted democratic socialist Salvador Allende in Chile. The oil country leaders continued to cater to themselves, as did the authoritarian low-cost industrializers in the Far East. Even though the United Nations was generally positive towards the New International Economic Order, the outcomes of negotiations were inconclusive and merely pieces of paper. Real power was turning to Margaret Thatcher, Ronald Reagan and transnational financiers and companies.

Democratic advances

Even though neoliberal governance and market-driven globalization gained hegemony in the 1980s, emancipatory politics was also in the air. Dictators as well as revolutionaries were overtaken by the new third wave of democracy, after the first slow wave in the nineteenth century and the second when colonialism retreated. In

April 1974, the fascists lost out in Portugal and its colonies. In July, Greece followed suit, Spain a year later. On the 30th of April 1975, the Americans fled Saigon. During the 1980s the wave spread to Latin America, and in the Philippines, 'people power' did away with the dictator Marcos. Even in Eastern Europe, dissidents began to organize, spearheaded by the Polish *Solidarność*. In 1989, on the face of it, the fall of the Wall in Berlin and the Velvet Revolution in Prague turned the world to the better.

It is true that earlier in 1989, the democracy movement in China lost out in Tiananmen Square and that in the following year the Burmese democrats – who had been capable of winning elections – were bitterly repressed. But at the same time, the better organized democracy movement in South Africa proved that negotiations were possible, even with racist dictators. In 1994, the African National Congress (ANC) assumed power after a landslide electoral victory. In 1996, renewal-oriented activists in the Indian state of Kerala convinced a mainstream leftist government to support decentralization, along with a 'People's Planning Campaign'. Meanwhile in Brazil, progressive unions, social movements, civil society and community activists, including adherents of liberation theology, built a rainbow party, made remarkable advances in local elections and built efficient participatory governance. In May 1998, the seemingly invincible Indonesian dictatorship collapsed and almost everyone claimed to be a democrat. In India, the centre-left governments from 2004 until 2014 acknowledged the need for social reforms along with economic growth. In Latin America, the potential of the 'Pink Tide' was signified by the first election (since the 1860s in Mexico) of an indigenous President, Evo Morales, in Bolivia in 2005, and by Brazil's participatory budgeting and successful fusing of growth and falling inequality under the Workers' Party (PT) and first-time President, Lula da Silva (2003–11).

New setbacks

During the following years, however, the further hope ignited by the protests against financial speculation, the breathtaking 'Arab Spring' and the landslide electoral victories of Aung San Suu Kyi in Burma (Myanmar) were steadily dashed. Similarly, most of the previous efforts in Latin America, India and the Philippines fell apart too. Religious identity-politics and right-wing nationalism returned to the fore, this time more averse to migrants and globalization than other nations and free markets. Mainstream social democrats adjusted and leftists did not advance. In the European Union, economic liberals gained ground by reducing political liberties and popular sovereignty in favour of judicial governance, and, as in Singapore, the power of meritocratic professionals – the latter being admired, in turn, by Chinese adherents of cadre-driven governance.

The puzzle

The cardinal question in this book is therefore why reformist social movements, civil society groups and 'their' parties were not able to make more of a difference in the context of the third wave of democracy. Why were they – and like-minded partners in the North – unable to generate viable alternatives to market-driven globalization, right-wing populism and technocratic governance? What are the insights in the South and the implications for the North? What can we do?

In retrospect

A few years ago, the setbacks made me want to sum up the studies of social democratic-oriented struggles that I had engaged in for close to half a century – in Indonesia, India and the Philippines, with Scandinavia and to some extent Brazil and South Africa as reference cases. My attempts to summarize these extensive writings, however, generated lengthy and dense texts. Finally, I gave up and developed an alternative.

In this new version, an initial definition of broadly framed Social Democracy in Chapter 2 allows for an open script that focuses in retrospect on the major insights gained and how to make sense of them. When the old pieces were thus put together and considered in wider theoretical and comparative perspective, there were also new insights.

To get there, I have also returned to my notes from interviews and conversations, as well as to logbooks and photographs, in order to reflect on a long journey with scholarly activists and political protagonists on how we addressed the mysteries of political change.[1] Further, maps and figures with historical timelines and some pictures have been added, while the lengthy footnotes have been replaced by an appendix with briefer references to the substantiation given in my previous studies, plus some updates.

As compared to a conventional research report, I hope the present book is thus crisper and more accessible to readers interested in understanding why it has been so difficult to renew Social Democracy, even in the context of the third wave of democracy, why this matters in the North too, and whether and how the basics can be reinvented.

Frame and logic

The architecture of the book is simple. Fruitful studies of the problems and options of Social Democracy call for the revival of history. There has been a lot of 'letting bygones be bygones'. One example is many liberals' accommodation of elitist practices as well as political amnesia regarding repression and massacres. Another instance is the new generations of leftists' obliviousness towards previous attempts at national liberation and democratic developmental states, in pursuit of immaculate new perspectives.

By contrast, this book begins with questions about the history and meaning of Social Democracy. There are three reasons for this: firstly to get a benchmark for discussing how the subsequent generations of Social Democracy have addressed old lessons; secondly, to answer the main question of how globalized economic growth

---

[1] Quotation marks are rarely used, however, as I always avoided tape recorders in favour of observations and detailed notes. Hence, reformulated statements and expressions ascribed to named persons are indicated by other means.

and elitist democracy have affected the preconditions for Social Democracy; thirdly, to also ask if these new conditions – which often differ from those that first shaped Social Democracy – have generated novel thinking and counter-movements.

There is little room for such queries today – either in the predominant discussion of identity politics or within the field of increasingly technocratic political 'science', with its special interests in free-floating international relations and quantitative indices of growth and democracy, beyond the realities and contexts where transformative politics have to be rooted and gain strength.

This book tries instead to reclaim the study of historical conflicts and processes in comparative perspective. We shall trace plausible causes and reasons for a number of universal but contextually framed problems and options of Social Democracy. I do this by asking questions of similar efforts in different settings. I shall return to details about Social Democracy and how to study it, but like Inspector Morse, the reader is invited to consider different hypotheses about what has evolved and why.

Fundaments of Social Democracy

Social Democracy is defined in terms of three generations, four cornerstones and five strategies. The details are in Chapter 2, but in brief, the first generation grew out of the industrial revolution in the North. The second generation was part of the emancipatory movements against colonialism, aiming at democratic developmental states. The third generation, since the late 1970s, is rooted in the struggle against authoritarian regimes and extractive capitalist growth, within the wider space created by the third wave of democracy. While the third-generation moderates had much in common with northern leaders like Tony Blair who tried to combine market-driven growth and welfare, its radicals wanted to build democratic alternatives from new popular movements and citizen action on the ground.

Our focus is on this third-generation Social Democracy, but we must also address the legacies of the first and second generations, as they have affected the third. And at present, the challenges of Social Democracy in the South are increasingly important for its revival in the North too.

Irrespective of what generation we are talking about, the general aims and means of classical Social Democracy involve development based on social justice – and these days, environmental equity as well – plus the popular and liberal politics needed to achieve this. These fundamentals may be thought of as a house that is built on four cornerstones, distilled from the literature on Social Democracy in the North as well as the South. The first stone is the formation, organization and coordination of democratic social and political collective actors with common interests. The second comprises efforts at creating equal citizens and making democratic linkages between them and the state. The third involves the struggle for social rights, related welfare policies and rights at work. The fourth concern attempts at economic growth coalitions (social pacts) between labour, agrarian producers and capital, often facilitated by public policies. The bulk of the general strategies to get there were recently well-framed by Erik Olin Wright in terms of dismantling, taming, resisting and escaping capitalism, while the fifth and most crucial one (which he forgot) involves combining these efforts by adding transformative politics and reforms. Together, that is Social Democracy.

Our prime mystery revolves around the challenges of the third-generation social democrats in particular, and their first-generation partners in the North, to defend and renew these cornerstones and strategies. By recalling the historical experiences of developing the fundaments, we can identify the crucial requirements. This is helpful when we search for possible causes and reasons for the current problems of maintaining and developing the foundations.

Contextual dynamics

In addition, these general problems and propositions are affected by the contextual legacies and dynamics of identities, interests and values. Given that they are many, complex and poorly documented, they can rarely be studied in any fruitful way by the quantification of a few variables. Correlations and regressions look like absolute science but may be absolute nonsense. The challenge one faces is, in my experience, like sailing in the Swedish and Norwegian archipelago. One knows the destination and can master the boat. But the charts are not always perfect and the weather and winds often unreliable. Also, the innumerable islands, skerries and underwater stones affect the winds, the waves and the currents. The boat and sails react to other factors as well, including breakdowns and the shortcomings of the helmsperson. In short, there are plentiful unknown influences and variations. An ocean racing friend who was also a computer expert tried to put them all in a program but gave up. And so, if we want to consider the problems and options of Social Democracy, the best we can do is study critical cases in contextual, historical and comparative perspective.

Thematic contrasts

There is one more challenge: we cannot rely on conventional types of comparisons. These either identify differences in similar cases in order to explain varied outcomes or focus on similarities in different cases to explain parallel developments. One reason why we cannot do this is that it is difficult to find perfect matches in reality. Another is that such studies tend to evade contextual dynamics. The various cases in this book are instead identified according to the idea of discussing crucial themes in contrasting contexts. Such cases form 'a kind of commentary on another's character', as Clifford Geertz phrased it when comparing Islam in Morocco and Indonesia. Or to put it another way, the cases in this book are selected according to ideas similar to those of Benedict Anderson. Some call him 'an Indonesianist', but he concluded in his memoirs *A Life Beyond Boundaries* that he was only able to write *Imagined Communities*, the path-breaking book on nationalism, when he was expelled from Indonesia and had begun to ask new questions from exile in Thailand.

The implications for this book are simple. The common theme is the challenges of Social Democracy, specified in Chapter 2. We search for new insights about these problems by identifying quite different critical cases where the challenges apply over time. Then we ask questions about puzzles in one case from the point of view of the others.

The cases

The meaning of critical cases is that they must be significant in relation to the theme one focuses on, and not deemed exceptional by acknowledged scholars. It has been possible to carve out such cases from my previous studies of progressive democrats in Indonesia, India and the Philippines, with references to the Swedish case of first-generation partners and to some extent Brazil and South Africa. In each case, I examine the contextual dynamics of the general challenges of Social Democracy. Chapter 3 provides an overview.

The first case studies offer historical background and analyse as briefly as possible the legacies of the second-generation social democrats. Chapter 4's focus is on the rise and fall of the world's largest reformist popular movement in Indonesia. Chapter 5 is concerned with the development and stagnation of Kerala's emancipatory politics, with some comparison with the Left in West Bengal. Chapter 6 addresses the dynamics of the inconceivable 'people power' revolution in the Philippines. Chapter 7 discusses the interactions with first-generation Social Democracy in the North, as in the paradigmatic case of Sweden.

The core of the book is the following seven chapters with case studies of the third-generation social democratic attempts at renewal and the puzzling challenges. These chapters concern:

- the Philippine experiments for a democratic Left until the early 2000s;
- the pro-democratic struggle in Indonesia until it was overtaken by elitist democratization after the fall of Suharto;
- the efforts to deepen Indonesian democracy, before the rise of new populism in the mid-2000s;
- the pioneering efforts to renew the Kerala model (1987–2001) by way of decentralized people's planning;
- the causes for the collapse of the Left in West Bengal but the rise of new citizen action in relation to the Indian centre–left government 2004–14, the subsequent anti-corruption movement and populist party in New Delhi, and the exciting new efforts to counter neoliberalization of Kerala;
- the rise and dynamics of the inconclusive liberal–left coalition in the Philippines 2010–2016, until the upsurge of Duterte;
- the growth and demise of what I shall call Indonesian 'reformist populism' from the mid-2000s until the present debacle;
- the current implications for the first-generation social democrats in Sweden, who tried, but failed, in the mid-2010s to develop an internationalist alternative to market-driven globalization.

Essence of conclusion

In the concluding chapter, the book returns to the general mystery of why Social Democracy is losing ground and if there are any openings. Social Democracy has always been particularly difficult in the South. Its initial cornerstones of popular-interest collectivities and equal citizenship and democracy had first to contend with colonialism and feudal-like subordination. Later, the major problems were authoritarian rule and uneven capitalist development. The third cornerstone of the struggle for social rights and welfare has been crucial in terms of self-help (such as cooperatives) and demands for specific public provisions. But comprehensive welfare state programmes have been unrealistic. This is because they have historically been combined with the fourth cornerstone of dynamic social growth pacts. And democratic social growth pacts, for their part, have been impossible to implement in the South. The major explanation is that in the North they presupposed effective democratic governance and comprehensive industrialization, generating broad and unified collective organizing for labour as well as for capital. Typically, these preconditions were absent in the South.

Second-generation dilemmas

This book shows, however, that aside from the Philippines – with a long-standing democracy entirely dominated by the oligarchy and the United States – social democratic-oriented movements in the other cases of Indonesia, and especially Kerala, proved that it was possible to build popular interest-based collectivities. The formula was to frame class struggles within broad efforts at equal citizenship and democracy.

This was undermined, however, when the second generation of social democratic-oriented leaders tried to compensate for the insufficient preconditions for economic growth by state planning and structural reforms via formally democratic, yet top-down, development states. The intentions were good but the results modest. Most importantly, progressives failed to analyse how private vested interests were hijacking public assets and resources and the political control of economic development. This was not curtailed by way of more democratic politics and governance. Authoritarian rule and unequal growth strategies gained ground, most seriously in Indonesia under Sukarno's 'guided democracy' and Suharto's 'new order'. But they also made headway in the Philippines under Marcos, and to some extent in Kerala too, through the channels of intervention from New Delhi, local party-driven clientelism and finally Mrs Gandhi's emergency rule.

Thus, the preconditions in the South for multilateral efforts at a New International Economic Order were also weakened. The floodgates opened for market-driven globalization, with severe consequences in the South but also in the North where the Social Democratic model was undermined. In spite of this, there was no effort to reinvent this model in an international context, only to adjust it to global neoliberalism in a way that would be 'socially acceptable' at home. But it was not, so for both reasons mainstream Social Democracy declined.

Third-generation insights

Meanwhile, however, there was also the positive third wave of democracy. Economic globalization substituted for parts of the old statist imperialism. In response to the protests, there was, therefore, some space for democracy. And within its framework there was new room for manoeuvre for, broadly speaking, third-generation social democrats. Moderates tried compromises with elites towards political democracy and inclusive economic growth. Radicals strengthened trade unions, civil societies, grassroots participation and tried to make a difference in elections. How did they fare?

Dearth of broad class-based collectivities

This book points to blind alleys but also to openings. The uneven development generates some industrial development but also growing inequalities and deteriorating employment conditions. This generates discordant interests and priorities among ordinary people, and weak progressive organizations.

Stalling democratization

Another frustration is that democratization has remained elite-dominated and is fraying. Efforts to counter this with popular participation in local governance have been difficult to scale up and relate to other levels and actors. Hence, the chances are slim for progressives to gain representation and even oversee implementation of the internationally celebrated Agenda 2030.

Bottom-up is not enough

Equally disconcerting is that it has been next to impossible in Indonesia, India and the Philippines to make a difference in national governance by combining and scaling up, in various innovative ways, scattered interests and local practices. This resonates with challenges for the more acclaimed ANC in South Africa and Workers' Party in Brazil too.

Broad alliances open up

More positively, the research suggests also that agreements and broad alliances of progressive politicians, unions, other popular groups and civil society activists, including some parts of the media, are feasible. The alliances are generally in support of acceptable urban development, equal rights to welfare, more jobs and better employment relations, plus non-corrupt provisioning. The agreements and reforms to these ends may also limit populism (in terms of a thin ideology about the 'common people', its 'general will' and identity, and direct relations between leaders and people). They may be transformative by strengthening the progressive movements. They may reinvigorate democratization by including representation of political and social partners in priorities, implementation and further development. And they may facilitate genuine interest- and policy-based parties. None of the actors in the alliances are strong enough to make it on their own. Even in comprehensively industrializing countries like Sweden in the 1930s, alliances were necessary to promote inclusive development and democracy. So in the South today they are even more crucial.

Populist obstacles

The typical obstacles are not structural, and thus inevitable. They relate instead to political shortcuts that may be altered. One is about insufficient cooperation between the progressives in the alliances. Another is the shortage of not just one comprehensive reform to support but whole series of them to continue to unite behind and make transformative by being designed to gradually strengthen popular capacity. Social Democracy is neither an attempt to smash capitalism by way of revolution nor a dogmatic struggle against markets and private ownership. But it is about democratic struggle for transformative regulations and reforms to nourish the aim of Democratic Socialism in terms of as much social equity, equality and welfare as possible as a basis for, and result of, sustainable development.[2] Yet another obstacle is poor democratic representation when the alliances negotiate with employers and the government. Direct negotiations between populist leaders and civil society organizations (CSOs)[3] and interest-organizations were promising but not institutionalized and made democratic. Thus they turned transactional and prepared the ground for right-wing populism.

Resequencing Social Democracy with rights and welfare reforms

In even grander terms, improved versions of such alliances for transformative reforms may clear the way for, as it were, a resequencing of social democratic development. Historically, the comprehensive welfare states in the North called for social pacts that stimulated inclusive economic development. The pacts in turn presupposed effective democratic governance and broad and unified collective organizing for labour as well as for capital – features which have been lacking in the South. This

---

[2] Thus defined in terms of political and socio-economic aims and means rather than philosophical principles and a communist-like utopia, as in Martin Hägglund's celebrated *This Life – Secular Faith and Spiritual Freedom*.

[3] In this book the term 'civil society organizations' (CSOs) refers to citizenship-based groups and often includes 'non-governmental organizations' (NGOs) but they may differ from interest-based organizations such as unions and popular groups among urban poor people themselves.

book suggests, however, that broad alliances for rights and welfare reforms that are universal, democratically negotiated and impartially implemented might serve as precursors to social growth pacts. In short, they may generate the much sought-after collective organizing of labour and capital, as well as participatory and democratic 'good governance'.

Fundamental for the North too

To get there, coordination and support from social democrats in the North are essential. This is not about benevolence but mutual solidarity for actual 'development cooperation'. Hence, thus it may not be entirely impossible. Enlightened social democrats in the North will realize that the revival of movements and parties calls for the internationalization of their nationally confined growth pacts and welfare states. Adjustment to the current globalization is insufficient. In the absence of alternative international governance, hard-hit people turn to 'national defence'. International negotiations are insufficient. Alternatives presuppose stronger partners in the South who can fight for inclusive and sustainable democratic development in their own countries, so that the space for extractive and exploitative globalization is reduced. Otherwise, how will it be possible for social democrats in the North to increase non-destructive exports and investments in the South, hold back climate change, reduce forced migration and fight pandemics? In other words, both partners must search for a new Social Democracy.

What is Social Democracy?

Before turning to the contextual mysteries it remains to account for how the search for new Social Democracy has been pursued. It is possible to appreciate the substantive chapters without knowing much of what shaped them. But as a point of departure it is helpful to know the fundamentals of Social Democracy and how they may be studied.

Characteristics

What is Social Democracy? Initial indications may be sought by comparing how social democrats, liberals and left-oriented populists relate to democracy. My main experiences in this respect are from co-directing collective studies during the years of Indonesia's democratization, with the international literature as a major reference. This was followed by a comparison with efforts at Social Democracy in India and Scandinavia. A major insight was that the aim of democracy is commonly thought of as popular control of public affairs on the basis of political equality, and democratization as the process of getting there. In actual fact, the main contentions concerned, instead, the constitution of the people (the demos) and public affairs, plus the preconditions for popular control and political equality.[1]

Social Democracy and liberalism

The major difference between liberals with a social mind and social democrats is of course that while the former claim that capitalism must generate growth before being taxed for welfare purposes, the latter argue that certain social rights and welfare reforms actually promote growth and are necessary to make it sustainable. This has implications for democracy. Social democrats claim that many more matters than conceded by liberals are of common concern, and should therefore be included in the definition of public affairs and subject to democratic governance. Social democrats are, for example, against the privatization of education and social security. They deem gender equality to be a public matter and advocate more public regulation of the market and working life. In short, Social Democracy wants the principles of democracy to apply more widely than liberals do.

---

[1] For more details, see the appendix with references.

A related difference is that liberals with a special interest in the question of effective governance often foster the judicialization of politics and stability. They are also more predisposed than social democrats towards 'the rule of experts' and market-oriented 'new-public management'. One example is the European 'ordo-liberals' who argue for strong managerial governance and judicial guarantees to foster free and dynamic markets. Another is the like-minded Singaporean technocrats. They are admired, in turn, by Chinese post-communists. This contrasts with the social democratic preoccupation with popular sovereignty as well as with the participation of workers, professionals and concerned citizens in fostering the best-possible public governance. In particular, social democrats are sceptical of the liberal's predilection for lobbying, networks and 'good contacts'. The alternative is democratically institutionalized consultation of interest organizations such as trade unions and employers' associations in public governance. The same applies to profession and issue-based groups such as those representing medical doctors or concerned with gender, human rights and environment.

Finally, social democrats and liberals agree on the importance of the freedom of citizens and their individual participation in public life. But social democrats argue that more equal and substantive civil and social rights are required if all people are to make use of such freedoms. In the same vein, social democrats support liberals with regard to human rights and the rule of law, but emphasize that implementation calls for popular democratic sovereignty, given that the most powerful actors are not to be trusted.

Social Democracy and left-populism

As for Social Democracy and populism, there is increasing scholarly agreement that the essence of the latter is, as Cas Mudde suggests, a thin ideology of the 'common people' and its 'general will', in contrast to established elites and their special interests. Populist politics, moreover, is rooted in the idea that 'the people' are defined by common identity, often against an enemy, and that there should be direct, rather than representative, links between leaders and people. Empirical categorizations include populist leaders based on movements (such as Modi in India), oligarchs and strongmen (like Duterte in the Philippines) and technocrats (as Joko 'Jokowi' Widodo in Indonesia). Currently, the most acclaimed left-populist additions to these fundamentals are Chantal Mouffe's 'agonistic politics' of posing 'popular sovereignty' against 'neoliberalism' and generating an 'hegemonic general will' by way of a common identity among emancipatory social movements against a common enemy. How does Social Democracy relate to the new leftism?

Social democrats and left-populists tend to agree on social rights and welfare. Left-populists, however, favour unmediated direct democracy – for example in terms of referenda and popular participation in public governance. In contrast, social democrats tend to only appreciate this on the most local level and otherwise prefer democratic representation of citizens as well as interest and issue organizations.

Similarly, left-populists say that mobilization on the basis of class is insufficient. The argument is that there are increasingly many additional forms of subordination of people and, thus, numerous social movements. This, the left-populists claim, calls for unifying identities and the sovereignty of 'common people' *against* dominant classes and elites – in effect turning the Thatcherite revolutions upside down. Social democrats certainly agree about the need for wide unity beyond narrowly defined class interests – actually, this was how they gained hegemony in Scandinavia in the early 1930s. But they tend to be sceptical of identity politics. The alternative is rather to favour broad alliances *for* realistic alternative policies. The major historical experience is the combination that evolved in the 1930s of Keynesian growth and radical welfare reforms, briefly in Roosevelt's United States and for decades in Scandinavia.

In turn, more authoritarian leftist populists, as in Venezuela, as well as rightists, as currently in Hungary and Poland, have a weakness for strong leaders – often elected in majoritarian elections – who embody and define 'the people' and its 'will'. At times this incarnation is in terms of ethnicity, as with the xenophobic European parties, or religion, as by Modi in India. In the worst scenario, the leaders claim that only *they* represent the people, while other leaders are illegitimate. They also select certain 'people' to supervise public administration, and thus enforce 'popular' proposals, at the expense of democratic representation, human rights and the rule of law.

Inclusive definition

The definition of Social Democracy is often reduced (by radical critics in particular) to the outlook of the mainstream social democratic parties that have adjusted, more or less, to elite democracy, judicialization, privatization, market-driven governance and globalization, and, most recently, even to nationalistic refugee policies. But while critique is helpful, strawman arguments (reducing the object of the study to the worst cases) are not. There is significant critique inside these parties. There are many positions and alternative groups. And the labels vary. Social Democracy is a wide stream of ideas, arguments, organizations and movements that have advanced and changed over time and context.

One example is those left-populists who wish to reclaim and emphasize basic elements of Social Democracy, such as radical democracy and firm opposition to privatization, increasing inequality and market-driven growth. Another is the Indian communists who abandoned their revolutionary strategy way back in 1951, while holding on to democratic centralism in their parties. Thereafter they supported social justice and firmly enhanced reforms and thus based development within India's democratic polity. Yet another example is the Philippine civil society groups that supported the 'people power' revolution against Ferdinand Marcos in 1986, and then tried to alter elitist democracy by way of more local popular participation as well as by building a social democratic organization to coordinate their actions and participate in elections.

Nevertheless, clear-cut analytical tools are needed. I have benefitted in particular from the insights of the concerned scholars who came together in a series of book-generating workshops between 1989 and 2015 to compare the experiences and options of broadly defined social democratic aspirations in such varied settings as Southeast

Asia, Latin America, South Africa and Scandinavia.[2] To identify the dimensions that applied over time and space, but varied with contexts and challenges, we revisited the literature in each context, as well as our own writings, and identified three historical waves of common dimensions and strategies. In my summary of these and further insights in the book on India and Scandinavia (*Reinventing Social Democratic Development,* co-written with John Harriss, amongst others), the conclusion boiled down to five propositions. While already alluded to in Chapter 1, here are the details.

First, that Social Democracy may be understood in the broad inclusive classical terms of economic development based on social justice – and now environmental equity too – by way of combining liberal democracy and transformative popular politics and policies through step-by-step advances.

Second, that this definition may be elaborated by specifying three generations of social democrats – one rooted in industrial development, another related to the anti-colonial struggle and the last as part of the third wave of democracy.

Third, that the general mystery and specific puzzles of Social Democracy lie in challenges to raising and developing the four cornerstones of democratic popular-interest collectivities, democratic links between state and a society of equal citizens, social rights and welfare, and social/economic growth pacts.

Fourth, that there are a number of typical strategies to construct these pillars. Erik Olin Wright specified them, later on, as dismantling, taming, resisting and escaping capitalism. Our addition was transformative politics and policies to combine the other strategies and unify actors with varying interests, identities and values towards Democratic Socialism, understood as democratic politics for development based on full justice.

Fifth, that the cornerstones and strategies are ideal types that vary and intermix in reality and that analysis thereof may benefit from historical insights and theories about the conditions and political capacities that the advances required or lacked.

I follow the same roadmap in this book, but let us be a bit more specific.

Generations

First-generation Social Democracy grew out of the comprehensive industrialization in the North during the nineteenth and early twentieth centuries. It was a critique of three 'rivals' on the Left – the syndicalist proposition, Karl Kautsky's deterministic thesis of socialist development and Lenin's revolutionary politics. While the syndicalists asserted that the basis for transformation should be workers' management of industry, and Kautsky claimed that the crises of capitalism would inevitably generate socialism, the groundbreaking social democrats – from moderate Eduard Bernstein to leftist Rosa Luxemburg – argued for the primacy of politics. The kind of politics varied, however. Bernstein was a reformist parliamentarian while Luxemburg supplemented general elections with extra-parliamentary pressure from below, which was not

---

[2] For more details, see the appendix with references.

accommodated and ended in confrontation, Yet both disagreed with Lenin – and later Stalin and Mao – who, in backward Europe and China, added peasants (to workers) as the drivers of change and claimed that supposedly 'scientific' revolutionary politics and leadership were indispensable.

The first-generation social democrats were certainly slow in acknowledging the importance of small farmers. But in contrast to the revolutionaries, the social democrats insisted, thus, on undogmatic knowledge and believed that socialist movements had to have democratic principles at their heart. Progress, they claimed, depended on fighting for the advancement of liberal democracy, with popular movements as propelling forces. In other words, the long-term aim remained socialism (in terms of development based on full social justice) but with democratic politics and government to get there, that is, 'Democratic Socialism'.

European mainland social democrats, communists and syndicalists failed to really join hands in combatting the 'national socialists' (Nazis and fascists). But social democratic thinking influenced Roosevelt's 'New Deal' in the United States and Scandinavian leaders in particular. The latter developed broad alliances, including with the farmers, for enduring policies. The Scandinavian parties gained hegemony, which lasted until the late 1970s and did much to shape the Social Democratic cornerstones and strategies, to which we shall return shortly.

Meanwhile social democrats in the North were often ambivalent about colonialism. The countries in what is now called the Global South were major 'exceptions', given that their development was held back by authoritarian means. Hence, one argument was that colonialism might after all contribute to the spread of capitalism, which had to precede socialism. In contrast to this first-generation passivity in the North, a *second generation* of social democrats evolved in the colonies and the subordinated countries. Some activists here had very strong popular roots. In what became Kerala in southwest India, for example, they framed their struggle – against colonizers and foreign Brahmins – in terms of quests for equal civil and political rights and a culturally unified federal state. This was combined with social and economic issues of class.

More commonly, the second generation of social democrats granted that enlightened party and state-led paths to progress were indispensable to combat underdevelopment. But when democratic systems proved feasible – in countries like India and Indonesia in the early 1950s – most activists, including those who called themselves communists, adjusted to the new political system.

Even so, democratization was deemed less important than anti-imperialism, central planning and socio-economic issues. Singaporean socialists abandoned democracy altogether. And where even rudimentary democracy was unrealistic, militant resistance gained prominence, such as in Vietnam. Radical nationalists, communists and strong socialist leaders like Nehru, Ho Chi Minh, Castro and Mandela were crucial. They argued that 'political shortcuts' to progress were necessary. From the 1960s and for some two decades afterwards, the shortcuts were submerged by more authoritarian and capitalist development supported by the West.

Later, the globalization of finance and production began to generate economic growth in parts of the Global South. This substituted for much of the previous territorial imperialism with powerful states like the United States in the driving seat. Thus a third wave of struggle for democracy was possible, further enhanced by the end of the Cold War.

Dictatorial regimes held on when supported by hegemonic parties, as in China, and competing superpowers, such as in the Middle East and North Africa. But elsewhere there was wider space for democrats – especially liberal democrats but also a *third generation* of social democrats. They differed from the second generation by being critical of political shortcuts to progress. The new priority of the third-generation moderates was combining liberal economic growth with welfare. Meanwhile the radicals emphasized equal citizenship, bottom-up democracy and social rights as foundations for inclusive development. Few of them rejected the importance of political parties, but they were often more active in CSOs, radical trade unions and numerous social movements.

As compared to the comprehensive industrialization in the North, however, the economic development has been more uneven – based, as it is, on wild exploitation of people and nature, global value chains and a commodity boom driven by the growth of China and India in particular. In addition, the states are more inefficient and democratization more shallow. Social Democracy must therefore be reinvented in a way that is relevant to the new conditions. This is the core of this book.

Four cornerstones and five strategies across three generations

As already mentioned, the three generations of Social Democracy have four cornerstones in common – popular-interest collectivities, democracy, social rights and development based on these. Some of them have not been possible to develop fully in all contexts, but they are all strived for. Similarly, there are five not necessarily mutually exclusive major strategies to get there. In his last book, Erik Olin Wright' has defined four of them succinctly: (i) getting into office and then dismantling vital elements of capitalism; (ii) meanwhile, or instead, taming it with various reforms; (iii) resisting it through protests and alternatives in civil society; and (iv) escaping it through non-capitalist ideas and ways of living. The fifth strategy is to combine the others and unify movements and actors with differing identities, interests and values by way of transformative politics that creates conditions for more advanced reforms and thus nourishes Democratic Socialism.

If one lists the pillars and strategies along two dimensions and combines them, the result is a three-dimensional table with twenty combinations that vary during three generations.

It is not meaningful, however, to fill in all the boxes. In reality, the ideal-type cornerstones and strategies overlap in different ways. This remains to be studied historically in different contexts. Yet, the basic characteristics are helpful as a point of departure for systematic analyses. So let us elaborate on the fundamental cornerstones and discuss the strategies in relation to them.

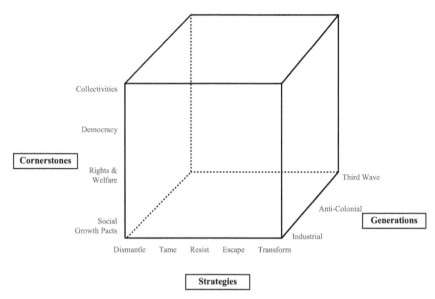

Figure 1 Pillars, strategies and generations of Social Democracy

First cornerstone: Democratic popular-interest collectivities

The bottom line is the formation and organization of democratic social and political collectivities. These are certainly rooted in the specific concerns of the working class. But in the first generation of social democrats' struggle for universal suffrage (for women too) and against fascism, the movements and organizations were broadened, often demanding equal civil, political and social rights among the people as a whole. At an early stage, trade unions were supplemented with a wide spectrum of popular movements – from day care centres, cooperatives and educational societies to funeral associations – to resist and escape capitalism. Labourism certainly prevailed for decades, but communities of popular movements also fostered broad alliances behind common demands and aspirations. In Scandinavia, for example, 'labour communes' – which congregated social democratic-oriented trade unions and other popular organizations and ran their own 'people's houses' for meetings and social events – served as the basis for building political parties and guiding them to participate in elections and parliaments. In the South, with limited industrialization, the working class and unions were of course much weaker, but class struggle was often framed by broader-based resistance to colonialism and caste oppression. How was it possible to develop the collectivities and what are the challenges?

The literature about social movements for democracy and socio-economic rights stresses three sets of factors that may help us identify causes for success and failure: (i) ideology and politicization, (ii) mobilization and organization, and (iii) the structural and institutional opportunities.

Ideology and politicization

The bottom line in the first set of factors is the importance of a joint ideology and vision about social democratic development and the policies to get there – a narrative. This has demanded programmes and reform proposals, but the crux of the matter has been to convince a lot of people of the necessity of turning the problems they share into issues of common concern, that is, to *politicize* them, even if they have hitherto been deemed private. In addition, these issues must be lifted to the top of the public agenda in general discussion and political debate, in stiff competition with many other actors' core issues. This is to gain 'discursive hegemony'.

How is it possible, for example, to encourage many people of different cultural and religious persuasions to accept that gender equality is not a private but public matter? And how does one convince a majority of the population that the difficulties self-employed poor labourers experience in getting a job and living a decent life are not just their own dilemma but also a problem for society at large, including for those with permanent employment? This is a fundamental challenge in the context of the uneven development in the Global South, but also, increasingly, in the North.

Similarly, how can social democrats, in the South as well as the North, convince those who have not gained from market-driven globalization that ethno-nationalism is not a solution, but that global finance and markets have to be regulated in favour of inclusive and sustainable growth and welfare programmes? How can social democrats convince – not least themselves – that it is unviable to rely on fossil energy even though it is the most effective way, for the time being, of increasing the general standard of living? How can alternatives to this be nurtured that do not increase the burden of the least privileged sections of the population?

Mobilization and organization

The second set of crucial factors in building democratic popular-interest collectivities revolves around the capacity to mobilize and organize broad groups of people. Mainstream leaders in the Global South, in particular, tend to incorporate people in politics by patronizing certain individuals or groups, including by clientelism that involves the exchange of supposedly mutual services. Clientelism calls for reliable links between leaders and supporters. This is difficult to sustain in times of socio-economic change and urbanization, especially where majoritarian first-past the post-electoral systems, requiring massive numbers of voters to win, are in place. Hence, more direct populist relations between leaders and 'the people' have become increasingly important, along with 'identity politics', that is, leaders' identification of people's commonalities and enemies. Our main question is therefore about the capacity of social democrats to navigate these waters, and at times build alliances by developing their own collectives based on issues and interests in different sectors and on local and central levels.

Structural and institutional opportunities

A third set of factors, then, is the institutional and structural conditions. These are often analysed in terms of opportunity structures. In the context of the comprehensive industrialization in the North, the first generation of social democrats benefitted from a number of favourable factors. The question we need to ask is therefore about the capacity of subsequent generations of activists to handle institutional constraints and take advantage of related opportunities. If repression and authoritarian rule prevent social democrats from organizing in workplaces and participating in elections (as under apartheid in South Africa), do they have the ability to locate other options and allies? If the electoral system makes it next to hopeless to run in elections (as in Indonesia even after Suharto), how are they able to move ahead and foster change? If most people (as in India) do not have real citizenship rights, aside from the chance to vote, how do social democrats work to extend such rights, as an alternative to patronage politics?

The favourable conditions in the North included comprehensive industrialization, common workplaces, working conditions and residential areas. Another asset was the enduring links between urban and rural communities. Yet another was the general education and the unifying effect of a common public school system. In Scandinavia in particular there were certainly vast inequalities, but feudalism was not dominant. Historically, Sweden, for example, was characterized by a triangular relation between the king (along with the Protestant Church), the lords and the independent peasantry (together with leaseholders of state land). Those without property were certainly excluded, and their numbers increased, making Sweden one of the most unequal societies by the late nineteenth century. But there was a long history of pre-democratic citizenship in parishes and municipalities that included propertied peasants and the state-leaseholders.

Generally in Protestant northern Europe, it was helpful that central governments were, potentially, more viable sources of social security than wealthy ethnic and religious organizations. In Scandinavia from the 1930s, this nourished broad alliances in favour of universal welfare state programmes. They were vital in containing fascist alternatives. Many of the programmes encouraged more effective production too. However, stateism and, later, market-driven liberalization stepped into the breach as many such popular rights-based movements faded from the scene.

Meanwhile Social Democracy in the South was held back by state-led imperialism, weak industrialization and divisive interests among subordinated and repressed labourers. The struggle for national independence, along with equal citizenship, was imperative. When nationalism was genuinely rooted in the struggle for equal political, civil and social rights, it was possible, in spite of everything, to build broad alliances and democratic social and political collectivities. One example is in the 1930s in today's Kerala; another is during the struggle against apartheid in South Africa. Usually, however, unified action was overwhelmingly difficult – given the repressive regimes and the subordinate classes' different interests and weak political capacity. This caused endless debates on what interests among labourers and/or peasants would be the best points of departure. Another major trend was to compensate for the divisions and feeble capacities by adhering to top-down political leadership and charisma. Such leadership was often strengthened by the mobilization of people through the provision of 'leftist patronage' as an alternative to patron–client relations between landlords or strongmen and their subordinates. These dilemmas caused severe setbacks and opened up for the rise of authoritarian regimes.

Subsequently, however, a third generation of social democrats gained ground within the resistance against authoritarianism and in the context of the new wave of democracy. The radicals of this generation insisted on the imperative of building collectivities and equal citizenship from below, despite the obstacles, and of resisting the commodification of one's own life. The thesis was that these aims would be facilitated by decentralization and campaigns for a number of key rights, along with organization through unions, social movements and civil society groups. The remaining problems of unified action and of scaling up from below are crucial themes in this book.

Collectivities to gain power

In other words, much of the effort to create broad collectivities is about gaining alternative political power. The French sociologist Pierre Bourdieu has provided an analytical structure that (in a slightly extended form) is useful to frame our studies of the social democratic challenges in this respect. In this view, power is about the legitimacy and authority to act on behalf of people. To achieve this, there is a need for resources. A general or a guerrilla leader can promise change by means of *coercion*. An oligarch can use *money* to buy a TV channel that boosts his ideas and reputation. Well-connected people with *privileged networks* can use them to expedite deals and gain recognition as leaders. A bishop or Ulama, an artist, or an expert with seminal insights, might use their '*cultural capital*' in terms of respected knowledge to gain authority. But what can social democratic activists do? Are they able to develop 'people power' in the streets, as the pro-democrats in the Philippines did in 1986, thus preventing the military from cracking down on dissidents? Do they build strike funds and unemployment insurance to increase their economic bargaining power and authority as leaders? To what degree can they connect with many people and communities, thus compensating for their limited access to people in power? Can they draw on better knowledge of how society works – and can work – and disseminate it in reliable media? Can they link up with progressive intellectuals to develop alternative reform proposals, education and culture to gain popular authority?

Second cornerstone: Democratic links between the state and a society of equal citizens

The second cornerstone for social democrats is to cultivate strong and democratic links between the state and equal citizens in society. Given the primacy of democratic politics (rather than revolutionary means), democratic control of the police and military but also private security forces and militias is fundamental. Otherwise, the top priority is to promote impartial (non-corrupt) public institutions that people can turn to, and rely on, in their contact with the state, so that they do not have to call on patrons and other mediators. This calls for public governance that is as close as possible to the concerned people through decentralization and democratically regulated self-management. In addition, social democrats in power would prefer to reach out to people on the ground by way of effective and impartial institutions rather than by providing privileged contacts and protection to their own followers. The same argument relates to the judicial system – the rule of law must apply, guaranteeing to equal justice to all, and be independent of those with political and economic power.

It takes democracy

To build 'good governance' in this sense, social democrats have no illusions. Many professionals and businessmen may be in favour of just and effective institutions between the state and equal citizens, as well as the rule of law, but they rarely stand a chance against the most powerful actors. Rather it takes many more people to make a difference and implement effective and impartial administration and the rule of law. It takes democracy.

As previously mentioned, the aim of democracy is commonly thought of as popular control of public affairs on the basis of political equality. And democratization is the process of getting there. But it is necessary to be more precise.

Social democrats are sceptical of procedural definitions, according to which democracy is only a form of government based on a limited number of institutions (rules and regulations) such as nominally free and fair elections. Rather their position is instead to foster both liberal democracy and a number of other institutions to make freedom and fairness real. When I was involved in constructing a framework for assessing the problems and options for activists to promote such a substantive democracy in Indonesia, the following aspects were basic – in addition, of course, to the activists' own capacity to mobilize and organize.

Firstly, civil, economic and political freedoms – including of critical knowledge and expression as well as organization in bodies such as parties, citizen associations and trade unions – best summarized in the Universal Declaration of Human Rights. Secondly, the 'rule of law' with an independent judiciary on the basis of democratically decided laws and equal justice for all (no matter the class, religion, ethnicity or gender of the individual or whether they are a citizen or not). Thirdly, the substance of the institutions in terms of their quality and scope, beyond the formalities, as well as the extent to which powerful actors really adhere to the rules and regulations.

Fourthly, and particularly important for a substantive liberal democracy – representation. The right to vote is fine but the right to voice is equally important. Democratic political representation may be defined as authorization with a mandate and the obligation of the representative to be accountable, transparent and responsive, through the citizens' own party structures and organizations, and free and fair elections.

In the context of the third wave of democracy, the numerous deficits in this respect have been of special concern. Strong businesspeople, ethnic and religious leaders, the military and the political elite have been assuaged and able to sustain their power. Radical social democrats in particular have therefore tried to focus on reforms that enable more equal chances for all to participate and make a difference in elections. Thus it has been deemed necessary to augment political representation through elections with citizen participation and the representation of issue and interest organizations (from trade unions and employers' associations to environmental or educational groups) in public governance concerning matters that affect and engage them.

This representation must not be by appointment from above, but democratically from the bottom-up. Historically in the North, such channels of consultation and representation have been set up as democratic alternatives to, on the one hand, guild systems and state-imposed corporatism (such as fascist or communist institutions), and, on the other, to 'privileged contacts' and liberal lobbying, often sponsored by private business.

Human rights and citizenship

Human rights are certainly crucial in that they apply to each and every person, while the democratic governance of society is based on citizenship. The struggle for human rights usually precedes democracy, but historically it has taken authentic democracy to enforce human rights on a grander scale. Politically, therefore, along with battles for human rights, the bottom line is equal citizenship, in terms of legal status as well as membership, participation and rights.

From the social democratic perspective, the people with citizenship who decide on public matters should be based on habitation rather than on birth or, worse, ethnicity or religious identities. Habitation is the ideal, because birth, ethnicity and religion tend to come with inequalities in public life. The public affairs that citizens decide over, moreover, shall be matters beyond private life, religion and culture. Therefore, Social Democracy is in favour of the modern nation-state when democratic and with direct relations between state and equal citizens, meditated by citizens' own organizations.

These qualifications are crucial, because nation-states are not all the same. As brilliantly analysed by Ben Anderson in his *Imagined Communities*, there are different nationalisms. Over the years, some social democrats lost their compass, such as during the lead up to the First World War and regarding colonialism. By contrast, modern anti-colonial nationalism was rarely ethnic or religious nationalist with elements of xenophobia but internationally oriented – in search of solidarities for civic nationalism based on equal citizenship against global capital and empires and their indirect, often racist, colonial rule. Similarly, later on, northern social democrats like Olof Palme defended the rights of small nations against rival empires and free trade on equal terms against colonial and other monopolies.

Those priorities are fundamental reasons why progressive social democrats support modern national liberation in the South. This is in contrast to, for example, indirect colonial governance with autocratic rulers at the helm, dominating leaders of ethnic and religious communities and clans with different and unequal citizenship. The same applies to the more contemporary state leaders who govern in cooperation with leaders in ethnic and religious communities.

Generational priorities

In the North, the first-generation social democrats fought hard for equal citizenship, universal suffrage, the best-possible popular representation, as well as to study and practice democracy within their own movements. Women's pivotal importance in the struggle for full civil rights and everybody's right to vote expanded the idea of substantive citizenship and democracy.

Once in governing positions in state and local governments, radical social democrats tried to dismantle and tame aspects of capitalism by introducing public management and regulation of vital economic sectors as well as furnishing an extensive welfare system. Moreover, Swedish strategist Nils Karleby sketched a most influential framework for what was later known as 'functional socialism'. This did not focus on formal ownership (which was deemed as merely one of several institutions necessary to control the means of production) but on transformative policies to strengthen popular organizations, alter the destructive elements of capitalism and thus create conditions for more advanced reforms, aiming at Democratic Socialism.

Hence, it was also crucial to control and improve the instruments of governance. In Scandinavia in particular, the major means were public oral and written hearings on central and local government proposals, and citizen participation in the drafting of such policies. Particularly important, there was democratic representation of interest organizations such as unions and employers' organizations (along with professional and issue-based groups) in the development and implementation of public policies. Some of this is still in place, even if undermined by lobbying and new public management.

By contrast, the second generation of social democrats was more preoccupied with creating preconditions for democracy through national independence and state building. Struggles against imperialism for national economic development and land reform were deemed fundamental for substantive political and social equality. This was considered more important than democratic freedoms and procedures 'as such'.

Even eminent leaders like Nehru, who staunchly defended liberal democratic elections, gave priority to top-down centralized governance by the few elected actors. And the Singaporean socialists discarded democracy altogether, as did their epigones in Indonesia. Consequently, social democrats had no viable alternative to the West's Cold War obsession with 'middle class coups' or to the East's focus on (statist) 'national democracy', both drawing on military support.

The third generation of social democrats emerged among the radicals who stood up against rightist, as well as leftist, authoritarianism in the context of the liberal wave of democracy. Subsequently moderates more attracted by Blairite 'third way policies' gained the upper hand and negotiated compromises with reform-oriented sections of the elite. But in the view of the radicals, substantive democracy was fundamental and had to be built from below by way of decentralization, locally based citizenship, strong civil organizations and direct participation in government. Representation via elitist parties was not to be trusted.

The record of many civil society organizations, however, shows that they have acted on behalf of others without being accountable. And lobbyism has tended to be dominated by activists with 'good contacts'. The challenges have been overwhelming and many activists have resorted to unmediated representation by populist leaders. Typically, this has involved individual horse-trading, scattered reforms without strategic plans and protests against the 'establishment' that have been hijacked by competing right-wing leaders. Much of this book focuses on the causes of these dilemmas and whether and how there are feasible alternatives.

Third cornerstone: Social rights and welfare

While the first cornerstones of Social Democracy are sequential and focus on building popular capacities and democratic conditions for further advances, the remaining two may alternate and are policy oriented. Mainstream social democratic actors are often criticized for lack of strategy in terms of the already-mentioned transformative reforms and actions that strengthen crucial actors so that they are able to strive for more advanced aims – in the final instance for Democratic Socialism. This transformative approach was integral to successful historical projects, and it remains a critical question for the more recent efforts at new Social Democracy too.

The third cornerstone is about struggle – on the basis of common popular interests – for social rights, related welfare policies and rights in working life. This was already important for the first generation of social democrats who tried to resist and escape capitalism, including by self-help (e.g. through cooperatives) and demands for local government reforms. But primarily, radical leaders emphasized preparations for gaining political power whenever capitalism was in crisis to replace or at least dismantle capitalism by introducing elements of a socialist alternative from above that might prove more effective.

The turning point was when this focus on radical political change did not make sense in the face of the overwhelming world economic crisis in the late 1920s and early 1930s. The activists had, as it were, run offside. The staggering suffering among people in general called for immediate action. The idea of the working class grabbing power and proclaiming socialism that might help at some point in the future was unfeasible. Labourism prevailed for a long time but the answer was broader social and political alliances and early Keynesianism, including decently paid public works programmes and general support to stimulate consumption and thus production. Ideas of resisting from the grassroots and dismantling elements of capitalism when elected into government were thus combined with measures to tame, and slowly transform, it.

This is when work through the state and increasingly universal public programmes overtook the insufficient efforts at welfare in municipalities by self-help. The fundamental idea, then, was to instigate transformative reforms that would strengthen unionized labour, of course, but also a broad alliance between urban and rural labourers (and later on small primary producers and lower level professionals too). Thus they would be able to campaign for more advanced reforms. Additional rights related to working life, such as ensuring decent labour conditions and democracy in the workplace. Even though the employers were granted the right to manage production (in exchange for collective bargaining agreements), a number of participatory rights and practices were strived for, as were various ideas of co-ownership and cooperatives, at least initially.

Advances and challenges in the South

Self-help was even more important in the South. Moreover, social democratic-oriented activists in Kerala proved that it was possible to at least initiate inclusive economic development on the basis of commercial agriculture and advanced professional education. Generally speaking, however, comprehensive welfare state policies and rights in working life were only possible, as in the North, within the framework of the next cornerstone: attempts at growth coalitions (social pacts) between sections of capital and labour in the widest sense of the words, as well as between labour and agrarian producers. Comprehensive welfare programmes could only be expanded – and financed – when production was modernized. This was crucial for productivity-driven entrepreneurs too. Examples of measures that also benefitted them include the education, training, mobility and health care of blue, as well as white, collar workers, unemployment insurance (promoting flexibility) as well as kindergartens and other measures to facilitate workforce participation among women in particular. A major more recent dilemma is whether and how to combine 'handouts', including conditional cash transfers to strengthen poor people's individual capacities, with efforts to provide better jobs and support collective measures such as public social security but also cooperatives. Another is the unresolved challenge during the third wave of democracy – such as in India, Brazil, South Africa and the Philippines – to combine world market-oriented growth with transformative welfare reforms.

Fourth cornerstone: Social growth pacts

The most advanced Scandinavian social pacts were of two kinds. The first meant that the social democrats, in organizing not just urban but also rural labour for decent jobs, finally also acknowledged the progressive potential of small farmers. Agreements were negotiated between, on the one hand, the social democratic party and the labour movement at large, and, on the other, the farmers' parties and the agricultural cooperative movements. Farmers' support for social democratic governance was vouched in return for decent living for rural people too. Family-based agricultural units were protected against the full onslaught of the market and the concentration of land ownership. Hence, family farmers were shielded against 'accumulation by dispossession', a common occurrence in the context of the expansion of capitalism in the South. Equally important, this reduced the potential for rural support for fascism and Nazism, which was otherwise a decisive feature in central Europe.

The second pact was between the national confederation of trade unions and employers' associations. Both wished to avoid legislation as well as to reduce the excessive industrial conflicts that characterized Scandinavia during the early twentieth century. The crux was that unions' gained the right to broad nationally coordinated collective agreements in return for acknowledging the employer's right to manage production.

This was later supplemented with various workplace rights, and even demands for co-management as well as cooperative forms of ownership and production. But leftist social democrats lost steam in the 1970s. And self-management was never a priority.

In any case, the broad collective agreements meant that wages were compressed between different companies and sectors. This fostered both unity among workers and the competitiveness of the export sectors. Representatives from the export industries dominated the centralized unions as well as the employers' associations. The result was economic growth as well as more jobs.

Meanwhile workers in sectors that could have negotiated higher wages were, of course, less supportive. They were in strategic businesses such as docks and in sectors less exposed to international competition like construction. Employers in these sectors were able to compensate for higher wages by increasing prices. Yet the disgruntled workers also gained from general economic growth, and their friends and family members often worked in export production.

Equally important, it was the workers in less modern sectors that tipped the balance by supporting the pacts. They gained better wages thanks to the collective agreements. Their employers, in turn, certainly had to raise productivity in order to survive, and some failed. But laid-off workers got decent unemployment support while waiting for new jobs in the competitive sectors, which expanded quickly – also benefitting from increasing international demand for their products.

Prerequisites

The social growth pacts presupposed strong and unified organizations on the part of both labour and capital, and unions benefitted from low unemployment. Equally important, there had to be interest-based representation of both parties in public governance related to economic, labour market, welfare and research and education policies. The combination of the growth pacts, the welfare state system and the interest and professional representation served Scandinavia extremely well until the early 1970s. This is when its foundations in national citizenship and governance began to be undermined by the market-driven globalization of finance and production, along with neoliberal national economic politics and new public management of the public administration. Norway has so far been a partial exception, primarily because its oil revenues have been well managed. This was much thanks to the application of social democratic principles and interest representation – in total contrast to, for example, the way in which Venezuela's left-populist military has abused its country's revenues.

Challenges for the second- and third-generation social democrats

For the second generation of social democrats in the post-colonial world, similar growth pacts and dynamics were next to impossible. Specific demands for the welfare of labourers with fixed employment, and therefore strong bargaining power, were fought for, but universal schemes were not viable. Hence, various self-help projects via unions and cooperatives, in addition to ethnic and religious associations, were crucial. Economic development was weak and uneven, having been subordinated to colonial priorities for centuries. Organized capital and labour were marginal. Collective agreements between them as a basis for social pacts were unrealistic.

Instead, the first main priority was land reform. This was to weaken the power of landlords, who did not encourage the modernization of production and society, and to facilitate instead farmers' citizenship and productivity. The result would be more jobs and increased demand for industrial products. The second priority was state-directed planning for general growth and industrial development. Social rights and welfare measures had to wait. In the case of Singapore, the socialists even abandoned democracy, thus renouncing the basics of social democracy.

One of the few partial exceptions was the Indian state of Kerala. A comparatively consistent land reform was implemented in Kerala, but industrial development was poor. In fact, export and service-led growth might have been a better option – given that the broad struggle in Kerala since the early twentieth century for equal civil and social rights against the oppressive caste system and colonial rule had not only generated land reform and workers' protection, but also encouraged public healthcare and, especially, internationally competitive education. But rights-based export production did not fit well with the state-led industrialization and import-substitution envisioned by Nehru and most leftists outside Kerala.

Third-generation social democrats continue to grapple with these issues of rights, welfare and sustainable growth. The question is if there are any alternatives to, on the one hand, the authoritarian developmental states in East Asia, and, on the other, the stumbling attempts in South Africa and during the Latin American Pink Tide. The East Asian advances are subordinated to global capitalism and ignore issues of environmental sustainability, universal social rights and, in most cases, political rights too. The 'democratic developmental state' strategies during the Pink Tide and ANC governance in South Africa drew on a commodity exports boom and fused protection of organized labour with liberal economic policies, in addition to some efforts to increase productivity. But these strategies were not environmentally sustainable and could only provide social support to the disadvantaged, not generate increased employment throughout society in the context of viable inclusive development. Most fundamentally: while the northern social pacts did not have to grapple with huge numbers of unemployed people and could focus on ensuring decent jobs, the southern challenge is also to create more jobs.

For all these reasons, Social Democracy in the North as well as the South cannot be reinvented within the undermined national frameworks. There must be a more international alternative. As will be obvious from the case studies, this is basic for the renewal of Social Democracy, though difficult. Difficult, but not impossible. As sustainable economic development in the South, based on social justice and by democratic means, is also fundamental to fighting global warming and the causes of forced migration, as well as to reviving social democratic politics in the North.

3

Cases and contextual puzzles

Studying attempts at new Social Democracy calls for case studies from contrasting contexts (Chapter 1). Having specified the common themes in terms of the dimensions, strategies and challenges of Social Democracy (Chapter 2), the next step is to identify critical cases of such dilemmas. The idea is to advance our understanding by asking questions about social democratic puzzles in one case from the point of view of others. To qualify as critical, the cases must be significant and unexceptional. For several decades, I have followed efforts in this direction in the three very different contexts of Indonesia, India and the Philippines, as well as in the Swedish case of the first-generation partners. The experiences in Brazil and South Africa, as well as those of Norway and others in the North, have also been kept in mind. This chapter provides an overview of these historical legacies and experiments in renewing the social democratic cornerstones, and the related mysteries that we shall address in the major parts of the book.

Timeline of cases

1940s–1968
- The rise and fall of Indonesia's democratic Left.

1930s–1987
- Kerala's emancipatory unity and political stagnation.

1960s–1988
- Philippines' inconceivable 'people power'.

1960s–2010s
- Implications in the North: Sweden from internationalism to 'Social Democracy in one country'.

1986–2001
- Inventing Philippine Social Democracy.

1970–99
- Rise and demotion of the Indonesian democracy movement.

1999–2009
- Dilemmas of deepening democracy after Suharto.

1987–2001
- Kerala's renewal of Social Democracy.

c. 1985–2020
- Counter-movements in India: West Bengal – all-India – Kerala.

2001–20
- Inconclusive left-of-centre politics in the Philippines.

2004–20
- 'Reformist populism' in Indonesia.

2010s–2020
- Implications in the North: the Swedish stalemate.

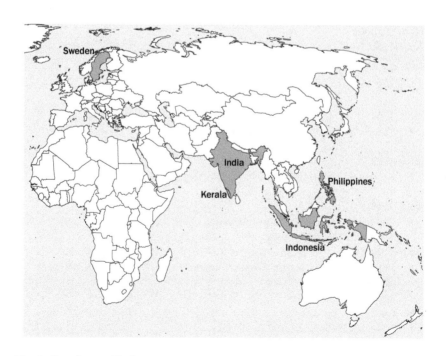

Map 1 Grand map with the cases.

Legacies of the second generation and effects on the first

In the background part of the book, four chapters identify the rise and fall of second-generation Social Democracy and implications for the first. This is to pinpoint the often submerged legacies and discuss whether and how the earlier dilemmas affected the efforts of the third-generation activists, and if they were able to take heed of historical lessons. The critical cases about the second generation are from Indonesia, India and the Philippines. There are also references to the North, Sweden in particular.

The specific puzzles are:

(i)   why the largest reformist popular movement in the world at the time – in Indonesia – was immensely successful until the 1960s but was then eliminated;

(ii) why the Social Democracy-oriented leftists in the Indian state of Kerala were initially even more successful but then suffered setbacks, and what we can learn from a comparison with the Left in another Indian state, West Bengal;

(iii) why many leftist (especially Maoist) perspectives disregarded democratization in the Philippines; and

(iv) why social democrats in the North failed to build an international framework, within which like-minded projects in the North and South could have supported each other, adjusting instead to market-driven globalization.

The rise and fall of Indonesia's democratic Left

The Indonesian case is found in Chapter 4. It commences with the leftists' remarkable achievements in the 1950s, in the framework of building broad democratic movements for civil and social rights. It then focuses on their giving in to populist nationalism under the 'guided democracy' system, and the subsequent catastrophe and massacres in 1965–6. How was it possible that the populism and 'guided democracy' that made President Sukarno and the reformist communists ideologically hegemonic could end in a devastating conspiracy and the annihilation of the world's largest reformist popular movement?

Kerala's emancipatory unity and political stagnation

Chapter 5 takes us to India, especially Kerala. Here outstanding achievements at civil emancipation and reduced inequalities from the 1930s onwards were rooted in anti-colonial and anti-upper-caste popular movements. Quests for equal civil and political rights, plus a unified Malayalam-speaking state, framed the struggles for land reform, workers' rights and welfare programmes. After a crackdown in 1959 by New Delhi on Kerala's first democratically elected government, the Left gradually stagnated. This was associated with faltering economic development and elitist horse-trading at the expense of the previous broad alliances. It is instructive to compare briefly with West Bengal on the other side of the country. Here the Left was more successful during the late 1970s and early 1980s in combining land reform and decentralization. But it was not as democratically rooted in popular demands for emancipatory civil and social equality.

Philippines' inconceivable 'people power'

Similarly, Chapter 6 addresses the particularly instructive case of the Philippines in the 1980s. The revolutionary Maoists had been hegemonic within the Left in the struggle against President Marcos' emergency, arguing that democratization and other advances presupposed armed revolution. Other leftists were also reluctant to prioritize democracy. The 'Hard Left' became less relevant, however, when liberals in particular gained ground in the struggle for democracy and the 1986 'people power' Revolution. Why did leftists miss the train? The road ahead was difficult. Yet, the activists pioneered the third generation of Social Democracy in Asia.

Cornered Social Democracy in the North: The case of Sweden

The setbacks for the second generation in the Global South aggravated the weakening of social democrats in the North. This is analysed in Chapter 7. Radical social democrats had become aware of the importance of the anti-colonial struggle, also of the freedom of small nations in the North against the superpowers. Sweden was a paradigmatic case in point from the mid-1970s onwards. The breakdown of the Bretton Wood agreement on international monetary management, the oil price increase and the rise of a new international division of labour and subsequent neoliberal governance began to undermine nationally confined growth pacts and welfare programmes. In addition, the backsliding of kindred partners in the South made it difficult to resist the new dynamics. From the 1970s, it was increasingly difficult to sustain the idea of bilateral development cooperation with progressive regimes and movements on the ground, such as within the non-aligned movement or with Vietnam. Thus, the concept of a 'New International Economic Order' and 'a North-South Programme for Survival' proved futile too. Subsequently mainstream Social Democracy adjusted to market-driven globalization and neoliberal governance, mainly opting for cooperation within the moats of the European Union and for aggressive exporting to 'emerging markets' in the South.

Third-generation mysteries

At the same time, the increasingly market- rather than state-driven globalization provided wider space for multilateral liberal and, to some degree, social democratic efforts. These included more human rights, 'good governance' and peace and democratization. The third and major part of the book is about the challenges faced by the third generation of social democratic activists in using this new room of manoeuvre to advance progressive politics. Critical cases are analysed in six interrelated chapters.

Inventing Philippine Social Democracy

Chapter 8 asks why it was so difficult, even after the successful Philippine 'people power' revolution, for the new social democrats to develop a viable alternative to the political and economic elite. There are five sub-cases of innovative projects. One is about the former commander of the New People's Army, Bernabe 'Dante' Buscayno, and his idea that class-based democratic change was possible. Dante wanted to try this out by organizing a huge farmers' cooperative among his original followers during the armed struggle and their relatives in his – as well as President Corazon Aquino's – home province of Tarlac.

Secondly, renewal-oriented 'popular democrats' tried to foster local community work among former Maoist supporters as an alternative to armed struggle.

Thirdly, social democratic activists tried to cultivate broad politics sprouting from progressive civil society organizations (CSOs) and trade unions. The 'three little pigs' of social democratic groups and the popular democrats (against the Maoist wolf) tried to make a difference in the 1992 presidential and senatorial election. To this end, they formed a non-party political alliance in support of progressive liberal candidates.

A related fourth attempt was made during the following years by the same groups, augmented by defected Maoists. Together they attempted to build a more coherent movement-based citizen action party, *Akbayan*, constituted in early 1998. A major source of inspiration was the successful rise of the new Workers' Party in the Brazilian local elections. In the Philippines, however, the prime room for manoeuvre stemmed from a constitutional amendment that enabled participation in national elections for a limited number of seats in the Congress on a separate party list.

Meanwhile several leaders were looking for something more ambitious and attempted – in that same year – to build a broad popular movement behind a potentially progressive presidential candidate with charisma and anti-imperialist inclinations. He was Joseph 'Erap' Estrada, an iconic movie star who – at least in his films – had sided with ordinary people. The idea was to exchange activists' support and labour for strategic positions in his administration in relation, for example, to agrarian reform. Estrada was indeed elected in 1998, and a few leftists gained ground. But nothing prevented other parts of his government from deteriorating. An ideologically mixed counter-movement succeeded in impeaching him in 2001 and conservative leaders got the upper hand.

Indonesia's stumbling multitude of creative pro-democrats

Chapter 9 is about the rise of the Indonesian democracy movement from the 1970s until the fall of Suharto in 1998, and its subsequent marginalization. The challenging question is why it did not do better? The reformist popular movements had been all but eliminated in the mid-1960s. Subsequently, any independent popular organizing was banned. The only exceptions were students and intellectuals who, back in the mid-1960s, had supported anti-communist officers like Suharto in the misguided belief that they would back civil liberties and democracy. The new dissidents' focus was on corruption, limited freedoms and the selling out of the country's resources to multinational companies. An alliance with nonconformist military leaders was brokered, but no popular organization developed. Following riots in January 1974, the opposition was curbed.

A subsequent younger generation of activists was increasingly influenced by dependency theory about imperialism and underdevelopment. They acted more cautiously via non-political CSOs. The aim was to foster alternative agendas and to support victims of repressive development, but most activists remained scattered and socially marginalized. Others limited themselves to study groups and analyses of class and power. By the late 1980s, however, several of them opted for political organization and sought leadership of the entire nation to stand up against the authoritarian exploitation. In reality though, there was no broad counter-movement to spearhead, only diverse protests. These activists' new emphasis was on a common enemy composed, in their view, of military and bureaucratic crooks, along with crony capitalists. This focus became crucial. A wider number of CSOs, students, intellectuals and some private professionals were also convinced of the urgent need for democracy. Finally, sections of the old political and religious elites joined in as well. Reports from progressives in the Philippines, South Korea, and later Berlin and Prague were reassuring. And more foreign support for civil society was available. This was the birth of the 'real' democracy movement. It remained polycentric, however, and without a solid social base and coordinating leadership, despite gaining strength during the economic and political crisis from 1996 until 1998. How did this happen?

Successively, the consistent activists lost out in the transition to elitist liberal democracy. Chapter 10 addresses the attempts to consolidate the scattered parts of the social democratically oriented movement after the fall of Suharto. This proved even more difficult than in the Philippines. Numerous actors joined mainstream parties and were co-opted. The new electoral laws made it next to impossible for economically weak dissidents to build parties and participate in elections, even on the increasingly important local level. Most genuine activists took refuge in CSOs and related social movements. How could this happen? It was not until the early 2000s that innovative attempts were made to regain the political initiative. They will be addressed in Chapter 14.

Kerala renewal by arduous participation and novel investments

The efforts at new Social Democracy in the Indian state of Kerala, analysed in Chapter 11, evolved under quite different conditions. It was obvious by the early 1980s that the old Left was deteriorating. This was in spite of land reform and efforts to sustain public welfare programmes. Renewal-oriented activists, inside as well as outside the organized Left, pointed to the need for broader alliances based on common interests and active citizenship rather than party-political affiliation. The idea was to combine this with efforts at new inclusive development agendas, as well as social rights and environmental concerns – spurred from below rather than through top-down planning.

The promotion of decentralization, active citizenship and people's planning was not unique. It recalled, for example, the ideas of participatory budgeting in Brazil. Yet, the activists wanted to renew, not replace, the old movements in Kerala. Their visions of inclusive alliances based on joint interest were rooted in the successful politics of the 1930s (analysed in Chapter 5). The new campaign took flight under the auspices of a State Planning Board, led by committed scholars. They had negotiated significant room for manoeuvre under a new Left Front Government. The Kerala case is thus one of renewing old social democratic-oriented policies and politics rather than replacing them. There is a double mystery involved: one, that the campaigns were possible and initially quite successful, and two, that subsequent challenges became overwhelming.

Fallen leftists in Kolkata, central-level campaigners and new Kerala efforts

Chapter 12 addresses three additional, but different, sub-cases in India of broadly speaking new attempts at Social Democracy and the efforts to build an alternative to neoliberalization in Kerala. One of the cases grew out of the previously identified political and economic stagnation in West Bengal (Chapter 5). The stagnation made the elitist Left negotiate rapid industrialization in cooperation with big Indian and foreign companies, in order to initiate inclusive, job-creating development. The informally employed labourers and small farmers were, however, not part of the equation, especially not those depending on fertile land subject to expropriation for 'development purposes'. Hence they jumped ship, along with many other frustrated Bengalis. As a result, the Left suffered humiliating losses and were voted out of power in 2011 after more than thirty years in office. How could this happen?

Another sub-case concerns several of the non-party-driven social movements in the country. These are often found among informal labour and related CSOs for decades having tried alternative organization from below. Meanwhile well-connected activists have advocated equal citizenship and social rights, along with welfare reforms, via the judiciary as well as reformist politicians, that is, within the Congress party under Sonia Gandhi. A number of vital social reforms were implemented during the left-supported Congress governments from 2004 to 2014. But were they successful?

Meanwhile, other activists focused more on issues of shallow democracy and corrupt governance. Frequently this implicated the Congress-led government. Bringing to mind the more recent Brazilian debacle, the liberal-leftist Indian government was thus voted out of power in favour of right-wing Hindu populists. Meanwhile, however, sections of the 'India against Corruption' movement that had turned against Congress's abuse of power managed to form a new 'Common Man's Party' (*Aam Aadmi Party*, AAP) and to win local elections in New Delhi with landslide margins, in 2013, 2015 and 2020. Local participatory practices and anti-corruption were made integral aspects of impartial public reforms. Yet, internal democracy suffered and the potential transformative outcome was less impressive. Why?

Finally we come to the exciting recent efforts to counter neoliberalization in Kerala. Already from the 1990s, the increasing rates of economic growth in Kerala were related less to local-level planning than to the liberalization of the Indian economy and the remittances from the millions of migrant labourers. Kerala's remarkable emphasis on human development based on public action has, thus, been taken advantage of mainly by individuals who export themselves rather than products and services. Non-leftist governments from 2001 made attempts at modern sector-based growth but failed, one reason being corruption. The leftists suffered from internal conflicts, opposed the new trends and tried to defend the weak sections of the population but lacked an alternative.

The Left government from 2016, however, has focused on reviving local production and strengthening public welfare and education, whilst simultaneously fostering public and private investment in modern sustainable production and services. The challenges include how to mobilize and negotiate welfare – and public as well as private investments – both locally and at larger scales, whilst maintaining democratic forms. These tasks became even more formidable with the severe flooding in late 2018 and the pandemic in 2020. Initially the calamities were fought successfully thanks to the previously introduced democratic decentralization. Later, however, state-wide coordination proved insufficient. Meanwhile, a hostile central government has raised fiscal constraints, to which the Left Front government has responded by extensive borrowing and fundraising. In addition, New Delhi supports rightist religious and caste-based populism, plus, along with the Congress-led opposition, corruption allegations. The Left stood tall, however, in the late 2020 elections to the local councils, focusing on better-coordinated state and local efforts to guarantee livelihood and combine welfare and development. This was certainly not enough to fight community transmission of Covid-19. But in sharp contrast to the otherwise gloomy dynamics in Modi's India, it has energized an exciting five-year budget plan, in face of State Assembly elections, to combine, on the one hand, productive and job-creating welfare measures and, on the other, investments in infrastructure, education and value-added production towards inclusive knowledge-based development. The dynamics are analysed in view of the insights presented in the following chapters, gleaned from studies of similar efforts and threats against progressive governments in other contexts, such as the Philippines, Indonesia, South Africa and Brazil. Against this backdrop, a major remaining challenge in Kerala is how to build democratic partnership governance of the new efforts and, meanwhile, to win the upcoming elections.

Frustrations of liberal-leftist cooperation in the Philippines

Chapter 13 analyses a more advanced case of liberal-left coalition building which materialized in the different context of the Philippines in the early 2000s. The efforts to form a popular front behind President Estrada ended, in 2001, in humiliating defeat (Chapter 8). While some leftists clung on to Estrada until the bitter end, claiming that he stood up for the poor, others took part in demonstrations against him. Years of radical leftist demonstrations against subsequent conservative governments followed without a breakthrough. Finally the protests ignited a coalition between progressive liberals and social democrats in the 2010 elections. The son of recently deceased Corazon Aquino, Benigno 'Noynoy', was elected president after Arroyo. The advances were not sufficient, however, to prevent the rise in 2016 of authoritarian right-wing populist Rodrigo Duterte. The dynamics were reminiscent of the end of the liberal-leftist government in New Delhi two years earlier, where new rights and welfare measures also did not lead to more inclusive economic development. In addition, the frustrated liberal-leftist ideas and rise of Duterte foretold the ascent in late 2016 of populist right-wing identity politics in Indonesia, as well as the fall of the leftist-liberal Brazilian coalition under Dilma Rousseff, followed in 2018 by the victory of right-wing populist Bolsonaro. How was this possible?

Indonesian experiments in 'reformist populism'

In Chapter 14 we return to the efforts of social democratically oriented Indonesian activists, now from the late 2000s. The consistent pro-democrats had been politically marginalized in the context of elitist democratization. They had either joined mainstream parties – typically being co-opted – or taken refuge in CSOs, which usually lacked roots in social movements. The conclusion from concerned research undertaken with the activists (co-directed by this author) became famous under the slogan 'Go Politics'. This was a challenging but feasible task. Even after the fall of Suharto, organized politics and public discussion were almost completely devoid of any leftist dimension. Innovative activists tried a number of strategies but nothing really worked. Given the context of uneven development, it seemed impossible to overcome – from the bottom up – activists' weak social base and the fragmentation of issues, interests and groups.

New opportunities had emerged from around 2004. Direct elections of political executives made mainstream leaders cast their nets wider, complementing clientelistic, individual relations with wider populist methods. Unions and respectable civil society leaders and their followers were useful too, thus gaining more influence than earlier by negotiating agreements of favours in exchange for votes and rallying behind the least objectionable politicians.

Meanwhile enlightened union leaders realized they had work to do beyond rallying in the streets and signing contracts with local politicians for better wages and employment conditions. They had to cater to the interests of casual workers too and contain low-wage competition, as well as linking up with CSOs, the urban poor, farmers and progressive politicians for more public welfare. This is how a successful broad alliance developed for universal public health reform in the early 2010s.

Meanwhile 'Jokowi' (Joko Widodo) became the country's most successful mayor (of Solo/Surakarta) and later governor (of Jakarta) by negotiating urban development plans, including welfare schemes, with business, CSOs and urban poor organizations. He was even elected president in 2014, assisted by the anti-corruption commission in scrutinizing, as far as possible, potential cabinet members and senior bureaucrats.

Chapter 14 analyses the potential but also the sad fate of these efforts. The groups slid back into individual negotiations about special interests, at worst with whatever politician was the highest bidder – including 'Indonesia's Trump', Prabowo Subianto, an abusive former general and son-in-law of Suharto. Finally, the Governor of Jakarta after Jokowi, 'Ahok' (Basuki Tjahaja Purnama), who in spite of being Christian and ethnic-Chinese was widely appreciated for efficient governance, lost the 2017 elections as a result of a successful campaign by hostile elites who utilized Muslim identity politics and accused 'Ahok' of blasphemy. As the 2019 presidential elections approached, with Prabowo again as the main opposition, Jokowi retreated, trying to retain his position by handouts and agreements with nationalist officers and conservative ulamas. Having secured a second term in the Palace, moreover, Jokowi enforced a top-down neoliberal 'Job Creation Law' to attract investments at the expense of environmental protection and labour regulations. What were the major stumbling blocks that brought down the reformist movement? And what are the chances for new student and popular counter movements to reclaim the struggle for welfare and democracy?

During this period there were also remarkable achievements in the westernmost province of Aceh. Aceh suffered from decades of conflict with the central government, and finally also from the devastating tsunami of December 2004. Subsequently peace and reconstruction were enabled by an agreement guaranteeing autonomy and democratization, including the right to form local parties. As analysed in Chapter 10, democracy-oriented actors won local elections in late 2006, but many of the opportunities were squandered. Chapter 14 addresses the reformists' initially promising, but subsequently ineffective, efforts to regain the initiative. The degeneration was partly due to the priorities of Jakarta and the international community. And the major question is of course, why?

The northern stalemate

The final substantive Chapter 15 returns to the fate of the first-generation social democrats in the case of Sweden. As discussed in Chapter 7, the attempts in the 1960s and 1970s to erect alternatives to the rise of market-driven globalization, by way of close cooperation with like-minded partners in the South and a New International Economic Order, foundered. Priorities changed in favour of structural adjustment to the neoliberal order and the liberal third wave of democracy, along with export promotion and Europeanization. After some initial fascination with Blairite 'third way policies', Social Democracy suffered badly, but by 2014 the Swedish social democrats managed to limp back into office, in coalition with the Green Party. Attempts were made to revive the idea of rights-oriented foreign policies and international Keynesianism. The new priorities included a 'Global Deal' on fair trade, investments and labour conditions along with the strengthening of international unionism and social corporate responsibility. Within two years, however, most of the efforts had petered out. In face of the influx of many refugees from the economic and political crisis in the South, there was no internationally oriented alternative to the rising tide of right-wing nationalism. Similarly, the leftist efforts to fight growing inequalities and rebuild the welfare state are quite inward. How did this happen? As Chapter 15 explains, it was not an inevitable surrender. Social Democracy can do better.

Part Two

Legacies of second-generation Social Democracy

4

Progress and demise of the world's largest popular reform movement in Indonesia

'Why are you delving into the boring rigidities of the old Left when there are emancipatory movements out there?' my very good friend, anarchistic Professor Jim Scott, teased me. Because, I replied, we must get history right, especially since the problems of the old movements did not disappear with them. There are lessons for the new activists too.

In any case, this is now the reason for Chapter 4.

The second-generation social democrats were part of the struggle against colonialism and racism, from the early twentieth century onwards. Northern friends were not very helpful. Their struggle for Democratic Socialism presupposed industrial capitalism and basic political liberties, a rarity in the colonial world. Communists, by contrast, claimed that avant-garde parties could substitute for a unified labour movement and impose political shortcuts to progress, as in the Soviet Union. They were more relevant in the South. Still, liberation movements like the Indonesian were mainly fighting colonialism. Their prime demands were equal citizenship and economic and social rights, in modern and democratic nation-states. At times, communists joined in.

Once in power, however – Nehru in India is a classic example – second-generation social democrats combined democratic elections of leaders with enforcement of central plans for industrialization and state-level plans for land reform. Industrialization was brought about more in cooperation with nationalist businessmen than with workers. And land reforms, to the extent that they were implemented, were more with tenants than agricultural labourers. More substantive democracy would have to wait, as well as social rights and welfare. International politics, by contrast, gained top priority. The aim was political and economic independence of the East from the West. The 1955 Bandung conference in Indonesia, with Nehru and Sukarno at the forefront, fostered the global non-aligned movement.

Most communists, in India as well as Indonesia, adjusted to this trend by enlisting pressure politics to push for more radical reforms and priorities. Moreover, the joint answer to domestic economic setbacks and resistance from old colonizers and new US hegemons was to boost nationalism and state leadership. Such was the thinking behind Sukarno's 'guided democracy' in 1959 and Indira Gandhi's 'war against poverty' ten years later.

The subsequent Indonesian catastrophe in 1965 was among the first and most deadly of the counter-blows against this route. India's 1975 State of Emergency was serious but resisted by broad oppositional movements – (flawed) democracy prevailed. What brought about these and similar failures of the second-generation social democrats? What are the legacies? We begin in Indonesia.

The rise of a democratic Indonesian Left

After the Second World War, the Japanese gave up Southeast Asia and the colonial powers tried to get back in. The British and Americans defeated militant nationalists

---

Timeline Indonesia 1910s–1970s

1910s
- Rise of the independence movement.

1942
- Japanese occupation.

1945–9
- Japanese leave – British arrive – Dutch return.
- Republic proclaimed – Sukarno president.
- Socialist united front government.
- Political and various militia struggle for liberation.

1948
- Dutch on the offensive.
- Radicals split.
- Moderates form new government.
- Communists repressed.
- *Darul Islam* revolt for Islamic state.

1949
- Round table agreement with Dutch.
- United States of Indonesia acknowledged.

1950
- Unitary Republic of Indonesia proclaimed.
- Conservative government.

1951–5
- New communist leadership.
- Communist support of nationalist government.
- Rapid advances for reformist communists.

1955
- Birth of Non-Aligned Movement in Bandung.
- Free and fair parliamentary elections.
- Remarkable communist gains.
- Inconclusive results and weak nationalist government.

1957
- Regional revolts – Emergency laws supported by the communists.
- Sukarno introduces coalition government, inclusive of communists.
- Communists win local elections in Java.
- UN refutes Indonesian claims on West Papua, but Sukarno stands tall.
- Radical unions occupy Dutch companies.
- The army gains control of the companies.

1958
- Regional revolts increase, with US support.
- Occupied companies nationalized but army retains control.

1959
- National elections postponed.
- Sukarno and army proclaim 'Guided Democracy'.
- Communists excluded from government, but considered and supportive.

1960–3
- Left-nationalists and communists focus on land reform and anti-imperialism.
- Unions supressed.
- Sukarno proclaims NASAKOM unity: Nationalists, Muslims and Communists.
- West Papua integrated in Indonesia.
- Confrontation with British-style independent Malaysia.
- British and other foreign companies taken over (by army).

1964
- Local conflicts over land reform.
- Sukarno instructs communists to retreat.

1965–6
- Rural conflicts continue.
- 30th September Movement with communist leaders against conservative generals.
- Ignorant communist party and left-nationalists scapegoated.
- Army-led political genocide along with rightist militias against leftists.
- General Suharto gains control of government.

1967–8
- Sukarno deposed as president, replaced by Suharto (1967).
- Maoist-style uprisings crushed.

Map 2 Indonesia.

in Malaya and the Philippines. But the French tried in vain in Indochina, while the inexperienced Americans – perceptively depicted in Graham Greene's *Quiet American* – were only able to postpone the denouement. And the Dutch must give up Indonesia.

Towards the end of the Indonesian liberation struggle, the leftists – the communists in particular – were hard pressed. Conservatives had taken the lead in the new Republic. The radicals in Solo (Surakarta), Central Java, and Madiun, East Java, failed to resist the decommissioning of their militias, and many were killed and arrested. In return, the United States and the Dutch agreed to an independent Indonesian federation.

Soon enough, however, President Sukarno and the nationalist party regained the initiative by speaking up for the consummation of national liberation and a unitary state. From 1950, just as in India (Chapter 5), a new generation of communist leaders adjusted, thus assuming much of what constituted second-generation Social Democracy. They provided critical support in return for protection. They added mass-based pressure politics. Initially with only a few thousand members, the Indonesian Communist Party (PKI) became the fourth largest party in the 1955 national elections and won partial local elections in Java and South Sumatra in 1957. By the early 1960s, about one-fifth of the population were members or sympathizers, organized in interest and issue-based mass organizations. Along with the leftist nationalists, they constituted probably the world's largest reformist popular movement.

In the early 1960s, the Cold War escalated and China added militant anti-imperialism to the mix. The Americans became more entangled in Indochina and conflicts mounted in Indonesia. In 1965, the '30th of September Movement', with dissident officers at the helm and secret support from communist leader D. N. Aidit, tried to dethrone seven top army generals, but failed. Their putsch (against the generals not the president) became the scapegoat for a military-led campaign to annihilate the entirely unprepared progressive movement, way beyond the hard-core communists. The campaign was remarkably successful. More than half a century later, Indonesia has still not regained a significant leftist dimension in politics and social life.

The mysteries

That afternoon in Jakarta in 1979 was not as warm as usual, and my destination – a bungalow in affluent Menteng – was rather close by, so I decided to walk. Yet, I had to stop along the canal to prevent sweating. I was nervous, verging on scared. What would the senior intellectuals say to this young researcher, a fake Indonesianist?

No interest in Indonesian culture had brought me here, only a political debate. Since the early 1970s, I wanted to call the cards of the Maoists around the world who kept saying that their idea of a peasant revolution was confirmed by the defeat of the reformists in Indonesia. Over the years, I had also become sceptical of the opposite argument, that the Indonesian Left had been so successful that there were no reasons for its leaders to engage in the conspiracies in 1965, which the military used as a justification for its massacres and elimination of the entire popular movement. To venture into this, I should, ideally, have undertaken field studies. But given the Suharto regime, that was impossible. So I had to focus on theory and strategy, and base myself on literature and limited archives. In the late 1970s, however, almost fifteen years after the massacres, as the few surviving leftist leaders were finally released in Jakarta, I thought I simply must find a way of getting into the country and asking their views, before concluding my PhD thesis. But how would that be possible, without an Indonesian studies milieu in Scandinavia to fall back upon? There were friendly hints from concerned colleagues, at home and in the Netherlands. But as field studies had not been on the horizon, I had even neglected my language studies, rather spending time with books and articles about similar problems in other contexts, to learn of Indonesia by comparison. And now I was to meet, among others, the foremost progressive poet, Sitor Situmorang, freed from the imprisonment he had endured after the fall of Sukarno.

So I carried on, like a country boy in the city, dried the sweat from my forehead, rang the bell at the gate and was relieved. We understand, Sitor said. You are welcome. There are so few scholars who can examine our experiences, and we need comparisons. We will connect you to some key individuals and they will take it further.

***

Subsequent conversations during the next few years, with recently released leaders in Indonesia and exiled leaders in Europe, confirmed my doubts and added new ones. Remarkably, the typical answer was that the communist party was not really involved (in the putsch), but that Aidit (the chairman) and a few others were: Aidit was worried by the rural conflicts (…) He thought the alternative was to sow divisions among the military and other enemies (…) And, finally, since the party was not informed about the conspiracy, there was no plan B on how to act if it failed. So everyone was exposed to repression. And everything collapsed.

But if so, what were the root causes?

Joesoef Isak was a superbly connected senior journalist back in the day, before being imprisoned for ten years after the fall of Sukarno. Now, from the late 1970s, he was editing outstanding leftist author Pramoedya Ananta Toer's novel quartet, drafted in the Buru island concentration camp. Our conversations were invaluable. After a while,

Isak sighed deeply, tried several formulations and finally concluded: You see, Aidit was inspired by the recent coup in Algeria against Ben Bella, which had benefitted radicals.

I wanted to dig deeper into this, of course. But all information was off the record, and sufficient substantiation was not available. Many released leaders lamented: one does not want to be called a traitor or revisionist (…) or be accused of blaming the victims (…) But things went wrong (…) Now we cannot stop thinking about it (…) And why is there no new movement, in spite of all the exploitation and oppression?

It took almost three decades until fine historian John Roosa, among others, could confirm the role of the communist leader, D. N. Aidit, in detailed and well-documented studies. Yet, my early doubts and insights in the late 1970s helped me identify, at least, what I continue to deem the major mysteries. *If* the Maoist critique of the PKI for being reformist was right, what explained the unprecedented advances of the reformist Left until the late 1950s? *If* the communist leader was involved in an elitist putsch, what were the problems that made him abandon mass politics? And, *if* there is something to historical materialism, why have not Indonesian exploitation and subordination generated a new progressive movement, such as occurred after political disasters and killings in other countries, such as Spain?

Why was reformism successful until the late 1950s?

Indonesia was not primarily liberated on the battlefield. From late 1945 – when the Japanese were defeated elsewhere and left Indonesia, and the Republic was proclaimed – local militias and some regular troops were certainly important in fighting the Dutch, who returned and tried to regain control. But essentially, the country became ungovernable. How?

The way the Dutch had governed Indonesia combined central despotism with indirect rule through local communities, dominated by feudal-like leaders and strongmen. The Dutch lost because this was made impracticable by the liberation movement. The major progressive part of the movement was no war-machine or even a central committee. It was rooted in a secular and quite plural congregation of modern nationalists and their associations, many of them with a long history since the 1910s. Even though they had different religious and ideological beliefs, and even though the activists fought for their own livelihoods and different interests, they educated ordinary people and tried to practise equal rights and active citizenship. They even fostered a unifying new Indonesian language. In the mid-1940s, a direct link was thus forged between fledgling citizens and the new independent government and state apparatus, set up in August 1945, as a tentative alternative to the indirect colonial governance. When workers in sugar plantations, for example, got together in democratic unions to reclaim land and grow food to eat, they undercut the basic colonial subordination of people and extraction of resources. Yet, what would be the new form of government?

The Dutch tried to recover some indirect control by enforcing a federation of self-governed provinces in return for acknowledging Indonesia's independence. But as already mentioned, once Indonesia was recognized worldwide in 1949, the principled national leaders hit back immediately. The new state was made unitary, complete with intensive campaigns for an ethnically neutral version of Malay as the national language.

Still, the struggle for a civic and democratic alternative to colonial rule was far from over. Some of the anti-colonial militants wanted independent Indonesia to be based on Muslim communities rather than equal secular citizenship. Several of them joined rebel movements. In addition, many leaders who had instead fostered modern citizenship to undermine colonialism did not find the popular organizations that had emerged from that process to be powerful enough to advance their personal interests within the new Republic. Hence, these leaders often rehashed the positions of the former 'traditional' heads of religious, ethnic and local communities. Thus they were able to provide common people with patronage and contacts with the new state in return for tributes and votes.

At the helm, President Sukarno certainly practised the art of divide and rule in negotiations with these leaders. Primarily, however, he bypassed them by reaching out directly to the 'ordinary citizens' as the supreme populist mouthpiece of an emancipatory nationalist vision that applied to everyone.

The communists added critical support. Their demands were varied, including better conditions for workers and tenants, rights for peasants to reclaim land from plantations, and nationalization of foreign companies. But all the demands were brought together under the unifying umbrella of fulfilling the ideals of national independence, on the basis of equal citizenship and democracy.

To this end, the communists also built impressive educational, cultural and cooperative movements. And they supported women's rights and full citizenship for the ethnic Chinese. In the early 1950s, the number of communist followers increased rapidly. Organizations and chapters multiplied. Plans were drawn up for further expansion in the villages, beyond the strongholds in urban, industrial and plantation areas. There is almost unanimous scholarly agreement that the communists built the only modern party and mass movement in the country's history, while also gaining from Sukarno's populism. In addition, more generally, Indonesia benefitted from dynamic debates and vibrant popular organization in the build-up to the most free and fair elections (in 1955) that the country has ever experienced.

However, while the combination of class and citizenship explains the unprecedented advances, the achievements also proved dangerous. From next to nothing, the communists became the fourth largest party in the general elections in 1955. Moreover, the overall results were inconclusive and no stable government could be formed. The communists made further gains in the 1957 local elections in Java and South Sumatra. Most other parties feared the communists' electoral momentum and cooperation with the president. The contending leaders wanted to postpone further elections. Some of them even initiated regional revolts, with American support. To counter this, Sukarno asked for more presidential powers. Moreover, radical unions gained ground in nationalizations of Dutch companies, as part of the campaign for the western part of New Guinea (Papua) where the Dutch retained control, but the military replaced the Dutch managers.

This was a watershed. The communists agreed, reluctantly, to support more central state powers. These included emergency regulations along with territorial organization of the Army down to the very village level, with parallel civil and military governance of public affairs. New elections were postponed, the existing parliament was dissolved and the parties that had supported the regional revolts were prohibited. In 1959 Sukarno proclaimed 'Guided Democracy' and was supported by the Army as well as by the communists.

From then on, the president and his supposedly loyal generals were at the helm, only consulting top-down appointed representatives of privileged organizations. This, and the way in which the communists tried to strengthen their own positions, takes us to the second question of why Aidit, the communist leader, took part in the devastating putsch six years later.

What problems of mass-based politics led to the engagement in an elitist conspiracy?

The communists wanted equal citizenship and democracy, along with a number of class-based reforms, but they had agreed to the introduction of 'guided democracy', including parallel civil and military governance, and the postponement of elections. The only option they had left was that of gaining anti-imperial and anti-feudal ideological hegemony, in addition to actual power within the state, including among soldiers and military officers, through popular pressure politics. This was based on the strength of the unions and peasant organizations and could best be done in alliance with Sukarno, within the framework of his decrees and campaigns.

One campaign was the struggle against the Dutch for the incorporation of the western part of New Guinea (Papua), the remaining part of their colonial empire in the region, into Indonesia. Later on there followed confrontation with the former British colony, now the 'neo-colonial state of Malaysia'. A vital component was the nationalization of Dutch and later British and American companies. Another major campaign was the implementation of a new Basic Agrarian Law. Yet another was participation in public governance and company management by appointed representatives of the nationalist, religious and communist parties and movements (*NASAKOM*) that adhered to 'guided democracy', supervised by the president and the military. Along with ideological hegemony, this afforded some influence, protection and space for pressure politics but how much?

The anti-imperialist campaigns did not really undermine their opponents

According to the increasingly Maoist-inspired communists at the time, the main adversaries were the equivalents of private 'comprador businessmen' within politics, administration and the military. They were labelled 'bureaucratic capitalists' for all practical purposes meaning those collaborating with foreign business and western powers. However, unlike the private compradors, the 'bureaucratic capitalists' of higher officers within politics, administration and the military were deemed not to have a class base of their own in production and trade. Ultimately, their power was instead supposed to rest with the private 'comprador businessmen', foreign companies and the West. Consequently, the calculation was that the anti-imperialist campaigns and nationalizations would severely weaken the 'bureaucratic capitalists'. But did this work?

It did not. Many officers and senior bureaucrats were sceptical of the leftists and their anti-imperialism. Yet, they did not reject the nationalizations of the foreign companies. Control of production is not just about formal ownership. While not actually owning the companies, the officers and senior bureaucrats controlled them as well as the workforce even though the unions staged protests. In this regard, the emergency laws, the army's territorial organization down to the village level and the joint civil–military governance were crucial. Those in command of public offices and companies did not have the right to buy and sell firms or shares, but they could negotiate and provide services in return for benefits. And the military itself became economically self-sufficient.

Suparna Sastra Diredja was founding member and senior leader of the plantation workers' confederation (*Sarbupri*) at the time. By 1980, when we met, he was exiled in a bleak Dutch suburb, reflecting: the military were in command of the companies (…) we could demonstrate against imperialism and 'bureaucrat capitalists' and ask for representation in management. But the party had called off strikes to prevent repression, so we had very little to put up against them.

The land reform struggle turned divisive

The communist route to new strongholds in the villages by campaigning for the Basic Agrarian Law proved equally troublesome. The law had been advocated by communists and leftist nationalists. Its rationale was to increase production by easing the plight of the sharecroppers and by distributing 'surplus land' (from large holdings) to the landless tillers. The communists and leftist nationalists, often inspired by Maoism, added that the most important aspect was to alter the balance of power by mobilizing the peasants and their allies against landlords and the other 'village devils'. This would be possible through quite legal campaigns for the implementation of the law. But was it?

Dr Ina Slamet, the scholarly director of the communist party's study of the rural class structure, reflected: our team was of course expected to legitimate the campaign, but we did also point to the complicated forms of exploitation and the shortage of 'surplus land', neither of which was well-considered in the law (…) Our political leaders asserted, however, that this would not prevent the party and peasant movement from mobilizing people and increasing their power – after which we could solve the problems with the imperfect law.

In reality, the overriding problem proved how to unify people in favour of the law, given the various interests coalescing around private and community ownership of land, tenancy relations and debts. Meanwhile there were few big landowners for most peasants to unite against, aside from plantations, not covered by the law. Perhaps worse, the better off in the villages could utilize their powerful connections within religious and conservative nationalist communities to mobilize support against radical peasants.

Djadi Wirosebroto was a senior leader in the communist peasant organization *Barisan Tani Indonesia* in the early 1960s. After the crackdown on the popular movements in 1965–6, he joined a local Maoist uprising in 1967–8. This he soon found impractical and defected from, but he staunchly defended the previous actions. And just out of prison in 1980, he hit the nail on the head in an intense conversation: don't blame my organization, we followed the law, and we mobilized many people. (…) But the law did not help us to handle all the demands and conflicts among people. And yes, therefore the peasants' own committees were frustrated (…) We had initiated these committees, but we were not in control. The committee leaders asked for more than was in the law, as they thought it was insufficient, which it was. And then the committees acted unilaterally (…), but their adversaries were able to hit back, forcefully.

In late 1964 the conflicts were getting out of hand, and in December Sukarno ordered the actions to be cancelled, immediately.

A few months later, moreover, the risk of military intervention prevented Sukarno himself from favouring leftist-nationalists and communists, and marginalizing conservative members of his National *NASAKOM* Front.

Struggle for equal citizenship and democracy downgraded

In short, the major problem from the late 1950s onwards was the diminution of the equal citizenship-and-democracy aspect of the previously successful reformist struggle. Without a focus on democratic control of public assets and resources, in the last instance by way of elections, radical nationalism could not hope to undermine the real strength of the 'bureaucratic capitalists', who were in political command of these assets and resources. On the contrary, these adversaries could even capture them and contain the workers' struggle, by way of 'guided democracy', including parallel civil and military governance and nationalization of foreign companies.

Similarly, in the rural areas, the land reform law did not help many of the rural poor. They were divided by much more varied tenancy relations, working conditions and size of ownership than considered in the law. Worst, the previously unifying framework of citizenship and democracy had been neglected. Thus it was no longer strong enough to help them stand up to the local strongmen. And the latter's source of power was, in turn, not just the control of land but also dominance of the village and town councils, wielded in cooperation with the military, as well as through the often religious old communities and loyalties that had served as the basis for indirect colonial rule.

Leaders cornered

In short, while the communists and radical nationalists gained ideological hegemony and many followers, their strategy to reduce the strength of their main adversaries (the civil and military 'bureaucratic capitalists' and the rural strongmen) was undermined. Thus, the third pillar of success – to gain influence within the state, including the military forces – was also weakened. So there *were* reasons for the top party leaders to contemplate alternatives. The preferred option was that party leader, D. N. Aidit, would rely on the party's unofficial special bureau (which since the early 1950s had developed networks among progressive officers) to encourage an internal military putsch against the most anti-communist generals (but certainly not President Sukarno). This was a strictly limited putsch that would neither involve nor put at risk the vulnerable party and the huge popular movement. But it backfired.

Historical roots of belated new leftism

Currently there are two major answers to the question of why the thorough expansion of capitalism in Indonesia during more than half a century since 1965 has not given rise to a notable leftist dimension in social and political life, even after the end of Suharto's dictatorship. One is the shallow social foundations and fragmentation of the new interest organizations and other pro-democracy groups. This proposition is important and we shall return to it in subsequent chapters, but it is short of a sufficiently long historical perspective. In the first view, history seems to begin in the 1970s, with the first student protests against Suharto. The other explanation is more convincing. It stretches further back in time, to the destruction of the Left after the 30th of September Movement in 1965, and calls for a more detailed discussion.

Aside from probing the details of the 30th of September Movement, the major focus of research about the catastrophe in 1965–6 has been on how the extensive pogroms and killings were possible, and how they were carried out. Some scholars stress the involvement of religious and other militias and vigilantes, especially in East Java. Others agree this was important but point to the leading role of the military. There is now convincing evidence in favour of the latter position. As shown by Jess Melvin in particular, Suharto could draw on readymade military plans to curb and exterminate what he and his men considered a major threat against the state and nation. There were certainly regional differences, but the suppression was nationwide. There were overlapping conflicts concerning land, religion and related actors, but these were not new and concerted pogroms and killings came as a surprise. So although the social and political conflicts had intensified in the early 1960s, and even though equal citizenship and democracy (as means to reduce and handle them) had deteriorated, the role of the military was paramount. In short, there would not have been a political genocide without Suharto's central command, which saw to it that the regional and local military served as instigator, legitimizer and facilitator.

The first step was control of media and psychological warfare. President Sukarno's (and of course communist leaders') were prevented from reaching out with their information directly to military officers, civil administration and the people at large to oppose the fake news about a communist coup d'état and plans to kill their adversaries.

Secondly, the role of the military in the annihilation of the communists and radical nationalists was certainly played out in different ways, but there was a pattern. This related to its capacity.

Where the military was solid – that is, not diluted by progressive sympathies and prepared to follow the instructions of President Sukarno – and had access to sufficient troops, as well as was reluctant to grant arms to previously rebellious Muslim militias, the repression and killings were swift and extensive (as in Aceh) or contained (as in West Java, and, initially, in Riau and South Sumatra).

Where the military was weakened by internal divisions and insufficient numbers of reliable troops, the suppression and killings were delayed but sparked off when anti-communists were provided with enough support (e.g. in North Sumatra). Where the military itself, and the civil provincial and local administration, included significant Sukarno and communist loyalists – most typically in Central Java and Bali – spearheading troops were sent from Jakarta to enforce suppression and killings. Thanks to admirable historical research, we know now that the initial pogroms and killings by the military, in cooperation with anti-communist militias, were typically public and complemented by mass detentions of everyone associated with the communists and the leftist nationalists. The progressives were unprepared and without any instructions other than to stay calm and rely on President Sukarno's ability to solve the crisis. At times, local progressives even preferred detention to mob violence, hoping for decent treatment by the authorities. Thereafter the most extensive killings involved the secret executions of 'disappeared' detainees, carried out under the supervision of the military and the civil militias.

All this points to a state-directed political genocide (in contrast to the ethnic and religious genocides acknowledged in the UN conventions) of about half a million people (i.e. not 'just communists') – plus the detaining of others for decades and the depriving of their relatives' civil rights. However, it does not explain why Indonesia differed from other contexts such as Spain, Germany and parts of Latin America where renewed leftist perspectives entered social and political life after similarly brutal and extensive repression. How to solve the mystery, then, of why the effects of the killings and repression in Indonesia have been so enduring?

My initial entry point is that although the military did play the leading role, it has to be admitted that the Indonesian genocide also came with the particularly extensive participation of local militias and vigilantes, combined with political, religious and ethnic identity politics. Most importantly, it is the symbiosis or, with historian John Roosa, the triangular relations between the central and local military and the militias that need to be further explained.

My second vantage point is that this is about more than military command and orders. The Indonesian state's capacity to implement its policies was limited. The military did not have a popular base in a movement or party, as, for example, in Hitler's National Socialists. And there was no hard-core ethnic, religious or even utopian framework for the campaigns. Hence, the military had to adjust to local sentiment and work with civilian groups and militias. But how?

Ironically, some leads came out of a lengthy conversation with the anti-communist General Nasution. Nasution was the most senior general at the time and the only one to escape arrest and assassination by the mutineers. I felt uneasy meeting and talking with a mass murderer. Afterwards, actually, an exiled leftist leader and friend refused to see me. But in early 1980, Nasution had just signed a critical 'Petition 50' to Suharto. Most importantly, he was eager to talk about his long adherence to modern nationalism and professionalism, in contrast to Suharto: I was more inspired, Nasution insisted, by Tito's unification of Yugoslavia than by the Americans who were backing up technocrats and abusers of power like Suharto (…) and I wanted to curb the communists as legally and professionally as possible, as in West Java. Others did not.

This was a reminder of the different nationalisms and types of governance. The Indonesian liberation struggle in the 1940s was brutal and localized, with many militias involved. As Geoffrey Robinson has stressed, its legacies explain some of the brutality of 1965–6. Yet, one should also recall the differences between two types of freedom fighters, hinted at in the beginning of this chapter. On the one hand, there were those whose ideas of independence were rooted in patrimonial leadership and differentiated citizenship, mediated indirectly through ethnic, religious and local communities. But there were also others who aimed at a secular modern nation-state based on equal citizenship meditated directly by citizens' own parties and interest and issue organizations.

When Indonesia's independence was internationally recognized in 1949, those in favour of indirect citizenship maintained many of their militarized task forces and communal organizations while the leftists and their militants were defeated by the new Conservative-led national army.

After 1950, however, a new generation of leftists made a fresh start by opting for peaceful and democratic means to sustain the ideals of equal citizenship. They were opposed by officers and local leaders who staged regional rebellions. But the then new Army Chief of Staff, General Nasution, stood by the unitary state. He curbed the rebels and later fostered 'guided democracy', along with Sukarno. And the Left adjusted.

President Sukarno's left-populism and 'guided democracy' – supported by the PKI and in tandem with Nasution's statist nationalism – thus sustained the idea of a modern nation-state with direct relations to its citizens. But the democratic mediation of citizenship was abandoned. Hence, the conflicts could only be fought by way of, on the one hand, conservative might and horse-trading and, on the other, radical mass mobilization and pressure politics. Moreover, as we know, the radical campaigns did not really undermine the strength of the adversaries. So a few leftist leaders fomented the '30th of September Movement'.

How did General Nasution act after the putsch on 1 October 1965? As anti-communist Chief of the Armed Forces – but without either direct command of troops or Tito's popular following – he preferred arrests to mass murder but soon set aside his 'statist nationalism' and joined instead the less principled generals in favour of indirect governance.

Nasution's decision may best be described as akin to that of the Dutch in the 1920s. Gerry van Klinken has drawn my attention to the way in which the Dutch at the time contemplated more modern forms of governance but also, among other challenges, had to suppress the emerging liberation movement. Hence, they returned to the basics of indirect colonial rule – governance by central despotism allied with the affirmation of strongmen and local leaders of communities who mediated unequal citizenship and control of the 'subjects'. In 1965, the anti-communists and the military did likewise. Both colonial and military rulers retained central command but built alliances with local strongmen and their militias and vigilantes, as well as with heads of ethnic, religious and local communities. To sense this synergy between the military and the 'civilians' it may be useful to combine Joshua Oppenheimer's revelations of the military-directed violence in his celebrated films *The Act of Killing* and *The Look of Silence*, with Fons Rademakers' visualization of indirect rule in his drama *Max Havelaar*.[1]

Subsequently, Suharto's 'new order' promoted the rise of capital. The regime was consolidated by combining his patrimonial despotism with new elements of centralized modernism. This was to some degree at the expense of local strongmen and religious, ethnic and local communities, as they were no longer indispensable in fighting the Left. However, this modernism was of course without equal and democratic citizenship. Ordinary people were left 'floating', deprived of any other state–society mediation than statist corporatism and centrally subordinated communal groups and their leaders.

We shall return in subsequent chapters to the challenges faced by the dissidents in analysing and resisting these dynamics. They never gave priority to the reclaiming of the demoted primacy of active democratic citizenship among ordinary people – even though old adversaries like liberal Marxist intellectual and renowned publisher, Goenawan Mohamad, joined forces with Joesoef Isak and Pramoedya Ananta Toer to stress its urgency. And the lacuna remained in spite of efforts at investigative journalism and participatory studies of democratization (which I had the privilege of taking part in).

In short, I would argue, the persistent absence of a leftist perspective in Indonesian social and political life may be explained in three steps: one, the undermining under 'guided democracy' of the long struggle, dating from the inception of the modern nationalist movement, for equal-citizenship-and-democracy; two, the powerful resurgence in 1965 of central despotism combined with indirect governance, some of which was retained under the 'new order'; and three, the failure of pro-democrats to address this symbiosis.

The devastating demotion of the struggle for equal-citizenship-based democracy

In conclusion, the second generation of social democratic-oriented politics in Indonesia made rapid and remarkable advances by undermining the Dutch indirect rule and building up the country. But this worked only as long as it combined the national liberation movement's efforts at equal-citizenship-based democracy with class-based demands for social rights and justice. The turning point was the giving up of the equal-citizenship-and-democracy-part of the equation: the democratic mediation between state and citizens.

Under 'guided democracy', the struggle continued within nationalist campaigns, but nationalism did not really sap the strength of the major adversaries, as they were more based on undemocratic capturing of public resources than on Western imperialism. Similar problems arose with the mobilization of the rural poor for the Basic Agrarian

---

[1] Even though Rademakers' film was, of course, based on Multatuli's novel of the same name about the previous generation of indirect rule during the Dutch cultivation system.

Law. The law was insufficient to solve the problems of the poor peasants, which bred conflict. Worse, support for 'guided democracy' at the expense of claims for equal citizenship and democracy meant that it was no longer possible to unify and strengthen many people behind such campaigns and visions, and to thus to target and reduce the adversaries' sources of power in control of religious and local communities.

Finally, as the mass-based strategies proved unworkable and prevented the progressives from gaining solid influence within the state, including the military, some leaders tried to create an opening by secretly engaging in a putsch, which failed. The military leaders and their allies returned, then, to full-scale central despotism, combined with indirect governance, as the primary instruments of a political genocide and subsequent subordination of people under the 'new order'. This, and the inability of the pro-democrats to address the new dynamics, most fully explains the enduring absence of a new progressive movement.

5

The rise and stagnation of Kerala's Emancipatory Left

On the way from Jakarta in mid-1984, I stopped over in India to prepare a comparative study. The Indonesian movement's basic problem had been how to sustain its combination of class struggle and efforts at equal citizenship and democracy. Did that resemble in any way the leftist challenges in the very different context of India?

Having been accustomed to Indonesia's non-inclusive yet dynamic economic environment while studying its political depression, the encounter with New Delhi's unbearable heat and Eastern Europe-like rigidity – in addition to the economic and social stagnation of socialist governed Kolkata – was far from auspicious.

Moreover, half a year later I realized that the recent major setback for the labour movement in Britain – the defeat of the miners' strike, and the victory of Thatcherism more generally – had been preceded in Mumbai more than two years earlier by the subduing of the world's largest strike – a year-long revolt of some 250,000 workers in the city's run-down textile mills. This was followed by the victory of *Shiv Sena,* a provincial brand of xenophobic Hinduism, at the expense of dissident union leader Datta Samant's political campaign. All of which confirmed, again, that it takes broader unity and comprehensive politics to foster an alternative to structural adjustment and right-wing nationalism.

This was easier to conclude, however, than getting a railway ticket beyond the Deccan. I was saved only by a Bangalore mystery of getting access to special quotas for non-show-up-dignitaries. Thus I was even awarded what many travellers deem the best first-class sleeping car ticket. Meaning in a non-AC compartment, with a window that could be opened when slowly passing the Western Ghats, early next morning, as the fog lifted in the valleys where women in colourful clothes were starting work in the paddy fields. Half-awake, I was back in Java. But a bit later there were also the sights of Kerala's palm fringed backwaters. And in the following days, vivid conversations with intellectuals and leaders of my own age. Dynamic scholarly activists who were relieved of north India's, at times, hierarchical arrogance, and even self-deprecatingly cracked jokes about their grand ideas of how to alter Kerala's less attractive sides. How come? What was Kerala about?[1]

---

[1] Portions of the following text have been retrieved from a joint chapter with John Harriss (with much advice from Michael Tharakan), in my and John's anthology, with Neera Chandhoke and Fredrik Engelstad, *Reinventing Social Democratic Development;* further information about which is in the appendix with references.

Timeline Kerala until the 1990s.

Late nineteenth century
- Socio-religious reform movements in Travancore-Cochin for citizenship and educational rights.
- Princely tenancy reforms in Travancore-Cochin against large landowners.

Turn of the century
- Broader unity among the reform movements for *equal* rights.

World economic crisis 1930s→
- Socialists/communists provide better organization for equal rights plus issues of class.
- Struggle in Travancore-Cochin with that in Malabar against feudalism combined.
- This together is also combined with struggle against the British and for united Kerala.

1956
- The unified Malayalam-speaking state of Kerala established.

1957–9
- Reformist communists win first state assembly elections.
- Land reform laws and a bill for more equal education.
- Anti-communist protests (with US support) against the laws.
- New Delhi oust the government and proclaim presidential rule.

1964
- The communist movement split into CPI (Moscow) and CPI-M (independent).
- Political clientelism causes corruption and division in popular and civil organizations.

1967–9
- Kerala CPI-M leads coalition government.

1967–8 & 1969–70
- West Bengal CPI-M in militant struggles and coalition governments.
- West Bengal Maoist insurgencies

1969–79
- Kerala cooperation between CPI and Congress party – CPI-M in opposition.

1970
- Kerala tenancy rights land reform implemented.
- Economy does not expand, however.

1975–7
- National state emergency rule.

1977→
- West Bengal CPI-M wins elections and forms leftist government.
- West Bengal tenancy reforms combined with political decentralization.
- From the 1990s, however, economy does not expand.
- West Bengal CPI-M tends to dominate central and local administration.

1980–1
- Kerala CPI leaves Congress for CPI-M-led Left Democratic Front (LDF) government.

1987–91
- Kerala renewal-oriented LDF government.
- Kerala reformist CSO expands.

Kerala, while in India, has its own special history. Even some of the tradesmen from Judea who arrived in the mid-500 BCE were impressed enough to stay on, as were the Christians in the first century. They were followed by Vasco Da Gama, who landed near Calicut, having discovered in 1498 the European sea route to India, and several years later was initially laid to rest in Cochin. There was intensive production of export crops along with food. Centuries later, the unifying struggle against the British cemented relations with North India. Yet Kerala remained dynamic and outward oriented.

The social democratic promise embedded in the Constitution of India was pursued with inadequate determination by the Nehruvian state. This is also what the Communist Party of India (CPI) sought to achieve more consistently and in practice, much like its Indonesian counterpart, after the final defeat of its brief attempts to pursue a violent revolutionary strategy in 1951. Ever since, the communists have held on to Marxist–Leninist principles of leadership and organization, but their achievements towards greater social justice have been within the framework of India's democratic polity and aimed, basically, at realizing the unfulfilled early promises of the Congress party.

Kerala, in turn, has sometimes been described as 'India's Scandinavia'. The reduction of poverty as compared to per capita income has been comparatively positive, and the state stands first in India in regard to most human development indicators. It has always had the highest level of literacy among the major states, and the quality of health care has generated the highest life expectancy in the country. Some of the legal underpinnings for labour organization and capital–labour relations remain in place. Moreover, these achievements are largely due to high levels of citizen awareness and participation through organization in civil society. Yet, *Dalits* (the oppressed, including members of 'scheduled castes'), tribals (*Adivasi*, indigenous people) and fishing communities have often remained marginalized, and the neoliberal growth pattern

Map 3 India.

during recent decades has undermined the Kerala model of justice-inflected economic development. Now, the state's inequality in consumption levels has no parallel among Indian states. How did this happen?

Defining the problems

Back in 1985, when I arrived, the signs of stagnation were obvious. The figures on economic development were depressing and there was no sight of a longstanding leftist government. Senior researcher and activist Thomas Isaac, who was later to

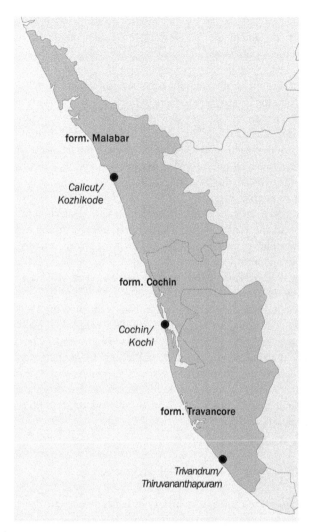

Map 4 Kerala.

initiate the world-renowned 'People's Planning Campaign', immediately set aside unnecessary doctrines and hit the nail on the head: you know, the agrarian question is not yet solved, in spite of our land reform, which was the least worst in India. There are loopholes, there are many people whose problems were not addressed, and worst of all: those who benefitted are not always increasing production. (...) So we must find an answer to this, without causing serious conflicts among people and movements.

Added equally stunningly outspoken and charming Nalini Nayak, youthful Marxist-Catholic civil society activist, one of Kerala's many well-educated women: even here in Kerala the Left neglects many unorganized sector labourers (...) Take the fisher folks, they cannot be included by top-down party decisions; we have to support *their* efforts. Teasingly she added: and please don't just pass by here, as most students do, on their way to metropolitan seminars, to test their theories and pick up our insights (I complied.)

Late at night, I thought of abandoning the comparison of the old Left's saddening problems and focusing instead on the more exciting younger activists' work in Kerala. Yet, all reformists were not of my own age. Most senior leaders were hesitant, but there were crucial exceptions. Outstanding leader E.M.S. Namboodiripad, for one, born in 1909, told me he supported reinvigorating the Kerala model. Most importantly, the reformists wanted to renew, not discard, the old movement. So a historical perspective was indispensable to probe their exciting challenges.

Concerned economic historian Michael Tharakan, whose aristocratic family conceded their land during the agrarian reform but not their manners and eloquence, made me anxious: the renewal must of course be rooted in our experiences back in the nineteenth and early twentieth centuries, which you certainly know of. (Oh dear, I was pretty ignorant.) Fortunately he added: it might be both useful and fun to discuss similarities and differences with Indonesia, and even with Scandinavian Social Democracy. (We still do.)

Our first conclusion was that the early Kerala movement in the 1930s might be one of the best cases of successful struggle for Social Democracy in the South, combining class struggle with unifying efforts at equal-citizenship-based democracy. This was similar to the Indonesian movement until the late 1950s, but more thorough. It even resembled, in certain important ways, the early history of Scandinavian Social Democracy. Since the 1960s, however, Kerala represented a sorry case of stagnation. Leftist leaders had chosen top-down coalition building, undermining the previously unifying priorities. How come?

Roots of progress

Most scholarship on the comparative history of social democratic development draws attention to the importance of relative cultural homogeneity and socio-economic equality, as was the case in Scandinavia (though its equality has been exaggerated). In view of Kerala's religious diversity and historically extreme caste and feudal systems, the emergence of its social democratic development is thus a puzzle.

Kerala's different religious communities (about 60 per cent Hindu, 20 per cent Muslim and 20 per cent Christian) have been able to live side by side and cooperate in vital aspects of public life through a 'cultural symbiosis', best explained by economic interdependence. Further, Kerala's system of caste differentiation, the most rigid and elaborate in the whole of India, was confronted by social reform movements in the princely states of Travancore and Cochin (in south and central Kerala, respectively) and anti-feudal struggle in British-governed Malabar (in the north) from the mid-nineteenth century. The southern movements in particular were remarkably similar to the liberal educational, religious and temperance movements of Scandinavia at about the same time.

In Kerala, there were three reasons why the princely governments had to comply with the reform movements' demands for more equal citizenship and basic education. First, because Christian mission activity had encouraged a sense of self-worth among subordinated people that could not be neglected.

Second, because the princes had fostered agricultural development by tenancy reforms, generating many smallholdings, to counter the powers of upper caste *Nayar* aristocrats and large landowners. This was much like the Swedish kings who at times linked up with independent peasants against the landlords. The economic growth that took place in turn called for educated people in the expanding services and trade, and in the colonial and princely bureaucracies, as well as for basic literacy among the smallholders cultivating tapioca, coconuts and rubber, along with coffee and spices.

Third, because there was a shift by the turn of the century from competition among subordinated communities for education and government jobs to joint demands for civil rights and services for broader sections of the population. For example, radical leaders of the extensive low-ranked *Ezhava* caste joined forces in the early 1930s with Muslim and Christian organizations to demand equal rights and opportunities for members of all these disparate groups. There were also reform activities in the higher caste communities and among the Syrian Christians. This was the birth of Kerala's celebrated civil society.

Broad alliance for Social Democracy

Scandinavian Social Democracy developed by the turn of the twentieth century by combining the liberal popular movements' achievements with workers' interests and demands in the context of rapid industrialization. Something similar happened in Kerala during the world economic crisis of the 1930s, when the struggle against evictions and for redistributive justice and decent wages and employment conditions became even more important. The efforts were facilitated by the then Congress Socialist Party, with leaders such as E.M.S. Namboodiripad, who later joined the communist party. How did they manage this?

The unification of the movements rested, firstly, with the leaders' ability to offer more effective mass-based organization and leadership than the individual caste associations. These included the *Pulaya* and *Ezhava* caste movements of often bonded labourers and toddy tappers, respectively[2]. The relative absence of class distinctions within the *Pulaya* caste was crucial in this regard; and while the *Ezhava* caste was more diverse, many only had a little land of their own and wanted stronger action. The same applied to workers in the coir and cashew factories.

Secondly, it was possible to combine their struggle in Travancore and Cochin with the peasants' movement against unreformed feudalism in Malabar, in the North, where the mainstream Congress party let them down.

---

[2] Toddy tappers scamper up palm trees to fill earthenware pots with sap from the trees. It is used to make a potent fermented drink.

Lastly, the broad alliance was consolidated in the joint opposition to colonialism and the dominance of non-Malayali Brahmins for a unified state of Kerala along linguistic and cultural lines.

Remarkably, the essence of this Kerala project was thus similar to the two most successful instances of the rise of democratic popular movements in the world at that point. Firstly, the development in Scandinavia, where the social democratic labour movement, in the context of rapid industrialization, first stood on the shoulders of the liberal citizenship-oriented reform movements, and then, by early 1930s, included more rural people – and later on professionals too – in an inclusive development strategy based on a 'people's home' with equal rights and productive welfare schemes (Chapter 2). Secondly, the largely civil rights and educational-oriented struggle for national liberation and the development in Indonesia in the 1950s (Chapter 4). This became one of the world's largest organized popular movements by furthering class-based demands along with modern nationalist citizenship and democracy, until it was cornered and subordinated to the 'guided democracy' of Sukarno and the Army.

Why stagnation?

Many Kerala communists, socialist intellectuals and trade union leaders retained their popular influence during the struggle for a unified Kerala in the late 1940s, in spite of the central party leaders' prioritization of trade union-driven revolutionary politics in Mumbai and Bengal and an agrarian revolt in Telangana on the eastern Deccan Plateau. As in Indonesia, the new communist priorities from the early 1950s of working within democratic structures in pursuit of a credible strategy for fostering social democratic development were unmatched by any other party in Kerala. This made it possible for the Left to win office in Kerala's first elections in 1957.

It was not possible in Kerala, however, to move from broad popular movements for equal citizenship and democracy plus social rights, to introducing anything comparable to the Scandinavian growth pacts between capital and labour. Such a *modus vivendi* between capitalists and workers could have been the basis for a viable welfare state, people's enhanced wellbeing as well as the springboard for effective production. However, industrialization in Kerala was lagging behind; and, even though there were relatively strong business groups and unions, unevenly developed production and trade generated diverse interests and insufficiently unified organizations.

It might have been possible to make initial progress on the basis of Kerala's own comparative advantages of high levels of education and export of agricultural products – as happened, for example, in Mauritius and Costa Rica. But the communists' initially successful strategy of 'unity and struggle' with the Congress, in line with Moscow's recommendations, implied compliance with the national government's development strategy of import substitution and heavy industries.

The Kerala government tried instead to adjust to the local conditions by way of a growth pact among labour, peasants, farmers and industrialists based on land reform and more inclusive education. This was expected to increase production and incomes, strengthen democracy, and serve as a foundation for industrialization. But even though the land reform was cautiously designed in line with the Congress party's 1949 policy recommendations, it was resisted by most of the larger landholders. Moreover, the emphasis on more inclusive state-led education for the benefit of underprivileged sections of the population was equally contentious, given that it would affect the privileges of many powerful groups and their state-supported educational institutions. The opposition came together in an anti-communist 'liberation struggle', supported by the United States. In 1959, the central government under Nehru imposed presidential rule; this decision was swayed by Indira Gandhi in her role as chair of the Congress party.

There is no doubt about the relative success of the leftists in Kerala, who were in power from 1957 until 1959 and in left-of-centre governments from 1967–9, 1970–7, 1978 and 1980–1. The main achievement was the implementation in the early 1970s, after much hesitation, of India's most consistent land reform. During these periods, there were also social democratic-oriented welfare reforms and, remarkably, the major advances were widely acclaimed enough not to be entirely undone when the Left was out of office. The results depended substantially on the strong legacy of citizen and social rights reforms along with popular education and associational activism. Moreover, the intense electoral competition between leftist and more conservative parties made both leftists and rightists sensitive to popular scrutiny and priorities. The expansion of Mother and Child Health Centres, for instance, continued because all parties knew that people wanted them. Many other welfare reforms were introduced and kept alive over the years: unemployment relief, pensions for agricultural and other workers as well as their widows, subsidised housing, public distribution with subsidised prices of essential food, meals in schools and preschools, minimum wages and more.

Meanwhile, however, the leftist United Front strategies were no longer driven by clear-cut socio-economic interests and popular demands from below for specific policies. Left-led coalition governments rested instead on compromises within the elite between the special interests of the various parties and their leaders. This process generated corruption as well as divisiveness. The larger Communist Party of India-Marxist (CPI-M), formed as a result of the split in the communist movement in 1964 and taking an independent position in-between Moscow and Beijing, retained most of the organized popular base and used it to confront rivals at the polls. Meanwhile the Communist Party of India (CPI) remained loyal to Moscow and cooperated with the Congress party, even supporting the all-India State of Emergency in 1975.

Various parties in coalition governments used perks to grow membership and separate interest organizations. These were among small farmers, tenants, agricultural labourers, labourers in the informal sectors and industry, as well as with workers and white-collar workers in the public sector, in addition to women's and youth organizations and cooperative associations and cultural and educational groups. And contractors and other businesspeople provided 'contributions'. Increasingly, many independent civil society associations, too, moved closer to influential politicians and parties. The special interests of the various groups were often given priority over unifying state policies and rights for all, regardless of organizational affiliation. Moreover, the benefits and welfare measures were chosen irrespective of their effect on economic development, which stagnated. Several activists said: the unity for common advances that we knew of from the 1930s is no more.

There were similar problems with regard to state–civil society relations beyond the parliamentary electoral system. In Kerala, as in Scandinavia, the participation of different interest groups in policymaking and implementation had evolved on the basis of decades of social and political struggle. But in contrast to Scandinavia, where this struggle was rooted in pre-industrial representation of various propertied interests, and where it was made inclusive of all the non-propertied and democratized by liberal associations and the labour movement, Kerala's state–society relations beyond elections were increasingly dominated by parties and individual politicians and bureaucrats, susceptible to corruption.

These disparate interests among the Left's following affected development strategies, too. Land reforms as already noted were finally realized in the 1970s, but these, as well as the remarkable advances within health and education, did not reach the weakest sections of the population and did not foster alternative inclusive development to the extent that was expected. The reforms did away with landlordism but mainly benefitted the tenants, who often developed special interests of their own. Moreover, there were exemptions for plantation owners and agricultural labourers were granted rights only to their huts and small plots on generally infertile land, and tribal people and fishing communities were completely outside the reforms.

Most importantly, perhaps, the reforms were not followed up with measures to boost production. Many new owners developed interests in less labour-intensive crops and even engaged in land speculation. In addition, the reforms were implemented during a period of conflict between the CPI and CPI-M.

Thus, better-educated, privileged groups could develop new and profitable ventures and secure good jobs outside agriculture. Meanwhile the former tenants from lower-ranked communities gained education and land thanks to the reforms and welfare measures, but did not always focus on the needs of production. A young female agricultural extension officer, for example, who received me in a local council office to discuss the improvement of production, was charmingly dressed up as for a party. She somewhat suspiciously examined my more rustic clothing (meant for what I thought would be a discussion while walking along the paddy fields) and seemed most eager to hear of Ingmar Bergman's films, which she had studied whilst dreaming of working in the media.

In short, the privileged groups rarely developed agricultural and other production activities of the kind that would generate new and better jobs for the underprivileged sections of the population. They remained marginalized, even if they now had the ability to read and write and enjoyed some access to health services. Moreover, even well-educated women repeatedly reminded me that efforts at gender equality were only in the public sphere.

Finally many investors avoided Kerala, claiming it was difficult to cooperate with its strong trade unions. And, from the mid-1970s, many better-educated and trained Keralites and their families sustained or improved their standard of living by becoming migrant workers, in the Gulf countries in particular.

Conclusions in comparison with West Bengal

Kerala's successful social democratic politics with roots in the 1930s had therefore stagnated by the 1960s and reached a dead end by the early 1980s. No stable Left government was in sight. Unevenly developed production and trade, along with divisive interests and organizations, blocked economic growth pacts. An alternative roadmap might have been based on human resources and agricultural export, but it was politically impossible given the all-India focus on import substitution and heavy industrialization. The land reform was crucial, as were many social rights, welfare and education programmes. But they did not include the weakest sections of the population. Nor did they combine with efforts to increase production or align with democratic decentralization.

There was also a shortage of institutionalized democratic representation of various interests. As a result, negotiated coalitions among progressive leaders and parties substituted for the previous unity from below that had been based on demands for common citizen and social rights. This gave rise to special interests, even corruption, and divisions between popular movements and civil society organizations along party-partisan and leadership lines.

That said, the new dynamics primarily operated through networks of politically dependent organizations and leaders, augmented by businessmen, rather than by means of populist appeals or a hegemonic political regime (or both, as under Indonesian 'guided democracy'). So in spite of the negative effects of party-clientelism, the Kerala communists had to consider various interests, and in doing so retained a substantial following.

These were the challenges that the renewal-oriented activists tried to address in 1985. We shall return to their imaginative efforts in Chapter 11. But first, let us compare briefly with the advances in West Bengal which the Kerala Left looked to for inspiration.

Said many activists: nothing can be copied, but the Left in West Bengal has managed to combine land reform measures with democratic decentralization. Thus it gained political hegemony, so now it can, perhaps, move on to other progressive programmes.

Party dominance

The most convenient way for me to reach the impressive Kolkata headquarters of the Marxist Communist party (CPI-M), in crammed Alimuddin Street in the midst of the old city, was by a hand-pulled rickshaw, even though the feeling was less than comfortable. Inside, most leaders, too, were different from Kerala, demonstrating assuredness and power. Indeed, they were in a dominant position since 1977 occupying the grand offices of the West Bengal state government in the British East India Company's old Writers' Building. And even though there were worries about deteriorating traditional industries, and thus reduced support among urban labour, they were emboldened by advances in rural areas, which impressed their counterparts in Kerala too.

Their Kerala friends were certainly aware of the differences. West Bengal's political economy had never generated anything like the Kerala tenancy reforms of the nineteenth century. The caste system was less rigid, elaborated and congruent with class. Hence, the social reform movements were also not as vital as in Kerala. More leftist leaders were from among the educated, the *bhadralok*. They had rarely emerged from within the broad Congress movement and many of them had rather been involved in anti-colonial terrorism. Moreover, they related primarily to the metropolitan working class, petty bourgeoisie and administrators, in addition to the occasional rural revolts. Building trade unions was, thus, more important for the communists than engaging with the urban poor, often immigrants from East Bengal and Bihar. Explained several assertive leaders: many of them are unreliable 'lumpen elements' and cannot be efficiently organized; it would take too many activists.

Extreme leftists inspired by Mao's Cultural Revolution in the 1960s (labelled Naxalites after the village in Darjeeling of the first local revolt) related to neglected tribal populations in particular but also engaged in urban terror. At the time, mainstream leftist leaders opted for militant actions too, including occupations to enforce land reform and the encircling of factory managers (*gherao*) to gain better wages and work conditions. Hence, the brief periods in office the communists enjoyed – as part of coalition governments in 1967–8 and 1969–70 – were followed by repression under conservative governments, direct Presidential rule from New Delhi and particularly the all-India State of Emergency, until 1977.

What was quite attractive to the Kerala reformists, however, were the advances that occurred in West Bengal after the Emergency. Most Bengali communists (CPI-M) had vehemently opposed it, standing out as champions of democracy, and thus being elected into the Writers' Building in 1977 by a wide margin. Once in office, moreover, their politics and policies became more social democratic, favouring less divisive agrarian reforms and, most notably, an innovative campaign to register and safeguard the rights of sharecroppers, *bargardars*. Importantly, this 'Operation Barga' was combined with political decentralization to three levels of locally elected councils, in order to promote fair reforms and increased production. From an almost non-existent rural base, the communists thus made impressive electoral advances. These milestones were transformed into powerful positions with regard to conflict resolution as well as the distribution of resources to foster economic development.

In fact, the reforms and decentralization kept them in power in Kolkata, uninterruptedly, until they were humiliated in 2011. We shall return to the causes for this collapse in Chapter 12, but some of the fundamental problems were visible already by the mid-1980s. And since they strengthen our converging conclusions from Indonesia and Kerala, it is useful to account for them briefly already at this stage.

First, it is true that the agrarian reforms and decentralization of governance in West Bengal encouraged production. This was less due to the insufficient land reform measures than to better irrigation, inputs and technologies, but the more democratic local governance bolstered the distribution and management of the inputs. By the early 1990s, however, the statistics pointed to stagnation. And top-level leaders and experts were afraid already by the mid-1980s that the advances would not be enough to stop labour migration to Kolkata, where unemployment and social problems were already serious. Worse, the progress would probably be insufficient to generate the increasing market demand for inputs and consumption goods necessary to stimulate industrial, not just agricultural, development. Typically, those concerned concluded: we must find other ways of spurring industrial development and generating more jobs.

By the second part of the 1980s they were still debating, however, how to go about it – all the while keeping an eye on China's and Vietnam's adjustment to the global markets. We shall return to their final, devastating decisions.

The second major challenge was the character of democratic decentralization. As already noted, the political and administrative decentralization in West Bengal took place earlier and was better synchronized with tenancy reforms and support for agricultural development than in Kerala. But the combination of equal citizen rights and class struggle that had engendered success in Indonesia and Kerala until the late 1950s was never at the heart of things. In West Bengal, aside from the unions, the party was paramount. While their Indonesian counterparts became subordinated to Sukarno and his generals, and the Kerala popular movements suffered division along party-partisan clientelistic lines, the West Bengal party (and loyal bureaucrats) gained hegemony – in Kolkata as well as in the local councils and villages. Yet, most straightforward leaders and experts agreed: given the weak citizen rights struggle, there was not much of an alternative.

In particular, there were very few Kerala-like popular emancipatory movements. The party seemed to be the only way ahead. Worse, therefore, added senior economist Ashok Mitra ('for scholarly purposes'), West Bengal Minister of Finance at the time: there is cocksure arrogance (…) there is a lack of strategy (…) there is insufficient consciousness, especially among middle level cadres (…) there is corruption (…) there is laziness (…) So like it or not, there is no alternative to Stalinist discipline. It's not fun to stand with it, but without it, we fall apart.

6

The 'people power' mystery in the Philippines

Through two decades of fraudulent elections, President Ferdinand Marcos seemed invincible. He held on to power, along with crony capitalists, by autocratic and corrupt control of public assets, resources and regulations. He abused massive foreign lending, pleased the United States and strengthened the army. And he relied on emergency powers and (from 1972) martial law. This was lifted in 1981, but repression continued. In 1983, opposition leader Benigno 'Ninoy' Aquino was murdered and the following year's election was fraudulent. The predominant leftist message that the only way ahead was popular revolution gained ground. The rapidly advancing Maoists claimed that peasants, led by the New People's Army, must encircle the cities, supported by a National Democratic Front. In Mindanao, Muslims rebelled and leftists tried urban insurrection, inspired by Central American counterparts. As international criticism increased too, and the economy went from bad to worse, Marcos announced snap presidential elections for early 1986 to prove his popularity.

This time the opposition was better prepared. Liberals and social democrats formed counter-movements. They were unified by the widely respected Cardinal Sin (the archbishop, not the sin), with Corazon 'Cory' Aquino, Ninoy's widow, in the lead. The United States would retain its military bases, for a while, but political prisoners would be released, democracy restored, corruption fought, the economy privatized and foreign debt renegotiated. Again, however, the Maoist Left, in particular, chose to boycott the vote, claiming that the elections were futile and that the liberals represented no one but landowners and capitalists.

Yet, people voted. And as Marcos was deemed the winner, as usual, people stood up as never before. Computer operators in the Commission of Elections resigned in protest at cheating. Catholic bishops pointed to unparalleled fraud. The civic poll-watching organization (Namfrel) substantiated the allegations with documentation and figures. In Washington, even Ronald Reagan hesitated. Corazon Aquino launched a civil disobedience campaign and there were discussions with the Left to ramp up the pressure further with a general 'people's strike' (*welgang bayan*).

The latter initiative was pre-empted, however, during 22–24 February, as Defence Minister Juan Ponce Enrile and RAM (the 'Reform the Armed Forces Movement' of young officers) cancelled an attempted coup and staged an army revolt instead, along with the Deputy Chief of the Armed Forces, Fidel Ramos, who had been sidelined by Marcos. Most importantly, Cardinal Sin called on priests, nuns and people in general to protect the mutineers and their men against an onslaught by Marcos and army loyalists

---

Timeline the Philippines until the 1990s

Early twentieth century – Second World War
- The United States wins the Philippines from the Spanish.
- US-like electoral system installed gradually.

Second World War
- Japanese occupation.
- *Hukbalahap* small farmers' based resistance movement.

Post-war
- *Hukbalahap* and other leftists continue to fight US imperialism.

1965→
- Ferdinand Marcos president turns increasingly repressive.

1968–9
- The Maoist Communist Party of the Philippines (CPP) formed.
- New People's Army (NPA) formed.

1970
- 'First quarter storm' student protests.

1972
- Marcos enforces emergency powers.

1973
- Maoist-led National Democratic Front (NDF) formed.

1977
- Horacio 'Boy' Morales defects government, joins NDF and turns its leader.

1983
- Liberal opposition leader Benigno Aquino assassinated.

1986
- Marcos announces snap elections.
- Massive opposition against cheating.
- 'People Power' revolution ousts Marcos.
- Maoists lose out.
- Political prisoners released.

1986–8
- Traditional democratic elites regain prominence.
- Radical social democrats regroup and gain some ground.
- Leftists marginalized in elections.

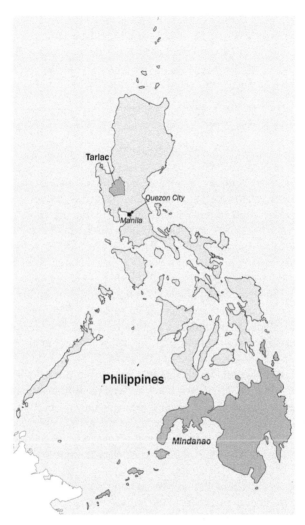

Map 5 Philippines.

by way of a peaceful 'people power' manifestation along the Manila EDSA Ring Road which ran alongside the rebels' headquarters. Thus, Manila was made ungovernable. On 25 February, both Marcos and his loyal Chief of the Armed Forces, Fabian Ver, fled the country, as people ransacked the palace, exposed the extravagant luxury and celebrated in the streets.

How was it possible? Leftists of various persuasions had been on the offensive, deeming democratization impossible, short of a revolution. Yet, the third wave of democracy had now reached the Philippines from southern Europe and Latin America, making the revolutionary Left look irrelevant. 'God, we missed out again', was how liberation-theology-driven rebel, Edicio 'Ed' De La Torre, summarized the situation on his release from prison.

The Maoists, however, would only admit to a 'tactical blunder'. They abstained from supporting progressives behind Aquino in drafting the constitution, and even from seriously supporting their own soft candidates in elections, who thus failed miserably. Meanwhile dissident socialists engaged but were unable to make much of a practical difference in the construction a new democratic polity. Why and how did this also happen?

The context

Ever since the late 1970s, discussions of the contentious issue of electoral boycotts often went nowhere. However, an enchanting May Day dinner conversation in faraway Canberra, hosted by senior Philippine activists and professors Francisco 'Dodong' and Anna Maria 'Princess' Nemenzo two weeks ahead of the 1984 elections, was different. While disputing the role of democracy for the Left, we agreed it might be useful to interrogate the Philippine debate on the basis of previous Indonesian experiences. So I did.

The Spanish who reached the Philippines in the seventeenth century found no gold but good trading ports, and land and labour for sugar planting. They ruled by means of force and the Catholic clergy, building a loyal local gentry. The Americans took over in the early twentieth century, implanting US-like elections of public officials but by men only.

Dissidents asked for universal suffrage, but given the initial American-led democratization, they had less reason than in Kerala and Indonesia to fight against indirect rule, and to demand equal-citizenship and democratic relations with the state via organizations of their own. The Philippine peasants and labourers fought primarily for land and better conditions, as well as against Japanese and US imperialism. There were no equivalents of the huge popular civic/class movements in Indonesia and Kerala.

Hence, there were elections, but not very free and fair ones. Much of the Philippine polity turned into almost a caricature of the individualizing, personality-oriented and ideology-resistant American settler-democracy – exported to a colony and then taken advantage of by feudal-like clans and bosses, who retained some remnants of Spanish and Chinese cultures.

The communist party loyal to Moscow (which Marcos asked for support for state-led development) focused on anti-capitalist struggles against US imperialism. Said its old secretary general, Dr Jesus Lava in 1990 – while enjoying a mah-jong party with, among others Casto Alejandrino, former commander in the originally anti-Japanese *Hukbalahap* (Huk) peasant guerrilla: our native classes are only pressure groups within the US Empire, like the farmers in the United States. (…) Democracy may be fine in theory but it's of little use until imperialism has been fought.

Student protests culminated in the late 1960s and early 1970 with a 'first quarter storm' of anti-government demonstrations against economic crisis and US imperialism. This was the breeding ground for various socialist groups but also the Maoist communist party under Joma Sison, formed in 1968 with a programme formulated in Beijing. (Another copy was used by the Indonesian Maoists.)

There was also an agreement between urban intellectual Sison and educated peasant leader Bernabe 'Dante' Buscayno from rural Luzon. Dante was raised within the post-war Huk rebellion against the American-controlled government and was the founding father of the New People's Army. Sison wanted a rural base and found, he said, a 'good tactician, not a strategist'. Dante wanted an urban partner, but told me he discovered 'an adventurist compiler of books'.

Maoist stereotypes

Dante was hardly a democrat but close to the Aquinos in Tarlac, Central Luzon. When released from prison after the 'people power' revolution he rethought his socialist priorities. He participated in the 1987 elections and set up an innovative cooperative project, to which we shall return in Chapter 8.

Sison, by contrast, preserved the doctrines and his Maoist party. How was it his party and the National Democratic Front lost out in the 'people power' transition to democracy? Why was it they held onto the idea of a peasant-based armed revolution to encircle the cities, and thus essentially boycotted the rise of democracy? There were several reasons.

One was that most critics of the Maoist orthodoxy within the movement were only in favour of alternative non-democratic strategies, such as the combination of military and political struggle during the war of liberation in Vietnam and Latin American insurrections.

Another reason was the generally accepted thesis among the Maoists and many other leftists that the conditions for a genuinely democratic polity – one that granted meaningful space for people to compete for power – were not at hand. In this view, the civil and political freedoms were unreal and the elections were a sham. The bourgeoisie was much weaker than in Europe and North America, and thus unable to grant basic freedoms. Feudal remnants and US dominance must be fought directly. Since that was not possible 'democratically', and since the 'national-bourgeoisie' and working class were not strong enough, armed revolution based on anti-feudal peasants and other supporters was the only option.

Said Sison: ordinary people do not stand a chance even in a democracy managed by Cory (Corazon Aquino) and her friends. Conversely, we could invite them for elections in our liberated areas, and who do you think would win?

When I asked why it had anyway proved possible to overthrow Marcos with the limited freedoms available, Sison altered his argument: that was exceptional, much thanks to military defections, and only very briefly. We made a tactical blunder. (…) We should have taken advantage of the crisis and openings (…) But just look what happened immediately afterwards (…) Cory couldn't but return to the old rules and practices (…) And when our supporters tried to run in the 1987 and 1988 elections, they didn't stand a chance.

Asked if the Maoist party and New People's Army had really given Aquino a chance, and had provided their 'national-democrat' candidates with the necessary backing, the answer was evasive: we were so busy debating the boycott issue at the time.

That was an understatement. There was close to uproar among the 'national democrats' – a furore which was repressed. In fact, an additional reason why the rise of democracy had been boycotted by the mainstream Left was a lack of internal democracy. There were no regular congresses, only purges. Critics had even been assassinated, others shortlisted for such a fate. After the fall of Marcos, moreover, several of the dissidents who chose critical participation in the new democratic order claimed that the typical top-leader response was: 'why give Cory (Aquino) a chance when she can't take it'. Sison himself indicated in our conversation that the clearance for Maoist participation in the 1987–8 elections was to conclusively finish the debate about voting to allow the dissidents to lose and thus prove themselves wrong.

The most fundamental reason for avoiding democratization, however, lay in how the Maoists analysed the sources of power of the political bosses, their crony capitalists and others elected or appointed to executive positions in state organs. In accordance with the Beijing format, these were all labelled 'bureaucratic capitalists'. As we know from the Indonesian case, where the same markers were applied, the 'bureaucratic capitalists' were deemed neither a class nor even faction of a class with a basis of its own in production. Their power was within politics and administration which also enabled them to gain some control of economic, military and human resources and oversee regulations. But ultimate power was supposed to rest with landlords, imperialists and their local partners.

In other words, fighting the bureaucratic capitalists by way of politics and elections did not, in this view, help much, given that more democratic control would not undermine their masters, who possessed the 'real' power. Sison concluded: just look at who remains in ultimate control in the Philippines, even after Marcos.

Dissidents for tactical unity

More puzzling was that the quasi-dissident Maoists in charge of the semi-legal National Democratic Front also did not focus on democratization. Their most celebrated leader, Horacio 'Boy' Morales, had defected from his executive secretary position in Marcos' development academy in the late 1970s. Ever since, he actually tried – along with numerous friends, including liberation theology activist 'Ed' De La Torre – to build a plural democratic forum for like-minded peaceful sectoral and issue-oriented organizations. One task was certainly to gather funds for the armed struggle, but their prime focus was peaceful extra-parliamentary actions, and at times to support progressive candidates in elections. Three factors prevented, however, the implementation of this plan as well as giving full priority to democratic control of public affairs.

One aspect, Morales admitted, was that their initial response to reprimands from the central-level party leaders was limited to references to, as he put it, the importance of especially Communist International leader Dimitrov's old theses (1934–9). They were about anti-fascist popular fronts among ordinary people 'from below' which communists would find ways to dominate anyway.

Another factor was that the dissidents' outwardly exciting attempt at attaining what came to be called 'popular democracy' was difficult to put into effect. Beyond ideas of broader unity, they remained short of an alternative vision and strategy and the leading proponents were soon imprisoned. In fact, the foundations for the further development of their ideas were drafted in a prison study circle in the early 1980s. Morales, De La Torre and others produced a series of 'Plaridel Papers'. These were named after a late-nineteenth-century progressive intellectual, Marcelo H. del Pilar, whose pen name was 'Plaridel'. According to Morales et al., Pilar struggled peacefully for reforms but remained open to the revolutionary option.

In the 'Plaridel Papers', the popular democrats abandoned their previous focus on Dimitrov's ideas of a communist-led popular front but sustained the importance of broad united action against 'Marcos's fascist regime'. The importance of party leadership was downplayed to the benefit of a broad and plural coalition of progressive groups and individuals, especially in civil society. This would also appeal to revolutionary groups whose different tactics and strategies could converge. Still, when the ideas were put to the test, they immediately proved difficult to carry out. Politically correct National Democratic Front activists claimed leadership positions in the new coalitions and alliances. Moreover, De La Torre confirmed: we never developed an alternative strategy (...) only a tactical focus.

The final factor behind the weak focus on democracy among the semi-legal National Democratic Front activists was that those of a similar persuasion who participated in the 1987–8 elections with a new related party (*Partido ng Bayan*) never got substantive support from the Maoist top brass and the movement at large. Hence, the candidates and campaigners found few reasons to engage in serious democratic competition, rather confining themselves to propaganda. The propelling force in the election movement, Etta Rosales, commented she 'remained frustrated', and according to Dante, the main candidate, it was only meaningful 'to ask people to listen, not to ask for their votes'.

Socialist focus

Meanwhile the leftist critics of the Maoists and their softer united front allies were rather few, had different backgrounds and mainly only one thing in common. That was the conviction that capitalism, rather than remnants of feudalism, was predominant in the Philippines. The implication was that socialism – based on labourers and the urban poor – should be on top of the agenda, not some Maoist peasant-based revolution. The issue of democracy was vital but secondary.

Insurrectionists

One strand of these new socialists could be found among the dissident national democrats in Mindanao. They related to the rapid expansion of capital in urban areas, as well as within agriculture, on the island. Their leading theorist, Marty Villalobos, later wrote a brilliant PhD thesis about the Philippine Left under his real name, Nathan Quimpo. In the early 1980s, he joined local cadres in 'people's strikes' (*welgang bayan*) to make society ungovernable. The Indian term for the same tactics, *bandh*, first developed in the freedom struggle under leaders like Gandhi. But in Mindanao the source of inspiration was the more recent insurrection in Nicaragua, and people's strikes were thought of as a first step towards such a general insurgency.

In Mindanao, where capitalism expanded quickly and urbanization was fast, it was possible to engage formal as well as informal sector workers, in addition to migrants from rural areas, in 'people's strikes'. They all lived in the bustees. There were similar experiences in parts of Negros and Bataan. This was innovative, and initially the activists were quite successful, even though military leaders typically instigated local violence to bring down the strikes. As previously mentioned, there were also thoughts of launching a *welgang bayan* in Manila in late February 1986, along with the civil disobedience of the liberals led by Corazon Aquino, against Marcos's cheating in the elections. But the negotiations were inconclusive and overtaken by the military revolt followed by the 'people power' demonstrations. Equally important, the focus on democracy and self-governance was not a major priority, insights about which could have been picked up from India. Later, however, Quimpo (alias Villalobos) backed attempts to combine interest-based struggles and democracy. We shall return to this in Chapters 8 and 13.

Democratic socialists

Another cluster of new socialists were former communists and radical social democrats of different hues. They certainly agreed on democracy as an ideal, but not as a major strategic aim at the time. Why? A major reason was that few of them thought it was possible to fight Marcos through elections and by democratic means – even if they were also hostile to Maoist analysis and priorities.

For some of these socialists this was mainly about anti-communism; for others it was more about Christian ethics, liberation theology and the idea of struggling 'along with people' instead of 'for them'. An additional priority was research to prove that dependent capitalism was coming to the fore, rather than semi-feudalism as the Maoists claimed. Another was therefore to propagate socialism, generally and in the context of union work and civil society campaigns such as within Aquino's protest movement.

Socialists of various persuasions were instrumental in the 'people power' movement. Several of them criticized the moderate, anti-communist and often authoritarian 'old leaders', especially those in the Philippine Democratic Socialist Party, PDSP. The most innovative organization was the Movement for a Socialist Philippines, *Pandayan*, which emphasized deliberative democracy, gender equality, Christian ethics and work with popular movements and action groups.

Other more independent Marxist and socialists were also prepared to join hands with the popular democracy-oriented national democrats associated with Morales and De La Torre. But when the Maoists claimed control of a broad coalition (Bayan), initiated by the popular democrats in late 1985, *Pandayan* stayed out and the independent socialists formed their own pre-party coalition *Bisig*, the Union of Filipino Socialists. Some in *Bisig* also kept in touch with progressive officers. Founding Chairman Dodong Nemenzo, for one, never ceased emphasizing that Aquino did not acquire power by way of a fair election but through extra parliamentary struggle and the role of dissident officers.

All the socialists contributed, though, to the efforts for a new polity under Aquino. A core idea was that none of the major classes – however defined – were strong enough to dominate the state. The concept for this was that the state was 'relatively autonomous', implying that there was room of manoeuvre for progressives within politics and administration. But aside from *Pandayan*'s focus on 'democracy from below', democratization as a strategic concept did not gain prime importance until later on, a development we shall return to in Chapters 8 and 13.

Neglected roots of power

In short, there were major differences between the early Philippine Left and its counterparts in Indonesia and Kerala. In Indonesia and Kerala, the demands for equal citizenship and democracy against indirect colonialism served as a unifying frame for the class struggle among workers, peasants and others. In the Philippines, by contrast, citizenship was primarily about anti-imperialism to gain national independence, and about anti-feudalism, while issues of emancipation and elections were hijacked by the ruling groups.

However, there are many similarities after the introduction in Indonesia of 'guided democracy' in 1959. In Indonesia as well as the Philippines, the Left did not manage to analyse the roots of political and military power. The Maoists failed to go beyond landlords and imperialists. The socialists focused on dependent capitalism.

In Indonesia, historically, the roots of power were in the despotic colonial bureaucracy and indirect governance. These structures were later captured and adjusted by nationalist leaders and officers. They gained control of public assets and resources, state powers and regulations in cooperation with landowners and businessmen.

Historical Philippine governance was rather via native officials selected and supervised by the Catholic clergy. Thereafter, under the Americans, officials were elected by a narrow elite. In contrast to Indonesia, this stratum gained access to economic and coercive resources and regulative powers by way of elections. And despite universal suffrage, they retained control of the votes. Those running in elections cooperated, of course, with landowners and businessmen. But as effectively drawn attention to by John Sidel, the central and local-level ruling classes in the Philippines did not dominate the state by means of pre-existing extensive control of land and capital. Rather they assembled sufficient resources to get elected into executive positions within state and local governments, and then used the poorly accountable bureaucracies to accumulate power and wealth. Concentration of land ownership did not correspond with the ability to get elected and stay in power.

In brief, beyond the activists stressing Social Democracy 'from below', the Philippine Left either focused on the powers of the landlords or of the capitalists, plus imperialism. In the process, the issue of control of public assets, resources and capacities was neglected. The dominant actors primarily acquired such control by getting into executive positions, often via elections. The positions were then used to gain access to the basic means of production and trade and to subordinate labour – the essence of the 'primitive accumulation' of capital. Thus the Left lost out in the 'people power' protests against dictatorial control of public affairs and for more democracy. It failed to either foresee them or make them more substantial once they broke out. In Chapter 8, we shall consider the efforts at making up for this neglect.

Effects in the North: From Swedish internationalism to 'Social Democracy in one country'

What were the effects in the North of the setbacks in the South? The first two generations of Social Democracy grew out of different types of capitalisms – industrial and colonial. The generations were made interdependent, however, by imperialism and globalized markets. So in theory, their priorities should have been complementary. Just like trade unions in high- and low-productivity sectors must coordinate, and organize among unemployed workers too, in order not to lose out. In practice, however, how did the challenges of the second generation affect the first generation and vice versa?

Sweden, a critical case

The most successful and enduring first-generation cases are the Nordic countries. The essences of social democratic policies have been similar. But Finland was late. And compared to Norway's natural resource-led development, and Denmark's and Iceland's extensive agrarian and fishery sectors, respectively, plus medium and small businesses, Sweden – with its large-scale and internationally oriented industrialization, along with radical urbanization – stands out as the most critical example.

For much of the nineteenth century, Sweden – in its previous guise as a regional empire – was among Europe's poorest and most unequal countries, even though family farmers retained their independence. By the late 1860s there was even starvation, partly because the better off did not forward relief to those in need. From 1850 until 1930, moreover, some 1.5 million people (out of some 5 million inhabitants) migrated in search of better lives, especially to North America. By the 1970s, however, Sweden had become the fourth richest country in the world. Most remarkably, the wealth was more equally distributed than anywhere else. Equality, despite the precepts of neo-classical economics, was obviously no hindrance to growth. The efficient economic development had rather been based on efforts at peace, effective and impartial institutions, equity and increasing equality. This was propelled by social democrats in particular.

Timeline Sweden until the 1990s

1860s→
- From starvation to increased state capacity and rapid industrialization.

1910→
- Liberals and social democrats for democracy.
- Militant labour movement.

1930s→
- Social democrats build broad alliances for social growth pacts and welfare state.

1970s
- Sweden world's fourth richest country, and most equally distributed wealth.
- Olof Palme new prime minister.
- Support for national independence movements in the Global South.
- Coup against Allende in Chile, but fascism overthrown in Spain and Portugal.
- Attempts with Willy Brandt et al. at NIEO (New International Economic Order) and a 'North-South Programme for Survival'.

1980s
- NIEO fails, partly due to weak partners in the South.
- Floodgates open for neoliberalism and market-driven globalization.
- Sweden adjusts to 'the new realities'.
- Social democratic welfare state and social growth pacts weakened.

1986
- Palme assassinated.

1989→
- End of Cold War.
- Sweden joins European Union (EU), hoping it will serve as regional substitute for failed NIEO.
- Also hopes third wave of democracy and better institutions will discipline markets.
- Both hopes fade away and adjustment to neoliberal globalization turns major priority.

National internationalism

The Swedish model had two international pillars. One was national independence based on equal citizenship and the ability to decide on its own priorities. This called for neutrality during the Second World War and then alliances of like-minded countries and movements to contain imperial powers. Most famously, during the

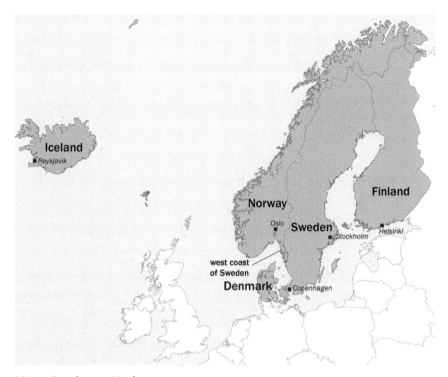

Map 6 Scandinavia-Nordic.

Cold War, this stance included engagement in favour of all countries' – and colonies' – right to national independence and to develop their own reforms. Sweden, with leaders like Olof Palme, was in the forefront, not being part of the North Atlantic Treaty Organization (NATO).

The other pillar was successful export industries. Besides access to iron core and forests and international demand, industrial competitiveness was based on innovation and high productivity. This stemmed from the social growth pact between capital and labour, initiated in the 1930s and complemented by strategic public procurements, representation of unions and employers organizations and other concerned parties in state governance, and productivity-oriented education and welfare.

Export promotion was based on the idea of free trade on equal terms, embodying opposition to colonial and imperial monopolies. Hence, this did not undermine the first principle of supporting genuine national independence in other countries too as long as these countries could develop their own social and economic policies and thus withstand negative business pressures. Besides, Swedish export industries were rarely involved in the developing countries where progressive development was at stake. And when they were, as in South Africa, social democrats were often in the vanguard of support to progressive forces, such as supplying a major part of the funds for the African National Congress (ANC) and United Democratic Front. Conversely, where private business stayed out but investments were needed to build political and economic independence, as in North Vietnam, Sweden took the lead, becoming the first Western country to recognize North Vietnam's independence. When the United States engaged in terror bombardments, strategic support was given for industrial and social development.

Hence, the essence of the two pillars was free trade and investments that did not undermine national priorities, plus bilateral agreements on development cooperation with like-minded developing countries.

Failed attempt at a New International Economic Order

But times had already begun to change. In the late 1950s, when I was shunted from my grandparents' farm in the decaying inner west coast archipelago to attend school in the dynamic country town at the end of the fjord, my single mother worked in its renowned garment industry and most men were employed in the seemingly ever-expanding shipyard. When I left for university twelve years later, it was all in crisis. Generally in Sweden, first textile and garments, then basic sector industries and shipbuilding were shifted to countries with 'firmer governance' and lower wages. Deindustrialization and internal Swedish migration to 'more competitive' cities were extensive and swift. When resettling in the outer archipelago many years later, economists had conceptualized some of my home tracts as 'potential waste areas' – aside from the summer months when tourists come. I shared the local anger; it is under my skin. What happened?

Initially the troubles could be handled in accordance with the model operative between unions, employers and the government since the 1930s – that factories with low productivity and thus problems of paying the same wages as other sectors were closed down, while the released workers were re-educated and shifted to more competitive production and services. But this presupposed expanding markets and growth by way of Keynesian economic policies, and in the 1970s conditions changed. The turning point was the disbanding of the Bretton Woods agreement on fixed currency exchange rates in relation to the US dollar in 1971. This was major warning that the space for national economic governance was shrinking. Social democrats had to go beyond their nationally confined models. While friends in former empires like the United Kingdom and France contemplated economic cooperation with their former colonies, progressives like Olof Palme and Willy Brandt tried instead to construct a New International Economic Order along with a 'North-South Programme for Survival'. This meant, primarily, additional cooperation with countries that were not aligned either to West or East in the Cold War. According to basic Keynesian thinking, less unfair terms of trade for the developing countries, and better conditions for their poor people, would – aside from other effects – increase demand for their products from the North too.

Four factors in particular undermined these efforts. One was that the kindred counterparts were quite unstable. Liberation movements were economically fragile.

Social democracy in countries such as Sukarno's Indonesia, Nehru's India and Nyerere's Tanzania had failed or ceased to progress. Secondly, China was engulfed in a devastating cultural revolution and in other countries popular democratic movements suffered from interventions from the West or the East. Thirdly, the leaders in the oil-producing countries increased their prices but looked after their own short-term interests rather than supporting inclusive development, which would have boosted demand from the North for products other than weapons and luxury goods. Lastly, the globalization of capital and finance, along with improved communications, enabled a number of authoritarian countries, especially in East Asia, to bet on low-cost export-oriented industrialization.

In short, it proved impossible for Palme, Brandt and others to use the United Nations (UN), multilateral organizations and the nonaligned movement as platforms for building a forceful social democratic alternative to the new market-driven globalization. The forces behind this globalization – transnational corporations, financial institutions and figures like Margaret Thatcher and Ronald Reagan – were too powerful. Agreements in the UN were just pieces of paper.

Retreat to adjustment

Increasing competition from newly industrializing countries, and even higher oil prices, was no major problem for Swedish social democrats as long as there was rising demand for exports and investments in new job-creating sectors, and socially responsible structural adjustment to adapt to the new lay of the land. However, much of that was now unfeasible – without a New International Economic Order that could have set the stage for global Keynesianism and rising demand. By implication, Swedish aid to the South – which aimed at strengthening political and social rights as well as welfare to thus promote inclusive development, just like the welfare state at home – turned into a cost rather than an investment in rising markets. Business (and often unions) branded the supporters of welfare in the South 'idealists in need of a sheltered workshop', arguing it was necessary to focus instead on expansion and profits within market-driven globalization.

In addition, the unions were strong and asked for better wages, but Keynesian stimulation of demand in Sweden meant more imports than investments. And deregulation of international finance facilitated tax evasion and capital flight.

Blue-collar workers unions suggested wage-earner funds to gain better control and encourage long-term investments. But this caused divisions in the social democratic movement while the bourgeois parties united and joined hands with business. Business leaders even rejected the enduring system of social partner representation in public governance by unions and employers.

Within Sweden, moreover, businesses with low productivity had long been told to either increase productivity and pay wages according to universal standards, or close down and advise those thrown out of work to find new jobs in the more competitive companies and sectors. This worked for the primary and secondary sectors, but was less feasible in the labour-intensive service and growing public welfare sectors, which had huge numbers of comparatively low-paid employees. Who would pay higher taxes so that they would get better wages? Meanwhile the welfare sectors were starved of funding and run-down by neoliberal management. This was especially true of care for the elderly and recently caused terrifying numbers of deaths during the Covid-19 pandemic.

Additional problems of migration

Another dilemma was migration. The welfare state model was inclusive of all citizens but did not really consider immigration. After the Second World War, 'import of labourers' was necessary: Swedish industry was intact and its products in great demand for reconstruction elsewhere. This 'labour import' was stimulated and organized jointly by the state, employers and unions. As long as the 'new labourers' contributed to the welfare state, they were granted the same social and cultural rights as everyone else. The problems appeared as market-driven globalization and liberalization within the EU-generated increasing numbers of temporary migrant labourers subject to social dumping, as well as to refugees who had difficulty finding work. The principle of equal social rights for all with decent jobs and the payment of taxes became increasingly difficult to combine with equal human rights for all. Refugees from failed attempts at progressive transformation, such as after the coup in Chile, were still welcome, but when numbers increased from first Eastern Europe and then the former Yugoslavia, there were restrictive measures. Aside from the right to family reunification, social democrats wanted closer examinations of whether there was a need to expand the workforce and strict application of the UN refugee convention with regard to asylum seekers plus assistance for them to return, when possible. Meanwhile the root causes of forced migration would be addressed through support for peace and democratization.

When the moderates and liberals won elections in the early 1990s, however, they combined labour migration supported by business with liberal human rights supported by leftists. Worst, not just centre-right governments but also social democrats tended to deprioritize over the years the struggle against the root causes of forced migration and for a comprehensive refugee policy, first advocated by, among others, the Norwegian UN High Commissioner for refugees, leading social democrat Thorvald Stoltenberg.

Radical deregulation of credit market

In 1983 President Mitterrand of France made a U-turn away from his socialist-oriented programme. In Sweden Palme was depressed. In 1985 he even lost control of his Finance Minister, Kjell Olof Feldt, who radically deregulated the credit market. The floodgates opened for financial and real estate speculation. This exacerbated the basic problems of market-driven globalization and the failure to provide an alternative.

Subsequent governments had to repay huge public debts. Welfare spending was reduced, including the support for those badly affected by structural adjustment. Privatization and business-like new public management gained ground, as did privatization of public welfare and services. Some two-thirds of the population with fitting education and skills, mainly in the big cities, benefitted from good jobs and cheap loans, which facilitated speculation in housing. The 2008 financial crisis hardly affected them. The losses were 'socialized', that is, paid by the most vulnerable citizens, including those in run-down suburbs and the rust belts.

Social democrats lost badly already in 2006, faced internal divisions and were short of alternative policy proposals. They did not return to power until 2014, limping back into office with the support of the Greens. (We shall discuss these more recent efforts in Chapter 15.)

The European substitute fails too

Meanwhile it certainly remained necessary to defend national independence and to promote, somehow, international demand. After the fall of the Berlin Wall in 1989, however, the European Union seemed to be a better point of departure than the unfeasible New International Economic Order. The Norwegians were oil-rich enough to defend their sovereignty and many Swedes were unconvinced of the benefits of the EU. But business, export sector unions and the bourgeois parties were all positive. Sweden joined in 1995, and social democrats supported Tony Blair's supposedly 'Third Way' of combining centrist (and centre-right) economic policies with centre-left social policies. Thus, efforts at nation-state social rights, and growth pacts between capital and labour, were deemphasized in favour of forging a 'Social Europe' within the EU.

This vision generated some optimism and electoral advances for social democrats in several countries, but as in the Global South in the 1970s, sympathetic partners within the EU were not strong enough to foster anything like a European Keynesianism or even much of a 'Social Europe'. Social democratic ideas first lost out to 'ordo-liberal' regimes that added judicial guarantees and strong governance to underpin free and dynamic markets and austerity policies and then, over the years, to right-wing nationalists too.

In face of the refugee crisis, the EU was even unable to develop a common policy for shared responsibility – only agreeing on maintaining a Mediterranean moat against unwanted migrants; much like Donald Trump's wall against the South along the Mexican border.

New internationalism and the third wave of democracy

Meanwhile, however, new liberal internationalism gained ground. There were two pillars. First, the increasingly market-driven globalization. Beyond the prioritization of EU, most social democrats – committed to sustaining Sweden's competitiveness – found no other way but trying to please investors and supporting exports and investments in the expanding 'new markets' (in the South).

The old idea of at least preventing trade and investments that contradicted local attempts at progressive change was mostly swept under the carpet in favour of what one might characterize as 'Social Democracy in one country' (an allusion to Stalin's 'Socialism in one country', which awarded priority, in international matters, to the special interests of the Soviet Union, when the efforts of socialists in other countries faltered). The Swedish Prime Minster, Göran Persson, even expressed his admiration for China's 'stability' in 1996 – only seven years after the massacre in the Tiananmen Square.

Norway, in partial contrast, made most of its money offshore. In large part due to social democratic-inspired governance of the revenues, it also avoided the Dutch Disease of overspending, Brazilian-like corruption and the Venezuelan disaster. But rather than investing the oil revenue-based pension funds in inclusive development in the South – which in the long run would have been good for Norway too – Norway opted for quick profits and, like Sweden, 'Social Democracy in one country'. Among the darker moments of Norwegian Social Democracy's grand old lady Gro Harlem Bruntland's tenure as prime minister was when she summed up a visit to promote Norwegian business in Suharto's Indonesia in 1995 by stating that his country was a 'source of global and regional peace and stability'.

The second pillar of the liberal internationalism was democratization. In addition to popular protests against repressive regimes, the more market than imperial-state-driven globalization also paved the way for a third wave of democracy, first in the South and, after the fall of the wall, in the former Eastern bloc too. It lasted for almost four decades, except where dictatorial regimes were supported by hegemonic parties, as in China, or competing global powers as in the Middle East and North Africa. Elsewhere, the third wave was an opening for social democrats, in the North and the South.

The wave commenced already in the mid-1970s, with the transitions from authoritarian rule in Portugal, Greece and Spain. Initially, social democrats and other leftists were crucial spearheads, and their like-minded friends in Sweden provided support via the Socialist International. This was when Olof Palme tried to hold on to international cooperation among kindred partners as the alternative, coordinated via the Socialist International and the UN. The efforts included principled support for, for example, the anti-dictatorial struggle in Latin America, the anti-apartheid struggle in South Africa and meditation in conflicts such as between Iran and Iraq. International solidarity via trade unions reinforced the solidarity.

But with the assassination of Palme in 1986, most of these priorities lost steam. Outside Sweden too, in the years to come, liberals in the new democracies accommodated the powerful groups and promoted elitist pacts rather than popular-driven negotiations. Swedish social democrats questioned the scope of the transformations, but supported the processes, for lack of an alternative.

Meanwhile the increasingly powerful Swedish liberal and conservative parties showed little interest in the role of unions, social movements and radical parties, such as those led by Lula in Brazil or Mandela in South Africa.

Separately, radical social democrats provided support from their own pockets to like-minded activists, trade unions and social movements, such as in South Africa, Brazil and the Philippines. The Olof Palme International Center in particular did sterling work.

In contrast, Sweden's official development cooperation emphasized mainstream advisory think tanks, elitist reformists and civil society watchdogs and resisted, with great fanfare, bilateral agreements (including support for human rights and democratization) with countries that were not deemed democratic, such as Vietnam, making them even less interested in democracy.

Over the years, market-driven globalization gained further importance, while the third wave of democratization petered out. Even the efforts in South Africa, the Philippines and Brazil were not as successful as expected. We shall return to the details in the main part of the book, but generally the admirable centre-leftist regimes and movements in these countries did not stand out as a solid footing for any new attempt at the social democratic internationalism of the kind that had been visualized by Palme and others.

Less interest in change

In the process, Swedish social democrats lost much of their interest in the fate of cognate movements elsewhere. The mainstream wisdom that global market-driven economic growth had eradicated absolute poverty was accepted, although even UN's Special Rapporteur on extreme poverty and human rights called attention to dubious World Bank poverty line standards, increasing hardship for informal migrant labourers in particular, and growing inequalities. Another typical argument was now that the Global South had at least partly industrialized and transformed into a competitor; it must handle 'its own problems' of repression and exploitation of people and nature.

Aside from international trade unionism and demands for human rights, plus the signing of ILO conventions in return for free trade agreements to prevent social dumping, there was, in this view, little Sweden, or any Northern nation, could do. International aid should focus on poverty, disasters, supporting elections and civil society watchdogs. Hence, the demand for contextual knowledge of the problems and options for potential partners in the Global South faded away. Higher education and research, for example, fixated, beyond human rights, on free-floating international relations, 'global governance' and quantitative indices of growth and democracy – far above the realities and contexts where transformative politics must be rooted and gain strength.

Picture 1 (private) Joesoef Isak was a superbly connected journalist under Sukarno who was imprisoned for ten years under Suharto and then edited Pramoedya Ananta Toer's novel quartet from the Buru island concentration camp. He put me on track: in 1965 PKI leader Aidit was inspired by the coup in Algeria against Ben Bella, which had benefitted radicals. We need to ask why this was considered necessary in Indonesia too in spite of a mass movement.

Picture 2 (private) Beginning in the 1980s, when this picture was taken and Kerala's social democratic development was losing pace, young scholarly activists, such as Michael Tharakan in civil society (left) and Thomas Isaac within politics (right), fostered change from below, culminating in the renowned People's Planning Campaign in the 1990s.

Picture 3 (private) Nalini Nayak, Marxist-Catholic civil society activist and one of Kerala's many well-educated women, has spoken up since the 1980s: the Left neglects many unorganized sector labourers (…) Take the fisher folks, they cannot be included by top-down party decisions; we have to support *their* efforts.

Picture 4 (private) In the 1992 Philippine elections, outgoing President Corazon Aquino ignored the democratic Left. Hence it opted instead for an alliance with progressive liberals. On my arrival, however, scholarly activist Karina Constantino-David smiled: I am sorry to let you know that we will fail as the NGOs are not committed. 'Randy' David added: and we do not have the funds.

Picture 5 (private) After the 'People Power Revolution', the founder of the New People's Army, 'Dante' Buscayno, tried peaceful class-based change through a huge farmer's cooperative, assisted by Fatima Penilla. The eruption of nearby Mt Pinatubo was certainly devastating, but essentially there was no solid class of farmers, and Dante failed to unify them by democratic politics.

Picture 6 (private) As liberal allies had proved short of funds and campaign workers in the 1992 Philippine elections, scholarly activist Joel Rocamora (left) and socialist organizer Ronald Llamas (right), among others, concluded that the democratic Left must build a citizen action party of its own –*Akbayan*.

Picture 7 (private) Fisher folks on the small reef of Pandanon in the Visayas built a successful cooperative but said that was to help the members, not run the island. So they kept losing elections and did not know how to reclaim their beautiful beach from a Cebu businessman who brought wealthy tourists, particularly struck by a temple structure 'possibly erected for a pornographic Japanese film'.

Picture 8 (private) Having criticized Sukarno's 'guided democracy', Arief Budiman was the first to oppose Suharto too. He wrote a PhD thesis in the United States about Salvador Allende and became an architect of the democracy movement. Religion was not important to him, but ethics was. He offered drinks to the bored, plainclothes cops outside his house and kept aggressive geese for security, as watchdogs were less appropriate in a Muslim community.

Picture 9 (private) Human rights lawyer Handoko Wibowo was among the remarkable democrats who facilitated local popular organization, in part a rebuke to 'metropolitan action maniacs'. Handoko supported the struggle of north Central Java farmers to reclaim land lost under Suharto and build inclusive development. Here, representatives from the villages gather to decide what local politicians they will support in a forthcoming election. The major challenge was to build alliances based on a joint programme.

Picture 10 (private) Dispossession of people's means of livelihood is widespread. But on Pulau Laut in southeastern Kalimantan, poor fisher folks with former pirate Arbani as their brave boatman leader had won a battle against a Korean factory and local bosses who had wrecked their fishing waters. He pointed out however – when the discussion was shifted inside as the tide receded and the smell from the mud became evident – that while the fisher folks could win a battle, their poor formal education meant they were legally prohibited from engaging in 'democratic politics' by standing in elections.

Picture 11 (private) 'Indigenous populations' often prefer customary rule (*adat*) to democracy dominated by the elite. However, senior civil society and political activists Maria Ngamelumbun and Pieter Elmas in *Kei Kecil*, southeast Moluccas, caution against restoring feudal powers: *adat* is good at local social relations and conflict prevention but not democracy and governance. Moreover, Pieter smiled from his end of their living room, Maria can gain votes by drawing on her clan and the mythology of mothers protecting the community, but I must rely on promoting customary rights through good governance in the official system.

Part Three

Challenges of Third-generation
Social Democracy

Philippine experiments for a democratic Left

Philippine democracy got a new lease on life with the ousting of President Marcos by the manifestation of 'people power' in February 1986 along the Manila EDSA Avenue (Chapter 6). Ironically, thereafter, the staunchest opponents of the dictatorship and suppression, the leftists, were in a shambles. Progressive liberals and socialists of various leanings were active in civil society, but short of forceful political organization to make a difference in the 1987 legislative elections. The Maoists were much stronger, but their main leaders claimed nothing fundamental had changed with the 'people power' transition towards democracy – it was just a conflict within the elite. Hence, they concluded – after long debates and purges of dissidents – that the old strategies must be reaffirmed, including the protracted armed struggle from rural bases. Meanwhile leading renegades like Bernabé Buscayno, 'Dante' to everyone, the founder of the New People's Army, and Horacio 'Boy' Morales, the prime so-called popular democrat, wanted to try their luck in the elections, but were humiliated. One reason was that the Maoists provided minimal support. In the guerrilla heartlands, tickets and votes for others were traded for money for the armed struggle.

Among the candidates of the Left in the elections, 'Dante' was the least bad performer. But on 8 June, the events took a new course. As 'Dante' was leaving a television studio in Quezon City – where he had discussed the results as a guest in socialist Professor Randolf 'Randy' David's live late night talk show – his car was ambushed by still unknown perpetrators, forced up against a wall and riddled with M-16 and .45 calibre bullets, plus a hand grenade. As a seasoned fighter, 'Dante' threw himself on the floor, escaped with wounds only and rushed for help. But some of the other participants in the talk show who travelled with him suffered badly, including Professor Danilo Sibal, who was killed, and his pregnant wife, activist Fatima Penilla, who doctors thought would not make it either.

Yet she did. Fatima Penilla survived for more than two decades (with constant pain) and gave birth to daughter Dana who a few years later did not mind taking a nap between the office computers in the new farmers' cooperative which Penilla helped 'Dante' manage. Morales and the other 'popular democrats' also did not give up, opting for radical community development and ten years later for the election of populist, somewhat leftist, President, Joseph 'Erap' Estrada. Meanwhile, talk show host Professor Randy David, along with socialist friends, fostered civil societies and unions, and later on a citizen action party, *Akbayan*. During the coming years, the priorities of 'Dante', the 'popular democrats' and the socialists stood out as the most innovative experiments for a democratic Left.

Their common view was that 'people power' was a step towards democracy but far from a social revolution. Accordingly, and in spite of the ambush, there were important new freedoms and crony capitalism had diminished. But the oligarchs and the social and political elites remained dominant. So irrespective of what detailed programme a new democratic Left preferred, a viable electoral agenda presupposed more solid foundations outside parliament. The question was how to get there.

The priorities differed among the democratic-oriented leftists. In retrospect, it is clear to me that the winding discussions and practices at the time boiled down to the following five projects: (i) class, (ii) community, (iii) citizen action and unions, (iv) party-building and (v) potentially progressive populism.

Arguments could be made for all of these. We shall examine them, in theory and praxis, one by one in the following sections. The excitement was how they would fare, what results would ensue, what lessons would be learnt. I decided to contrast the priorities over time, from the late 1980s until the early 2000s, arriving at quite unexpected stories.

Timeline the Philippines 1980s–2000s

1986–7
- 'People Power' Revolution.
- Maoist Left loses out.
- Political prisoners released.
- Traditional democratic elites regain prominence.
- Radical social democrats regroup and gain some ground.
- Leftists marginalized in elections.

1987→
- Ex. guerrilla leader 'Dante' Buscayno ambushed and forms huge farmer's cooperative.
- Ex. Maoists 'Boy' Morales, 'Ed' De La Torre and 'Gani' Serrano opt for 'popular democracy' and community development.
- Socialist groups *Bisig* and *Pandayan* plus CSOs consolidate and expand.
- 'Popular democrat's' community development with combatants fail, must start anew.

1991
- New code for CSO participation in local government.
- Mt Pinatubo erupts, causing crisis for Buscayno's cooperative.

1992–3
- Corazon Aquino opts for General Ramos as candidate in presidential elections.
- Buscayno rejects Ramos and forms local coalition, which fails, as does Buscayno's cooperative.
- *Bisig, Pandayan* and 'popular democrats' opt for radical liberals in elections, but fail.

1993–8
- Full-scale crisis and conflicts in Maoist movement.
- Former Maoists in *Siglaya* come close to *Bisig-Pandayan*-'popular democrats'.
- Dynamic activities among these groups and radical CSOs.

1998
- The same groups build citizen action party *Akbayan*.
- *Akbayan* wins one seat in national parliamentary elections and advances locally.
- 'Popular democrats' help making populist Joseph Estrada president and gain 'access'.

2000–1
- Estrada accused of serious corruption and ousted.

Map 7 Philippines.

Class

To learn more about efforts focusing on class at this decisive moment for the Philippines Left, I opted to visit Dante's and Fatima Penilla's farmers' cooperative in the dry plains of Tarlac, Central Luzon. Although perhaps prosaic in comparison with guerrilla fighting in the mountains, this was a key example of efforts to build solid support for 'people power' in the Philippines after the ousting of the dictator Marcos. A beaten bus took me out of Manila. This was 1990, so past Marcos' grand motorway, the mountain ranges of the Mt Pinatubo volcano that would soon erupt explosively built up in the northwest. There were also glimpses of the Clark Air Base, from where the Americans used to send bombers to Vietnam. In the nearby restaurants of Angeles, 'Dante' worked as a young man. Just after Capas town, one could discern *Voice of America's* gigantic masts, where he and his rebels used to slip in, disguised as construction workers and security guards, to pinch communication equipment for quite different purposes.

Not so far away, 'Dante' was born into a poor peasant family with many siblings, and a father who had fought the Japanese but who had to put up the kids for adoption when their mother passed away. Yet, 'Dante' managed to get a high school education when serving as a houseboy in Manila. Having fought the hacendados, then, along with other plantation workers, he joined the remnants of the Huk guerrillas that had fought the Japanese and later on the Washington-dominated government in Manila. They put him in charge of education, and he taught the classics of Marxism. Eventually he even practised the books – by abandoning the corrupt commander and forming the New People's Army. So from the late 1960s until his arrest in 1976, 'Dante' educated and organized guerrillas in the mountain ranges all around the country.

Earlier, in Tarlac, tenants living under serf-like conditions had protested against their appalling conditions, for example, by setting fire to the sugar cane fields of Hacienda Luisita, owned by the Cojuangcos' who turned pro-Marcos. However, this was also where young Lady Corazon grew up. 'Cory', as she became known to everyone, married an equally privileged son in the nearby hacienda in Conception, Benigno 'Ninoy' Aquino. He turned radical liberal, fought President Marcos and developed close relations with popular leaders like 'Dante'.

Upon their death sentence in 1977, finally equals, 'Ninoy' Aquino and 'Dante' took an oath that if either survived, they would care for the other's family. So when Ninoy Aquino was assassinated in 1983, 'Dante', while in prison, supported 'Cory' Aquino in ousting President Marcos. And when 'Cory' Aquino later on released 'Dante', she also facilitated huge loans for his cooperative. Later on, however, their loyalties became more complicated, even devastating for the project. But when disembarking the bus to revisit Tarlac-Tarlac, nobody knows, of course.

Small farmers against capitalist markets

The heat vibrated in the air along MacArthur highway, in front of 'Dante's' and Penilla's modest residence, so we took refuge inside, behind a fan.

'Dante' had prepared a mini-lecture: it's capitalist destruction out there now, not the feudal-like landlordism we used to fight and which 'Joma' (Sison, the Maoist leader/Chapter 6) remains obsessed with. Marcos is out, so we have freedom to act. And thanks to our previous struggle, there was a partial land reform where maize and rice are cultivated. So many sharecroppers are now small farmers (…). However, they are exposed to the disadvantages of capitalist markets. The farmers are short of effective inputs. The mill-owners and middlemen buy cheaply and sell dearly. Farmers are heavily indebted. They run the risk of losing their land. Workers, moreover, are given miserable pay, and there is a shortage of jobs. Yet, they fail to do something together. (…) That's why we initiated the cooperative. We started with the royalties from a silly film about my life. We also got loans, partly thanks to 'Cory' (Aquino). And there were some 500 loyal former combatants. You know, these are my home tracts. Now there are advances, and many more are interested. But the drought is bad (…) We dig for water (…) Besides, we should have windmills instead of generators to pump it up. Can you connect me to the Danish environmentalists? I'm told they have practical solutions.

Having returned to the immediate realities, 'Dante' rushed to supervise work on the new rice mill, soon to be inaugurated. Penilla shook her head: he always claims to be 'flexible'. As the more NGO-ish administrator,[1] I have to keep some order.

Small mice chased each other under the computer as she quoted and commented on various documents: by now, some 4,000 people are interested. Their family plots are individually owned but all together larger than sugar cane-growing Hacienda Luisita. We have seventy-seven local leaders in twenty-three groups, with one coordinator and technical adviser in each. We are the largest cooperative in the country. To prevent infiltration, we only employ local people. We provide inputs, help with land preparation, and collect and handle the harvest of rice, maize and beans. We market and sell for good prices, deducting the loans. It works. We have also initiated fishponds, production of organic fertilizers, cooperative shops and a canteen. There is more to come. The problem is growth pain.

Politics when needed

The main office consisted of a few long tables in one of the empty factory halls, rented cheaply, otherwise used as a warehouse. Seated on some rickety chairs, I challenged 'Dante': Have you turned into a progressive moneylender with good contacts, or the managing director of a cooperative? Can it be replicated? What are the politics?

'Dante' replied that he was sick and tired of both the old Maoists and the new 'community concientizers': they just talk and lecture. But we won't be naïve; we must be able to defend ourselves. And I have some authority (…) and the conditions for activists in Tarlac may be better than in some other places. Still, there are freedoms and room for manoeuvre now. And the farmers know their interests and enemies. We do not need to tell them. Yet, they will not act politically until they are prevented from making the best out of their situation. So we try to take them there, to the new

---

[1] In this book the general term civil society organizations (CSOs) is preferred to non-governmental organizations (NGOs) – except when 'NGO' is used in an expression by an organization or an informant.

frontline, as quickly as possible. They make money now. But if the cooperative is blocked by the businessmen and gangster politicians, the farmers will resist. And I will take up politics again.

When I followed up by asking if he could, in the meantime, run all these cooperative ventures as an army of farmers when there was no visible enemy, he smiled: I know what you mean. You have a conspiracy with Fatima. Yes, we shall be more democratic as soon as possible.

Hell breaks loose

Only about a year and a half later, two catastrophes changed everything. On 15 June 1991, Mt Pinatubo exploded next door, the second-largest terrestrial eruption of the twentieth century. Ash and lahars were everywhere, worsened by a typhoon and thunderstorms. 'Dante's' cooperative in Capas was northeast of the worst-affected areas, but agriculture was badly hit, especially rice and other crops dependent on water. Deep ploughing, moreover, was expensive. People became increasingly reliant on relief and political support. 'Dante' had to return to politics earlier than expected.

Then came the next disaster. President Aquino decided not to run in the 1992 elections, endorsing instead General Fidel Ramos. 'Dante' was dependent on protection and funding to stand a chance if running as a candidate for the governorship in Tarlac. In such a position, he would be able to save the cooperative and provide an alternative for the province. But he could not support General Ramos – an old enemy who had imprisoned him. Moreover, he was bound by the promise to Ninoy to support 'Cory' Aquino. So 'Dante' was also prevented from opting for the support of a contending politician with sufficient resources. Hence, he lost out. When I arrived for another visit in late May 1992, just after the elections, difficult discussions were in the air. Good for critical research, but painful for friends.

The most obvious problem was the debts. After Pinatubo, farmers were up against the wall. If they delivered their poor harvests to the cooperative, some of the returns would be deducted to pay for their loans. Some of them delivered to private businessmen instead, competing with the cooperative. Hence, the cooperative suffered problems too of servicing its loans to creditors who refused to write some of them off in spite of the natural disaster. New efforts were made to include the farmers in running and caring for the cooperative, but many did not want to share the responsibilities. A common refrain was that they had thought 'Dante' was strong and would support them, but now he was weak and unable to help.

Additional attempts were made to diversify the cooperative and engage in other businesses, to provide employment and make money to pay back the loans. Some ventures were successful but not good for popular organizing. When taking up sugar production that called for less water, it was increasingly difficult to engage both farmers and workers. They did not have to attend daily, as they did with intensive agriculture.

Moreover, 'Dante' responded positively, of course, to President Aquino's call for him to oversee the post-Pinatubo rescue operations in the area at large. These included constructing huge resettlement camps and industrial parks to attract businesses and provide jobs. His engagement was not just to help Aquino, it was also an opportunity to gain the initiative in rebuilding Capas and Tarlac. But he was never granted sufficient powers and resources to deliver. Once again, ordinary people deemed him responsible but weak and unable to help. And in trying to prevent the looting of equipment and an entire electricity plant (in the O'Donnell part of the previous US air force base) – which could have been the backbone of production in the area – he became the 'main enemy' among shady businessmen.

'Dante' got angry and hired private security guards to protect the remaining gear. (They politely saluted me too when I documented the damage.) Most importantly, he decided he had to engage in at least local politics in spite of the promise to 'Cory' Aquino to stay out of the fray after having snubbed Ramos. 'Going politics' was the only chance to save the cooperative, and the Capas municipality, and to foster new leadership. Friendly experts helped in drafting a model plan for the municipality. 'Dante' mobilized and backed a coalition of progressive local candidates. Campaigning commenced. The cooperative, the imaginative visions, and to some extent the rescue work were the backbones. Yet, they failed. Cheating and vote buying were there, of course, but the progressives were not strong enough to contain them. Why?

Divisive farmer's interests and insufficient democratic work

Fatima Penilla answered by recalling our argument that one cannot direct farmers like an army when there is no clear-cut enemy. Her mantra was there had to be firm democratic management – tragically confirmed by the deterioration of the cooperative when she was not replaced as senior administrator upon leaving, for private reasons, in late 1993.[2]

'Dante' accepted the argument but did not follow up. He thought the problems were even more fundamental. As we returned to his basic analysis, he agreed he had been wrong in assuming that the farmers had sufficient mutual interests in engaging in cooperation to resist the drawbacks of the capitalist market. On the contrary, now that neoliberal finance was entering rural markets too, each family, to make a living, had so many other jobs and small businesses and class interests got confused. People kept various options open, not just the cooperative.

In his darker moments, 'Dante' muttered there should have been stricter business principles, so that farmers had not turned beggars relying on his kindness. Later on, he de facto followed that line. But in our discussions in 1992, he still thought that an even more diversified cooperative might have helped, if there had been better democratic management (regretting Penilla's departure) and if they had succeeded in gaining political power.

In short, we agreed there was a need for more than just democratic management. The scattered class interests and issues had to be negotiated, for example, by way of political model plan for Capas – a plan with popular participation at its heart in both drafting and implementation.

---

[2] Penilla never recovered fully from the painful wounds she incurred in the 1987 ambush. She passed away in 2012.

The last time we met, in a hut on his own fields in 1995, as he was now a consultant only in the declining cooperative, he returned to the point that when political intervention was delayed – and finally failed – and when the Capas model plan they had suggested came to naught, nothing else was left. He was hoping to resume work, learn from the insights and regain contacts with socialist friends in Manila. It did not materialize.[3]

Community

While Commander 'Dante's' point of departure for renewing the Left was the perceived class interests of his farming mates, celebrated technocrat Horacio 'Boy' Morales, from a landed political family in the same province, thought otherwise.

Morales had defected from Marcos' Development Academy for the National Democratic Front (NDF) in 1977 (Chapter 6). This act of outstanding integrity was not only to counter the then death sentences of Maoist party leader Sison, New People's Army commander 'Dante' and main liberal dissident 'Ninoy' Aquino. It was also to support semi-legal development organizations as a supplement to the armed struggle. These organizations would in turn promote progressive local development along with the pillars of 'national democracy': peasants, agricultural and other workers, small farmers and businessmen.

The new ideas did not gain much ground, however, as Morales, like so many other leaders, was soon hunted down and put in prison. But while confined between 1982 and 1986, plans were drawn up among like-minded leaders in the same camp – radical Catholic and Christian activists, Edicio 'Ed' De La Torre and Isagani 'Gani' Serrano. They shaped what came to be known as the 'popular democratic position' by engineering and sponsoring community development, later on adding populist leadership. The operational base would be the somewhat run-down, and previously CIA-supported, Philippine Rural Reconstruction Movement (PRRM). Still it was one of the largest CSOs in the country, and Morales had been offered the chance to take it over, once released.

House of cards

Serrano, 'the resident poet of the Camp Crame prison' and Morales' deputy at PRRM, was a remarkably honest, soft-spoken and rethinking former executive member (in the 1970s) of the Maoist communist party's central committee. In one of our discussions in 1992, he was particularly on the mark: once out of prison, we worked effectively according to the plan, but it collapsed a few years later. Peace negotiations broke down and government resumed repression. Many of the militant popular organizations, where

---

[3] On another visit in 1998, we failed to meet, as he had suffered a serious accident in a brick factory. He recovered and continued to work, low profile, on his own farm and with business-oriented cooperative ventures.

we had tried to base new development efforts, such as credit cooperatives and peasant organizations, were of course vulnerable. However, we did not expect them to fall like a house of cards as soon as the leaders were threatened. Admittedly, the organizations proved mainly campaign machines within the framework of revolutionary national democratic struggles.

Charismatic popular democrat and liberation theology-driven educator, 'Ed' De La Torre, concurred: cooperation with the combatant leaders did not work. They were out to agitate and rally protests only, nothing constructive. And we couldn't work with only them. Primarily we wanted to work with the common people. So we had to form a basic organization on our own.

While 'Dante' in Tarlac concluded that building an economically competitive cooperative and gaining local political power were crucial to fostering democratic development, the 'popular democrats' – for example, in Serrano's nearby province of Bataan – emphasized the need to strengthen community development. In their view, this would enable people to make good use of the education and resources provided by the PRRM.

Building community

For the time being, the idea was thus to live with the harsh political situation and play down different interests within the communities. The focus was on issues that most people could agree on and manage themselves. One method was to help people to map their own problems and potentials. Another was to introduce democratically governed cooperatives, for instance, within a village. Small businessmen were also brought in. Moreover, environmental destruction was often so urgent that many people's livelihoods were threatened. These issues called for integrated local and regional programmes.

Similarly, the 'popular democrats' tried to promote coalitions and councils where civil society organizations and popular movements could come together. Said 'Boy' Morales: please don't call them dual power structures. Rather, we are inspired by the original idea of direct popular governance through pluralistic soviets, not dominated by communists.

The liberal government enacted a new Code for Local Government in 1991 that envisioned the participation of CSOs. Hence, the 'popular democrats', among others, took up the challenge for *their* partners of being accepted. Working relations with the 'actually existing politicians' were cultivated in order to gain access to local governance and, if possible, expand the space for popular initiatives. But radical political change was not on the agenda.

Non-political

All the related programme documents were obviously designed to fit the international jargon of civil society of the time – being against the state, in favour of participatory community development and promoting green agendas. It was quite slippery, so in an attempt to understand what it meant on the ground, I tailed behind Senior PRRM

Manager Lisa Dacanay during one of her field trips in Bataan, in mid-1992. She professionally (and patiently) answered all my provocative questions and guided me to numerous projects and discussions with participants. Yet, it was rather her community organizers' reaction during, I'm afraid, a quite boyish Philippine bar-session that illustrated the contentious character of the choices made. When they found out I did comparative studies, they asked me what had enabled the celebrated participatory budgeting in Porto Alegre, Brazil. Hearing my answer that it had taken enforcement by a successfully elected Workers' Party mayor, as civil society had not been enough, they paid for the next round of beer.

The PRRM certainly did some electoral education and encouraged local activists to participate as candidates and supporters, especially on the village (*barangay*) level. But as an organization it stayed neutral, never really endorsing candidates. Communities supported by the PRRM got people elected as *barangay* leaders, but *barangays* were supposed to be non-political. As far as I could find out, there was no clear-cut causal relation between the self-managed community development and progressive local politics. Even the later attempt at such an alignment – the 'Pinatubo Party' – remained a non-starter.

Transactional and populist substitutes

Successful politics was rather by lobbying, transactions, and later, populism. This was in order to gain access to the crucial central-level resources as well as international support. The 'popular democrats' were not alone. They competed with other civil society-oriented actors such as liberals and various social democrats. PRRM's and 'Boy' Morales' connections were vital. One example was Juan Flavier, a former president of the PRRM. As Secretary of Health in President Fidel Ramos' new 1992 government, Flavier fostered extensive joint projects. Later, moreover, Morales served as Flavier's successful campaign manager in the 1995 senatorial elections and facilitated close connections with the Department of Agrarian Reform. This cooperation was intensified when Morales (along with 'Ed' De La Torre) finally managed Joseph 'Erap' Eastrada's successful Presidential campaign in 1998, in return for the position of Secretary of Agrarian Reform. We shall return later to this populist project. It ended in disaster.

Citizen action and unions

After the 'people power revolution' in 1986, a constitutional referendum in 1987, and the following legislative, local and *barangay* elections, many analysts suggested that the Philippines had merely returned to the illusory democracy under the semi-feudal political bossism that preceded Marcos and his state of emergency. That is, to a situation when the guerrillas had been marginalized, and the oligarchs ran their own armies and mobilized the votes of all those dependent upon them – thus getting relatives elected as legislators, governors and mayors, who, once in office, made use of public means, assets and resources to pay back their sponsors and enrich themselves, while keeping in touch with the American Embassy.

On a closer examination, however, the old structures were falling apart while new solid forms had not yet appeared. Much of the old landlords' influence had diminished already with the growth of President Marcos' centralized rule. Capitalism expanded in urban as well as rural areas. Tenants and workers managed to gain some freedom of action, and significant numbers of peasants got their own land.

So when Marcos' state-authoritarianism finally collapsed, and a new code for local governance was introduced – along with liberal economic policies and a myriad of CSOs – it was not possible to return to the old days. Even if many of the new businessmen had their roots in haciendas and huge plantations; and even the new small farmers were impoverished.

In addition, the number of migrant workers had increased drastically, and inside the Philippines many people had moved to the cities. Contacts, patronage and political bossism were still vital, but skill and education mattered. Family loyalties and traditional ideas and authorities including the Church(es) remained significant, but journalists and movie- and TV-stars were becoming increasingly important. This applied especially to the almost 50 per cent of the electorate below middle age. Meanwhile the Americans had started to evacuate their military bases, and state-socialism was falling apart in Europe while becoming commercialized in China.

New opportunities but what should be done?

In other words, the old Maoist Left was getting increasingly irrelevant. And while political machines remained crucial, the traditional politicians seemed dated too. So there should be new opportunities for innovative democratic leftists to engage in elections. But how?

'Dante', as we know, had failed to compensate for the fragmentation of farmers' interests with more democratic cooperative governance and broader political intervention and programmes. When Mt Pinatubo erupted and his loyalty to 'Cory' Aquino prevented viable political alliances, his project fell apart. Morales, Serrano and other 'popular democrats', moreover, failed to foster radical development (and politics) that, ideally, would have enabled semi-legal Maoist organizations to engage in, for example, peasant cooperation. The Maoist vehicles proved to be campaign machines only. And the 'popular democrats' own alternative community development did not generate clear-cut political openings.

So what did the progressive social democrats in *Pandayan* and the independent socialists in *Bisig* (Chapter 6) have to offer? One of them was concerned scholar and journalist 'Randy' David, whose televised talk show before 'Dante' was ambushed had evaluated the performance of the Left in the 1987 elections. Did the socialist attempts fare any better?

'Three little pigs'

To answer, one must recall the messy political preconditions (Chapter 6). The Philippine New Left grew out of a student revolt in the late 1960s. It was a militant equivalent to the concerned activist part of the 1968 generation in Europe (and North America). But the

Philippines is Latin America in Asia. Hence, most activists opted for Maoism while the socialist minority studied the rise of dependent capitalism in Latin America. Thus, the Maoists linked up with 'Dante's' revolutionary peasants in 1969, and the radical social democrats in *Pandayan* fostered resurgent citizenship among the urban poor and union struggles in industries and plantations.

The 'old' moderate socialists rejected this approach. Some were in the Philippine Democratic Socialist Party (PDSP) and were thought particularly authoritarian. Others were accused of horse-trading in the elitist political firmament, flirting in particular with the Liberal Party or the then similarly oriented and personality-driven PDP-Laban. The critique became uncompromising when the moderates acceded to the retention of the US military bases in the country and supported General Fidel Ramos and business oligarch, Sergio Osmeña, in the 1992 presidential elections.

A few years earlier, in the mid-1980s, independent radical socialists such as Professor Randy David also came out against the unprincipled 'old' socialists. David and other new leftists had, as we know, built a socialist bloc (*Bisig*) with unionists and renewal-oriented ex-communists, including founding chair Professor 'Dodong' Nemenzo. A decade later, moreover, 'Dante', 'Boy' Morales and others defected from Maoism, calling themselves 'volunteers of popular democracy' (VPM).

The saying was these blocs – *Pandayan*, *Bisig* and the 'popular democrats' – were the 'three little pigs against the Maoist wolf'. With respect to democracy, *Pandayan* focused on popular participation and deliberation on the ground, and *Bisig* as well as the 'popular democrats' argued democracy was fine, in principle. They wanted to counter the dominance of oligarchs and political bosses by electoral reforms, to foster more issue and programmatic-based parties and politics. However, the 'three little pigs' were adamant that the basic sources of power were outside state and politics, and thus not subject to electoral competition. 'Real power' must instead be fought for by unions and civil society, by pressure politics to gain supportive public resources and favourable policies and, according to *Pandayan* in particular, by way of progressive ethics and alternative democracy 'from below'.

Last minute deal

In spite of the disputes and priorities in civil society, the first comprehensive democratic transfer of political power in the Philippines since Marcos grabbed power could not be neglected. In May 1992, some 88,000 candidates would be involved in synchronized elections. About 30 million voters would elect a president, vice president, 24 senators, 200 congressmen and women, some 14,000 provincial and municipal councillors, 73 governors and 1,600 mayors. The financial resources of the candidates as well as vote buying would remain as important as usual. But the new freedoms were there, the Commission on Elections was expected to do a decent job and the professional coup-plotters were likely to keep a low profile. The electoral arena was gaining legitimacy and becoming increasingly important. The 'popular democrats', and especially the leftist socialists, were interested in democracy as a precondition for equal citizenship and peaceful strategies. What should they do?

Radical civil society organizations had tried in vain since 1990 to decide how to engage in electoral politics. Several of them made now a second attempt. They agreed on promoting political consciousness, electoral reforms and 'people's platforms', but not on endorsing candidates. Unions were reluctant too. In 1992, moreover, *Pandayan* and *Bisig* as well as the 'popular democrats' refused to support President Aquino's endorsement of General Ramos and businessman Osmeña as candidates for president and vice president. In the last minute before electoral registrations, leading activists decided instead to form a coalition, *Akbayan,* which would be able to at least promote a few progressive national-level candidates and put vital issues on the agenda.

Among the presidential candidates, the *Akbayan* coalition supported the widely respected liberal senators Jovito 'Jovy' Salonga, ex-speaker of the senate and responsible for carrying through the anti-US-bases treaty campaign, and Aquilino 'Nene' Pimentel, the prime force in decentralizing state powers. The main senatorial candidates were liberal nationalist Wigberto 'Bobby' Tañada and liberal social democrat Florencio 'Butch' Abad with roots in *Pandayan* as well as coming from an influential political family.

These candidates had already built an alliance. Hence, they would bring money and their electoral machine while the radicals would add dynamic activists. The key words were national independence, promotion of people's interests, participatory democracy, sustainable development and genuine structural reforms. Similarly, local activists would provide progressive candidates for congress, municipalities and executive positions. Might this be the first breakthrough for a new democratic Left?

Another challenge

On the contrary, as the votes were counted, the 'soft Left' was humiliated. Very few people chose honest politicians who represented their interests. Fidel Ramos, the head of the Constabulary under Marcos, won the presidential race by a thin margin, ahead of a Miriam Defensor-Santiago, who suggested all evil was due to corruption and would be curbed if politicians were locked up and businessmen given all possible liberties. Third was Marcos' foremost crony-capitalist Eduardo Cojuangco, the favourite, moreover, of controversial sect *Iglesia ni Cristo.* Even Imelda Marcos got more votes than leftist liberal Jovy Salonga. A comedian, Vicente 'Tito' Sotto, got the most votes for the Senate, while 'NGO candidate', Butch Abad, lost badly.

Already on my arrival in late April, a few weeks ahead of the elections, friends told me this would happen. Scholarly socialist and civil society activist Karina Constantino-David smiled: I'm sorry to let you know that we will fail. The NGOs are not committed. 'Randy' David added: we don't have the funds. Gerry Bulatao, directing the politically friendly CSOs' political intervention, said: the project has stalled. Ever so devoted 'Ed' De La Torre added: in Bataan, even the PRRM is unable to take a stand.

When I asked, in response, why the Left had allowed neoliberal Miriam Defensor to monopolize the issue of anti-corruption, which was so crucial in Indonesia, the answer was that after Marcos and his cronyism, most activists focused on 'the basic conflicts' of urban poverty, agrarian reform and workers' conditions.

While their depressing messages were clear, I could not grasp the dynamics. To understand why their calculations had proved wrong, I had to get out of the seminar rooms, the drummed up campaign meetings and the May Day demonstrations in metro Manila.

The Cebu mysteries

To be fair, I asked for a case that the *Akbayan* leaders themselves thought was promising, and I could therefore analyse critically, rather than a failure they did not deem representative. Thus, I was invited to *Bisig*'s stronghold around Cebu City, in the economically dynamic central part of the country. I was warmly welcomed to the downtown office of the coordinating civil society group (Forge), where intense activity and stacks of materials and schedules displayed serious commitment. Reflective Director Gwen Ngolaban said: yes we focus on the elections, but not all our friends and groups do. And there is a shortage of funds. And we started too late. Every day we normally try to help people help themselves. Electoral politics is not part of that routine.

I said I was interested, precisely, in the connections between their everyday efforts and politics. Gwen nodded and asked friends to take me in two directions: a well-established fishing cooperative in the small island of Pandanon ('which is also a very nice place') and campaigning with urban poor and workers in *Bisig*'s central city stronghold.

The cooperative is not for running the island

The crowded, speedy ship heading for the major Bohol island in the south could not land at the small reef of Pandanon. Passengers and luggage were taken onto the shore in local *bankas*, to be greeted by hordes of children. *Bankas* for fishing and their equipment were everywhere along the beach. We found the main track and headed northeast. On every available piece of land there were people and houses, under the occasional palm trees, until we approached what I first thought was the end of the island. But from the wooden house where I would stay, there was an open view of an abandoned stretch of untouched white dunes, and at the end of it, the contours of an attractive Greek-like temple structure, designed for sunrise and sunset. This lovely tip of the impoverished and crowded island, however, was not for the locals, anymore. Rather, I was told, it was rented by a Cebu businessman who gave tours to wealthy tourists. And the open temple-structure had been constructed for a 'possibly pornographic Japanese film'.

If this was one part of the Philippine political economy, another was people's efforts to alter it. The cooperative was multi-purpose, my hosts explained. Everything but fish must be brought to the island, including fresh water and ice. And the catches must be traded off the island. The fishing waters too had been overexploited, including by dynamite fishing. Whatever was left of the reefs should now be protected.

Exchanging experiences from living in fishing villages (as I also do), I asked who decided on Pandanon? And why was it, I added, that they had not (yet) been able to gain power in spite of their well-functioning cooperative, already enrolling about half the households? That was a trickier issue. We kept discussing it during another visit a few years later.

One occasion I raised the matter was when I had, admittedly, just disturbed a cooperative meeting by causing great laughter trying to sail one of the participant's *banka*. The boat did not have a rudder, only a paddle and the leaders said I had to learn to handle it as flexibly as politics – by moving forwards to get it up against the wind.

Then they made three points. One, the cooperative was to help the members, not to run the island. Two, candidates for the *barangay* and municipality elections must consider many other concerns, beyond those of the cooperative. Three, they had tried to launch some candidates, but there was vote buying: even our people take money (...) they do not think they harm cooperative interests, because the local government and the cooperative are separate.

So the obvious conclusion, I thought, was that as a cooperative was not enough to engage in local government, they had to also form a political association. But then there was more laughter. Maybe, they said, but the vote-buying problem would still be there. If some of our friends think others sell their votes, they will also. Yes, I commented: that is what my colleagues call a 'collective action problem'. They spend a lot of time studying game theory to overcome it.

My friends' response was: let them theorize (...) the simple fact is that people must be able to keep an eye on each other. So our first priority will be to arrange a fiesta late at night before the next elections because that is when people tend to sell their votes.

Urban poor communities and unions are not the same

In Cebu City, Gwen Ngolaban and Timmy Tejedor introduced me to the socialists' stronghold among poor communities: we are not primarily building campaign machineries to confront bulldozers and reject everything, they said. After Marcos, there are possibilities to work out alternatives, for daily livelihood but also to alter Cebu's master development plan. It is undoubtedly designed by the oligarchs and their politicians, but if we can gain some political power in the municipality and province, things might change. This may be one of the missing links between local self-help and politics.

Moreover, Ngolaban asserted: such issues might unify the urban poor without fixed jobs and unionized workers, who otherwise have different priorities. *Bisig*-related unions and civil society groups among the urban poor have therefore decided to support a progressive young labour lawyer as their councillor, Arman Alforque.

Hence, I joined Alforque and his local campaign team. In addition to noisy tours up and down the streets, there were also evening meetings with local leaders, and lengthy promenades to meet people in the winding alleys in the shanty compounds. Arman invited conversations, listened politely, far from cocksure. Some women said he was good looking. Everybody took their time. There seemed to be mutual trust. I was impressed.

Asking later about his chances to win, he said the campaign was too late. There had not been enough electoral education. There had been conflicts between the leftist politicians, civil society groups and unions – and within them too. Plus a shortage of funds. Moreover, he added: people listen and nod to our ideas, but then they have other concerns as well. Urban poor groups and unions have different priorities. Informal, contract and permanent workers compete on the labour market.

Alforque lost – in the urban poor stronghold. He did not run again in 1995, disturbed by the chronic problems of managing the relations between funded CSOs and penniless unions. Also, he had taken a stand on the primacy of unions, explaining: urban poor groups and unions must coordinate their various issues, but in terms of mass organization, those of the workers are most solid. Besides, many of the workers live in poor urban areas.

Next stop a party

Back in Quezon City, witty socialist organizer Ronald Llamas, not knowing how to spell to 'giving up', was already summarizing and planning for the next elections: we will lose now but have won several lessons. The 'magnificent' liberal candidates we supported delivered neither funds nor machines. We could just as well have done this on our own. Worse, the CSOs remained hesitant and fragmented. And the unions quarrelled. We must have a party of our own.

Party-building

Notwithstanding the debacle, increasingly many democratic leftists did agree there was a need for a political organization, perhaps a party. Still, their points of departure and priorities differed.

Plural civil society

Civil society activists focused on special issues, such as human rights, gender equality, poverty alleviation, agrarian reform or labour education. Or they worked in specific territories, such as in urban poor communities. The activists wanted, of course, as many people as possible to unite on 'their' issues, or within 'their' communities – irrespective of ideologies or party loyalties. Donors, moreover, had to be supplicated by way of opportune project proposals and were notoriously worried about political links. Using project funds for political activity was not accepted. But employment and temporary work for CSOs were crucial for nearly full-time political activists to earn a living. Similarly, the groups wanted the best-possible contacts with influential politicians (irrespective of party), and 'their' administrators. In that context, idealists and leftists were nice but usually devoid of power and influence, and thus of no avail. In other words, the activists might well wish a progressive party existed, but not at the expense of their own work.

In addition, the activists engaged in some joint projects. One example was trying to get access to the local development councils and their funding, stipulated by the new Code on Local Governance. Another was promoting 'good governance' in supposedly non-party political *barangays*. This was in tune with donors' priorities, so generous funding was available. But by the late 1990s, there were signs of reduced foreign funding and thus problems for sustained activism. There were also frequent coalitions on crucial issues, such as demanding consistent land reform or resisting American military bases and the country's international debt. Most campaigns rejected existing policies and suggested different priorities.

Less emphasis, however, was placed on the development of alternative reform proposals which might be negotiated and implemented jointly by central/local government and issue and interest organizations. State, government and participatory practices were rarely trustworthy. Moreover, there were limits to ideological pluralism. For example, leftist civil society groups related to different 'NGO-coalitions' – socialist-liberal oriented or popular democratic. Maoists, liberals and others certainly ran their own 'federations of NGOs' too.

With regard to political party building, it was therefore common among civil society activists to think of a coalition that might collect a basket of issues to agree on and promote. Still, as Gerry Bulatao of the '2001 NGO-project' put it: we keep in touch with several decent parties and candidates and inform people about them, but we can't link up with a certain party exclusively or endorse specific candidates.

Civil society activists who were more favourable to party building anyway remained worried about strong leadership. Karina Constantino-David's mantra was: all these centralist short cuts take such a long time, let's build local parties and confederate. 'Ed' De La Torre was unusually categorical: I'm for a strategic party beyond short-term tactics, but only if it doesn't coordinate and guide everything.

Divergent blocs and insufficient movements

At the other end of the table were four non-party political organizations or political blocs. These comprised the radical socialists (*Bisig*), the local democracy-driven socialists (*Pandayan*), the 'popular democrats' (in various setups) and now also some Maoists who had recently left their party and formed *Siglaya* (*Siglo ng Paglaya*; Century of Freedom). The 'three little pigs' had thus become four. Prominent figures among the 'renegades' included 'Etta' Rosales, who had directed the Maoist's electoral work, and former politburo member Ricardo 'Ric' Reyes with roots in rural mass movements. Staunch metro Manila labour leader, Filemon 'Popoy' Lagman, had also defected but was only interested in occasional cooperation, primarily planning a Leninist cadre party for himself.

Another challenge was the relative weakness of popular organizations within the democratic Left, especially among farmers and workers. Unionization by factory rather than industry/sector nourished divisions, as did different employment conditions. Exacerbating the discord, most unions were subordinated to the patronage of employers and traditional politicians, or to Maoist leaders. Radical socialists remained in minority positions, even though they made advances and built promotional civil society organizations. As the Maoist hegemony diminished, the field opened up, but the 'renegade' leaders who defected rarely brought members and movements with them.

Hence, 'popular democrat' Joel Rocamora – who negotiated much of the party building – concluded that the mass organizations were insufficiently strong to build an ideal social movement-based Workers' Party, like Inácio Lula's in Brazil.

Institutional barriers and one opening

Based in a popular democratic think tank in the vicinity of academic and activist life in Quezon City, Rocamora was also concerned about the institutional challenges. The Philippine political system is modelled on the American and, worse, based on an even more unequal social and economic structure. Hence, there is competition and transaction between political machines and personalities on all levels. A process thoroughly dominated by oligarchs and political bosses. There is no space for programmatic party-politics, at best for progressive individuals.

According to Rocamora it was therefore unviable to launch a new progressive party – it wouldn't stand a chance. Echoing Political Science Professor 'Dodong' Nemenzo, he also argued it was unrealistic to make use of the new Code on Local Government (stipulating the devolution of funds and participation of civil society) without fighting the political bosses who were bound to dominate it. To put up a meaningful fight, there had to be much firmer work among the civil society activists than hitherto. For example, there was an internationally sponsored activist project to foster 'good local governance': the *Barangay*-Bayan Governance Consortium (humorously baptized Batman). This, it was asserted, had great potential if it did not remain merely a CSO-experiment – there had to be political coordination and intervention as well.

Leftist democrats agreed on the need to campaign for a parliamentary system with proportional elections. Yet, this was a double-edged sword, as the most ardent supporter might be an incumbent president who wished to stay on for several periods. One reform was granted, however. Starting with the legislative elections in 1998, 20 per cent of the House of Representatives would be elected by way of a national party-list system with proportional representation. The big machine-parties were not eligible to run, only small parties, interest groups and the like. They would get maximum of three seats each. Obviously, this might cause further division among the progressive groups and open up for all kinds of shady projects. Yet, it *was* an opening.

The art of politics

'Politics is the art of the possible', remarked Otto von Bismarck. But, added Václav Havel, it must also be the 'art of the impossible'. By not giving up, the humiliated team that had fostered the *Akbayan* coalition in the 1992 elections honoured both views.

After the full-scale split in the Maoist party in 1993, additional dissenters joined the discussion. Improved tactics were tried out in support of a few local candidates in the 1995 elections, and some results were encouraging. A conceptual paper was produced, suggesting the formation of a joint party rather than a coalition. The ideas were mulled over in a series of national and local meetings with some 3,000 participants. Given the diverging points of departure among civil society activists and campaigners, trade unionists, political movements and (not to forget) personalities, it was a herculean task to arrive at something both imaginative and viable. Yet, it did happen. In January 1998, an *Akbayan* Citizen Action Party was founded.

The price was high, of course. Many activists were frustrated. Some told me in the days that followed that *Akbayan* was not even a democratic socialist party, merely an electoral vehicle. Others said it was an unholy marriage between various political blocs and personalities rather than a mass party. Many agreed there were no clear-cut criteria for what pillars should be represented and what weight they would get, adding: there is too much politicking at the top, and crucial people have been abandoned.

I made a long list of objections, and it was easy to understand the critique. Obviously, many dissenters would proceed along other routes among CSOs, or engage in separate party-list parties, such as a gender equality party (*Abanse*), a PRRM-based community action party and various local and interest-based groups. Similarly, militant unionist Popoy Lagman, who was one of the few Maoist renegades who had brought along his followers when defecting, had already opted for a more ideological party-list formation: *Sanlakas,* United Force and later on the *Partido ng Manggagawa,* or Labour Party. Would *Akbayan* really take off, catch people's imagination and make a difference?

It was easy to be critical, even cynical, but through my comparative lenses *Akbayan* was unique. In spite of the weak and divided social movements and unions, something in the new formation reminded me of the successful rainbow Workers' Party in Brazil, inclusive of different leftist perspectives, CSOs and social movements. Despite numerous notoriously quarrelsome groups and personalities, most delegates remained in the conference room in Quezon City, inaugurating the party. Many civil society activists certainly said they would give priority to their organizations, issues and campaigns. Yet, they remained open for cooperation, trying for example to avoid competition in the same electoral districts.

Probably most importantly, *Akbayan* stood out as *the* democratic Left-oriented alternative, given its comprehensive approach and vision, and ideas of how to get there. The other party-list formations were either community, issue or sector oriented, or else driven by pure ideology and avant-garde leaders.

The outstanding personalities who committed themselves to foster the ideas also testified to the determination behind the endeavour. These included internationally respected Professor Walden Bello as chairperson and Ana-Maria 'Princess' Nemenzo as his deputy, Ronald Llamas as president and Ric Reyes as his deputy, Carmel Abao (from *Pandayan*) as secretary general and Joel Rocamora as arbiter. Equally convincing, 'Etta' Rosales and labour leader Donny Edwin topped the list of candidates for Congress. Widely respected 'Ed' De La Torre told me he was happy too. Internationally, the Swedish Labour movement's Olof Palme Centre in particular was consistently supportive, resisting temptations to link up with the old social democrats who had lost their compass in the corridors of power. What I failed to understand was how *Akbayan* would consolidate.

Inclusive construct

Propelling leaders Llamas (*Bisig*), Abao (*Pandayan*) and Rocamora ('*popular democrat*') tried to convince me: the party is not ideological, they insisted, but the political blocs are. They can cooperate but also stimulate each other by forming caucuses. Together we are against a protracted people's war, but in favour of a protracted democratic transformation, by balancing state and civil society. We are plural in giving voice to various demands by progressive groups, but we shall also aggregate and make priorities. The party has an individual membership, but the blocs will bring their mass movements and related CSOs. They can cooperate in sectoral committees as well as coordinate with other movements and campaigns.

I remember responding that theirs was obviously a serious attempt to combine what was available, without excluding anyone. But it remained to be seen if it would work. Most urgently, would it be possible to make a difference in the forthcoming elections, only four months away?

Their surprising answer was beyond my comprehension: now we have a party and leaders plus committed activists, we are strong enough to leave the seminar rooms and abstract debates and go onto the battlefield, even engage in murky deals with moneyed local players. I said it sounded risky. They said: it's unavoidable, come and watch. I did.

In practice

I headed for the South, where *Akbayan* claimed advances. Already in my first stop – the economically expanding city of Bacolod, in traditionally sugar-producing Negros Occidental province – it was obvious that the problems of managing the campaign were overwhelming. A sturdy veteran leader, escorting us in a battered white American sedan, convinced me there was little space for programmatic issues and reform proposals. Even public information of the new party list system was scarce. Here as in other locations, campaigners had to provide basic information.

Ronald Llamas spent time explaining why activists should care about it. It would prove positive in the long run because there would be less 'bossism' and programmatic policies. But for the activists I encountered at a public meeting in an extended shade along a country road next to harvested fields, it seemed more urgent that a local mayor was threatening squatters with bulldozers if they did not vote him. Could this sort of thing be countered? Old Maoists had linked up with *Akbayan*. Did they have the requisite muscle? Unfortunately, some other former combatants had joined Lagman's party (*Sanlakas*), which had access to extensive funds due to his family connections. So what should be done?

Even within the broad Left, ideological differences were obviously less important than personal trust and access to money and projects. In Bacolod as well as in business-driven Cebu City, Central Visayas and General Santos (GenSan) in southern Mindanao, there were pressing shortages of funds, even though unionized labourers had donated a day's wage each. But *Akbayan* did also acquire funds and endorsements in return for – for example – campaigning for other not immediately competing candidates. Activists in Cebu, whom I joined for distribution of propaganda one evening, said they would thus get funds to pay their poll watchers. Besides, they could distribute material for *Akbayan* too, at the same time. Poll watching was also for sale to other candidates. It was unavoidable and it worked, they assured me. But why, they asked rhetorically, was it so difficult for leftist-oriented CSO activists to contribute more? Why did some of them even opt against *Akbayan* in favour of liberal groups and candidates?

There were other, equally troubling, issues. *Akbayan* politicians had also to be members of mainstream parties. This was to enable them to engage in local politics (and not just in the national party-list election) and gain access to the established parties' funds and electoral machineries. But there were other reasons too. Membership of mainstream parties was also necessary to get other candidates and parties not only to list in their sample ballots the individual candidates they commended people to vote for various positions, but also to endorse *Akbayan* as the party voters should choose in the party-list elections.

In the agribusiness and fishing-oriented GenSan in southern Mindanao, for example, *Akbayan* supported incumbent mayor, Losa Lita Nunez, a short but vigorous school teacher. She tried to convince me it did not matter if she was part of another party and if she was, in turn, endorsing quite shady politicians as long as the locals knew her own qualities. And when I followed up by asking what business people thought of a progressive candidate, she smiled and repeated her slogan of 'business for all, not just for some'. A lovely leftist twist.

Akbayan campaigners were more specific, admitting principled reform proposals should matter. One, they said, was the party-sponsored programmes for 'good governance' in the *barangays*. Yet the same activists soon focused again on the best tactics to gain access to the municipal *barangay* department. This was how they would secure funds and be able to build a constituency. They said: we are not an NGO with foreign funds and a blueprint for community development or good governance for locals to fill in. We wish to enter with partisan politics, and gain influence, then we can apply 'good governance'.

When I asked if that politics was just about protests and general demands or also based on constructive policy proposals, they said: yeah, yeah, we have ideas! But now people must trust us. And then, when we get into office, we can be more specific and deliver.

I think they were happy changing the subject, by kindly indulging my interest in the conditions of the fishermen and the type of boats they used. So I was taken to the landing and auctioning of more and larger tunas than I had ever seen. Overfishing for smart Japanese sushi restaurants. By now there is a serious crisis.

Stalling

Akbayan did reasonably well in the election, gaining a seat in the Congress and standing out as the embryonic progressive party – more comprehensive than the issue groups, broader than the extreme Left. Yet, the new party was of course – initially at least – an amalgamation of groups and activists with their own priorities and contextual challenges.

There were certainly also a number of successful mayoral and local councillor candidates, and *Akbayan* extended its local branches. But as a party-list-party, *Akbayan* remained associated with national issues and central-level direction, for good and

for bad. This became increasingly important during the turbulent struggles in metro
Manila between 2001 and 2010, over the presidency and abuse of power, to which we
shall return in Chapter 13.

Populism

In the meantime, while the party-building efforts were making slow headway, popular
democrat 'Boy' Morales, along with 'Ed' De La Torre and the community developers
at PRRM, was also involved in a quite separate populist project. This originated in the
trading of electoral campaign management for access to public resources and positions
in government. The assumption was it might also nourish community development
and, perhaps, a mass movement.

The turning point came in 1995, when Morales used PRRM's apparatus to back its
former President Juan Flavier in his successful campaign for the senatorial elections.
Later, as the 1998 elections approached, Morales accepted the task of also directing
then Vice President Joseph 'Erap' Estrada's campaign to become president. In addition
to Estrada's Philippine-macho attributes of drinking, gambling and womanizing, he
was known for somewhat left-leaning nationalism by having opposed the American
bases. Morales accepted the job in exchange for strategic positions in a forthcoming
administration related to rural development, poverty alleviation and more.

As an iconic movie star, moreover, Estrada used to side with ordinary people. Thus
here was a possibility to nourish some leftist populism to gain votes, but also to build
a broad movement. To this end, former preacher 'Ed' De La Torre styled Estrada's
speeches and appearances. Similarly, a mass organization was built to promote him.
This was labelled *Jeep ni Erap*, associating, of course, his nickname with common
people's means of transportation (the jeepneys), but also standing for Justice, Economy,
Environment and Peace (JEEP). Based on funding from the businessmen that Estrada
promised to honour as president, JEEP mobilized supporters and remunerated
campaigners who engaged in 'grassroots empowerment and governance programmes',
plus, of course, in election campaigning and poll watching. In Cebu City, for example,
I noticed unofficial coordination with *Akbayan*. Fortunately, however, friends of both
Akbayan and Estrada managed to prevent the inclusion of JEEP in the party-list, as it
would have exposed how traditional politicians could abuse the list, originally meant
for marginalized groups.

Shortcut to disaster

Estrada was elected. 'Dodong' Nemenzo provided friendly advice and a few other leftists
gained formal posts, including 'Boy' Morales who took up the position as Secretary of
Agrarian Reform, cooperating with PRRM. 'Ed' De La Torre was placed in charge of
technical education skills, Karina Constantino-David was to foster Housing and Urban
Development and 'Princess' Nemenzo was appointed representative for women in the
Anti-Poverty Commission. JEEP, however, was not sustained. 'Ed' De La Torre later
confessed: it was a serious mistake, but as a government official, I couldn't run it.

Estrada's otherwise conservative administration deteriorated quickly, and the progressives stood little chance of preventing it. In October 2000, the president was accused of receiving payoffs from an illegal gambling racket. Progressives stepped down while Morales and De La Torre stood by until the last minute. When an impeachment trial failed to convict him, a similar constellation of dissidents as in 1986 – though this time inclusive of above-ground Maoist activists – staged a second 'people power' demonstration along the Manila EDSA Avenue. Still, the democratic Left lost out. As the police and armed forces joined in, there was no alternative progressive regime and in the vacuum conservative Vice President Gloria Macapagal-Arroyo took office.[4] We shall return to the fate of progressive Philippine politics in Chapter 13.

Interim statement

In mid-May just after the 1998 elections, 'Randy' David invited me to come along with a few other academic and journalist friends to his Pampanga home tracts, just south of Mt Pinatubo. We wanted to know if there had been reasonable local information about the party-list system, and we wanted to get an impression of the reconstruction seven years after the volcano erupted. The common electoral malpractices faded away, however, as we witnessed how the region was still stricken by the calamity. The glorious sixteenth-century San Guillermo Parish Church in Bacolor, for example, remained half-buried, even inside, by several metres of lahar, on top of which provisional services had to be conducted immediately under the ceiling.

What I remember best, however, was a phone call thereafter to one of my travelling companions to Pampanga, Seth Mydans (of *The New York Times*), suggesting he was in the wrong place at the wrong time. The Indonesian regime was about to crumble. He must get there.

While in politically exciting Philippines, I had also not thought of Indonesia – my prime point of reference. So both Seth and I were a bit embarrassed, having thought it would take longer to get rid of Suharto. But now, Seth had to leave for Jakarta immediately, and my life changed. From now on, there would be less time for me than expected for comparisons with the Philippines, because of my commitments to colleagues and friends in the Indonesian democracy movement and our joint 'participatory research', which would last more than a decade and called for extensive work. But by 1998, what lessons did I bring along from the Philippines?

Firstly, 'Dante's' project testified to the importance of proceeding from peasants' struggle for land to cooperation. That was how to improve production and not lose out in the market. What was more, it also testified to the dearth of common class interests when landlordism faded away. Obviously, it was thus crucial to foster unifying democratic governance among cooperative members. Also, it was important to engage in politics, develop common policy proposals and build alliances with other people.

---

[4] Estrada was later (2007) found guilty of plunder but pardoned by Macapagal-Arroyo.

'Dante' lost out on all accounts. But in spite of analysing the problems better than most, he was unable to overcome them, given the balance of forces and the preoccupations among friends in Manila.

Secondly, the 'popular democrats' courageously abandoned the idea of substituting development aid for weapons to Maoist militants, because their organizations among the people proved 'little more than campaign machineries' without interest in popular cooperation and, moreover, fell 'like a house of cards' when the leaders got into trouble. The alternative intervention by way of masterminding community development fostered local self-help but created few political openings. Contentious interest-based demands and policy proposals were obviously deprioritized. In Indonesia, this part of the story was vital too, as we shall see in Chapter 9.

Thirdly, by contrast, many civil society activists and unionists really did, vigorously, promote equal and active citizenship, combined with issue and interest-based demands and proposals. They were not strong outside the major cities, however. And repeatedly they stumbled over problems of proceeding from, on the one hand, lobbying and transactions with influential actors and the compiling of assorted demands and ideas to, on the other hand, the political aggregation of issues and interests for joint interventions. Conversely, ideological formations or groups focusing on 'basic' issue and interests – such as gender equality and workers' rights – proved too narrow. The Indonesian activists were up against similar challenges, dilemmas we shall also return to, in Chapters 9 and 10 in particular.

Fourthly, it was easy for those negotiating the *Akbayan* party to preach the primacy of a broad party with references to like-minded activists in Brazil. They had managed to form a rainbow social movement party. They had managed to foster civil society-driven participatory budgeting by introducing it from above, after having won mayoral elections. However, vital preconditions were lacking in the Philippines. The political and social movements – and the trade unions – were not strong enough, especially in the local contexts. Hence, it was also much more difficult in the Philippines than in Brazil to make use of elections, and the law on decentralization, to undermine the oligarchs and political bosses.

The formation of *Akbayan* by so many different groups and personalities undoubtedly testified to the idea of 'politics as the art of the impossible'. But it remained to be seen whether and how the new party might be used to foster stronger movements and develop broad local alliances behind demands and alternative policy proposals. And, crucially, whether it could actually begin to win mayoral elections, and subsequently implement blueprints for 'good governance' and 'community development'. The Indonesian pro-democrats tried several roadmaps, including heeding advice from the Philippines. We shall return to this in Chapters 9, 10 and 14.

Lastly, the transactions with moneyed politicians combined with populism. This may well generate resources and swiftly mobilize huge numbers of people. But the case of the 'popular democrats' promotion of Estrada and the subsequent deterioration of democracy also testified to the weakness of populist politics. The lack of proper representation of the various groups and interests involved – along with inadequate checks and balances – may be a shortcut to disaster. It may even generate political crisis and the intervention of authoritarian forces, from both right and left. In Indonesia it took until about 2005, with the early rise of current President 'Jokowi', before the pro-democrats were attracted by similar ideas and subsequently faced parallel problems, to be analysed in Chapter 14. Meanwhile the Philippine Left tried to unseat the conservative leaders who replaced Estrada. They failed but later *Akbayan* formed a coalition with liberals, which won the 2010 elections. Chapter 13 will focus on these experiences.

The rise and decline of the Indonesian democracy movement

There were good reasons to be surprised by the telephone message in mid-May 1998, received when travelling in the Philippines, which alerted us that Suharto's regime in Indonesia was about to crumble (Chapter 8). Only two months earlier, the unanimous conclusion of the well-informed journalists and scholars in the Jakarta Institute for Free Flow of Information (ISAI) was that the democracy activists remained weak and did not constitute a realistic alternative, even though the Asian economic crisis had intensified. Leading publisher and author, Goenawan Mohamad, sighed: we have no organization and common programme, and we are short of time, so we need a figure, a symbol, to rally behind. But there are no Indonesian equivalents to the Philippines' 'Cory' Aquino and Cardinal Sin.

On 11 March, Muslim technologist B. J. Habibie was appointed vice-president and a few days later Suharto demonstrated his stubbornness by also forming an emergency government, including his daughter and staunch cronies. So the next question was whether this team would be able to suppress not just the pro-democrats, but also the globalized market, the worried middle classes and their frustrated siblings in the university campuses. In a taxi to the airport, Southeast Asia scholar John Sidel and I realized there was no point in splitting the bill as the value of the rupiah remained ridiculously low. So our instinct was that while Suharto would not survive, he would hold on for some time. We were half-right. The rats abandoned ship just two months later.

Even though Suharto stepped down in May, however, the prime dilemma of the weak democrats remained. Why? How was it possible that even a vaguely leftist dimension to the push for democratization had not really regained ground in Indonesia since the mid-1960s, in spite of the deep roots the Left had laid since the inception of the independence movement in the 1920s? Previously leftists had always picked up again after various setbacks, like in Spain or Latin America. Not now. Why had Indonesia become so different? To answer, we must follow the progressive actors and their efforts over the years.

Timeline Indonesia 1967–1999

1967–1970s
- Maoist uprisings fail.
- Leftists in general demoralized, scattered and repressed.

1970s
- Students criticize corruption and dominance of foreign companies.

1974
- Student and dissident officers' 'Malari' uprising supressed.

1980s
- Radical students/intellectuals form CSOs for Human Rights and alternative development.
- Extractive development supplemented with low wage export industries.

1988–mid-1990s
- Cold war over and contradictions in Suharto's regime over nepotism and favours.
- Suharto favours limited 'openness'.
- Socialist activists go outside campus to mobilize workers, farmers and others.
- Others focus on organizing 'victims of capitalist development' from below.
- Yet others support critique from regions of authoritarian centralist development.
- Cause-oriented groups blossom.
- Liberal and socialist 'players' form think tank groups, including Democracy Forum.
- Muslim intellectuals form think tank ICMI, trying to reform the regime 'from within'.

1994
- End of 'openness'. Liberal magazines *Tempo, Detik, Editor* closed.
- Suppression of critical academicians and students.
- Strikes and labour unrest.
- Sustained fragmentation of pro-democracy movement.

1996–7
- Dissidents in mainstream nationalist party elect Megawati Sukarnoputri new leader.
- Regime cracks down on Megawati-led party and pro-democracy supporters (27/7/96).
- Increasing protests. Dissidents try to form more united movement but fail.
- Attempts to rally against the regime in the 1997 elections fail.

1997–8
- Asian economic crisis hits Indonesia hard.

- Opposition still unable to form united front.
- Dissident leaders support student protests.

March–May 1998
- Economic crisis deepens.
- Student protests increase.
- Suharto resigns in favour of Vice President Habibie (21 May).

May 1998–9
- Intensive manoeuvring among leading actors.
- 'International community' opts for democratic elite transition.
- Radical pro-democrats lose out.
- Elections in June 1999 – dominated by mainstream parties.

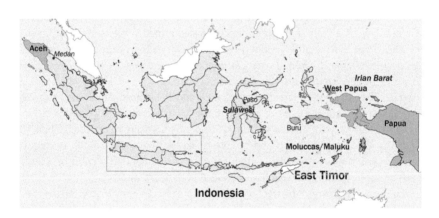

Map 8 Indonesia.

Map 9 Java.

Collapsed Left

Much of the weak resistance can be explained by the ways in which the reformist communists and Sukarnoists were supressed and thereafter the continued threats and surveillance (Chapter 4). But another aspect was the outright collapse of the leftist project itself. Several of the former leaders in Indonesia and Holland said: how could we organize effective resistance when the party leaders had kept us in the supposedly democratic movement in the dark about elitist political manoeuvres that might generate a massive crackdown? Even the leaders were not prepared to direct the organizations. We were all taken by surprise. And how could we claim basic civil and political rights when the decade-long struggle for democratic citizenship had been set aside since the late 1950s? Rather everyone had to search for protection among distant friends and relatives, away from the immediate neighbourhood where people know each other, or by going underground. But the witch-hunt was overwhelming.

Meanwhile the surviving party leaders who subscribed to an alternative Maoist perspective opted in the late 1960s for a 'long march' to remote and relatively safe 'old' party strongholds, such as in Blitar, East Java, and around Solo and Semarang in Central Java. But their attempts at peasant-based armed struggle made little sense. Once again, reactionary militias supported the military suppression, but this time the generals were anxious to uphold strict command, followed by state-led programmes to pacify and modernize the areas.

Hence, both the policy to support Sukarno and the Maoist model had capsized. Most surviving leaders whom I met in exile, or when they were released from prisons and camps, were broken stalwarts, frequently accusing each other of betrayal, quarrelling about old positions and unable to sketch alternative routes. A frequent recommendation was to 'organise without form'. Some sought protection by entering groups or public institutions that had participated in the repression.

Even human rights groups were afraid of being associated with the former *tapols* (political prisoners). It was easier for leftists outside the country to stand up for their human rights, but the activists had often given up on the old leaders' political clout, rather pinning their hopes on the liberation movements in East Timor (which Indonesia occupied in 1975), and in Aceh and Papua. As leading campaigner Liem Soei Long put it: maybe the liberation movements can 'encircle' and weaken the rulers in Jakarta.

Democratization, however, was not a top priority. And, until the mid–late 1990s, there were few attempts to connect the liberation struggle with the unfolding democracy movement inside Indonesia.

Failed rectification (1970s)

The first student revolt against Suharto (*Malari*), in January 1974, was supported by dissident officers and spurred riots but failed to dislodge the regime. Hariman Siregar, the foremost young leader, was imprisoned for six years along with his seniors. During our first conversation thereafter, desolation was still in the air in spite of his smart godfather looks. But now, in 1991, he sounded happier, even suggesting we should meet in a soccer stadium: you know, the intelligence keeps an eye on my network, but we have formed a football team to enjoy while talking freely.

I was excited to meet him for another reason too. In his capacity as an outspoken youngster among senior liberal-socialist activists, Siregar embodied the 1960s theory of celebrated American political science professor Samuel Huntington that there was a need for a 'politics of order'. Much like Huntington, Siregar and his mentors had been frustrated with the Indonesian communists' ability to mobilize people against the ills of colonialism and market-driven modernization, while liberals and socialists had lost out in elections and were unable to build the liberal democracy, rule of law and modern development they cherished. Theoretically, as social democrats, they were supposed to be the stalwarts of democracy, but in reality they remained weak. So their convenient conclusion was that democracy was premature. Initially there must instead be a 'politics of order' to withstand a communist-led popular upsurge by way of a solid state and rule of law. This in turn would pave the way for industrial development and democracy. In Singapore from 1959, liberals and socialists could enforce this on their own, but where they were less strong, assistance was necessary from the military and the United States. This was exactly what happened in Indonesia in 1965-6. Later on, the same tactics were labelled 'middle class coups' and spread around in the Global South, instigating more than two decades of authoritarianism. The CIA-backed plan to overthrow Salvador Allende in Chile in 1973 was even named 'Operation Jakarta'.

One problem with Huntington's theory was that there were still no signs of democracy even in Singapore, in spite of its solid state and rule of law. Another was that when the Indonesian military grabbed full powers in 1966, they did not allow the middle-class professionals to govern, only assist. So inspired by the more radical student revolt in Thailand in the early 1970s, Siregar and his mentors ran out of patience and instigated an uprising in January 1974. In other words, Siregar and his tutors were now questioning their own expectation that they, the enlightened middle-class professionals, would govern – not the rude generals and the multinationals. At times they even regretted having supported Suharto in the first place.

As for democratization, however, the dissidents held on to the thesis that it was premature as a route to change until there was sound capitalist development along with a solid state and the rule of law. While gossiping about their plans and tactics, Siregar asserted: the masses are unreliable and scattered (…) and yes, we remain weak in mobilizing genuine popular support. We are urban intellectuals with networks among businessmen, professionals and officers. Our chance to generate a critical mass that can support us is by sponsoring student movements. That is the only way to change the regime, gain some room of manoeuvre and, later on, when possible, build democracy.

Socialist students and alternative development
(late 1970s–late 1980s)

Another reason for the weakness of the democracy movement was that a new wave of critics changed their footing from supporting capitalist modernization to the opposite dependency theory. According to the latter, poverty was not because of too little capitalist development but too much, in collusion with multinational companies which called for repression to sustain the exploitation. So in spite of altering their theory of development, the dissidents still regarded democracy as impossible, until the suppressive dependent capitalism had been overcome by socialist-oriented development. And according to the critics, socialist-oriented development was not impossible because the Indonesian regime – portrayed in for example Rex Mortimer's anthology *The Showcase State* – was as dependent on foreign powers and companies as most other countries in the Global South, including the Philippines, and was thus unstable.

Ironically, the most important Indonesian scholar now putting forward this perspective was former student leader Arief Budiman. Budiman had first supported Suharto, then failed to reform the 'new order' and escaped subjugation thanks to a fellowship at Harvard in the United States where he wrote a PhD thesis about Salvador Allende's attempts at socialist development in Chile which had been snuffed out by the same type of Huntingtonian middle-class coup as that which brought Suharto to power.

Several months into 1984, the rain remained torrential in the beautiful hillside town of Salatiga, Central Java and the roof was leaking in Budiman's modest house on the grounds of the Christian Satya Wacana University. The television was all right, however, and an important sporting tournament was in progress. So without the polite Javanese manners both of us were suspicious of, Arief greeted me by shouting happily from inside that, while it was good to finally meet, discussions must wait until the match was over. Meanwhile I should squeeze in and watch carefully, because, he smiled: badminton is what Indonesia is good at in spite of Suharto.

As Budiman often remarked, his Chinese ethnicity disqualified him as an organizer. But he enjoyed some fame since the 1970s, a fairly independent position at the private university when returning from the United States, and support from the old dissidents in Jakarta (who had made their way as successful lawyers, editors and the like). Thus, he turned into an authority among the intellectuals who shaped the subsequent rise of the democracy movement. He had two priorities – firstly, to foster a new generation of rethinking critical students, and secondly to support victims of authoritarian development and promote alternative routes via cause-oriented CSOs.

Budiman, along with progressive colleagues like Ariel Heryanto, offered educational programmes in collaboration with foreign scholars. Study groups mushroomed in the major universities in Jakarta, Bandung and Jogjakarta, but also in distant ones like Salatiga. The literature was increasingly radical, including Marxist classics, the new critique of 'dependent development' and insights from kindred struggles in the Philippines, South Korea and elsewhere. Many student activists found their way to the groups, despite surveillance and crackdowns.

Meanwhile Indonesia's history was also reclaimed on a more popular level by the highly controversial release in the early 1980s of renowned author Pramoedya Ananta Toer's novel quartet about the rise of early modern nationalism. The books were drafted during his fourteen years on the Maluku prison island of Buru. Toer's team, with Joesoef Isak in the forefront, and liberal-socialists like Goenawan Mohamad and Budiman, who had criticized Pram's succouring of 'politically correct culture' under

Sukarno, reconciled over the importance of democratic citizenship, and international colleagues were supportive.

Many activists in the radical study groups were critical of Hariman Siregar's and others' previous organizing in the campuses. The new generation wanted to reach out to 'the people'. Their mentors too were becoming aware of the need to promote alternatives on the grassroots level. Hence, they established CSOs to criticize authoritarian development and support its victims. Human rights lawyers, for example, introduced 'structural legal aid' to address the roots of the problems.

This was, however, easier said than done. Fauzi Abdullah, for one, who pioneered the support for labour when Indonesia embraced low-wage-based export industries, stressed the importance of informal leaders and wider communities, outside the factory gates, to counter regime controlled-unions and efforts to split and repress the workers. Similarly, Kartjono, leftist nationalist head of the major rural development CSO *Bina Desa*, always reminded radical students of the regime's tight control in the villages. Alternative organizing was strictly prohibited. To begin with it was necessary, therefore, he argued, to strengthen vulnerable people through self-help, health care and the like, and not to just support the landless as it would be branded 'communist'.

Still the critics' focus on the victims of authoritarian development made little headway. The plundering of natural resources and grabbing of land for commercial purposes did not generate forceful resistance, beyond Aceh and Papua (and occupied East Timor). Suharto and his generals, bureaucrats, technocrats and business partners did not just extract resources and rents, they were also capable of effective governance and investments in productive ventures. Contrary to the general statements of dependency theory that the Indonesia was governed by a puppet regime, it really did not seem to be on the brink. So what would be a more accurate analysis and what should critics do?

Discordant democrats against the state (late 1980s–late 1990s)

Around the mid-1980s, analyses were refined and international conditions changed. Democratization became the main priority.

More attention was given to the role of state and politics. As oil prices fell in the late 1970s, the state facilitated export-driven industrialization and enforced a drastic 50 per cent devaluation of the rupiah. Merely by driving around in the new industrial areas outside Jakarta, I could literally see workers – who had very rarely, if ever, been on strike before – come together to demand compensation.

Similarly, the most common answer about rural conflicts during the first part of the 1980s was that they were less about landlords gaining access to the surplus produced by tenants or workers than against state-facilitated dispossession of the land and fishing waters of small producers. This primitive accumulation of capital was usually to pave the way for plantations, logging, mining, dams, industrial estates, roads and housing, or golf courses and car parks.

Nobody suggested that an East Asian kind of developmental state apparatus was under way in Indonesia. Framed by Suharto's patrimonial rule, Indonesian public assets, resources and state capacity to implement policies were instead captured from within by officers and politicians, and from outside by private actors. Hence, accumulation of capital was largely about access to public assets, resources, concessions, licences and the capacity to discipline labour to facilitate business investments. In the final instance, this was by agreements with the regional commanders of the territorially organized army and appointed village leaders.

Meanwhile scholarship on the Global South added more focus on control of resources and class relations to its previous preoccupation with international dependency. The timely catchphrase was 'bringing the state back in'. With regard to Indonesia, Richard Robison, for one, stressed the importance of state and politics in the rise of a domestic capitalist class and oligarchic rule. Others, like Harold Crouch, employed a more Weberian approach to emphasize the patrimonial character of the regime.

Still, these and other scholars agreed that democracy remained unrealistic, given the poor rule of law and governance, and businessmen's and professionals' dependence on the state. This was a convincing argument – to the extent that democratization had really rested historically with rising capitalists and middle classes only. But often it had not. Resistance and demands by the labouring classes were just as crucial, especially in countries, such as Sweden, where industrialization gained pace in conjunction with the first wave of democracy. Something similar happened in the Global South during the second wave of democracy, when popular movements for democratic citizenship were part of the anti-colonial struggle. And now, by the late twentieth century, even though the colonial rulers were no more, political and military coercion plus monopolization of public assets and resources remained seminal in countries like Indonesia.

From this alternative historical perspective, my own conclusion was therefore different to the scholars stressing the importance of capitalists and middle classes only. The struggle for democracy, in terms of equal civil and political rights and impartial governance of public assets and resources, might actually become pivotal. There were clear signs of this, as the counter-movements were mainly against political monopolization of the economy, repression, dispossession of people's means of production and new industrialization based on cheap and subdued labour.

Towards the late 1980s, moreover, the opportunities for pro-democrats improved. This was partly due to conflicts within the regime over Suharto's apparent reduction of the influence of the military, to the advantage of his siblings, loyal oligarchs and his devoted Muslim research and technology minister. His name was B. J. Habibie and he advocated Malaysian-like nationalist economic development. In making trouble for Suharto, the military and other dissidents opened up a space for radical critics too. Moreover, the international situation changed. In the late 1970s, the United States lost out in Indochina. In 1986, the Philippine 'people power' demonstration for democracy did away with President Marcos. The following year, the democracy movement in South Korea was victorious. In 1989, the Wall fell in Berlin and the Cold War came to an end. Human rights, democratization and support for civil society became major themes in Western foreign policy. Hence, there was more access to funding for Indonesian critics – if, that is, they adjusted to donors' priorities. In 1990, Suharto retreated, confirming there would be more space for open discussion, *keterbukaan*.

These developments gave rise to the genuine democracy movement. But who were the activists? Did they complement each other, thus generating a roaring river, or were there divisive tendencies? There were five clusters: popular instigators, local organizers, autonomists, cause-oriented and interest groups, and political players.

Popular instigators

The radical students' secretariat in Jogjakarta, Indonesia's Oxbridge and only remaining sultanate, was in a narrow alley, *Gang Rode*, slightly east of the palace. The building was low – and the heat inside stagnant – but the discussions lively. The activists reminded me of the 1968 revolt back home, when one tried for the looks of John Lennon and the women he charmed. The radicals were part of the Jogjakarta section of the study groups that Arief Budiman and others had supported since the early 1980s. A few years later, the participants were already well read in the concerned social science literature (and quite to my surprise even eager to discuss the pros and cons of my own writings, parts of which had apparently been translated). They were also informed of the debates among activists in the Philippines and reflective of their own experiences. Subsequently they decided to spread their message outside the campuses, among small farmers and the rural poor in particular.

The study groups in Jakarta were more preoccupied with workers and the urban poor. But according to Daniel Indrakusuma, senior leader in the radical CSOs *Skephi* and *Infight*, the focus outside the big cities and industrial areas was indeed on land conflicts. This was perfectly illustrated by a poster on the wall which caused much anger within the establishment at the time – a most amusing satirical cartoon calendar, featuring the luxury lives of Suharto with a massive belly and his wife in an outgrown bikini, while military and business partners helped them supress and dispossess the people of their means of livelihood.

The major case in point was the conflict in the late 1980s and early 1990s between the state and small farmers over the construction of the huge World Bank-sponsored dam in Kedung Ombo, Central Java, on the northeastern side of the triangle between Jogjakarta, Solo and Semarang, once a leftist stronghold. When metropolitan legal aid institutions retreated, students from Jogjakarta wanted to contribute to the spectacular demonstrations against Suharto. To some surprise, there was no massive repression, possibly because of the international attention and the conflicts within the regime, which made minor concessions.

The instigators' intention was to invigorate the rural victims, generate wider space for further struggle and challenge the regime in Jakarta. But the spark did not cause a fire, either in this case or in any of the similar ones around the country. In short, the instigators 'ran offside' by not considering the challenges of the locals or of embedded organizers. These remarkably committed activists had facilitated the locals' efforts for years. And they remained supportive in 1991 when I visited numerous desolate villages where some people stayed on as the water rose.

Subsequently many popular instigators tried to organize better, root themselves locally and facilitate education, including among the rural poor and industrial labour. For one thing, a People's Democratic Association was formed in 1994 and a party, PRD, in 1996. This was to guide activists' organizations among students, farmers, workers and others. Although the cadres split almost immediately, they began numerous actions that pointed to growing resistance around the country.

Local organizers

Students from Salatiga, supported by Budiman and his colleagues, and especially local organizers, were thus sceptical. Their explanation for why ordinary people did not rise up – even in an old leftist stronghold like Kedung Ombo and when instigators proved that the military would not crack down on their demonstrations – was weak bargaining power. Said student activist Stanley Adi Prasetyo, later on a pioneering investigative journalist: What could people do when the Jogja students had left?

Former leftists from the 1960s were even more worried. The highest-ranking surviving PKI leader from the 1960s, Sabandi Rewang Parto, who also tried a Maoist uprising in 1968, concurred with like-minded elderly activists around Solo and Semarang: people are so afraid, also the old leftists. Before they can engage, their capacity must be increased and the risks of being repressed must be reduced.

One of the local organizers was Johny Simanjuntak, a barefoot lawyer. While only five feet high in the office, he was tall in the field. Said Johny: the human rights lawyers focused on their propertied clients and only talked of structural legal aid, but when I practised it, they were nowhere to be found. The students studied Marx and some visited Philippine militants, but when I did that too, and added liberation theology and refused to hit-and-run like a petty guerrilla, they were already in their buses back to Jogja. The locals must survive. One must assist them to gain strength by studying and organizing. In addition, I can help by facilitating negotiations with strongmen and authorities.

Simanjuntak was one of the many radical local organizers – often reformist Muslim, Hindu, Christian or Catholic – who gained ground around the country. They promoted self-help such as cooperatives and education, as well as interest-organization, also among labourers and the urban poor. Their major challenge, however, was to unite the specific local efforts and connect them to broader concerns and organization, which they did not trust. We shall return to their attempts to overcome this.

Autonomists

The accumulation of capital by dispossessing people of their land and waters was particularly serious in the less densely populated 'outer islands', beyond Java and Bali. Radicals often agreed with Budiman's colleague in Salatiga, George Aditjondro: this oppression of people is because Indonesia is nothing but a colonial mistake (…) our founding fathers wanted to liberate the colonial territories, but in reality many of the territories were just conquered (…) and it got worse with Suharto. Liberation is a remaining task here, and it should be based on autonomous local battles, generating a federation.

The major Indonesian Forum for the Environment, *Walhi*, kept a rather low profile in these matters, but others joined in. In the late 1990s, the radicals built an Alliance of Indigenous Peoples of the Archipelago (AMAN) claiming that traditional leaders should uphold customary rights. Meanwhile freedom fighters in Aceh and Papua claimed similar rights to full independence as the former Portuguese East Timor.

Thus the autonomists' insistence that the struggle for liberation from colonialism must be fulfilled, and that customary rule must be restored among indigenous populations, often meant that issues of democracy and the abuse of human rights fell by the wayside. So democracy actors in Indonesia became worried that their work would be discredited by contacts with the autonomists and vice versa.

Cause-oriented and interest groups

The democracy movement is often indelibly associated with the networking issue organizations, which expanded through the CSOs that were established after the crackdown on dissidents in the mid-1970s. The prime mechanism was the legal aid institutions (LBHs and their national association YLBHI), propelled by senior lawyer Buyung Nasution and his friends. The idea of structural legal aid introduced in the 1980s meant not only representing clients in court but also supporting people's efforts at achieving human rights. By the early 1990s, this approach was radicalized in response to the student activism outside campus and by labourers and fledgling unions.

Consequently, there were conflicts between the radical supporters of the structural approach and more conventional litigators. The disagreements were toned down, briefly, when Nasution returned in 1993 from self-imposed exile in Europe, encouraged by the growing international support for human rights, civil society and democracy. Nasution proclaimed himself the 'locomotive of democracy' and toured the universities, along with the national director of the legal aid institutes and prime networker, Mulyana Kusumah. But when I asked, in an internal Jakarta LBH discussion about its new programme to support civil society, what actors would be nurtured, there was uneasiness, much contemplative smoking of *kretek* cigarettes, and no clear answer. Nasution cut through by saying it was a fair critique and that LBH would assist if Arief Budiman and I initiated a project to explore the issue of who would be the 'actors of democracy'. But while we did, LBH did not. Rather, the divisions in LBH intensified and Nasution felt that the radicals were taking over, so he put the breaks on, supported by the conservative board of trustees. And since internal democracy did not work, some of the dissidents formed their own legal aid and human rights organizations. We shall return to the dynamics and implications.

Meanwhile, democratization was never a major issue for the development-oriented CSOs. As Asmara Nababan, the then director of the International 'NGO Forum' INFID, pointed out: our focus is only to frame and agree on alternative development.

Many other issue organizations and networking groups mushroomed, including among women for gender equality. The religious reformists gained ground too, reinterpreting basic Muslim texts, but also Hindu, Christian and Catholic. This allowed for an appreciation of equality, tolerance, human rights and democracy.

From the mid-1990s, however, the major new centre of gravity in the democracy movement was media-oriented students and journalists. They were furious over the regime's banning in June 1994 of leading investigative journals *Tempo, Detik* and

Editor, after their having exposed mismanagement and possible corruption of one of Suharto's most trusted ministers and confidantes, B. J. Habibie. The crackdown terminated the period of relative openness, *keterbukaan*. As the most senior editor Goenawan Mohamad put it: Many of us had not been particularly radical. We thought the main task was to defend freedom of speech and the media. Now we realized that this takes democracy too.

Hence, the journalists continued to report, giving pride of place to the issue of democracy. They focused on militarism, mismanagement and anti-corruption in particular, thus reaching out to the aspiring middle classes. They fostered alternative media, culture and communication, including a radio station and an underground email news network (co-managed by my assistant). Outposts were set up around the country, printing out and forwarding electronic bulletins by conventional means. They educated grassroots reporters, started a genuine journalists' union, built an institute to promote their ideas and found places to meet.

Simultaneously there was a clampdown on concerned academic scholarship too, most conspicuously at the Satya Wacana University in Salatiga. Arief Budiman and his close colleagues were sacked and had to search for jobs outside the country or form independent 'NGO institutes'.

There were also signs of labour unrest, though organization was difficult. Unions were curtailed and informal leaders tried alternatives. Leading activist Dita Sari suggested a political breakthrough was needed in order to galvanize union activity, and legendary human rights activist Poncke Princen agreed to help. Princen was less easy to suppress, given his background as a Dutch anti-Nazi who had defected to the Indonesian freedom fighters in the war of liberation. So from his impatiently manoeuvred wheelchair, Poncke declared in 1990 an Indonesian equivalent of the Polish Solidarność, *Setiakawan*. As in the case of the land struggle in Kedung Ombo, however, the spark did not light a fire.

Two years later, 1992, labour lawyer Muchtar Pakpahan set up the first independent actual union, the Indonesian Prosperity Labour Union (SBSI). In 1994, local organizers in Medan, Sumatra, originally supported by Catholic and Batak Lutheran congregations, organized strikes among tens of thousands of workers. In Greater Jakarta, moreover, Teten Masduki with the LBH and others promoted a coordination forum, *Forsol* (Solidarity Forum), between labour leaders and supportive CSOs. So there was potential.

However, the cause-oriented groups did not always focus on issues and interests that grew out of popular struggles. Rather, they were often determined from above, in seminar rooms and in discussions with donors. To make matters worse, the centrally based CSOs competed for donor support and at best shared the funds with client CSOs outside Jakarta. In the case of the Kedung Ombo dam, for example, LBH prioritized litigation for clients losing land, while the local organizers' long-standing efforts to strengthen communities, including those without land, were ignored. Similarly, media-related campaigners such as in the student-driven information centre and action network *Pijar* felt they had to instigate dramatic developments to ensure mainstream media coverage, thus turning into 'action maniacs'. But as its leader Bonar Tigor 'Coki' Naipospos put it: the risk is that the issues become too diverse to generate broad and sustainable movements.

Political players

Senior dissident players in need of newsworthy actions for their manoeuvres were behind many of the progressive CSOs and popular instigators, who in turn depended on the dissident players' patronage, prestige and good contacts, inside as well as outside Indonesia. The links between them deepened when the period of relative openness (*keterbukaan*) came to an end in 1994 and the chances shrank for an orderly succession from Suharto, in which the players could participate.

The Petition 50 group from 1980 – consisting of widely respected retired officers, political executives and related intellectuals – represented an early cluster of political players with some interest in the pro-democracy communities. The petitioners met weekly in former Admiral and Jakarta Governor Ali Sadikin's grand residence to discuss and draft recommendations to the regime. Sadikin, who was also on LBH's board of trustees, told me in late 1994 that he was worried by the debates in LBH as he mainly wanted to improve the 'new order'. He was also concerned by the fact that some of his followers had been attracted by the devoted Muslim intellectuals organization ICMI (to which we shall return), which was supported by Suharto's right-hand man B. J. Habibie. Summing up the basics, the secretary of the group Chris Siner Key Timu, a catholic intellectual, put it succinctly: Suharto sits on the roof and would like to step down but there is no staircase, so a proper one has to be provided.

Meanwhile the Democracy Forum set up in 1991 by senior leaders and intellectual activists became more important. Most members were rooted in the student movement of the 1970s. Abdurrahman Wahid, nicknamed 'Gus Dur', later Indonesian president from 1999 to 2001, was an exceptional member by virtue of being both a radical liberal intellectual and the leader (by inheritance) of the world largest socio-religious organization *Nahdlatul Ulama* (NU). In a lengthy discussion in late 1994 on a delayed plane for Semarang, he said that co-member Arief Budiman was impatient and that while I was heading for discussions with Arief in his new fine house, he himself must visit some of the less radical, but more important, *pesantrens* (boarding schools): for them reforms must be incremental so that they can live with them. If they cannot, the country will be in danger.

Radical younger activists were also invited to join the Democracy Forum. But when asked about their role, Marsillam Simanjuntak, the forum's coordinator (and later on President Wahid's closest adviser, Minister of Justice and Attorney General), asserted: one has to topple the regime first to gain sufficient freedom. To be honest, social movements and CSOs can only be supportive and help delegitimize the rulers.

In short, the political players related to movements and CSOs primarily to gain support for their own priorities and were not accountable to people on the ground. In 1994, for example, self-proclaimed 'locomotive of democracy', Buyung Nasution, did not support protests against the banning of *Tempo*, *Detik* and *Editor*, preferring instead to sustain his relations with B. J. Habibie, whose dubious affairs had been exposed by the magazines.

Actually, one of the reasons for establishing the liberal, socialist and inclusive Democracy Forum was that Habibie's ICMI had been formed. ICMI fostered everything from a major think tank (CIDES), directed by former alternative 'development-NGO' leader Adi Sasono, to cooperatives among Muslim communities. Sasono told me he was inspired not just by Malaysian Prime Minister Mahathir bin Mohamad's successful nationalist development strategy favouring 'native business' against the Chinese, but also by Finance Minister Anwar Ibrahim's efforts to make it more democratic. (This was, of course, some time before Mahathir disposed of Ibrahim.) Moreover, ICMI was close to Amien Rais, the leader of the second largest Muslim organization, the theologically modernist *Muhammadiyah*, with numerous affiliated organizations, schools, universities and hospitals. A rival of 'Gus Dur's NU.

Meanwhile, reformists within Suharto's *Golkar* party, such as Marzuki Darusman, of the government's new National Human Rights Commission, and Gus Dur's ally Matori Abdul Jalil, of the only permitted Muslim party, the PPP, convinced me they combined contacts with pro-democrats, the mainstream parties and the military officers. Such pluralism, they said, was necessary in order to work towards a new regime 'that all can live with'.

Most importantly, additional reformists in the small Indonesian Democratic Party (PDI), in which former followers of President Sukarno and Christians and Catholics were supposed to cooperate, linked up with respected intellectuals like the economist Kwik Kian Gie and sympathetic generals. Solid proposals for alternative economic policies were rare among the critics, but Kian Gie was among the first to warn against the outrageous corruption and speculation bubble that burst in 1997, making the Asian economic crisis particularly serious in Indonesia.

Moreover, a number of generals close to PDI were instrumental in getting former President Sukarno's daughter Megawati Sukarnoputri elected new leader in a special party congress in 1993. This heralded broader popular following and links with radicals in civil society. Everybody realized the reformists were inspired by Corazon Aquino's rise to power in the Philippines. Suharto's blunt attempts to get Megawati ousted only increased her popularity. In 1996, soaring numbers of sympathizers inside and outside the party, including leftist activists in their newly formed PRD party, rallied in the streets and public forums. There were joyous scenes and my taxi driver did not mind being held up in a traffic jam next to the party office in Jl. Diponogoro, rather handing out some rupiah to the activists who were distributing leaflets.

A few days later, however, on 27 July, when I had left for interviews in Jogjakarta, concerned journalists telephoned from a rooftop in Cikini, Jakarta, to alert about an early morning crackdown by hired thugs and the subsequent street battles. Many scholars deemed the crackdown to be 'business as usual', arguing Suharto was safe in the saddle. They were wrong. Even Adi Sasono admitted in an intense conversation: this is a serious setback – reform-oriented actors like myself in ICMI have tried hard to suggest ways ahead (…) but 'the old man' has now displayed total inability to discuss orderly succession (…) so what shall we do?

Shared burdens: Blurred concept, propagating through division, attractive shortcuts

Meanwhile, most currents in the fledgling democracy movement shared three additional burdens, the first of which was the lack of a common vision, programme and strategy.

As leading lawyer and human rights campaigner, Todung Mulya Lubis, put it in late 1994: the crucial task of linking CSOs and activists will not be solved by themselves but, at best, via joint actions on overarching vital issues. However, there is a lack of them. The banning of media and scholars looked like one, but only for a while. It was not big enough. So we jump from issue to issue, without a concept to combine them.

Particularly serious was that, while there were lots of critiques of oppression and 'corruption, collusion and nepotism', there was no forceful alternative policy to rally behind with regard to the most fundamental issue of all – the exploitative, rent-seeking and speculation-driven economy, which collapsed in 1998.

By the mid-1990s two particularly promising attempts existed – *Forsol*, the solidarity forum between labour leaders and supportive CSOs, and *KIPP*, an electoral watch organization with the potential of unifying pro-democrats in face of the possibly fraudulent elections in 1997. But neither of their main leaders, Teten Masduki and Mulyana Kusumah respectively, both of the LBH, deemed the issues of the labourers and stolen elections to be related. So there was no coordination.

Another suggestion was to unite behind a leader, possibly human rights lawyer Buyung Nasution, labour lawyer Muchtar Pakpahan, or author and publisher Goenawan Mohamad. But everyone quarrelled about their individual pros and cons, including in private matters, instead of directing and keeping them accountable.

The second challenge was the tendency to propagate through division. Among the core pro-democracy groups, I cannot recall any that primarily tried to organize as many followers as possible in democratic movements. The opposite tendency was more common, as illustrated by legendary Human Rights activist Poncke Princen. When I asked him in 1994 about the fate of the independent union *Setiakawan*, he replied: yes, it is defunct now (…) but it can be reactivated (…) I am afraid of organization (…) many people, many problems (…) I can do my job with just a few people.

In other words, the popular instigators, cause-oriented groups and political players in particular typically discussed and quarrelled about the best theories, analyses, projects, connections and funding. As such, it was more difficult to strive for joint frameworks and keep the flock together than to form a new group with a few followers and new donor support. When instigators set up 'mass organizations', they mainly thought of wider groups of like-minded people guided by cadres, and the main point was to encourage action. Unions were, of course, in the business of attracting members, but they mainly relied on workplace bargaining power to block production in individual factories, not labour market bargaining power involving unifying as many workers as possible in different sectors and communities.

Finally, there was the common temptation of attractive shortcuts. When I asked why it did not make more sense for activists to try to achieve their aims by developing membership organizations, liberation-oriented autonomists answered that, of course, they had to give priority to force and security, while those favouring customary rights relied on inherited leadership. Other activists smiled and said they understood they should be more democratically oriented in their own work, but that it would take too long.

There was also another aspect to the preference for shortcuts. Buyung Nasution, for one, argued that the governance of LBH had to be guarded by a board of trustees: we must not take the risk of being hijacked by members, left or right.

When I asked if this could be avoided by strict rules and representation, the answer was: there is no trust in representation, and our critics only want direct democracy.

In short, the pro-democrats rarely developed democratic means of representation in groups and movements. They were certainly not unique. The parties and socio-religious movements acknowledged by the regime were thoroughly dominated by the elite. Even the election of Megawati, for example, had to be backed up by generals.

Lost in transition (late 1990s–early 2000s)

By cracking down on the pro-democrats on 27 July 1996, Suharto displayed his inability to accommodate even moderate dissidents and plan for succession. Yet, while protests continued around the country, the attempts at coordinating the more principled democracy movement were in a shambles. All aspects of its divisive dynamics blossomed.

The 27 July affair testified also to the incapacity of the democracy actors to congregate and build a viable alternative. Many of the reformist players who competed for influence with Megawati, and were afraid radicals would gain influence, had not backed her attempt to fend off the regime's intervention in the PDI. Megawati's own loyal party team had also not been the best coordinators, shunning sympathizers from outside, leftists and others. After the crackdown, the new-born movement was in a mess, and there was a witch-hunt for radical activists, branded as practically communists. Several of the other actors focused on saving their own skins, distancing themselves from the radicals, indicating they had no-one to blame but themselves. My short assistant stood tall, distributing underground bulletins at night, guiding me after lunch. But the situation was tense. A sympathetic PGI-guesthouse receptionist informed me he had prevented somebody from searching my room. Did I want to move to the second floor?

Meanwhile 'Gus Dur' undermined the Democracy Forum by waiting for the regime to split and temporarily cooperating with Suharto's eldest daughter, in order to counter ICMI, a rival of his own organization NU. The efforts of Mulyana Kusumah at LBH to connect Buyung Nasution – 'the locomotive of democracy' – with activists around the country had already come to naught. Nasution had altered his priorities, not joining the efforts to unite the movement against the banning of critical journalists and scholars.

The attempt to instead rally behind Megawati by building a radical electoral watch movement, *KIPP*, led by Kusumah and backed up by Goenawan Mohamad, stumbled too. One source of inspiration was, of course, the Philippine experiences. *KIPP* might unify the opposition against Suharto's expected cheating in the forthcoming 1997 elections. But the idea suffered from the 27 July crackdown and the moderates' resistance at LBH. In addition, *KIPP* was badly managed and poorly connected to other movements. Finally Megawati and her team retreated by eschewing efforts at creating a broad alliance between Megawati and reform-oriented Muslims in the

PPP ('Mega-Bintang') in the approaching elections. The idea was modelled on a quite effective campaign in the central Java town of Solo to weaken *Golkar's* and the Suharto government's attempts to dominate the area. Maverick Muslim politician, Mudrick Sangidoe, persuaded many people to paint over the *Golkar* party's yellow colour on public facilities with neutral white. Yet, Megawati herself even passively boycotted the elections. By implication, the radical pro-democrats lost their chance to learn and engage in electoral politics.

Endgame

As the Asian economic crisis unfolded in 1997, the media's exposure of corruption, collusion and nepotism intensified. The number of plain-clothed cops pretending to fish in the dirty river next to the office of the Alternative Journalist Association (AJI) proliferated. There was also intensive critique of the military repression against radical dissidents. But there was no general campaign for alternative economic policies and welfare programmes, and supportive groups and union leaders lost touch with the legions of workers who were laid off, more than a million within modern manufacturing alone. (About 32 million people, or 34 per cent of the labour force, were out of work in 1998.)

In other words, Indonesia was desperately short of the kind of liberal politicians, socialist-oriented activists and dissident religious leaders who all came together against Marcos in the Philippines. Moderate officers (such as future President Susilo Bambang Yudhoyono) and the *Golkar* party leaders (including Marzuki Darusman of the new National Human Rights Commission) lost steam. The modernist Muslim intellectuals in ICMI at least had a plan, inspired by the nationalist economic policies in Malaysia and the reformist (later to be sacked) Deputy Prime Minister Anwar Ibrahim. But in early 1998, Suharto sidelined, temporarily, the ICMI in favour of his oligarchs and generals. Possibly this made Amien Rais, ICMI member and leader of the second largest socio-religious organization *Muhammadiyah*, speak up. For a brief period, he looked like a potential leader for the opposition, but the contending players naturally hesitated. So, from late March, all of them instead sponsored various proxy agents among the increasingly angry students who in turn thought they could make use of the political players. Historically, students in Indonesia have had a special licence to protest, at least within the campuses.

In early May, as the economic crisis worsened, Suharto's team introduced even harsher austerity measures than IMF (and Washington and Canberra) had asked for. Meanwhile the students, backing various democracy-oriented political players, from Muslim leaders to popular instigators, filed out of the campuses to rally in the street, first in Medan, then in Jakarta, Solo and other cities. Many urban poor followed suit. To enable military suppression, rough elements instigated riots and a witch-hunt of Chinese. Fortunately, however, the students' occupation of the parliament and senior civilians' condemnation of the violence made the Commander of the Armed Forces, General Wiranto, abstain from another Tiananmen Square. And nobody of any standing wanted to be included in a new cabinet. Consequently, Suharto resigned.

Moderates consolidate old bases

After 21 May 1998, Vice President B. J. Habibie, the chief patron of ICMI, was thus in charge. The moderates' ideas in ICMI, *Golkar* and the armed forces of how to reform the 'new order' were set in motion, adding a timely new touch of democracy. In essence, this meant economic and political liberalization, lots of decentralization, negotiated peace in East Timor and quick elections. This was also to please the other key leaders – Amien Rais, Megawati and 'Gus Dur' – as well as to facilitate discussions with East Timor's imprisoned leader Xanana Gusmão. In a private conversation with Gusmão, when later in house arrest 'only', he appreciated the critique against too much emphasis on armed struggle and acknowledged that the liberation movement's belated cooperation with the Indonesian democrats was a crucial step towards independence for East Timor.

Habibie and his team were also in need of international endorsement and assistance. In August 1998, leading scholars and experts were brought together in Jakarta by the Institute of Sciences and the Ford Foundation to discuss how democracy might be crafted. A few troublemakers like Professor Daniel Lev and myself were also invited, but we hardly needed to express our reservations as the parachuted missionaries' message was simple enough. When local sceptics were worried about the applicability of the liberal elitist model on offer, with its roots in Spain and Latin America, comparativists like Professor Alfred Stepan cut through: 'We just give you the framework, you fill it in.' This was precisely what happened during the following months – the model was 'filled in'.

... while radicals are short of new

The numerous students who had radicalized wanted instead to kindle comprehensive democratic transformation. But they were confronted with three great obstacles, of which they were only able to surmount the first. This took the form of a campaign that portrayed them as immature muddleheads who mainly caused traffic problems with all their demonstrations, and who wanted a complete breakdown of Suharto's 'new order' but had no programme for what to put in its place. There was, to be sure, something to this. In Jakarta, at the time, I was often reminded of the student movement of thirty years previous in Europe. This too was not just pronouncedly political; it was cultural and anti-authoritarian as well. Yet that was nothing to despise; indeed, it was probably the latter element which had the greatest significance in Europe over the long run. In addition, there was among the new Indonesian students a still greater and more hopeful and dynamic power, which issued from the fact that they were not just breaking with authoritarian structures. They were also rediscovering history – which was forbidden – and opening up their society – which was closed. The students were the weeds that broke suddenly through the asphalt and burst into full bloom: beautiful but disordered. And most of them were, most assuredly, neither naive nor muddleheaded. Great numbers of them did read, discuss, analyse and come to democratic decisions.

Never, dare I say, have I encountered students with such questioning minds and such a thirst for knowledge as those who, in late August 1998, rescued me from the dinner party after the conference on how the elite should design democracy, by taking me off in an old borrowed taxi to meet with a larger group of young leaders from various campuses. They insisted on a marathon lecture on the political situation and the historical background and the hour grew late. Yet it seemed to me that the gathering burnt like a beacon in the Jakarta night. In the long run, the students should have history on their side. When the dawn broke, however, it was still over the same old Jakarta, and that made things harder.

The second problem faced by the students was the fact that virtually all the established forces tried to tame and use them. Habibie, General Wiranto and their cohorts in the regime were doing their best to keep control and to acquire new legitimacy by directing the reform process from above, and by marginalizing radicals like the students. In addition, leaders like 'Gus Dur', Megawati and Amien Rais took advantage of the fact that the students were putting pressure on the regime. This enabled those leaders to compromise with the weakened establishment, and to carry out cautious changes at a snail's pace. The moderates were also trying to tame the students so as to be able to contest the upcoming elections with a minimum of disturbance.

The radical sections of the students were at a loss as to how to deal with this. In November 1998 (in conjunction with the country's extra-ordinary People's Consultative Assembly) they failed to persuade the moderate leaders to unite and to go ahead on the basis of popular mobilization. The moderates agreed instead to swift elections with reinvented parties. These 'new' parties included Megawati's Indonesian Democratic Party of Struggle, PDI-P; Gus Dur's National Awakening Party, PKB; Amien Rais' National Mandate Party, PAN; along with supposedly reformed *Golkar* and the PPP. Most Muslim students obeyed, while the more radical groups tried to protest. But the radicals were beaten up and shot in the streets, by the military, police and an extremist *Pram Swakarsa* militia, sponsored by rough officers and Muslim leaders.

The crackdown was also an early signal of the diminished importance of the Muslim, Christian and Catholic reformists in matters of human rights, tolerance and democracy. Not so long after, for example, violent conflicts flared up in Poso (Central Sulawesi) and the Moluccas. And the radical politics of decentralization became a crucial linchpin for conservative local regulations, constraining gender equality and the rights of the LGBT community in particular.

These dynamics paved the way for quick elections in June 1999. By implication, only *Golkar*, and those leaders and parties related to the socio-religious organizations that had coexisted with Suharto, stood a fair chance. Hence, the students and their radical patrons were faced with a third problem of formulating a political programme of their own and building an independent political base. This was the hardest challenge of all. The students had functioned as a substitute for the lack of broad organizations among the middle and lower classes. But these democratic spearheads had no politics and policies of their own.

When revisiting radical student leaders and popular instigators in Jakarta in December 1999, they still insisted radical movements were gaining ground around the country, that they wanted to form popular councils and that they would try their best in the elections. Organization, they said, was taking root in several cities and there were local actions to replace pro-Suharto village leaders. Wondering what this really meant, I asked the view of sympathetic but less optimistic Johny Simanjuntak, whom we know as the local organizer in Kedung Ombo. He said I could join him for a while, in and around radical Solo.

Local impasse

In Solo itself, my meeting with the young activists a few days before the election was a bit tense. I wanted to discuss how they were trying to organize and mobilize voters, but they wanted me to give a talk about the Marxist classics and radical struggles in general. When I asked if that was not irrelevant given the immediate tasks, they said they were mainly propagandizing, not really trying to gain votes.

In the village of Gebyok, in Karanganyar district outside Solo, by contrast, the struggle was down to earth. A few dissidents had asked democracy activists from Solo to help them sue their corrupt *lurah* (village head). The advice was that nothing would change unless they themselves linked up with others and sought the support of the villagers in general. So this they did. A *komite reformasi* was formed to fight the *lurah* who had appropriated money for a fresh water project, over-charged people for land certificates and privatized public land in favour of his cronies. Demonstrations were held at the *lurah*'s and *bupati*'s (the head of the district) offices. The *lurah*'s office was occupied for two weeks, and a majority of the villagers came forward to prevent the military and the police from intervening. When the *lurah* was brought to trial and temporarily discharged, the committee continued its work with regular meetings and public gatherings. The committee initiated a cooperative to support agriculture, added the disclosure of local *Golkar* leaders' use of the public social safety net for their own political purposes and then discussed how to gear up by demanding total reformation of the local administration. The committee members were hardly revolutionaries. The chairman was a dynamic local factory mechanic in his mid-twenties. Other members included a retired schoolteacher who used to hunt communists in the 1960s but also a much younger and well-dressed and educated radical businessman, and a farmer-cum-agricultural labourer. Their party affiliations varied, some supported Megawati's new party PDI-P, others a small NU-based party and one a conservative Muslim party. But they told me: that doesn't matter, it is just traditional affiliations. The important thing is that we have agreed what should be done here.

My fear was that they would be co-opted and divided by the established politicians and administration on the district level. But their response was that they just wanted to hold on to their own programme and relate to similar committees in nearby villages, and if possible on 'higher' levels too. However, when I asked if they knew of any such committees 'up there' they said they did not.

Six months later, little of this had happened. On the 27th of November 1999 instead, just as I returned to Gebjok, the committee failed miserably. But the bitter, new lesson was important to learn. It had started well. *Golkar* lost massively in the June elections and the committee won its legal case against the *lurah*, so an election of a new head of the village would go ahead. But then there was political reconciliation among the elite on various levels. No common enemy was left to fight. Personal ambitions gained ground in the committee, which split. Two candidates were nominated. The PDI-P had won the June general elections but remained politically and organizationally weak.

So the victory on the central level did not help the local committee. *Golkar*, on the other hand, lost the people's sympathies but retained its organization, and remained in informal control of the local administration. Hence, *Golkar* skilfully prevented the strongest of the dissident candidates from running on legal grounds (formally he lived just outside the village). The politically less-experienced committee was unable to work out an equally smart counter-move, stubbornly opting instead for boycott. Even worse, it actually tried to prevent the election on that Saturday morning of 27 November when I returned and was stopped, of course, by the administration and the police, which, thus, appeared as defenders of democracy and the people's right to vote. And this people did, rather massively, in favour of the *Golkar* candidate.

It was possible to literally observe how even the initially best-possible local and popular reformist group turned out to be totally at a loss without ideological and political structure and the chance to scale up its work in cooperation with similar groups outside.

Democratization crucial but polycentric movements unviable

Why did the Indonesian democracy movement get lost in transition? When trying to put my thoughts together after the 1999 elections, it was useful to recall how the anti-Marcos democracy movement in the Philippines had lost steam too. In Indonesia, the previous leftist movements were certainly more thoroughly suppressed than in the Philippines, but in both cases, they had given up on the importance of democracy. Initially, moreover, the Indonesian critics of Suharto's 'new order' focused on corruption and authoritarian 'dependent development', much like the Philippine socialists. The argument was that since repression was necessary to sustain extractive and dependent development, this had to be fought before democratization would be feasible. It was only in the late 1980s – when it became obvious that the Indonesian regime was not just depending on repression, Western aid and multinationals but also, perhaps primarily, on the political facilitation of domestic capital – that many activists began to focus on the role of the state and the importance of fighting for democracy.

However, four major problems were also reminiscent of the Philippines. Firstly, that the democrats could not base themselves on strong, broad popular movements. The prime reason in the Philippines was that these had been suppressed and then dominated by the Maoists, and, in Indonesia, that oppression had been even more severe. Secondly, that uneven economic development had generated such diverse demands that it was difficult to build broad unified movements. Thirdly, that the pro-democrats themselves were ridden by divisive priorities and a dearth of unifying concepts and programmes. Fourthly, that the shortcomings were exacerbated by donors' normative short-term priorities. Consequently, the pro-democrats' innovative but scattered efforts did not generate a roaring river.

In 1996, contacts certainly intensified between pro-democrats in civil society, emerging social movements and progressive political players when the Suharto regime proved unable to reform itself, and the subsequent Asian economic crisis grew particularly serious in Indonesia. The players themselves were rooted in networks of frustrated officers, subordinated parties and socio-religious movements. Now they were eager to gain support from pro-democracy activists too. This was an open window for the activists, but since their divisive dynamics had blossomed and they were ill-prepared for how to handle the economic crisis and build democracy, it was impossible to forge progressive policies together with the reformist players.

Therefore, although the new generation of frustrated students certainly developed their own priorities and tried to remain autonomous in the endgame to oust Suharto, the progressive political players were able to use some of them as proxy agents. Opportunistic officers, oligarchs and political and religious leaders were able to recalibrate their relations, including through radical decentralization – with the support of the 'international community'. The formula was transition to basic liberal-democratic rules and regulations by way of a pact within the elite, while principled democrats were relegated to civil society watchdogs. Would it be possible for the progressives to reinvent themselves and find ways to promote more genuine democratization?

Dilemmas of deepening democracy after Suharto

The light in the Jakarta seminar room was as gloomy as the late 1999 atmosphere. The study initiated five years earlier about actors of democracy was finally being concluded. Its original aim had been to supplement the one-sided focus on civil society by also discussing actors, and there was much to learn from history. But the current logjam was also a good illustration of the divisive dynamics at work in the democracy movement. The post-Suharto movement lacked alternatives to the elitist accords for economic recovery and democratization, which had gained hegemony from 1998 onwards. The military was granted privileged political representation, the oligarchs were accommodated and the local elites – including religious conservatives – benefitted from decentralization of resources and decision-making. Meanwhile politicians could rely on the political parties and socio-religious organizations that had accommodated themselves to Suharto's rule and were thus able to dominate the new electoral system. (In 1999, PDI-P got almost 34 per cent of the votes, *Golkar* about 22.5 per cent, PKB almost 13 per cent, PPP almost 11 per cent and PAN about 7 per cent.) After the elections, moreover – and in spite of her party's victory – Megawati was outmanoeuvred as candidate for new president.

By contrast, the pro-democrats having tried to build the foundations for democratization – such as active and equal citizenship, human rights and policy-driven issue and interest groups – needed more time and resources to measure up in elections. Now, in the face of prompt balloting and a regrouped establishment, they were marginalized as juniors in the mainstream parties or humiliated (PRD got 0.07 per cent of the votes). Many deemed politics so dirty that they preferred to avoid it. Had the movement vanished? What were its current priorities? How would it be able to regain strength? Everyone in the seminar agreed we must find out, but how could we get an answer?

Given that first-rate academicians remained vulnerable, or were hired for good money in foreign donors' projects, we agreed to conduct a survey together with those who should know best by experience – investigative journalists and human rights workers around the country. The committed journalists could help us map the movement and (with some supervision) carry out critical case studies together with young researchers. In addition, Munir Said Thalib, Munir for short (the 2000 laureate for the alternative Nobel Prize), promised to give us access to the national network of the Commission for Disappearances and Victims of Violence (*KontraS*).

This was not just a vision. Within a year, the design was finished, the funding secured and the research teams formed. The survey of pro-democracy actors around the country was concluded in a few months, after which nineteen case studies of crucial actors were drafted in a year and a half. Activists themselves shared their experiences and added numerous illustrative stories. Senior scholars from Indonesia and elsewhere analysed the studies in view of comparative insights.

Timeline Indonesia 1990–2009

1999–2001
- Mainstream parties win elections – pro-democrats marginalized.
- Indonesia leaves East Timor.
- Abdurrahman Wahid president.
- Conflicts in Moluccas, Sulawesi and Aceh.
- CSO-facilitated peace negotiations on Aceh.

2001
- Megawati Sukarnoputri president.
- Indonesian government resumes offensive against Aceh freedom movement.

2002
- Research shows Indonesian democracy movement politically marginalized and socially rootless. Activists agree to 'reclaim politics'.
- Peace in East Indonesia, in return for dominant parties' business opportunities.
- Freedom movement in Aceh dominates c. 70 per cent of territory.

2004
- Research shows main problem of democratization is biased system of representation.
- Results ignored. Mainstream focus on anti-corruption and administrative reform.
- Susilo Bambang Yudhoyono new president.
- Tsunami in Aceh (26 December).

2005
- Huge international assistance for reconstruction in Aceh.
- Peace accord on Aceh by way of agreement about local democratization.
- Indonesian pro-democrats politicize issue-, interest- and community groups.

2006–9
- In Aceh, reformist combatants and CSO activists win Aceh elections.
- In Aceh, international support for reconstruction separated from democratization.
- Elsewhere in Indonesia, CSO activists fail to congregate and scale up.
- New progressive Indonesian parties fail to qualify for elections.

2009
- National elections: Susilo B. Yudhoyono re-elected and mainstream parties dominate.
- Pro-democrats try 'diaspora politics' by joining mainstream parties, with poor results.

Map 10 Indonesia.

Map 11 Java.

'Floating democrats'

When we all met in early 2002 to discuss the draft conclusions, everyone concurred the pro-democrats had lost out in the transition to electoral democracy. But in contrast to the mainstream analysts who deemed the movement to be in decay, we found much of it alive and kicking. Activists focused on the rights of workers, the urban poor, small farmers and women. Others strengthened local communities, worked in watchdog groups or focused on issues from human rights and corruption to the media. Civil society was indeed expanding. At the same time, however, many organizations and media were not based on equal citizens' ideas and interests. There were numerous 'uncivil societies', such as extreme religious and para military groups. Media were no longer censored by the regime but they were mostly dominated by moneyed actors. Pro-democrats in established parties were typically unable to make much of a difference.

Most importantly, our case studies indicated that the mainstream democracy promoters were mistaken. Their idea was to accommodate the elite who accepted basic democratic institutions, while confining radical democracy activists to civil society. The expectation was that the powerful actors would become democrats as they adjusted to the new institutions and that civil society would improve the system. Our results indicated, however, that the economic and political elite adjusted by using their privileged resources to dominate the freedoms and electoral democracy. This held back democratic advances. Meanwhile the pro-democrats in civil society lost trust in mainstream politics and the possibilities to improve the system. Disillusioned, some opted for militant struggle to alter the structural conditions or break-out of the nation-state. Others returned to the primacy of 1980s-style civil society work in terms of opposing stateism and 'dirty politics'. They supported victims of unequal development and lobbied for improvements.

Ironically, therefore, the pro-democrats were equally 'floating' by being fragmented and often as isolated from ordinary people as the masses under Suharto who were forced to stay out of politics. In the view of our studies, civil society activists should thus reclaim the process of democratization by resuming efforts at building broad movements and getting into organized politics. In short, they should 'go politics'.

Reclaiming democratization

Donor representatives in the conference smiled appreciatively when praised for not having intervened in our research but had blank looks on their faces when informed of the conclusion that pro-democrats must reclaim the process of democratization and 'go politics'. Later Norway, for example, designed its 'human rights dialogue with Indonesia' to align with the government's, rather than pro-democrats', priorities.

Admittedly, we were not very precise about the meaning of 'going politics'. The studies so far were fine in mapping the movement and defining its challenges, but insufficient as a basis for deciding what should be done. Commentators from the Philippines, Thailand, India, Nigeria, South Africa and Scandinavia added insights, but most Indonesian participants returned to their standard formulations. Popular instigators and liberation-activists said: there must be ideology, solid organizations and leadership. Local organizers and autonomists contended: we must rather start from concrete issues on the ground and then get more political. Cause-oriented activists and union leaders added: we should engage in taking vital issues to the politicians and parliament. Political players concluded smugly: all of you must back up us when we enter the parties.

A task force was appointed to suggest how we should acquire deeper insights and Asmara Nababan, the outgoing secretary general of the Human Rights Commission, promised to direct the new operation. It was easy to agree on following up the previous studies by focusing on three additional tasks: one, to analyse the actual state of democratization based on the insights of the pro-democrats so that they could reclaim the initiative in the public discussion about democracy; two, to specify the pro-democrats' problems and options to 'go politics'; and three, to use the results for discussions among activists about joint strategies. But would it really be possible to use participatory research around the entire country to bring the priorities of the pro-democrats back to the centre of the discussion, and nourish the essence of Social Democracy – democratic popular-interest collectivities, democratic links between the state and citizens, and strategic social rights and economic policies?

I had recently seen something similar happen in Kerala (to which we shall return in the next chapter). And the original basis of the Indonesian independence movement had been study and education. In any case, the most trusted democracy groups, and some leading personalities, backed the new research team and a new association was formed – *Demos*. A project proposal was developed, the Swedish and Norwegian agencies for international development were persuaded to provide basic funding, and the University of Oslo allowed me to supervise the research as part of my regular obligations. However, the International Institute for Democracy and Electoral Assistance (IDEA) exemplified the market-like competition among CSOs by withdrawing its commitment when we decided to work with pro-democrats on the ground and not just copy its assessment scheme. Thankfully, concerned officers with the Ford Foundation and Soros' TIFA Foundation stood by. So what was the outcome?

Designing an alternative analytical framework was challenging but relatively easy, as it could be done in seminar rooms. The best formula for assessing state of democracy (by David Beetham) was made more realistic and less biased in favour of liberal democracy, and questions were added about actors and social and political movements in order to consider the dynamics of democratization.

Given the unique trust in these efforts thanks to our cooperation with respected pro-democracy groups, it was also possible to identify reliable informants as candidates for an expert survey. There had to be as many as 800 experts to cover all the sectors and the whole country. They needed to have long experience from democracy work around the country in various sectors, such as human and workers' rights, anti-corruption or gender equality.

The uphill task was to reduce the number of questions and to phrase them so that they related to the informants' concrete circumstances. I well remember a senior journalist lashing out at me when she had tested a draft questionnaire: you are absolutely crazy professor, so many and so ridiculously abstract questions!

We tried to improve but the main solution was training interviewers to specify the questions by giving local examples. Still, complete interviews called for some six to eight hours discussion with time-pressed activists. Yet, a sign of the Indonesian pro-democrats' commitment was that they put up with it. In fact, there were very few dropouts.

The first time all the information was consolidated, we were jubilant in our little bungalow office in central Jakarta as we thought we had passed our baptism of fire. But we were wrong. It was not possible to insert the data in a statistical programme, lean back and mull over correlations. Most questions had been formulated to not merely examine the state of democratic institutions but also cast light on the problems and options of improvements, of democratization. This required qualitative analysis in view of different theories about the rise of democracy, which in turn called for quite senior analysts, whose services we lacked. Our young researchers had done a marvellous job of formulating relevant questions and assembling the data, but they were not well-read in the scholarly literature. And my own task, originally, was only to provide general supervision and analyses in comparative perspective, plus quality control. So we tried hard to also enrol concerned local scholars, but they were few and rarely available, at least not for the pennies we could offer. Our only option was internal education along the way. All my instructions, corrections and calls for reformulations must have been quite frustrating. But in order to be accurate and trustworthy, we simply had to measure up to international academic standards.

We did it, with some delay, but in the long run our researchers had to get additional education about theories of democratization, and there needed to be cooperation with committed local academicians. We tried to establish cooperation on education and training between the universities of Gadjah Mada and Oslo, but it was easier said than done. After two rounds of surveys, the *Demos* team split between those who wanted to go ahead on their own with less-qualified research and those who wanted to gain further education at UGM while continuing the research with senior scholars. While those scaling down the research lost steam, it was even more difficult for the uniquely experienced, but formally unqualified, researchers who held on to the original idea to be accommodated within the hierarchical and competitive academic world. Due to university formalities and donor injunctions, the barefoot and certified researchers were also unable to form an alternative autonomous unit or a CSO with common aims and equal conditions. The spirit of democracy suffered, and some of the quality of the research too. But we endured and most of the research was successfully concluded, albeit after delays. So, what was the new knowledge and did it make a difference?

The problem is representation

The reports from the two initial surveys until 2009 boiled down to one controversial conclusion and two recommendations (developments and results thereafter will be considered in Chapter 14).

The many academic colleagues and donor experts who had predicted that our studies would only confirm the vocal pro-democrats' opinions were utterly mistaken. The immediate joke in late 2003 when the first data emerged from our poorly air-conditioned office on a warm Jakarta afternoon was that we would be seen as pro-government because a clear majority of the informants had stated that there were great initial advances with regard to freedom of opinion and speech and other civil and political rights, except in Aceh. In actual fact, the major problem was that the advances were about freedom from state oppression but not freedom from private militias and business. Moreover, the capacity of powerful private actors and 'uncivil societies' to make use of the new freedoms – to influence the media for example –

was much greater than that of the pro-democrats. So exactly as the journalists had concluded when their magazines were closed down in 1994 – that democracy was needed to enforce freedom of speech – now more democratization was needed to ensure comprehensive human rights.

Similarly, the pro-democrats concurred with mainstream experts, diplomats and international business that the standard of the rule of law and impartial governance was very low, in spite of the new Corruption Eradication Commission (KPK). But the research showed that the equally poor popular representation in organized politics, as well as within civil society, was more fundamental. Just as in the case of freedom of the press and human rights, one could not expect the government, bureaucracy and private actors to make improvements without more substantive democratic representation of people.

Electoral democracy had certainly been introduced in 1999, and the military were about to lose their political privileges, but the acknowledged parties were dominated by the political, religious and economic elites. Ordinary people and pro-democrats without substantial economic resources were de facto prevented from building their own parties that could take part in the elections. Even participation in local elections required national presence with branch offices around one of the largest countries in the world (we shall return to the exception in Aceh).

With regard to the introduction in 2004 of direct elections for political executives, moreover, only the parties that were able to form coalitions comprising 20 per cent of the seats in parliament were permitted to nominate candidates for president, governor and heads of towns and districts. For an independent candidate to be able to run, it took immensely expensive campaigns to collect the required number of signatures. Even candidates for local positions needed comparatively advanced formal schooling, and to run in a village election one had to contribute to the administrative costs. On top of this, there were ineffectual checks and balances concerning the private funding of candidates and parties. And the possibilities for citizens and organized interests to participate in policy development were slim too. Local bureaucrats and politicians typically captured nice sounding participatory budgeting, and popular organizations were neglected.

In the view of our research, it may well have been necessary to accommodate the powerful groups and leaders from the Suharto period in a new democratic system, but this should not have been at the expense of the opportunity for organized interests, such as unions and pro-democrats, to foster active citizenship, membership and policy-based organizations and parties.

Equally bad, the second explanation for why these groups did not make a difference was their own weak culture of democratic representation at various levels and related ineptitude in building coalitions and alliances. Said dynamic human rights activist Poengky Indarti: for most of us the best way to make an immediate difference is to lobby, develop favourable contacts and get media attention (...) these methods are also necessary to formulate the tangible aims that donors impose on us, and later on to get more funds by showing that we have fulfilled the targets. Besides, we are not experienced in building organizations from bottom-up. Networks are all right for board members in the CSOs that I know of, but there is no trust in broad membership.

Similarly, local unions and similar organizations do not have sufficient means of keeping leaders on higher levels accountable.

Who cares?

The first recommendation was therefore that pro-democrats must campaign for rules and regulations to improve democratic representation in the political system as well as within and between their own organizations. But who cared?

When first briefing our main donor's representative, the Norwegian ambassador, he looked surprised. He listened politely but indicated that there was no strong reason to add the issue of democratic representation to those of the rule of law and human rights. Many academicians and democracy experts were also not interested, suggesting that our research was partisan – and when proven wrong, claiming that we should have asked ordinary people rather than grounded experts around the country. When we replied that the aim was best-possible study of the actual state of affairs rather than an opinion poll, they dropped the objection but insisted that we were naive anyway because popular membership-based organizations and parties were relics of the past.

For their part, several pro-democrats said they had given up on political parties. The organization for electoral reform (CETRO), for example, was obviously attracted by a US-like system with individual candidates in one-person constituencies and direct elections of executives. This, they thought, would undermine elitist parties. Our references to the drawbacks of political bossism in the US-inspired Philippine system were ignored. Meanwhile human rights and environmental activists repeated their arguments that better democratic representation was all well and good but lobbying and pressure politics were more effective.

In addition to human rights, donors' favourites were efforts at good governance and anti-corruption. Leading advocates in this regard, including Bambang Widjojanto, a previous executive director of LBH, asserted that elected politicians and parliaments were immersed in 'dirty politics' and prone to corruption. Hence, they believed, there had to be anti-corruption agencies and other means of 'horizontal accountability' within public administration before representation could improve. This must be enforced by policy development, lobbying, judicial action and pressure politics – plus support from the 'international community' – because elections were part of the problem. Confronted with studies showing that anti-corruption measures that ignored democratization often sustained authoritarian rule, as in Singapore, or that the early reforms against corruption in the North, such as in Sweden, were not only statist shock therapy but fused with pre-democratic local representation, Widjojanto and his friends resorted to 'the truth' – as contained in coloured booklets published by the United Nations Development Programme, the World Bank and the Asian Development Bank.

The most reflective local organizers, on the other hand, such as Wardah Hafidz, who supported the urban poor, believed political representation was not feasible yet. Better democratic representation, she reasoned, presupposed active citizenship, which in turn called for emancipatory community organizing and informal means to improve accountability and trust. Meanwhile, she said: we represent their issues.

But the most astonishing reaction was within our own research community, *Demos*. Having analysed the state of democratization and specified pro-democrats' problems and options, the additional task of *Demos* was to bring together the activists to consider the results and discuss ways of 'going politics'. There were workshops around the country with key informants, and some meetings with scholars and senior activists to polish our recommendations. But the contentious issue was whether or not *Demos* should also initiate an educational movement – a popular school of democracy.

The major argument was that this would be the most obvious way for us to follow up our own recommendation to improve representation and collective action within the democracy movement and that we were uniquely placed to do this. We had the backing of all vital pro-democracy groups and had, for a start, enrolled at least 1,000 committed informants and numerous interviewers around the country within all relevant sectors of democracy work. Like-minded donors were interested, recalling the history of liberal and social democratic educational movements in their own countries, and I pointed to the importance of the study and educational movements in Kerala. Still, the response of the *Demos*' director and most researchers and board members was negative: it is too dangerous to opt for a broad membership organization, because it would be easy to hijack the organization and its research. Besides, they added: voluntary activism as in Kerala does not exist anymore in Indonesia. And there are many other groups doing democracy studies and education that might deem us competitors.

The political bloc route

The second main recommendation was to promote non-party political blocs among pro-democratic groups and organizations. One reason for this was that the elitist democratization neglected the representation and participation of more genuine democracy actors who could not build viable parties. Another was that the pro-democracy groups themselves were fragmented and lacked ideas of how to get together and scale up. The proposal was therefore to promote blocs, or united fronts, of like-minded civil society groups and popular organizations, such as unions and urban poor organizations. When possible, as in Aceh, the blocs could form local parties, but otherwise the pro-democrats would have to unite on minimum common programmes and demands, and thereafter relate to mainstream parties and government, local and central. Only later – if they became stronger – could these blocs form parties of their own.

The political bloc idea was difficult to realize, however. During extensive discussions with our key informants and like-minded leaders around the country, I did not come across any important actors who were able to assemble from below based on joint issues and proposals. Rather, the groups went in two other directions. One was trying to broaden the support for the issues, interests and communities they had already given priority to. The other was immediate party building. Why was broad unity from below so difficult and what was the fate of the roadmaps activists opted for?

First actual route: Politicizing issues, interests and communities

The dynamics of politicizing previous priorities varied with the different issues, interests and communities the pro-democrats embraced.

Human rights as the focus

Munir, another tall little man in the democracy movement, almost disappeared behind his desk. So I usually found him standing in front of it, arguing heatedly and energetically but with good humour: Yes I support your conclusions that politics is too important to be left to the politicians (…) we can't build a better world in civil society only. But formal politics is now so muddy that one can't avoid getting dirty if engaging in it, so I prefer to act from outside.

Munir's words carried weight. Though only thirty-five when awarded the alternative Nobel Prize as a remarkably brave and innovative human rights fighter, he personified the best of the New Indonesia. In the early 1990s, he changed from being a militant Muslim youth activist into a spokesman for Muslim social values and universal humanitarianism, along with his labour-organizing wife Suciwati. In contrast to Buyung Nasution, who petered out as a self-labelled 'locomotive of democracy', Munir refused to bow to pressure. This earned him iconic status, especially among dissidents who were repressed for their decision to challenge the authorities.

Munir moved beyond the legal aid offices in Surabaya and Jakarta. He went into the field and encouraged victims to get organized in order for him to be able to help them fight abuse and in order for them to make a difference together. This was the manner in which he combined the fight for human rights with a pledge for better conditions for workers and for land for farmers. This was the way he campaigned against the abuses by the military and militias, from Suharto's death squads, the atrocities in East Timor and the ongoing violence in Aceh. In short, this was the way in which he and kindred colleagues at LBH wanted to transform elitist urban CSOs into democratic peoples' movements, especially *KontraS*. But when I asked how such groups could form blocs or broader united fronts with others to really make a political difference, he always looked at his watch, indicating there were more urgent questions to attend to: let's find more time to discuss later.

We never found that time. After boarding Indonesia's flag carrier Garuda Air's evening flight to Amsterdam on 6 September 2004, for a study visit, he was poisoned to death with arsenic.

Anti-corruption as a unifier

Teten Masduki personified another conclusion. Having invigorated LBH's support for labour organizing in the 1990s, inspired in part by the cooperation between students and workers in South Korea, he switched priorities during the Asian economic crisis. Many of the labour activists were thrown out of work and the issue that caught most people's imagination was the regime's collusion, nepotism and corruption. Bald-headed in more than one way, Teten Masduki was entrusted to form Indonesian Corruption

Watch (ICW). His priorities, though, were different from the technocrats and lawyers who claimed elected politicians were part of the problem, so therefore the efforts to fight corruption and foster rule of law must precede democracy. Said Maduki: ICW has no problem with democracy and politics, only with rotten politics. But resisting corruption calls for extensive resources, access to information and judicial action. So public action is not enough, we must colonize the state and its resources and promote a Commission against Corruption, just as there is a Commission for Human Rights. (…) As for our own organization, we do not want another paralysing conflict like in LBH about extensive membership or not, so our compromise is partnerships with other anti-corruption groups around the country.

Unions on the rise

The many new unions formed after the fall of Suharto also held on to their special focus – permanent employment and decent wages and work conditions. Popular instigators (including the radical Indonesian Front for Labour Struggle, FNPBI) insisted on overcoming 'economistic' short-term demands by adding education and general political issues, such as fighting neoliberal policies. But there was no alternative that addressed workers' daily problems.

Several of the conventional unionists appreciated the importance of 'going politics' too, but the question was how. Poengky Indarti monitored the priorities of the many unions and labour groups. Ever so patient, she spent hours with me drawing extensive maps with numerous boxes. The prime federations and confederations with international support later carried the labels of KSPSI (the previously regime loyalist Confederation of All-Indonesia Workers Unions), KSPI (the 'reformed' splinter Confederation of Indonesian Trade Unions) and KSBSI (the Confederation of Indonesian Prosperous Labour Unions of 1992). But there were also plentiful local unions and groups. Some of them came together in KASBI (Congress of Indonesian Labour Union Alliances) and other groups, at times trying to build a bridge between formal and informal labour. Yet others, like union activist Hemmasari Dharmabumi in Bandung and labour organizer Arief Djati in Surabaya, wanted to counter centralism and horse-trading by building more democratic unions from below. But when I asked them how the independent unions would coordinate and scale up, there was no firm answer. Dharmabumi, moreover, organized workers in transnational companies where it was possible to negotiate better deals than the minimum wages thanks to international, rather than national, coordination.

At the end of the day, Indarti and I could not but conclude that the diversity was less a reflection of exciting ideas about how to 'go politics' than more mundane factors – such as leaders' competition in plant-level negotiations, the differing issues in unevenly developed companies, varied employment conditions and, finally, horse-trading with employers and politicians. According to union facilitator Sahat Lumbanraja in Medan, moreover: plant-level issues that workers can agree on vary so much between sectors that they are not a good basis for wider unity, and the issues that are handled on higher levels are often controlled by leaders whom workers do not trust, as they cannot keep an eye on them.

One exception came in 2002–3. A union coalition – backed by supporters in civil society – formed around new labour legislation and benefitted from government instability and sympathetic insiders in the 'Ministry of Manpower' who were seeking labour votes for then President Megawati in the forthcoming elections. The result was the comparatively advanced Manpower Law of 2003, which took its adversaries almost twenty years to reverse (Chapter 14). Another emerging development related to Indonesia's extensive decentralization, which included local tripartite negotiations of minimum wages. To gain influence in the wage councils, which had limited numbers of seats, the unions had to network, agree on basic positions and stage demonstrations. Secondly, with the introduction in 2005 of direct elections of local political executives, unionists in extensively industrialized districts and provinces gradually realized they could also seal contracts with the politicians likely to take up seats in the wage councils. Unions delivered votes to successful candidates in return for better wages and other benefits. We shall return to these dynamics in Chapter 14.

Urban poor getting together

The number of urban poor increased significantly as a result of both the extensive dispossession of rural people's means of livelihood under Suharto and the extensive cut-backs during the Asian economic crisis. But while workers' potentially progressive role in development boils down to their capacity to act collectively in favour of common interests and block production, how do poor people, who are often without work entirely, get together? Legal class actions were useful but presupposed decent laws and judicial system. Advising people on how to approach the authorities was fine but insufficient. Islamic feminist and scholarly propelling force in the Urban Poor Consortium (UPC), Wardah Hafidz asserted, innovatively, that the main task was to support the urban poor's different survival strategies in such a way that they could also agree on self-help and demands for what they all needed – housing, livelihood and basic public services. Said Hafidz: the weapons of the poor are informal, but people must get together.

While workers can close down factories, informal labourers and urban poor can certainly make a city ungovernable, as attempted in parts of Latin America and in the 'people's strikes' in the Philippines (Chapter 8). However, the challenge is how people in need of basic livelihoods can coordinate and develop more attractive alternatives than the patronage offered by politicians, religious leaders and businessmen in return for subjugation. Many urban poor organizers agreed with Hafidz that they did not want to engage in politics before people's own organizations were strong enough to make a difference.

Meanwhile the new direct elections of political executives represented a temporary fix. Urban poor groups could negotiate contracts with important politicians, just as unions could trade votes for higher minimum wages. If politicians with clout promised to support the major demands of various urban poor organizations, the urban poor leaders would deliver votes. To some extent, this worked. The urban poor in Makassar, South Sulawesi, for example, resisted eviction by negotiating deals with the mayor. And most famously, a broad cluster of urban poor groups in Solo, Central Java, were strong enough to negotiate a pact on less unfair urban development with the then Mayor, Joko 'Jokowi' Widodo. We shall return to this dynamic in Chapter 14.

However, the urban poor had to be strong enough to enforce the contracts. Moreover, various groups often negotiated different contracts with different politicians, thus increasing the divisions among the progressives, such as in Jakarta between UPC and the Citizens' Forum. And the contracts only applied to specific urban poor matters, not relating to other sectors of the population, so 'friendly' politicians could get away with otherwise dubious policies. There was something to Teten Masduki's complaint: the urban poor organizers do not talk of citizens, only of their specific groups, street children, *becak* drivers, fisher folks, etc.

Fisher folks fight back

The frequent dispossessing of rural people's means of livelihood did not end with Suharto. When asking activists in the environmental *Walhi* network for examples of popular resistance with the most democratic potential, they often pointed to the large island of *Pulau Laut* in Kotabaru district, South Kalimantan. Here poor fisher folks had won a battle against a Korean factory and local political bosses who had wrecked their fishing waters. It was irresistible to find out about their experiences.

Noorhalis Majid, *Demos'* key informant in Banjarmasin, said flights to Kotabaru were unreliable, but he wanted to know about the story too and could fix a car. Taking turns, we could get there in a day. The highway was all right while on the depressingly deforested flatland that had also been bulldozed of coal and turned a swamp. But then it turned a dirt road marked with huge potholes that occasionally caused even lorries to tip over. When we finally lined up for the ferry to *Pulau Laut*, the truckers around complained despairingly.

Land being expensive, the compact fishing village we were going to was on stilts in the sea. On the narrow boardwalks connecting the shacks, playing kids only rarely fell into the water and humorously chatting women were rinsing shrimps. Men cleared trawls and maintained engines in the small boats below. We talked of daily life, but as the tide receded and the smell from the mud became evident, discussions shifted inside.

Middle-aged Arbani, the obvious supremo, let his confidantes tell me about the history and himself, just adding a joke or making a brief point, only really engaging in the hard talk. Charisma is as difficult to describe as good looks (asserted by my female assistant) and it was bolstered by Arbani's background as a pirate. It was only after a stint in jail because of an unfortunate hijacking of a container ship that he took up fishing. Thereafter his main reputation became that of a brave boatman and crusader for everyone's right to the sea, including the poor fisher folks – not just the better off who wanted to divide the spoils among themselves. Hence, he was the self-evident leader of their organization, *Insan (Ikatan Nelayan Saija'an)*. *Insan* had been formed in late 2003 to demand that the debris that a cement company had dumped in the fishing waters when constructing a new harbour be cleared. Huge stones and blocs on the seabed deprived fishermen of their livelihood by destroying their trawls. *Walhi* backed them up, but as the local authorities refused to act, the activists realized that they were facing a political problem too. Hence, they organized a massive week-long blockade with their small boats of the company's harbour, engendering heavy repression by the police and navy. As some *Walhi* activists were also arrested, the issue came to the attention of international environmentalists as well as media and politicians in Jakarta. Finally the embarrassed central government instructed the local authorities to see to it that the seabed was cleared.

The subsequent developments were more complicated to navigate. Bribes had already been refused, including a free haji to Mecca for Arbani and his wife, but then there were donations too. Lacking an experienced organization to keep track of risks and temptations, the leaders' instinct was to say 'no thank you, our independence is not for sale'. As a partial alternative, they set up a modest cooperative to save on kerosene for the boats. Things became appreciably worse, however, when they came to realize that real improvements called for political engagement. In the local context, the poor fisher folks were at the bottom of the local social hierarchy, stigmatized by others, lacking education and quite dependent on the assistance of *Walhi*'s community organizers. Gaining ground by getting members selected by leaders of hamlets (RW) and neighbourhoods (RT) was feasible. But building a party and participate in elections was out of the question, given that it called for a national presence. To run in elections via an established party was impossible too, as few, if any, of the fisher folks measured up to the regulation that to stand in elections a minimum of a senior high school education was required. Democracy was not for them. Membership in *Insan* itself, moreover, was only for heads of households. Smiled Arbani's wife: I wouldn't mind being a member of a woman's section, if there was one.

On reflection, Arbani and his senior companions asserted: yes, we should widen our priorities and build broader alliances with other fisher folks and labourers within mining and others, but our specific aims and demands are not the same (…) and our communities are different (…) and there are few links with them that we could build on. So setting up everything from scratch will take a lot of time, and we must earn our living (…) and we are not experienced. Just imagine if there already was a broader organization with other progressive people too, not just a few *Walhi* activists coming here now and then …

Late one night six years later in *Walhi*'s South Kalimantan headquarters in Banjarbaru, Abu, one of the community organizers assisting *Insan*, told me: Arbani passed away not so long ago, much too young, possibly cancer (…) he never stopped asking me to run for them in the elections, as he could not, although he was an outstanding leader. But it wasn't my job. On the other hand, his superiority was also a drawback. He was never even elected in *Insan*, only appointed by acclamation. So certain matters were not attended to when he messed up his private life (…) It's so typical (…) activists themselves must democratize their groups to scale up.

Small farmers in search of allies

I was never able to answer journalists' question what a progressive new Indonesia might look like – until staying with Handoko Wibowo in his small inherited clove plantation, on the Batang hillsides, in north Central Java. Upon my first arrival in late 2006, the tastefully decorated rooms in the little modest old mansion had been renovated to also allow his extended family of activists to rest and recuperate. And there was a veranda for dining, serving as a meeting place for progressives in the area. They constituted a remarkably wide-ranging circle of people, from radical popular leaders to decent businessmen and politicians, and some local LGBT activists. In the roomy kitchen, supportive students were busy preparing food for about 300 representatives of several thousand small farmers in the district who were expected for dinner. The farmers were guided by Handoko in their struggle to get back the land they lost under Suharto. In the evening, the representatives – surprisingly many were women – gathered in an open pavilion in the garden. The subject was what demands they would make and what candidate they might support in the election of a *bupati* (head of district). After brief prayers and accounting for developments since the last meeting, there were intensive discussions and joint conclusions, followed by radical nationalist songs, a certain internationalist chant and informal dinner conversations. A moving glimpse of a new Indonesia.

As a socially competent and entrepreneurial young lawyer, Wibowo might well have become a successful academic or reform politician – had he not also been a supporter of homosexual rights and the son of an allegedly radical ethnic Chinese family who had been driven into bankruptcy, partly because Suharto's son Tommy monopolized the clove trade. Having weathered the economic challenges the only way it seemed possible – by drawing on 'good contacts' and sharing bribes in the Pekalongan court – Wibowo recalibrated his moral compass, dedicating his life to progressive change. His formative legal aid case was against local textile companies that dumped their waste straight out into the water and sea, destroying just about everything for the fisher folks. The victory was spectacular – thanks to Wibowo's harnessing of the fishing community's own energy, plus the media. Later on, soon after the fall of Suharto, he was also asked to advise the thousands of small farmers' households in Batang who were trying to reclaim their right to use the land that had been licensed by the dictatorial state to corporations and plantations, which often just kept it for speculative purposes.

Wibowo extended his method of popular-based legal action by supporting small farmers' organizing in the villages and by suggesting a joint Batang Forum for Small Farmers' Struggle (FPPB). There was an innovative repertoire of joint actions to facilitate broader collective organizing – from demonstrations in front of courts and occupations of land, to cultural events, education and support for the members' own agriculture and cooperative ventures. Cautioning against militant actions that could lead to arrests, priority was given to spectacular peaceful actions. Radical students from Semarang and Jogjakarta provided assistance.

The impressive advances were not without challenges, though. As in the case of Dante Buscayno's small farmer's cooperative in the Philippines (Chapter 8), there was a danger of Wibowo and the FPPB getting mired in the single issue of land because it was not the only concern. Several of the small farmers' family members also earned their living as labourers in the neighbouring towns or as migrating house maids in Jakarta, for example. Their additional common interests included better further education and impartial public services. This called for political engagement, but the trust the farmers' leaders had on land and farming issues did not automatically extend to the many other matters at stake in village elections. In addition, the nomination of candidates and mobilization of funds produced numerous conflicts. Depressingly, many members did not even vote for their leaders. Reliving the full story, Wibowo could not hold back the tears.

Equally complicated, Wibowo himself did not want to be elected, either in the small farmers' movement or in local politics, as his private preferences and Chinese background would be used for black propaganda. Hence he must act informally as the movement's senior adviser and as its mediator in contacts with senior bureaucrats, politicians and parties. In spite of the best of intentions and efforts at transparency, democracy in the movement was thus insufficiently institutionalized. Moreover, as the 2009 legislative elections loomed, other actors wanted to benefit from the small farmers' votes too. Party-building activists from Jakarta made frequent visits and students supporting the small farmers' movement opted for a new political party, with instigating activist Dita Sari in the forefront but with zero local roots. This caused a major rift and negative outcomes.

In a late night discussion afterwards, Wibowo said that because they had failed to build a political bloc by expanding the small farmers' movement, the only alternative now was to establish meeting points for the wider circle of groups involved. Wibowo added: the first, *Omah Tani*, a house for small farmers and their friends, may also serve as a neutral clearinghouse for actors to consider a political bloc. Did not you tell me that Scandinavian unions and popular movements built 'people's houses' in the early twentieth century to get together and thus form a party too?

For some years, Wibowo and like-minded activists were thus successful in building a bloc of small farmers, informal labourers, single mothers, homosexuals as well as human rights and anti-corruption campaigners. One priority was to support the least bad independent candidate for *bupati* (head of district) in the 2011 elections, Yoyok Riyo Sudibyo. In contrast to progressives elsewhere, no real political contract was signed. Said Wibowo a year later: what would be the use of it? The point is that Yoyok knows he must discuss vital decisions with us, otherwise he will lose our support, which he needs. Besides, we are also building alliances with other progressive leaders and unions, in the towns here in Batang and Pekalongan as well as in greater Jakarta.

The dynamics in Wibowo's clearinghouses were intriguing, but when I arrived again in the evening four years later, his lovely little mansion seemed almost abandoned. Next morning Wibowo served a sad story for breakfast: Yes, maybe our political bloc should have worked out a minimum programme, a firm platform. We just shared common norms and ideas, and then acted pragmatically (...) Thus it was easy for the *bupati* to build his own competing cooperation with others and dispose of us. Meanwhile, activists could not but link up with various political parties. Moreover, our union friends around Jakarta abandoned the idea of broad alliances. It was devastating.

Customary rights and democratic deficits

Given the weak democratic organization in Indonesia, many progressives tried shortcuts to broad interest-based collectivities – the prime foundation of Social Democracy – by placing their hopes on communities relying on customs and religion. My own understanding of this temptation increased significantly after experiencing the superb Catholic discipline and organization behind the huge, world famous Easter procession in Larantuka, East Flores, and then, next morning, facing again the chaotic public infrastructure, including unreliable taxis and cancelled flights.

Pro-democratic Muslims, for example, supported the idea of citizen forums (*forum warga*). The problem was who would be classed as a citizen? Activists in Bantul, Jogjakarta, said: our forums are rooted in the local *ummah* (Muslim community). Then we invite others too, but of course, the *ummah* is core.

In Bali, moreover, human rights and anti-corruption campaigner Wayan Sudirta, together with supporters, formed a CSO and community coalition for democracy, known as *KORdEM*. They were drawing on the practices of the esteemed religious-reformist Hindu Youth Forum, and reminded me of Mahatma Gandhi's ideas. However, while Sudirta was elected Bali representative to the politically insignificant Regional Representative Council in Jakarta, *KORdEM* as a political bloc was not broad enough to also get significant numbers of members elected into mainstream Bali politics.

Challenges were even harsher in the 'outer islands' where authoritarian means had always been used to extract natural resources – from colonial occupation and indirect rule to Suharto's authoritarian reign. Along with the radical decentralization after his demise, power relations were renegotiated, often fanning conflicts. As a last resort, people turned to different religious communities for protection, which in turn intensified the conflicts. In response Jakarta sent the military. Finally the then Vice President Jusuf Kalla offered the contenders business opportunities and power-sharing in return for peace, which generated more corruption.

In this context, popular organizations and democracy-oriented CSOs were not a viable alternative. In Poso and Tentena in Central Sulawesi, for example, the particularly ugly conflicts between militant Muslims and Christians made it difficult for human rights groups to make much difference, even when trying to unify ordinary people against repression and the disastrous exploitation of natural resources. As local activists put it: here is the reign of terror and corruption.

***

Increasingly many pro-democrats put their faith instead in customary law, rights and organization (*adat*) – aiming at reform from below. According to Abdon Nababan who led the Alliance of Indigenous Peoples of the Archipelago (AMAN): our political demands are based on customary rights (…) but the indigenous groups and their rights must be validated historically, (…) yes, blood relations, if you like (…) and to claim the rights, we must draw on the traditional leadership and international conventions.

Senior scholarly activist Roem Topatimasang supported customary rights too but was sceptical of defining indigenous populations by colonial sources: old feudal-like control of local communities was used by the Dutch to divide and rule. This must not be revived. Local communities themselves, not some old rajas, should be strong enough to negotiate with the government. Customary rights must be respected, but equal citizenship must be fought for too, because it is fundamental to empowering entire communities and building democracy.

What did these positions mean in practice? What, if any, were the potentials for Social Democracy? Probably the most innovative activists were in the faraway Moluccas, so I had to get there.

In an early 2007 conversation in *Kei Kecil*, southeast Moluccas, I congratulated astute village head Alo Jamlean on having been formally elected with a wide margin, asking him if he really would have preferred to rather be appointed in accordance with the *adat* system. His stunning answer was: yes of course I would! Our so-called democracy has been imposed by Jakarta, and it is corrupted by businessmen who grab our natural resources. It even generated civil war here, in which religious leaders got involved too. Only the *adat* leaders facilitated peace. People have more trust in customary rules. Besides, it is the task of my own superior *marga* (clan) to govern the village.

Ten years later, when I revisited Jamlean, he said elected politicians and their bureaucrats had pushed him aside for a while but that he was now back in office: so *adat* prevails and we shall sustain peace and protect communal land, the fishing waters and the world's best beaches.

But how original was *adat* and could it foster alternative development and genuine democracy? Outside the small community hall in a traditional village on Seram island where we were to discuss *adat* regulations, some villagers were sitting on the ground putting small stones in strange squares in the sand while rocking as in a trance to a rhythmic beat. Another old tradition? No, bingo.

In the veranda, however, community leaders and supportive CSO activists explained eagerly the benefits of the customary rules and leadership. That way, they said, they could sustain nature and ordinary people's livelihoods, and contain social conflicts. Also their ancestors' more specific spiritual protection was superior to the general religious blessings of priests or ulamas. The only negative aspect they could think of was that men wishing to marry had to prove their bravery by bringing a human head to the *baileo* (community hall), and two heads to become an *adat* leader. But they assured us that this was long time ago – more than a year, and far away, at least 100 km. (At this point my wife looked over her shoulders.) Since then, they smiled, it was decided that a symbolic red cloth on a silver plate would do: so you see, it is possible to adjust *adat* to some human rights. And now women are allowed to climb trees too.

Internationally recognized *adat* campaigner, Elyza Kyssya, chair of the customary legal authority in Haruku island which was next to Ambon, agreed it was difficult to apply the customary rules in cities like Ambon. Moreover, it was hard to combine them with human rights and equal citizenship: for example, there are not equal chances to education (…) I myself had to cancel advanced education by having to return home and obey the obligations of my *marga* to govern.

Yet he and others were unimpressed when I suggested it might be possible to learn from the experience of subordinated people in Kerala in the early twentieth century (Chapter 5). They held on to caste and tribal organizations with regard to special issues, but came together in common movements to fight colonial and caste oppression and well as social injustices. Kyssya's and others' counter-argument in the Moluccas was that *adat* is a holistic system of values and governance. If one only held on to customary rights to nature and local people's livelihoods, for example, while otherwise adjusting to equal citizenship and human rights, the capacity to sustain the customary rights would dwindle.

Interestingly, however, leading social activists Maria Ngamelumbun and Pieter Elmas in *Kei Kecil* disagreed. Many years ago they had established a CSO, *Nen Mas Il* and an associated People's School to protect the *adat* communities while also promoting development, welfare, human rights and gender equality. In the mid-2000s they engaged in organized politics too to further these aims. People's appreciation of their CSO activities, but also reliance on kinship, substituted for vote-buying and expensive campaigns. Elmas did not make it as an independent *bupati* candidate, but by signing up with a mainstream party both were elected to local and regional parliaments.

Said Elmas with a smile during another visit in 2014 (specifying his points in 2019): While Maria could draw on her superior *marga* connections as well as the mythology about mothers protecting the community, I had to primarily rely on my ability to promote customary rights through good governance in the official system. Actually, scaling up *adat* is not a viable alternative. It is good at local social relations and some conflict prevention, but not democracy and governance. We do not want to restore the powers of feudal-like leaders. It is easy for businessmen to split and co-opt *adat* leaders to pave the way for trawlers or cut down forests to plant sugar. There is a need for democratic politics.

Nothing is easy. Combining democratic politics to foster customary rights with efforts at both stronger and equally governed communities is difficult. In 2017, in a friendly dispute provoked by my questioning, Juliana 'Uli' Jamlean of *Nen Mas Il*, for one suggested that the *adat* administration and the official system should run in parallel, in order to foster complementarity plus checks and balances. Her community organizing husband, Henci Petrus 'Fes' Efraim, on the other hand, advocated the primacy of *adat* and two years later was appointed village leader by his *marga*, acclaimed by the residents and the *bupati*.

Second actual route: Party building

The obvious alternative to the difficulty of building political blocs 'from below' was setting up parties to organize the scattered people and groups 'from above'. Resources were scarce, but given the extensive decentralization, many thought it would be possible to start locally, as for example, the Brazilian Workers' Party had successfully done. Soon enough, however, as alluded to above, the already-elected politicians, supported by experts advocating elite-driven democratization, imposed rules to reduce the number of parties and prevent local ones. The ultimate argument was this was necessary to keep the country together, which, of course, was not very convincing in view, for example, of India's stability in spite of multiple parties at various levels. Pro-democrats in favour of party building had to therefore invent various methods to conform to the unfair rules. We shall return to their experiences, but first we must recount the story of the resource-rich Muslim stronghold of Aceh, which was the only province where the political elite was forced to make an exception and allow local parties. This enabled both peace and post-tsunami reconstruction, before democratization was curbed. How did that happen?

Lost opportunities in Aceh

Strategically located on the northern tip of Sumatra by the Malacca Strait, the former sultanate and now province of Aceh, which contained a population of almost 5 million, had been riven by conflicts since the mid-1970s between the independence movement, GAM and the army. After Suharto, Aceh was also demoralized by unsuccessful CSO-organized peace talks, and in late December 2004, it was devastated by the worst tsunami ever. But despite all this, Aceh turned into a remarkably positive case of peacebuilding that proved the dominant experts wrong – that is, those cautioning against 'contentious democracy' and favouring instead market- and elite-driven roadmaps. Quite contrary to their arguments, it was precisely the 2005 decision in the Helsinki negotiations to allow local parties and independent candidates in Aceh that gave peace, democracy and reconstruction a chance, and even prevented Indonesia from falling apart.

The background for this more social democratic-oriented peace accord was that a sufficient number of the otherwise conservative GAM leaders had been principled enough to withstand Indonesian Vice President Jusuf Kalla's power-sharing offers. These were based on the precedent from Poso and Moluccas of trading business deals for a ceasefire. In Helsinki, moreover, both sides agreed with former Finnish President turned acclaimed mediator, Martti Ahtisaari, on not negotiating all possible social and economic problems but agreeing on conceding weapons in favour of home rule and a democratic political framework. A framework within which these issues could be handled and many other actors, including CSOs, could take part. Finally, the democracy-oriented GAM negotiators were also able to argue convincingly that this would not work without local parties and independent candidates. Yet, the unique opportunity for democratic peace and development was wasted. Why?

The tsunami put pressure on the parties to settle on peace in Aceh and the international donors agreed to a massive assistance programme which was of similar proportions to Marshall Aid which had helped rebuild and democratize Europe after the Second World War. However, the donors conceded to Jakarta's resistance against democratization and good government as the basis for peace and reconstruction. So in contrast to Marshall Aid, both Jakarta and the donors separated reconstruction from democracy and good governance work, neglecting the last two. Aside from some anti-corruption efforts by the UNDP, only a very few and short-handed civil society groups stood tall, a depressingly brief list which included international donors Friedrich Ebert Stiftung (FES) and the Olof Palme International Center (OPC).

Fortunately, Jan Hodann of the OPC had for some time supported the pro-democrats in GAM, and in a battered Jakarta hotel after the tsunami we agreed that *Demos* might add to this by enabling – with my assistance – studies and education of civil society activists to facilitate their participation in the forthcoming elections. However, after a while, the funds for OPC dried up. And 'international community', including Sweden, refused to support *Demos*' proposal.

Meanwhile, by late 2006, Aceh was up for the first free elections of governors and heads of districts. Conservative GAM leaders held back the formation of a democratic local party, but reformist peace negotiators, Irwandi Yusuf, M. Nur Djuli, Bachtiar

Abdullah and Shadia Marhaban and others, supported a political bloc of independent candidates. The independents were from the commanders' transitional committee KPA – with Yusuf in the forefront – and the civil society network SIRA, which had previously demanded a referendum on independence, with Nazar Muhammad in the lead, backed by activists like Taufiq Abda. Unexpectedly (according to mainstream observers), the independent candidates won a landslide victory. Irwandi and Nazar secured the gubernatorial seats with almost 40 per cent of the vote. KPA/SIRA candidates were elected heads of almost half of the districts/towns. And many associates gained positions as advisers.

The challenge was how to move ahead, develop feasible policies, support reintegration of combatants and facilitate civil society and popular movement participation in reconstruction without being trapped by corruption. Such policies would also reduce the importance of patronage and command structures in politics and governance, and open up for society-driven local parties. Discussions in probably the world's best coffee shops were intense. The scenario was difficult but not impossible, yet it failed. Why?

Banda Aceh was flooded again, this time by aid workers and experts. It turned a strange melting pot with sharia laws and canning in front of the main mosque, and tasty Italian food and wine in a roof-top restaurant nearby. Huge sums of money were spent on reconstruction, especially through the Agency for Rehabilitation and Reconstruction (BRR), in insufficient cooperation with the local government, while the reintegration agency (BRA) lagged behind. All the crucial actors looked to the institutions and donors for jobs and access, including professionals, CSO leaders, entrepreneurs and former commanders-turned-businessmen. Few funds were invested in good public governance, active citizenship and democratic organization.

Having lost out in the 2006 elections, the conservative GAM leaders and former commanders built their own Aceh Party (PA) based on old loyalties and new money. The reformists, however, were afraid of being labelled renegades and of losing support among the commanders. Hence they hesitated to build a party of their own with allies in civil society, a failure which proved devastating. Meanwhile the reformist leaders in government had also to please their own supporters, fellow commanders and business partners – plus negotiate a new law for the governance of Aceh and navigate Jakarta's and donors' reconstruction plans and ignorance of democratic governance. So notwithstanding their positions as governors, deputy governors and heads of many towns and districts, little happened in terms of innovative programmes and much talked of popular participation in development and implementation of public policies. Remarked Munawar Liza, the progressive new mayor with great ambitions for Sabang, the scenic and historic deep-water harbour island in the mouth of the Malacca Strait: advances should not have been impossible, in spite of everything (…) but I, for one, was simply not in sufficient command of my jurisdiction.

Meanwhile civil society leaders benefitted from good assignments but lacked a joint programme and an independent popular base, especially outside the cities. Electorally, their ideas of new parties and popular organizations remained non-starters. Finally Norwegian support was given to the participatory democracy studies I advised to facilitate civil society participation in politics and not leave the field solely to former combatants, businessmen and Jakarta loyalists. However – typically of Aceh and donors at the time (but unusually well documented) – a programme manager with prominent patrons prioritized better salaried side-work and enabled activists linked with conservative GAM leaders to hijack and alter the project. In spite of this, the donor deemed the whistle-blowers troublemakers and honoured the turncoat's patrons. So as the head of FES in Indonesia, Erwin Schweisshelm, concluded by mid-2008: the democrats have now been marginalized by donors as well as by powerful local leaders.

As the 2009 legislative elections approached, Governor Irwandi disengaged too. His own position was not at stake and he possibly wanted to pave the way for a deal with old GAM adversaries, in order to be re-elected governor later. In any case, the field was wide open for the conservative GAM-party (PA) to clamp down on the pro-democrats, especially in SIRA.

The election was devastating for democracy and personally humiliating for the civil society candidates, SIRA ones in particular. They were expected to make some gains but lost out entirely. Insightful and humble leader Taufiq Abda agreed his party had lost because the progressive reformists had failed to show outstanding results as partners in public governance and in building popular support for an attractive minimum programme. But equally important was that PA had branded SIRA its major enemy, harassing and cheating on it while previous allies like Irwandi Yusuf stayed away. Confirming the conservative GAM-leaders' view, their deputy campaign leader, Dahlan Jamaluddin, condescendingly corrected me: you must realize that PA won because it is the only party with a genuine nationalist ideology and roots in decades of struggle. SIRA is just a youth and student offspring that functioned as a legal tool when GAM could not form a party. Thereafter SIRA lost its importance.

Thus the uniquely democratic peace accord, the international support for reconstruction and the successful election of an alliance of progressive GAM leaders and civil society activists became lost opportunities.

Measuring up to the harsher rules in the rest of the country

Beyond Aceh, however, local parties remained barred. Pro-democrats who wanted to participate in elections without subordinating themselves to the elite-dominated parties, had to find ways of living up to the rule that a new party must prove genuinely present almost everywhere in Indonesia, a territory about as big as the European Union. (The regulation since 2009 is presence in all provinces, 75 per cent of the regencies in each province and 50 per cent of each district's sub-districts.) Would it be possible and what were the lessons?

Workers' party unworkable

The first of four major strategies was to draw on trade unions, the original base for most social democratic parties around the world. In countries like Indonesia, however, as we know, few labourers are organized and most of them work with heterogeneous employment conditions in unevenly developed companies and institutions. The immediate issues at stake are varied and many unions compete in local negotiations.

Permanently employed skilled workers and professionals have the best bargaining power and usually cater to their own interests. At times, they also need to gain wider support to defend their freedom of organization, negotiate minimum wages or contain social dumping, but this is exceptional. And when they have to influence politics, it is often deemed more favourable to negotiate with powerful mainstream politicians than to waste time and resources on a small new party.

Predictably, the results were thus bleak. Popular instigators within labour organizing emphasized education and politicization, but their parties did not aim at making a difference in elections, and the supplementary effort to organize informal labour and workers behind common issues was a long-term project. Muchtar Pakpahan by contrast, whom we know as the pioneer of the early 1990s labour movement in Medan and the first independent trade union federation (SBSI), convinced me he really wanted to gain immediate support of enough voters to negotiate with other political players. Yet, his labour party failed miserably in a series of elections.

Environmental party in waiting

In analyses based on the first participatory democracy survey, the *Demos* researchers made a tentative aggregation of issues and concerns among pro-democracy-oriented groups. One conclusion was that it should be feasible to build a social democratic and environmental-oriented political bloc. This inspired several activists, especially in the environmental *Walhi* network. However, as senior activist Ridha Saleh summed it up, self-deprecatingly: we all agree there is a need to engage in politics to save the environment, but only a quarter of us want to build a political bloc with others, and even fewer, perhaps 15 per cent, want to have a Green Party of their own. So the majority prefer to continue to lobby and get involved in various deals.

It was a never-ending debate, and neither the idea of a green political bloc nor a party took off.

Stumbling multi-sectoral party

Simultaneously popular-oriented civil society activists tried to build a political vehicle for local organizations and movements all around the country. On paper, it looked like it had legs. In 2005, after years of discussions, they abstained from a platform, became pragmatic, compiled their different priorities and formed a National People's Party (PPR). The leaders' prime task was to get a sufficient number of groups around the country to serve as local units with members, to make the party eligible to take part in elections. To convince local activists that the leaders were trustworthy, they promised not to be candidates in elections, only pave the way for representatives of people's own movements. When asking conciliatory coordinator Syaiful Bahari how the popular communities, organizations and CSOs would decide on the candidates and their priorities, and keep them accountable – without a joint coherent platform – all he could say was that there would be deliberative councils.

Most member organizations represented small farmers, fisher folks, minorities and the urban poor. Bahari himself was from the major rural development CSO *Bina Desa*. The following among middle classes and workers was much weaker.

The federalist perspective worked well in a province like Bengkulu, southwest Sumatra, where the party grew out of dynamic civil society groups organizing fisher folks and small farmers in particular and could relate to a popular human rights-driven politician, Muspani, having co-founded PPR. In this context, the PPR activists served as self-confident coordinators without immediate competitors. At times I had the illusion of touring a semi-liberated area.

In many other provinces, however, the initiators stumbled. One problem was that there were competitors with different party-projects and ideological priorities. When shuttling in 2007 between two groups' meetings in Palu, Central Sulawesi, for example, the answer to my question if they could ever unite was it might happen if one of their parties managed to be accredited for the elections but not the other.

Exactly like in the Philippines, another challenge was that many sympathetic CSOs, including Bahari's *Bina Desa*, were unwilling to engage in formal politics and spend money. This was partly because of donors' prescriptions but also because open support might cause divisions in their organizations and harm local work with various partners, as well as contacts with bureaucrats and politicians in power. And many CSO leaders had their own agendas and contacts.

Several potential allies told me that by supporting PPR they would only benefit – at best – on election day, so why should they invest a lot of time and resources on such an insecure and long-term project. Usually it was less risky and costly to cosy up to already-established politicians and parties who could offer something immediate in return for votes.

PPR initiators Bahari, Muspani and others were widely appreciated, but in October 2007 they were on the brink. Despairingly, they explained: in the world of CSOs and social movements, there is no culture of strict membership, and now we need registers to qualify for the elections, quickly. As local activists are not used to that, we have to send organizers from the centre, but we do not have the funds.

The PPR failed to reach the formal requirements of local offices around the country and collapsed. The activists and associated organizations sought temporary political avenues.

Ideological party-alliance in despair

Dita Sari was an outstanding PRD popular instigator whom I first visited when she was imprisoned in Tangerang under Suharto for militant worker organizing. Several years later we met to discuss elections in the rather different surroundings of a Jakarta coffee shop displaying tempting chocolate cakes. She said: I do not have to tell you, PPR's NGO-ish congregation doesn't work – there must be some ideological glue. In face of the 2004 elections, we tried to build a broad left party (*Popor*) by inviting various progressive groups – from student organizations and union activists to *Walhi* and radical NGOs. But our leadership was not strong enough and we did not gain accreditation. Now we must try again to qualify for the 2009 elections.

Dita Sari and her companions relied on the classical road map that there is a need for a common ideology and a well-functioning national organization. To broaden the framework, their leftist cadre party was transformed into a united front, with firm leadership. This time it was called *Papernas*, the National Liberation Party of Unity. It combined the old leftist 'front from above' tactics of uniting leftist organizations, and 'front from below' idea of rallying people behind ideological demands.

Half a year later, *Papernas* activists in Palu asserted that they could make things happen, while the PPR sympathizers were merely 'social workers'. However, the *Papernas* platform included more ideological markers and general critique of neoliberal politics and economics than convincing reform proposals. And even though many Indonesian progressives appreciated Sari and her friends' commitment and organizational skills, such admirers' standard disclaimer was they did not want to be subordinated to them. Like PPR, *Papernas* did not qualify for the 2009 elections.

Bottom-up and imposed Social Democracy unfeasible

So far, our search for new routes to Social Democracy after Suharto has thus boiled down to two discouraging conclusions, much like in the Philippines after Marcos. Firstly, that the innovative efforts at building broad and democratic interest-based collectivities from the bottom-up – the first foundation of Social Democracy – proved unworkable. At least when there was also no convincing alternative to the mainstream concept of elitist democracy and no persuasive ideas of how to foster welfare and inclusive development. Secondly, that the opposite attempts at organizing people and groups by compiling their demands or providing an ideological umbrella were futile too.

Having abandoned the original idea of political blocs based on broad interests and joint policy proposals, and having failed also to assemble people by politicizing single-issues and interests or providing a party organization, with or without a platform, the pro-democrats retreated in disorder. Leading figures approached whatever powerful parties and political figures they could find, so-called 'diaspora politics'. The result was mostly devastating. In Aceh, many progressive activists lost faith in local parties. Elsewhere, Dita Sari worked with a minor Muslim party (PBR), encouraging rural activists to campaign for her. In Batang, this caused serious divisions among the small farmers reclaiming land with the support of previously discussed local organizer Handoko Wibowo. One of the major PPR organizers in Bengkulu sought refuge in Suharto's armed forces chief Wiranto's *Hanura* party. Other PRR as well as *Papernas* leaders entered media tycoon Surya Paloh's new *Nasdem* party, exchanging their organizational skills for limited benefits. Yet others made deals with infamous general-cum-oligarch Prabowo Subianto and his *Gerindra* party. In East Kalimantan, a former *Walhi* activist, Abrianto Amin, even became special assistant to the thoroughly corrupt head of the district of Kutai Kartanegara (Rita Widyasari), and quite seriously tried to convince me this was the best way of making some advances. It was a sorrowful universal pattern. Some activists retained basic principles by linking up with Abdurrahman Wahid's pluralist PKB or Megawati Sukarnoputri's PDI-P, but many of them were either co-opted or isolated too.

We shall return to this in Chapter 14, because in spite of the major setbacks, there were also signs of life. One reason was the new direct elections of political officials such as mayors, governors and presidents. They needed supplementary support from civil society, social movements and unions, a symbiosis best illustrated by the rise of President 'Jokowi' and political executives' trading of locally improved minimum wages in exchange for workers' votes. A related factor was the increasing popular demand for decent pay and employment regulations as well as for public welfare programmes in the aftermath of the Asian economic crisis, far beyond what could be provided by self-management in civil society.

But first we must return to Kerala and the remarkable reinvention of the Kerala model of human development, a major source of inspiration for new ideas about rebuilding Social Democracy from the bottom-up.

Kerala's renewal of Social Democracy

'No, let's not take all the stuff out of the car right now', my friend said. 'Did you notice the headload workers hanging around at the junction? They will claim it's their job, and that we should pay them (...) It's crazy, but it would be wrong to betray them until there is a better way of protecting their right to work.'

Finding that 'better way' is, in a nutshell, what the efforts in Kerala at broadly defined new Social Democracy were all about, from the mid-1980s until the early 2000s.

The attempts differed from those in Southeast Asia where yesterday's progressives had been defeated. In The Philippines and Indonesia the first task was to overcome Marcos' and Suharto's repression through democratization rather than resorting to Maoism or urban insurrection. Thereafter, the focus was on alternatives to elite democracy and neoliberal economic growth (Chapters 8–10). The same applied in most other contexts, such as in Brazil against authoritarian capitalism and in South Africa against apartheid.

In Kerala, however, the historic achievements had stood tall, in spite of the unseating by New Delhi of Kerala's socialist-oriented first government in 1959, and the imposition of national emergency rule in the mid-1970s. The major challenges were instead that sluggish economic growth persisted after land reform and that, beginning in the 1960s, the Left deteriorated by turning to horse-trading and clientelistic politics (Chapter 5). In short, there were serious problems with the major cornerstones of Social Democracy. But first, let us recall the achievements, setbacks and lessons.

Dynamics of decline

In the 1930s, although increasing numbers of people in what is now Kerala came together under socialist and communist leadership to push for equal civil, social and political rights in public life, they retained affiliations with religious and caste reform movements in family and community matters. This dualism has endured, so recently, for example, religious principles about access to temples have lent themselves to the rise of conservative identity politics. Why was that? Originally, when the issues of equal rights and land reform were top of the agenda, the common characterization of the popular aspirations was that every village had a socialist-oriented political committee, another for peasant and labour issues, and a third for education and the library. But this system declined from the 1960s, as the committees multiplied and became divisive. How did this happen?

First-generation Social Democracy in the North was rooted in industrialization, workplace and labour market organizing against capital, later expanding to embrace wider issues and broader politics. By contrast, the second generation in the Global South had to organize scattered labourers and peasants without common workplaces and employment conditions. Labour organizing remained weak, especially in the informal 'unorganized' sectors (i.e. family labour or, in India, with less than ten workers) where most people worked. In Kerala, however, progressives also organized informal, 'non-registered labour' – working in small-scale factories, loading/unloading trucks, carrying luggage in railway stations, etc. This was partly by the control of hiring practices by unions and professional associations (so-called closed shops). But it was achieved also by giving precedence to unifying political demands such as for decent labour laws, minimum wages and tenancy regulations. There was a saying that 'the best organised labour is in the unorganised sectors'.

After the central Congress government's imposition of presidential rule in Kerala in 1959, divisions mushroomed. The conflicts were mainly between the Congress party (and its allies) and the Left, but also between factions in each bloc (Chapter 5). In 1964 the rather ecumenical Communist Party split between the pro-Moscow CPI and the more independent CPI-M. The CPI was in favour of cooperation with Congress and joined its Kerala United Democratic Front (UDF). The CPI-M emphasized mass-based class struggle and retained most members.

By implication, the various parties and the two electoral fronts they formed competed for followers by hijacking or forming their 'own' unions, peasant organizations, credit cooperatives, educational organizations and so on – exchanging favours for votes. Several years later, towards the end of the 1970s, the CPI resumed cooperation with their old comrades in CPI-M as part of a Left Democratic Front (LDF). But the divisive pattern was still there.

In short, while a common problem among civil society activists in the Global South is scattered groups with a focus on single issues, Kerala's particular dilemma is top-down party-politicization of special interests.

Looking back, the early party clientelism of the 1960s increased when the common enemy of landlordism evaporated after the 1971 land reform. Instead, there were divisions between the plantation owners who were exempted, the tenants who gained land, the agricultural labourers who got (at best) the plots around their huts, and the fisher folks, tribal populations and others who received nothing. Labourers asked for better pay while the beneficiaries improved their education and often invested elsewhere. Agriculture stagnated and unemployment increased. Others became migrant labourers in the Gulf countries, thereafter consuming and investing in construction and speculation.

An additional explanation for why manufacturing remained poor was that Kerala never benefitted from India's emphasis on heavy industry. In the 1980s, moreover, when New Delhi contemplated neoliberal deregulation, even the protection against foreign competition of Kerala's cash crops such as rubber and tea was threatened, as was production of local necessities.

In comparison with the four cornerstones of Social Democratic development (Chapter 2), Kerala's broad social and political collectivity was thus divided; equal citizenship and democratic links between state and society suffered from clientelism; social rights and public welfare were more targeted than universal and not related to production; and land reform did not generate common interests in inclusive economic development. In other words, actual existing Social Democracy became increasingly divisive and unproductive.

Worst, most people depended on political favours and were unable to alter the dynamics. Radical political leadership seemed lacking. Kerala's ecumenical radicals seemed to be as much a spent force as the northern social democrats who adjusted to global structural adjustment, and the crumbling leaders in the Soviet Union and its satellites. Just as among the stumbling social democrats, in the North, the cardinal question in Kerala was whether it was possible to foster reinvention without undermining previous achievements.

Timeline Kerala 1980s–2001

1980s

- Economic and political stagnation.
- CSOs and political activists develop reformist agenda.

1987–91

- Left win elections with focus on development.
- Rural development focus on group farming.
- Reformists in civil society and state engage in total literacy campaign.
- Constitutional openings for decentralization followed up in Kerala.

1991

- Rajiv Gandhi assassinated.
- Left in Kerala has little time to follow up decentralization – loses election.

1991–4

- Reformists in civil society and politics campaign for group farming, alternative technologies, resource mapping and showcases of participatory local planning.
- Support from legendary communist E.M.S. Namboodiripad – others often critical.

1994

- Major congress with scholars, activists and politicians generates new framework for bottom-up democratic development – turns *the* Kerala alternative.
- In contrast, West Bengal communists opt for urban market-driven industrial development.

1996
- Left wins local and state elections.
- People's Planning Campaign launched and decentralization of politics and economy.

1997–88
- Successful initial phases of campaign.
- E.M.S. Namboodiripad passes away (March 1988).

1999
- Hurdles in implementation of campaign.
- Political crisis with Left government on direct vs representative democracy.
- Crisis resolved by allowing political party leaders more say in campaign.

2000
- Progress of campaign celebrated in major international congress.
- But, Left loses in local elections, including where campaign had been successful.

2001
- Critique of campaign intensifies and Left loses State Assembly elections.
- Traditional Left cracks down on reformist campaigners.

Change from below

From the mid-1980s, however, there was an opening for new ideas. Some communist leaders were aware of the need to encourage development, not just struggle over how the pie was split. CPI-M's then Secretary-General, E.M.S. Namboodiripad, Kerala's initially Congress-Socialist and later communist patriarch and first chief minister, convinced me he was favourable. The tall peasant leader from the rapidly developing state of Punjab, Harkishan Singh Surjeet, who would replace E.M.S. in 1992 as CPI-M leader, was also eager to renew the party–and himself, even trying to swim without his turban off the Swedish west coast.

Back in Kerala, E. M. S., as he was known to everyone, supported proponents of change who criticized the primacy of class struggle as well as the perception that Kerala's human development ('the Kerala model') had been possible without economic growth. The remarkable achievements in terms of health and education, they argued, had only been possible thanks to social and political transformation, which in turn had paved the way for inclusive growth. But thereafter politics and development stagnated. Said E.M.S. in early 1996: even after land reform, our economy remains neo-colonial. Hence, we must promote growth within agriculture and relate it to manufacturing.

Beyond the notorious power struggles among party and union bosses in Kerala, there were two principled ways of thinking about this. Both emphasized the need to promote production. On the one hand, technocrats and union leaders in manufacturing and public administration wanted to reinvigorate Nehru's state-led development by learning from the industrialization in East Asia, including China. On the other, reform-oriented intellectual activists in civil society and popular movements argued that one must help 'ordinary people' improve their lives. Back in time, they said, progressives had done this by leading the struggle for equal citizen rights and land reform. Now that the major conflict over landlordism had been solved, the next step was to promote people's own development cooperation by involving them in local democracy.

E.M.S. was sceptical, he told me, of 'romantic ideas against technological progress' but still supported the reformists. In addition, several of the reformists were themselves

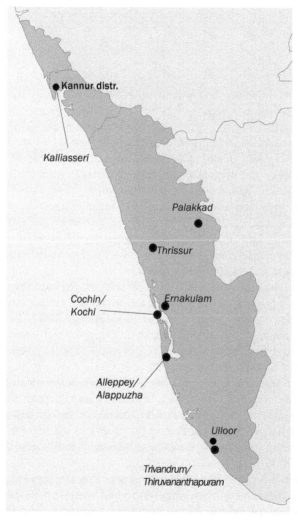

Map 12 Kerala.

renowned scholars and public intellectuals, including economist Prof. I. S. Gulati, political economist Dr T. M. Thomas Isaac, neurosurgeon and health worker, Dr B. Ekbal, and nuclear expert turned alternative technologist, Dr M. P. Parameswaran. Some of them were party members too, who linked up with former student movement comrades and intellectual full-timers in the CPI-M.

Since the late 1970s, these party activists had also built 'a room of their own', along with non-party allies like ecologist Prof. M. K. Prasad, economic historian Prof. P. K. Michael Tharakan and senior public servants, numerous educators and students. This was the People's Science Movement (KSSP) – a popular educational group that grew into a world-renowned mass movement with a green-left agenda and slogans like 'science for social revolution' and 'democratic deliberation'. KSSP's tens of thousands of core members and many more affiliates in towns and villages echoed the third pillar in Kerala's old Social Democracy – the library and education movement (Chapter 5).

Priorities

Intentionally, the reformists had no comprehensive programme or otherwise settled critique of other leftist leaders. Said M. P. Parameswaran: we are few and short of power in the party [CPI-M]. In addition, it is ridden with power struggles that rarely relate to our issues of democratic development (…) Theoretical debates would also not be fruitful (…) Besides, I am not a Marxist theoretician. It is better to offer constructive alternative analyses and proposals, plus to demonstrate in reality that our ideas are feasible through projects and village level experiments.

Those who were more eager to link up with organized politics were even more circumspect. Thomas Isaac, for one, kept reminding me, with a smile: it is stimulating being challenged to spell out my ideas, but we have many voices, and we do not want to be trapped in the competition between party leaders, so avoid quoting me at this point and just use me to make your own interpretation.

To make sense of the reformists' vision and strategy, one must therefore combine documents on various projects and add notes from conversations and visits in the field. Finally, one evening – along with the mosquitos in the Centre for Development Studies' guest house – I managed to summarize for myself the reformists' ideas and priorities by way of numerous boxes and arrows on the back of a poster. In retrospect, the essence may be distilled into four points.

Firstly, that production and productivity must increase to promote competitive agriculture, manufacturing, services and administration. This calls for cooperation among small-scale producers as well as social security for workers who must find new jobs. Leftist parties and unions must accept that more jobs will be lost if they continue to resist modernization. Actually, there was growing unity in this regard, even in some unions.

The second and more controversial point was that the increasing numbers of people outside the competitive economic sectors had to engage in joint efforts with the 'insiders'– for example by restoring the irrigation systems and introducing alternative technology and products for sustainable production and self-help. Public health and education could also be improved through popular participation. Leftist parties and unions should be convinced to get involved in this without providing special favours for their members. Orthodox leftists claimed that these views negated class struggle and were close to World Bank and liberal ideas that civil society and the poor should not ask for public welfare but take care of themselves. But the reformists countered that their points were only in line with the broad agreement to promote production in competitive sectors by combining modernization, welfare and better wages. Besides, they were not in favour of privatization in civil society but decentralization to democratic local governments (*panchayats*), which could encourage people to cooperate.

Thirdly, those who did not benefit from the land reform must be given special livelihood and educational support through the *panchayats*. Thus, they would also be less dependent on religious and caste communities and free to vote for leftist parties. The leftists, in turn, would be less dependent on horse-trading with communal candidates and parties. In Kerala's tight competition between UDF and LDF in one-person constituencies, a few percentages might tip the balance.

Finally, the reformists expected that the many people who would benefit from engaging in local development cooperation would constitute a 'critical mass', which could alter the destructive party-politicization of popular organizations and unions, and reinvent the 1930s' ethos of social democratic development 'from below' (Chapter 5). It remained necessary, however, to enforce top-down devolution of resources and decision-making according to universal democratic standards – in order to facilitate local actors of change and contain the conservatives.

While immensely attractive in my eyes, the model seemed more like a vision than a feasible strategy. I was wrong. The reformists almost made it. Here is the story.

Pioneering cases

Much to everybody's surprise, the embattled LDF managed to win the 1987 state elections by a tiny margin. The swing in its favour was mainly due to divisions in the UDF and dissatisfaction with its rule, plus speculations in the media that K. R. Gowri, the widely respected senior Communist leader with wide support among women and in her subordinate *Ezhava* community, was a possible new chief minister (she ended up as minister of industry and welfare). But the campaign against previous tactical alliances with communal parties might also have won votes, in addition to the argument for less focus on class struggle and more constructive growth, employment and welfare policies. So the reformists gained some momentum and, after lengthy debates, the LDF ended up with a dualistic approach. The majority would focus on union-interests in combination with industrial growth, while the reformists would promote decentralization and popular participation in rural development. How did the latter prevail?

Group farming

CPI's dynamic Minister of Agriculture, V. V. Raghavan, took it upon himself to implement the idea of increasing production through group farming among the propertied beneficiaries of the land reform. A few years later when the LDF was out of power again and we met for a long conversation, Raghavan was more humble and reflective than most senior leaders: ironically, our original assumption was that the tenants would increase production when they got rid of the landlords. But then the workers asked for better pay and many farmers preferred to invest in other sectors and to speculate, even in land. The credit cooperatives, moreover, had come to focus less on loans for agriculture than for weddings and the like.

When I asked why speculation was not fought head-on, the answer was straightforward: all voters were crucial for us, so we could challenge neither the farmers nor the workers. And producer cooperatives as well as new leasing arrangements were politically impossible. (…) Hence, we could only talk to the farmers' organizations and the union leaders, and promise support for joint farming, so that production was more profitable and it was less burdensome to pay better wages.

When I pointed to similarities with classical social democratic growth pacts, Raghavan smiled and added: group farming had not advanced that far (…) admittedly, most farmers were interested only as long as they got more subsidies than the profits or rents in other businesses. Similarly, the unions agreed only if their members got jobs with better pay. And their respective organizations agitated for more benefits and remained attached to different parties.

Asked if group farming could have done better by relating to decentralization and local planning, Raghavan nodded but sighed: decentralization and local planning were not yet implemented. For a start, I even had to fight to get some of my central level experts to work in the village offices and promote cooperation with other departments (…) You know, pumps may be there but not a well or electricity.

Total literacy campaigns

By the late 1980s, Kerala, with altogether some 29 million inhabitants at the time, was of course the most literate state in India. In spite of this, about a fifth of the adult population could still not read and write and hence were prevented from taking active part in development efforts, to say nothing of their difficulties in making full use of civil and democratic rights and their sensitivity to patronage and communalism. So if this could be altered, the vote base of progressive candidates might widen.

KSSP had tried literacy drives on its own but had come to realize that civil society intervention was insufficient. It was necessary instead to engage in broad cooperation and joint actions with as many social and political organizations as possible, as well as the government. In the late 1980s the LDF government in Kerala and the National Literacy Mission in New Delhi were both positive. Hence, the KSSP could design a feasible pilot project in close cooperation with its former vice president who had become the chief administrator (district collector) of Kerala's main commercial and industrial district, Ernakulam-Cochin.

The district's 2.3 million literates and 235,000 illiterates were all saturated with information, cultural performances, etc., and offered various opportunities to contribute by studying or helping others to study. The project's implementation was de-linked from the regular bureaucracy but backed up by the government and popular committees, with the KSSP as the backbone. To be able to carry out a quick mass campaign with committed participants without vested interests, the operation lasted for only a year and the KSSP itself produced teaching and learning materials. About 50,000 trained volunteers conducted a literacy survey that covered the roughly 600,000 households. Thereafter, some 18,000 instructors looked up who the illiterates were and held classes at their convenience, rather than – as usual – the other way around. There was a maximum of fifteen learners per class, as against the normal thirty. All illiterates between six and sixty years of age were included, in contrast to the standard practice of filtering out anyone over thirty-five. To afford all this and to promote commitment, most instructors and others involved were volunteers. Those employed knew they had to work virtually around the clock and were taken on secondment in order to have a job to return to.

The first part of the programme was a success story. The reformists gained much influence and an international reputation. In early 1990, the then Prime Minister of India, V. P. Singh, declared Ernakulam-Cochin the country's first fully literate district. A similarly gigantic programme for all the other Kerala districts turned some 1.5 million people into neo-literates within another year.

The programme testified to the potential of joint popular and government action. It showed clearly that it was possible to mobilize almost the entire state and society, and to make Kerala fully literate in record time. A supportive Literacy Society was established, overseen by the chief minister, cabinet ministers, senior officials, eminent personalities and representatives of political parties, mass organizations and voluntary agencies. Many local government officials, about 800,000 volunteers, and between 300,000 and 400,000 instructors were out in the field.

However, the results varied with the commitment of the district chief administrators (collectors), and the backbone was the people's committees and the local project offices. It was often difficult for activists to cooperate with the government. Most importantly, the much-applauded participatory management was limited and neither institutionalized nor firmly linked with the plans to decentralize government and administration.

The post-literacy activities were the most crucial aspect. The plan was to extend the activities of the volunteers and of the newly literate, into similar improvements of school education and primary health care. But while the campaign generated the prerequisites for democratic development, the follow-up by the state and local governments was a different matter. Moreover, the people's organizations and political parties did not take the opportunity of participating and influencing people. While most instructors were women and they conformed nicely to the cultural and religious background of the learners, the majority had no political affiliation. The further development of the campaign's civic and political potential was thus left mainly to comparatively apolitical and uncoordinated voluntary organizations, including not yet very authoritative young women.

Moreover, when Kerala as a whole was declared almost literate in March 1991, the second-phase activities were postponed to allow party activists and administrators to focus on state and national elections. So while the social activists had humbly restricted themselves to creating preconditions for more democratization and development, the government and political activists did not build on their achievement. Therefore the reformists decided that it was necessary to persuade politicians to finally move ahead with decentralization, which might open up for widespread popular participation and local democracy.

Initial decentralization

As senior Professor M. A. Oommen put it: the fact that almost all politicians claimed to be in favour of decentralization suggested that nobody was serious about it.

New Delhi had given its blessing for more decentralization, but state-level politicians and parties were afraid they might be bypassed and insisted they had 'more urgent things to handle'. In reality, nobody wanted to give up positions and powers, the trade unions in the public administration included.

Off the record, reformists were certainly worried that local elites might hijack decentralization, but concluded that since the landlords were no more it should be possible to open up for popular action. Some confessed that 'at worst a new party is unavoidable', while other radicals were more stoic, like humorous Bishop Mar Paulose: 'The Party [the CPI-M] is not much better than the Church, but at least it does something for the people.'

Unsurprisingly, there was much foot dragging, long discussions and little action. It took some three and a half years of missed opportunities before a Kerala Act on Decentralization was finally passed and district elections took place in early 1991. The Left won in most districts and E.M.S. stated that 'there should be no authority for the state government to intervene in the powers handed over to the District Councils'.

Yet, decentralization stalled. The dynamic Palakkad district Council President A. K. Balan, for one, concluded: it was not quite clear how we should go about the decentralization after the elections (…) we could have been much better prepared. So during the following three months, we were mainly studying the functions of the district (…) No, there were no clear ideas and preparations for this even in the party [the CPI-M] or the LDF (…) so we did not have time to formulate our own identity and show results before the next elections.

Nonetheless, the top leaders thought there was enough momentum and announced quick State Assembly elections. They were wrong. The LDF lost. Factors other than slow decentralization were that the UDF leaders had consolidated their divided house and there was sympathy for the Congress party after the assassination of the former Prime Minister Rajiv Gandhi a few weeks before. In any case, the setback was serious. Decentralization crumbled as did government support for post-literacy and other campaigns. Would the new ideas and dynamism endure despite losing governmental power?

Dynamic examples, close to hegemony

Although the reformist policies had not delivered votes, this was largely due to their critics' (in the party and unions) lack of interest in following up the literacy campaign and implementing decentralization. Besides, the critics themselves had not been overly successful in the promotion of manufacturing to create new jobs. So the crucial question after the debacle was who would develop the most effective politics and policies in opposition. In this respect, the critics' agitation was insufficient while the reformists had imaginative and constructive ideas. These ideas could not be fully implemented without government support, but they could be propelled outside parliament by dynamic activists and proven viable in concrete cases. Hence, the reformists gained ground, in the CPI-M in particular.

In addition to advocacy for decentralization, their three priorities were to develop alternative technologies, map local resources and showcase democratic planning. Informally, the wild expectation was that by bringing together experiences, proposals and knowledgeable activists, it would be possible to formulate an acclaimed platform for how to develop Kerala that nobody would be able to put up an effective alternative to. Amazingly, that is what happened. How?

Viable technology

Many of the reformists were green-leftist pioneers, arguing that alternative technology was necessary to sustain the environmental conditions for further development, to enable even poor people to acquire and use sustainable techniques, and to contain neoliberalism.

Being sceptical of anything with a smell of dopey hippieism, I was already hesitant on my way to KSSP's Integrated Rural Technology Centre outside Palakkad, in central Kerala. But after a few days, KSSP's smokeless stoves, solar and wind energy techniques, simple latrines, artificial reefs and advice on vegetable production, animal husbandry, water regulation and drinking water won me over. They were as convincing as, previously, the cultural workers' plans for alternative media and communication, or famous architect Laurie Baker's cheap and beautifully designed brick houses that do not require expensive air-conditioning. Moreover, rarely have I, in the midst of young activists, met such dynamic senior public administrators, engineers and researchers, happily telling me that after formal retirement they were finally able to 'work more intensively than ever with meaningful solutions and education'.

Resource mapping

The Panchayat Level People's Resource Mapping was modelled on the literacy campaign. The aim was to supplement group farming with comprehensive watershed planning, plus coordination with activities beyond the interests of the individual landowners. This called for massive recording and widespread knowledge about the local resources. Concerned scholars from the Centre for Earth Science Studies and the KSSP tried out the mapping, mobilized funding in New Delhi and gained political patronage in Kerala. The scientists would lead the project, systematize all information and map the land and water resources in each village *panchayat*. But the mapping of land-use and local assets would be carried out by volunteers organized by the KSSP, in close contact with those who actually used the land and cared for it. Many of the capable retired persons, teachers and unemployed students who can be found in the often semi-urban villages of Kerala were engaged.

As soon as the data had been collected and processed, all the parties involved would take part in the formulation and implementation of action plans – such as for land and water management, drinking water systems, flood control and local infrastructure, as well as the generation of agriculture, forestry, animal husbandry, energy, fisheries and small-scale industries. This would be the foundation for locally based integrated planning as against the prevailing centralized and compartmentalized practices. As soon as real decentralization of powers came about, the thinking went, the people would also support politicians in running efficient local government with popular participation, beyond unfruitful and divisive political, caste and religious divisions.

Predictably, conservative leftists were critical or simply not interested. When I asked around about its importance, the comment of widely respected communist leader Mrs Gowri, for example, was even 'Resource mapping? What's that?'

CPI-M as a party never approved of the mapping and the limited LDF government support ended when it lost the 1991 election. But the activists sustained the pilot projects in twenty-five village *panchayats*, established good examples and garnered numerous insights.

One that I often observed was that although the government had approved of the mapping, the ministries' local representatives – including the agricultural extension officers charged with fostering group farming – did not necessarily contribute, not even in LDF-governed villages. Another was that the elected village *panchayat* presidents lacked executive powers. And the campaigners kept telling me they felt ignored by local politicians and peasant and worker leaders, who were less engaged than expected in confronting the unproductive use of land and neglect of irrigation systems. Similarly, several volunteers without a job said the campaign was fine but wondered if there was something in it for them. Now that landlordism was history, there seemed to be new divisive interests around how to make a living. Obviously, resource mapping rested instead mainly on the dynamic action groups of committed scholars, KSSP campaigners and volunteers.

Showcase Kalliasseri

Some of these challenges were addressed in the reformists' showcase of Kalliasseri in Kannur, north Kerala. Although the local council was entirely dominated by the CPI-M (nine seats) and the CPI (one seat), landowners were reluctant either to intensify their own cultivation or to let others use it. Similarly, the farmers who were offered qualified assistance to team up and convert the swampy parts of their land into a promising prawn cultivation wished rather to persist with other activities, collect rent from outside investors and not involve local agricultural labourers who could have invested their own labour 'but might take over'. The Kalliasseri way of handling this was to have the *panchayat* leaders to provision a separate Development Society with 180 directly elected members (in ward-level meetings) and twenty ex-officio members to implement a local action plan. Thus it was possible to, for example, improve the availability of fresh water for everyone and reduce unemployment. The lovely local school, moreover, was exemplary – thanks to devoted teachers and engaged parents. But the prawn farm was a lost cause (and not because of environmental precaution).

In Kalliasseri as elsewhere, the problematic issues of different interests, economic priorities and actual control of resources remained untouchable. For the time being, leaders and activists argued they could not but convince landowners of the need to give priority to production by making opportunities as attractive as possible. For example, they would ask them to let unemployed youth and women temporarily grow vegetables on fallow land, in order to demonstrate to the owners that they could make good profits and employ some of those currently without work. Similarly, they would convince migrant labourers in the Gulf to use their savings more productively at home. The expectation was that popular bargaining power would increase with more democratic decentralization of resources and decision-making. If this came about, actors with special interests would have to listen more carefully and adjust to democratically decided plans and projects.

Gaining momentum

Summing up my information and observations during 1993, there were, thus, reasons to be excited that the reformists would be able to generate a 'definite' development model and gain momentum, but a residual scepticism was warranted.

When the invitation to an international Kerala conference a year later reached me, it was certainly a positive sign, but on my way there, I became worried. During a friendly competition for space to take a nap on the uncomfortable airport benches in Mumbai with fellow invitee Oxford professor David Washbrook, he told me more than a thousand participants might attend. We both shook our heads, wondering how it would be possible.

But it was. More than 1,500 scholars, knowledgeable activists and leaders from all-around Kerala, elsewhere in India and some other countries, discussed about 600 papers in numerous panels and workshops about insights and options – thanks to efficient use of local resources and the organizational skills of the AKG Centre for Studies and Research, supported by the CPI-M. Scholarly and political authorities, with E.M.S. in the forefront, contributed and lent their support. Trade union activists provided food, cultural workers contributed entertainment and everyone was given housing. It was a breathtaking demonstration of knowledge and capacity, in honour of freedom of expression and open discussion. Even the predominantly UDF-leaning media paid attention.

Of course, the reformists were not able to follow up with as many regional seminars as had been planned. And local development programmes were conspicuous by their absence when LDF formulated its manifestos for the forthcoming local *panchayat* and State Assembly elections. But the discontent with UDF's rule was massive. The progressive politicians had pledged to institute decentralization. The Kalliasseri model was the subject of serious academic discussions. And although the academics' engagement in further experiments was delayed, the activists themselves gained momentum and the Left made substantial gains on all levels in the 1995 local elections to district, block and village *panchayats*.

Said E.M.S. in what turned out to be our last conversation: If we win the State Assembly elections too, we shall overcome bureaucratic rule with democratic decentralization and encourage not just the followers of my party but also many others to engage in the *panchayats* and cooperatives. (...) No, I cannot tell you exactly how to get there. This is a pioneering endeavour, so one must get started before being able to analyse all the problems and options. Yet, we shall get there, even (he smiled and stuttered as always), even if I am now too old to be in touch with the daily activities.

The Left did win the 1996 State Assembly elections. In the negotiations about the new government and its priorities, the reformists had a much better starting point than in 1987. The politicians were on record as saying they would be supportive, and the activists themselves had amassed a great deal of knowledge about alternative development from below. In fact, theirs stood out as *the* development model. Before the forces of hesitancy were able to put obstacles in the way, leading reformists were able to present complete and comprehensive plans – which they did rapidly and with great tactical skill – for what should be done under the aegis of the Kerala State Planning Board. The road was now open for renewed efforts at alternative development at the local level.

Top-down campaign for planning from below

At the time, the term 'shock therapy' was associated with neoliberal policies such as in the former Soviet Union. In Kerala, however, the notion was turned on its head by the 'shock-therapeutic decision', as it was widely called, to promote democratic decentralization and popular participation. At least 35 per cent of the planning budget, up from virtually nothing before, would be devoted to investments through local governments – the *pancyahats*.

Over a few years, the centre of gravity shifted from the civic society activists and their critics in parties and trade unions to the State Planning Board, under its new Vice Chairman Prof I. S. Gulati, and its democratic people's planning from below, directed by Dr Thomas Isaac. Five years earlier, the literacy campaign in Ernakulam-Cochin had been scaled up to Kerala as a whole in a joint effort between volunteers and the government and with the backing of an all-inclusive Literacy Society. In the same vein, the lessons from group farming, alternative technologies, resource mapping and experimental local planning in Kalliasseri would now be applied in all *panchayats*, coordinated by the planning board and patronized by a grand committee of all concerned partners, chaired by E.M.S. How would they fare?

Jumpstart

The progressives' mantra was that since Kerala's land reform had not been implemented in conjunction with decentralization, as in West Bengal, it had not benefitted from popular participation. Rather it had suffered from bureaucratic and legal delays. This must not be repeated. Those with vested interests in the present centralized system must be balanced by concerned people on the ground. Yet, there must also not be any populist romantic blather about it but universal regulations. They should not be implemented by 'the party', as in West Bengal, or by several parties, as would have been the norm in Kerala, but by the Planning Board – to contain partisan politics and horse-trading.

Before applying for funds, all local governments had therefore to prepare a plan based on instructions from the Planning Board about priorities and the participation of people and organizations concerned in addition to politicians and officials. The general priorities were to increase productivity in small-scale sectors and improve the quality of public services, with special emphasis on women and marginalized sections of the population. Initially, the needs would be identified in ward-level assemblies (*grama sabhas*). Thereafter, inclusive development seminars would map and assess the local resources in historical perspective and suggest feasible sector-wide recommendations on what should be done. Well-trained resource persons, typically volunteers, would facilitate the work and help summarize the major points in development reports. The third and fourth steps were that local task forces, including expert officials, would prepare detailed project proposals, after which the elected bodies would decide on local plans. In the final stages, the local plan proposals would be coordinated at the block, district and central levels, followed by final decisions and implementation.

All along the process, there would thus be new spaces for popular participation, together with input from members of various interest organizations, officials, other experts and elected politicians. There would also be continuous training of all participants, carried out by resource persons on the central, district and local levels. Some 15,000 elected representatives, 20,000 officials and 75,000 volunteers were given training. While still insufficient, it was one of the largest-ever informal education programmes in India.

My logbook from a revisit in December 1996 is optimistic. The commencement of the campaign was swift and successful. Several of the development reports that had already reached the Planning Board read like good master's theses. The many experienced KSSP and other activists around Kerala with know-how from the literacy campaign and onwards had obviously compensated for the overwhelming need to train everyone involved on the local level and the slow deployment of competent persons from the central-level ministries.

My particular worry related to the Committee on Decentralization of Power (the 'Sen Committee', after its late chairperson Dr Satyabrata Sen), which was appointed by the Kerala government to get the rules and regulations right. The committee had agreed on general principles for decentralization about autonomy, subsidiarity, role clarity, complementarity, uniformity, people's participation, accountability and transparency. But the specific institutionalization – such as on how direct and representative democracy would be combined and social auditing carried out – was delayed. Even the activists were not very interested, arguing that this would have to follow when the campaign had achieved its aims. One of our mutual jokes was that they were 'movement maniacs' while I suffered from 'rigid constitutionalism'.

Hurdles

During the following years, the problems piled up as the questions turned from planning to decisions and the distribution of funds. When I returned in 1999, my notes based on archived media reports and local informants generated a long list of challenges. Most ministers and trade unions were reluctant to adjust to decentralization. The squabbles were typically about who would decide on what, and what would be left for cities and villages. Locally, party and union activists seemed not very interested in the public meetings, discussions and planning exercises. The implementation of the Sen Committee's general recommendations on institutionalization was deadly slow. Education and training of local staff and elected representatives remained insufficient. Unsurprisingly, project implementation was thus sluggish and ministerial programmes, such as group farming, remained separate from the attempts at integrated local planning and the promotion of production. Many complained that more funds were spent on handouts than welfare combined with production. The attempt to counter the closed exchanges between politicians, bureaucrats and contractors with new beneficiary committees was fine, but many committees degenerated at times into little more than a partisan division of spoils. Other critics added women were not given enough support to engage and that there was nothing for unemployed educated young people. The attempts at alternative communication and documentary films were inadequate, and mainstream media was filled with allegations of corruption and leftist dominance.

All these troubles might have been manageable, but improvements and hard work were held back by another dilemma. It possibly began when E.M.S. passed away in March 1998. The major patron of the campaign and one of its propelling actors was no more. Soon enough, as close research partner Michael Tharakan put it, echoing the French saying from 1789, the revolution began to devour its own children.

Political crisis

In spite of the severe challenges, the campaign was doing well enough to make mainstream politicians and union leaders of all persuasions worry they were losing out. So Congress leaders said the campaign was dominated by the Left; CPI leaders said that they were being cheated by the CPI-M (within the LDF), and, ironically, all of them – including CPI-M politicians – claimed they were being dethroned by the Planning Board campaigners.

Veliyam Bharghavan, the new state-secretary of the CPI, was furious when we met: the Planning Board is acting unconstitutionally (…) and its Vice Chairman Gulati and members like CPI-M's Isaac, who is at least an economist, but also E. M. Sreedaran, who is only E.M.S.'s son, have established a parallel government that is not subject to democratic control and is partisan at that. Now they have even engaged numerous partisan voluntary experts who bypass officials and elected representatives and reject good projects they do not like.

From the other point of view, Thomas Isaac, who doubled as campaign leader at the Planning Board and a member of CPI-M's high command, was frustrated with those politicians who claimed to support the campaign but did not deploy enough experts to enable the projects to function. Said Isaac: now the CPI in particular is even complaining about the volunteer experts who offer themselves to save the planning from below by speeding up clearance of the projects.

Insightful analysts argued that the CPI was challenging the campaign to compensate for its limited number of local activists as compared to the CPI-M. The CPI was defending the privileges associated with the political positions in local and state government it had negotiated thanks to the party's ability to tip the balance between the political coalitions. Three years later, CPI's young star, Binoy Viswam, conceded: our critique regarding the democratic principles was mainly correct, but the campaign was basically good, so we should have done more to defend and support it (…) I'm sorry about that.

What was going on in the villages?

Meanwhile it was hard to know the situation in the villages, beyond the leaders' backbiting in Thiruvananthapuram. In addition to CPI's critique, mainstream media was flooded with allegations of dysfunctionality and corruption. Was the campaign capsizing? Had I myself become too embedded?

To get the view of some outsiders, I turned to the best editors in the media, asking what they thought, based on local reports and investigative journalism. Their answer was that they really did not know because there was very little reliable local journalism. 'And, you know, there are more than 1,000 villages, so it is impossible to cover them all.' I replied that we could perhaps get together, make a sample of villages and tour around for a week, from early morning until late night. Thus, we would get a reasonable picture, in lieu of reliable surveys, which did not and might never exist. Would they be interested? No, they would not.

Hence, I asked instead the exhausted campaign leaders if they could loan out 'for about a week' one of their best-informed and critically reflective experts to guide me. Encouragingly, they were more interested than the editors. So designated expert, Rajmohan, and I, collected background data, made a sample of villages, hired a battered Ambassador ('The King of Indian Roads') and got going. We were joined by an assistant and by my wife, who helped with documentation and, from her own experience, kept asking local leaders the pertinent question 'why have all you progressives not been able to handle the issue of simple toilets, at least for women'.

Distances are not huge in densely populated often semi-urban Kerala. We drove some 1,500 km in eight to nine days, on the plains and up on the hills, interviewing and discussing with village leaders and activists in three politically different *panchayats* per day – comparing notes and analysing while on the road. Some of 'our villages' were among the 25 per cent of the altogether 1,045 that the Planning Board said were doing well, some belonged to the 50 per cent deemed mediocre and a few were from the 25 per cent of laggards. I benefitted, of course, from getting the best-possible briefing and immediate access to leaders and activists. Moreover, fortunately, they, in turn, were straightforward as they were eager to communicate frustrations and suggestions to the Planning Board expert. The discussions were as open as in an academic seminar, but often better informed. The only special favour was when we met a magnificent procession along a highway and expert-cum-driver Rajmohan, who knew of my wife's obsession with elephants, jumped out and got hold of a local leftist leader who immediately understood what had to be done, mustered his authority and blocked all traffic until the sympathetic honourable lady had taken her pictures.

Summarizing from my logbook, the good news was that the belittled campaign seemed alive and kicking. Moreover, nobody had any complaints about the voluntary technical experts that critics in Thiruvananthapuram had tried to stop. (Actually, the same opinion was expressed just before our village trip by an outstanding District Collector.) A major theme was instead the lack of sufficient training and devolution of administrators from the centre. Irrespective of political affiliations, the local leaders were thankful for the voluntary experts. Another common complaint was the lack of clear rules and regulations. A lot of time was spent searching for applicable rules, and when they were found wanting or too general, negotiations were needed on what could be done and how.

The most embarrassing situation was interviewing a woman who had obviously been selected for a leading *panchayat* position to fill the quota for females, but who was not given the chance to say anything by the men around, until I stopped them. Women were rarely in the forefront.

Concerned teachers and local experts, mostly related to the KSSP, were obviously crucial in expediting the local planning. The quality of cooperation between them and the village leaders seemed to explain much of the differences between the best-performing villages and the others.

With regard to popular participation, we were told that poor villagers kept attending meetings to gain benefits. In contrast, the middle-class residents had typically lost interest, having found that few perks were available for them. The educated youth in search of employment were also not very engaged. A common remark was that they wanted white-collar work rather than opportunities in 'simple local production'. Several village leaders also said workers, farmers and their leaders felt ignorant at times about the planning and did not participate very much. In spite of invitations, there were few union and farmers' leaders around in our group discussions.

In particular, we tried to ask about plans for production, but in my notes there are only showboating remarks from the villages that had done well, including one with a dynamic UDF leader. Otherwise infrastructure improvements and the distribution of inputs, including livestock, and the provisioning welfare dominated. In reply to my question about cooperation with private investors and industrial projects, the answers were usually negative, even puzzled, including remarks like 'we can only plan how to use public resources, not theirs'.

The issue of partisan decisions and outright corruption seemed equally difficult to handle. The common statement was that nepotism and contractors were fought but that there were new challenges to select the beneficiaries and to get them engaged in carrying out checks and balances. Depressingly, there were no signs of firm social audits.

During the subsequent years, more systematic and comprehensive studies by colleagues pointed to similar pros and cons. Back in early 1999, my general conclusion was that the voluntary experts were appreciated and necessary so that the campaign remained dynamic but it had lost its magic. While having caught the imagination of huge numbers of people in the mid-90s as *the* fresh alternative, many seemed now to have found that there was not so much in it for them in the short run, and that the plans and projects had been infected by 'normal politics'.

Debacle

Ironically, it was only when CPI-M's arch-rival the CPI confronted the campaign that the CPI-M, together with its stalwart leader V. S. Achuthanandan, came out in defence of it. But would CPI-M get its cadres and politicians to engage in the campaign and respect its aims and principles? Or would it impose its own authority, as the ANC had come to dominate the 'civics' in local South African politics?

The CPI was granted more influence through a new executive committee to oversee the campaign, in return for accepting that the volunteer technical experts were essential to the implementation of the local projects. Thomas Isaac and E. M. Sreedaran, among others, remained optimistic, but KSSP activists like M. P. Parameswaran were worried that the efforts at non-partisan local development were being diluted.

International fame and great expectations

A year later – in May 2000 – when I returned for updates and a grand conference on democratic decentralization, the campaign had obviously gained fame among international scholars of social movements and participatory politics, from the United States to Porto Alegre in Brazil. Their enthusiasm was in the air, and the Planning Board summarized achievements such as innumerable participants in *grama sabahas*, 8,000 km of new roads, 100,000 new houses, 50,000 wells, 20,000 public taps and 15,000 cleaned ponds. Recently, they had also initiated poor women's organization in labour groups, sponsored by local government rather than by private civil society. These *Kudumbashree* groups, which became a success story, could, for example, grow vegetables on land that owners had left fallow but could not lease out individually given the land reform laws.

After the conference – while international visitors toured local projects with celebrated US Professor Erik Olin Wright in a new tropical suit at the helm – research partner Michael Tharakan and I hid out on one of the new houseboats in his backwater home district to compare more disturbing observations and analyses. On the cabin top, after having moored for the night in a channel, it was easy to understand why 'God's own Country' would become one of media's 'lifetime places to visit', but also to worry that the campaign might lose out. Four months later it did.

Electoral disasters

During the conference in May, there was much optimism about the looming local elections in September. The expectation was that people would support the bold efforts at decentralization, local development planning and new projects by voting for the local progressives who had made them possible. Mainstream media and UDF leaders who claimed that the campaign was biased in favour of leftist voters were also predicting that the LDF would win. But it did not. The results were humiliating. LDF lost out even in villages where the campaign had done particularly well. Why?

Two set of factors stand out. Firstly, many people obviously felt that decentralization was a long-term project that all parties had now accepted, but that production had not improved and that there was actually not much for them in most projects. Secondly, the parties appointed their own favourites as local candidates, often at the expense of people who had become generally appreciated and deemed trustworthy in the campaign. Most of those who the LDF bosses had allowed to run again did win, but Thomas Isaac publicly bemoaned the fact that other candidates had replaced a fifth of the incumbents in highly successful *panchayats*. The usually restrained E. M. Sreedaran was disgusted: we were told not to undermine the authority of the local party units (…) but their petty party-political interests came in (…) this is not even worthy of talking about (…) I do not want to specify, you know what I mean.

In contrast, the opposition got a shot in the arm for the impending State Assembly election, which was due in May 2001. In addition to general dissatisfaction with certain educational reforms and the prices for agrarian products that were beyond the LDF's control, the UDF managed to unite its factions and Muslim partners, the LDF top brass was indeed guilty of financial mismanagement, even causing delayed payment of wages, and the UDF and mainstream media focused on the shortcomings of the decentralized planning. In short, the opposition managed to create a general feeling that the government had not done well enough. According to post-poll surveys, the LDF government was simply not popular. The result was disastrous, not so much in terms of votes but the loss of seats in closely fought constituencies.

Crackdown

Since the inception of the Planning Campaign, the reformists, together with E.M.S., had encouraged activists in parties, unions and farmers' organization – among others – to participate in the campaign by proving their abilities and ideas, and thus gain followers, rather than by providing special favours. They were to achieve this by implementing decentralization and supporting the principles of the campaign on the ground. After the electoral defeat, however, numerous critics within the CPI-M blamed the reformists for having been naïve, claiming that they had not understood the necessity of favouring potential voters to win elections and they had negated class struggle in favour of participatory development. Similarly, these critics argued, the participatory project had conceded to neoliberal ideas of decentralization and civil society, and it was based on cooperation with foreign scholars supposedly associated with the World Bank and the CIA.

The self-revealing allegations came with a purge as well. E. M. Sreedaran, fifty-five, passed away from cancer within a year, but others, such as senior campaigners and public intellectuals M. P. Parameswaran and B. Ekbal, were pushed aside or expelled. Many humiliated and – after two decades of campaigning – quite exhausted activists had second thoughts about democratic and socialist ethics.

Over the years, however, party leaders came to their senses as the reformists refused to engage in others' stupidity, authored the best analyses of the campaign and stood tall. Ekbal, for one, regained his membership and is now back on the Planning Board. Thomas Isaac proved his case by being elected to the State Assembly as well as by showing, in his home district, what local people could achieve, thanks to decentralization of powers to the *panchayats*. He was also the obvious choice for minister of finance in subsequent LDF governments (Chapter 12).

Conclusions in hindsight

Nobody interested in the reinvention of Social Democracy can avoid the experiences in Kerala. In Isaac's own recent assessment, the campaigns made decentralization real. People can now turn directly to local governments, fight corruption and promote development based on local needs. They can also sponsor productive workers' groups like the women's *Kudumbashree*. During the campaign, however, popular participation declined over time, especially among the middle classes. Integrated planning on various levels was limited. The mobilization of resources and investment in production was inadequate. Social audits were not implemented. Most seriously, the campaign was not institutionalized through sufficient deployment of staff and the creation of appropriate rules and regulations, and its aims and means deteriorated during the subsequent UDF administrations.

Isaac's points align with my own conclusions at the time, but in hindsight and in comparative perspective, some additions may be made.

Citizens' state

From the point of view of the cornerstones and strategies of Social Democracy, the most pioneering contributions related to the founding and democratization of links between state and more equal citizens in society. This included space for popular participation in democratic rule as an alternative to privatization. As compared to the liberal emphasis on less state involvement and more polycentric civil society, as in the Philippines and Indonesia, the Kerala reformists proved that both a strong state and an active civil society are needed, and that they can be combined. This was seen as an alternative to the clientelistic and partisan practices that had infected the Left since the 1960s.

However, the reformists' unresolved issue was how to also provide space for the positive aspects of party and interest organizations, which were now ignored or even undermined the campaign. The same applied to the public administrators. Unnecessary conflicts simmered between campaigners, party and interest-organizations as well as bureaucrats. Senior campaigner Dr T. N. Seema said the issue was difficult and not confronted. Nor was the combination of direct and representative democracy handled well. M. A. Oommen argued: these matters could have been discussed and negotiated during the follow-up of the general proposals by the Sen Committee [of which Oommen was a member] if anyone had paid any interest, including party bosses but also campaigners.

Rights and welfare

The contributions to the Social Democratic focus on social rights and welfare were also pioneering, especially the massive education and inclusion of downtrodden people. This recalled the historical struggle for equal citizenship in Kerala. But like the old efforts, the new ones utilized more targeted support 'for the poor only' than universal welfare policies. One result was that the middle classes, including unemployed but educated young people, shunned the campaign in favour of private solutions.

Many people agreed on decentralization and local democracy, but not on what it should be used for. Experiences from Indonesia suggest that one such focus could have been a unifying welfare reform, in which party and union activists might also get involved (Chapter 14). Such welfare measures are also not handouts but crucial to promoting productivity. Historical insights from Scandinavia in the late nineteenth century show, moreover, that local responsibility for the underprivileged became impossible when many of them left agriculture and worked elsewhere. Hence, the remaining farmers wondered why they alone should take care of the unfortunate labourers. The result was the rise of a welfare state underpinned by wider national reforms. This welfare state was universal by virtue of being inclusive of farmers as well as labourers and professionals, but also had a civic dimension so that people in many sectors and contexts could finance, support and perfect the reforms locally (Chapter 2).

Economic development

In terms of the fourth Social Democratic cornerstone about economic development, earlier efforts at social democratic-oriented growth pacts in the context of the Nehru's top-down directed industrialization and import-substitution had failed. The reformists' idea was rather to start from below. Group farming, for one, would be connected with other efforts within comprehensive local plans. This did not work, however. Given that at present the local economy cannot develop in isolation from even global neoliberalism, additional links must be made. Not even the authoritarian Chinese Communist Party was able to connect people's communes in what Vivienne Shue called a 'cellularised' economy, but conceded to Deng Xiaoping's market reforms. The social democratic alternative in Scandinavia forged strong institutional links between central and local public planning, rooted in the representation of employees and investors/employers in public governance. And at this point in time it must also address globalization (Chapters 2, 7 and 15). According to Prof. K. K. George, the reformists and the Planning Board put forward many good instructions for how to carry out local planning, but the focus was on public resources separate from private ones. Also, there was almost nothing about connecting the villages with the modern economy, including industry and the problems and options of so many people working and investing outside their home areas.

Democratic popular-collectivities

Ultimately, the prime social democratic cornerstone of democratic popular-interest collectivities and related strategies was the most problematic. The reformists certainly reinvented the educational and library movement of the 1930s, one of the pillars of Kerala's widely admired human development. Over some fifteen years – from the mid-1980s until the early 2000s – hundreds of thousands of democratically devoted activists all around the state engaged in campaigns for literacy, resource mapping and people's planning – in cooperation with government and numerous organizations of various persuasions. The liberal-oriented civil society groups in the Philippines and Indonesia were far behind. However, the wider mass movement that the campaigners tried to pave the way for never materialized.

Was it naïve to assume that class conflicts were less crucial after the land reform and that people might, thus, join hands and abandon partisan practices, when decentralization and spaces for popular participation had been established and people themselves could plan and develop local resources? Possibly yes, but not because class struggle was set aside, as extreme leftists argued. The major problem was not about the remaining class conflicts in production but that some people were more able than others to bypass the task of developing production and to opt instead for speculation (even in land), commerce and other ventures, or to work outside Kerala. As already indicated, this challenge was not addressed head on, and certainly not with the kind of unifying welfare and economic reforms, along with representation of the parties concerned, that has proved so constructive elsewhere, from Indonesia to Scandinavia (Chapters 2 and 15).

Leadership

Some of these challenges might have been addressed had the Left Front parties and mass movement activists got more involved in the campaign – by adjusting to its aims and principles rather than trying to impose their parties' dominance. The importance of leadership was also certified by the way participatory budgeting was made possible in Brazil and by citizens' engagement in South Africa. But in contrast to the ecumenical Brazilian Workers' Party, the party bosses in Kerala had deeply entrenched roots in local governance. Fortunately, though, they were not as dominant as the ANC in South Africa or the CPI-M in West Bengal, where Social Democracy became mired in deeper crisis. Kerala remains more open and promising (Chapter 12).

Counter-movements in India –
New openings in Kerala

Did others in India do better than the Kerala reformists and their foes? We need to ask before returning to Kerala and its exciting new openings. Generally, the playground changed from the 1990s. One factor was the central government's adjustment to market-driven globalization; another was the new identity politics, an outgrowth of new reservations (for representation in various legislatures, government jobs and enrolment in higher educational institutions) for underprivileged castes. In the 2000s, Hindu fundamentalists hijacked both processes. Being busy in Indonesia and Kerala, I was unable to resume close studies elsewhere in India but was supported by key informants and knowledgeable colleagues.

Timeline India with Kerala 1994–2021

1994
- West Bengal Left government focuses on outward-oriented industrialization.

2004→
- Left supported Congress-led central government (2004–14).
- Bifurcated policies of market-driven growth and social rights plus welfare.
- Resistance among workers plus small farmers and informal labourers around India.

2006–7
- Small farmer-based protests against Left government policies in West Bengal.
- Kerala Left win state election. Focus on anti-corruption and welfare.

2010
- Short of comprehensive alternative, Kerala Left loses state elections.

2011
- West Bengal Left government humiliated – first time voted out of power since 1977.
- Strong India against Corruption movement in Mumbai and New Delhi.

2013
- Local direct democracy and anti-corruption party (AAP) gains prominence in New Delhi elections.

2014
- Congress-led central government loses election to populist Hindu fundamentalists.

2015
- Landslide AAP New Delhi victory, but populist and short of comprehensive policies.
- Kerala Left wins elections to local councils.

2016
- Kerala Left wins elections. Tries to base economic growth on education and welfare.

2019
- Hindu-fundamentalists wins national elections again. Congress and Left humiliated.
- In Kerala, however, secular politics stands tall.

2020
- Kerala Left again wins elections to local councils.

2021
- Kerala Left wins second consecutive State Assembly elections.

Dynamics of demise in West Bengal

During a revisit to Kolkata, West Bengal's capital, in the early 1990s, Left Front officials celebrated increasing agrarian production and electoral victories in *panchayat* and assembly elections. 'Why are you so sceptical?' they asked, highlighting as well positive scholarly assessments. India-expert political scientist Atul Kohli, for one, had emphasized the Left government's progressive capacity – thanks to its, as he put it, coherence, commitment to constrain propertied interests, predictable rules and regulations for entrepreneurs and combination of central direction and decentralized policy implementation.

But there was a darker side too. This time several leaders and experts affirmed also that priority must be given to investments in manufacturing, because the land reforms and decentralization were insufficient to generate the necessary number of jobs and demand that could underpin wider growth. In addition, concerned analysts kept confirming my previous conclusion that the celebrated local governance was less characterized by equal citizenship and popular participation than by the dominance of the party and related local elites (Chapter 5). Hence, the electoral base of the Left might not be as solid as believed. Poor people might vote Left for the same reason that motivated people in other places to support reactionary parties – simply standing by the most powerful patron. Over the coming years, the significance of clientelism was well researched, including by economist Pranab Bardhan and his colleagues. And political scientist Dwaipayan Bhattacharya coined the concept of a 'party-society' to analyse how the *panchayats* were managed by bureaucrats under partisan control. The first and second foundations of Social Democracy – democratic popular-interest collectivities and democratic linkages between equal citizens and state – were obviously undermined.

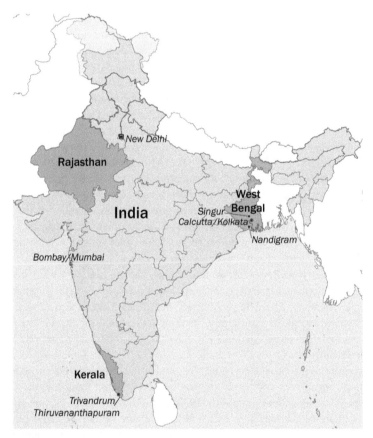

Map 13 India.

Banking on capital, not labour

While the reformists in Kerala in favour of rural development and popular planning gained the upper hand over technocrats and trade unionists advocating state-led industrialization (Chapter 11), the reverse took place in West Bengal. In 1994, the Left

Front decided officially that industrialization would be its top priority. For almost two decades, the major preoccupation had been tenancy reforms, decentralization and agricultural development. This had made life easier for many people and generated a broad voter base. Now the main leaders and experts returned, as it were, to their origins in the Kolkata unions, party headquarters, government offices and institutes of modern development. They referred to new figures (from 1992/3) about declining growth in agriculture. They concluded more jobs must be created in other ways, and since the central government had adjusted to market-driven globalization, West Bengal must follow suit. They pointed to lessons from East Asia, including China. Most importantly, they asserted that industrialization called for investors from outside and production for markets elsewhere as the risk for capital flight was high and local demand weak.

In other words, the conclusion was that since broad social democratic growth pacts between capital and labour, combining modernization and productive welfare reforms, were not practical, the Left Front promised that 'their unions' would comply and, with regard to others, that the state was fortunate to have India's largest and cheapest non-unionized labour force. As shown by sociologist Rina Agarwala, the majority of labourers, who worked in the informal sector, were particularly neglected. This applied to the rural scene as well. When the Left supported a new Congress-led government in New Delhi in 2004, and a National Rural Employment Guarantee Act (NREGA) was passed in 2005 that granted adults in every rural household the right to 100 days of waged-employment from the state, it was comparatively poorly implemented in West Bengal.

The advocates of land reform and welfare based growth resisted. In 1995, even Benoy Choudhury spoke up. The legendary peasant leader, member of the CPI-M politburo, second-in-command in West Bengal's government and Minister of Rural Development, Land Reform and Panchayats stated that 'this is a government of contractors, by contractors and for contractors'.

Chief Minister Jyoti Basu retorted that 'if that was the case, why did Choudhury remain in the government?' Hence, the only change was for the worse. Increasingly, as *New Left Review* writer Kheya Bag noted, party cadres acted like local mafias, 'collecting for the party' while enjoying immunity, thanks to police collusion. And in the end, the Left Front's efforts to attract national and international capital failed anyway because of a counter-movement.

By expropriating productive land for 'industrial development' without real negotiations and decent compensation, the Left Front acted more like the Chinese Communist Party than, for example, the 1930s' Scandinavian labour movement, which combined rapid industrialization with subsidies for the farmers. In 2006 and 2007, not far from Kolkata, the people in Singur and Nandigram had had enough. Their militant protests – also supported, of course, by cynical critics – prevented the Indian Tata Group from setting up a car factory and the Indonesian Salim conglomerate from establishing a chemical hub on occupied land. The movement snowballed. The Left Front suffered severe losses in the 2008 *panchayat* elections as well as in the 2009 Parliamentary elections, without heeding any lessons. In the 2011 Assembly elections, it was ousted after thirty-four years in the Writers' Building. Down and out – and still no convincing signs of reinvention.

New movements and activism

India's adjustment to market-driven globalization was late but spurred popular resistance and civil society activism, much like in the Philippines and Indonesia (Chapters 8–10 and 14). The old Left was sceptical. In the mid-1980s, in a small room in the CPI-M's Delhi headquarters in Ashoka Road, Prakash Karat, several years later the party's secretary-general, authored articles suggesting that the new civil society activists were even part of a new foreign-funded imperialist strategy. In fact, the Congress party, socialist groups, as well as the radical Left and their mass movements were all losing ground. In Kerala, the radical reformists reinvented the 'old movement' from the bottom-up but stumbled (Chapter 11). Thus, new diverse movements and organizations arose.

Broader labour movement

Given the adjustment to global neoliberalism, the capacity of labour to resist and build alternatives was crucial. India's structural transformation is only partial. Almost half of the labour force remains within agriculture, though only generating some 15 per cent of total GDP. Small farmers and agricultural workers are hard hit and stage protests and demand state support but are still separated from the non-agrarian labour movement. The unions then only encompass a small fraction of the labour force as a whole and are politically divided. From the early 1990s, moreover, the share of contract-labour in total employment increased even in the organized factory sector – from some 13 per cent to 33 per cent about twenty years later – and the number of workers in the unorganized sector rose too. Unions certainly resisted changes in labour laws promoting more flexibility. But over the years they have also tried to broaden their membership and issues, including by focusing on minimum wages, social security and regularization of work. Labour scholar K. R. Shyam Sundar reports that these issues, as well as the striving for dialogue between unions, employers and the government, have been central themes in several general strikes. By 2013, the CPI-M-affiliated confederation (CITU) pointed to emerging social movement unionism by claiming that most trade unions members were from the unorganized sector. The Congress government reacted by at least establishing a special ministerial committee to look into the question, but the subsequent Bharatiya Janata Party (BJP) governments have only talked to 'sympathetic unions' and practised divide and rule by decentralizing responsibility to state governments.

India missed the first train of labour-intensive industrialization and international competition is intensifying, so growth remains 'jobless'. In fact, there has been a loss of permanent jobs (some 11 million only in 2018), there are about 8 million new entrants to the labour market every year and unemployment continues to increase. In March 2018, *Reuters* reported, for example, that 25 million applications were submitted for 90,000 jobs advertised by Indian Railways. The number of labourers making a living as day labourers or self-employed has risen too, as has the number of educated youth who must work as freelancers. A shortage of permanent employers and increasing unemployment has led many of them, as reported by Rina Agarwala, to find new ways of organizing, such as turning to local governments for welfare and regulation of working conditions.

One may certainly agree with political economists Supriya Roy Chowdhury and M. Vijayabaskar that seeking state intervention for welfare and work regulations is a way of avoiding wage-related demands and conflicts with employers and contractors in workplaces, clearing the way for capital accumulation. But from the point of view of social democratic experiences, expanding the pie is as important as sharing it. So the challenge is to get government to regulate and engage employers in sharing the costs, and make new productive investments which generate jobs, as well as developing social security and unemployment schemes and regulating employment and work conditions that increase both productivity and workers' bargaining power. The Indonesian experience suggests that universal public health reforms, for example, may cultivate a broad unity among labourers in general and even the middle classes (Chapter 14). In India, the terrible effects of Covid-19 make productive-oriented welfare even more crucial.

Primitive accumulation and citizen rights

Market-driven global development did not just depress agricultural production and stimulate low-wage manufacturing based on environmental destruction. As in Indonesia (Chapters 9 and 10), it also intensified the primitive accumulation of capital by dispossessing small producers of their land and other means of production. This paved the way for profitable, often private, infrastructure projects (from motorways to dams), the extraction of natural resources and speculation in real estate. The state-facilitated expropriation of productive land in West Bengal for private industrial development was a case in point. In most instances, however, the battlegrounds were distant from the major unions and farmers' organizations. In remote areas, those immediately affected were typically either Dalits or tribal populations. In urban areas, they are informal labourers in the slums. Maoist-Naxalite groups are active in some of the remote areas. Many other activists have come together in the National Alliance of People's Movements and social and human rights groups extended support.

One bridging factor has been activists' growing concern with civil and social rights. As discussed by political scientist Neera Chandhoke, the struggle for social rights was set aside in the final stages of the struggle for national independence. Leftists preserved several of the movements, particularly in Kerala, although often focusing on regular workers and farmers, and giving less priority to Dalits and tribal groups. The Nehruvian priorities were political rights and state-led development to enable substantive citizen equality and social rights 'later on'. This kept being extended further into the future. With the adjustment to global markets, it was obvious that progressives had to start anew. Organizations for broadly defined human rights such as the People's Union for Civil Liberties, the People's Union for Democratic Rights, the People's Science Movement and the *Mazdoor Kisan Samiti Sangathan* (Association for the Empowerment of Labourers and Farmers) in Rajasthan were among the pioneers.

Politics of rights

For the civil society activists who rarely made a difference in electoral politics, lobbying and judicial activism was as crucial in India as in the Philippines and Indonesia. The Supreme Court was receptive but never proclaimed a doctrine of social rights and was unable to do anything about implementation. After the 2004 parliamentary elections, however, there was a new window of opportunities as the left of centre parties were able to form a United Progressive Alliance (UPA) with a minimum programme. This combined liberal economic reforms, plus efforts to increase productivity, with several welfare schemes during two Congress led-governments, until 2014, even though several partners, including the Left, dropped out along the way. Most importantly, Italian-born Sonia Gandhi, who inherited the leadership of the Congress party after the assassination of her husband Rajiv, appointed Manmohan Singh prime minister in order not to provoke Hindu nationalists but exerted great influence and formed a National Advisory Council (NAC) with social activists and concerned scholars and administrators to foster an ambitious social reform agenda.

In 2005, the agenda included the Right to Information Act, which mandated government agencies to release information about their activities to citizens upon request, and the remarkable Rural Employment Guarantee Act (NREGA), which ruled that adults in every rural household had the right to 100 days of waged-employment from the state. A year later, there was also the Recognition of Forest Rights Act, giving tribal communities the right to traditionally cultivated land and protecting and conserving forests, and in 2009 there was a law making education for children under 14 free and compulsory. These policies also inspired a 2011 bill on citizens' right to timely delivery of goods and services and redressal of their grievances, but it was never enacted, only applied in several states in quite watered down forms. The Food Security Act in 2013, which aimed to provide subsidised food to some two-thirds of the population, was, in spite of resistance, more effective.

The NAC initiatives were lauded as bold initiatives that provided some welfare and improvement of migrant workers' and rural labourers' bargaining power. Similarly important, they cleared the path for equal citizenship by stipulating transparency and enabling popular participation and accountability of public services through social audits and public hearings.

Much of the support was targeted, however, not universal. This was possibly one of the reasons for the limited enthusiasm among the growing, aspirational middle classes, for whom there was not much in the programmes.

Worst, perhaps, was that the rights and welfare measures neglected health and education and were separated from the liberal economic policies rather than transforming them into a welfare-based economic strategy. Political scientist and anthropologist Partha Chatterjee, and others suggested that the programmes were mainly designed to manage poverty and resentment. According to political scientist and historian James Manor, some wealth was redistributed during the time of the UPA alliance but it did not prevent income inequality and unemployment from continuing to mount.

In terms of implementation, moreover, the schemes suffered from the generally poor standard of public administration. And following the Left's poor performance in the 2009 elections, activists and beneficiaries could not do much to improve things. This impotence worsened after the BJP gained power in 2014 and even diluted the programmes. Equally serious, as well put by political economist John Harriss, the impressive schemes were more top-down than anchored in the experiences and commitments of the popular movements and organizations. Even in terms of support, NREGA, for example, was sponsored by the Left at the central level and effectively combined with the dynamic *Kudumbashree* women labour groups in Kerala (Chapter 11), but, as we saw, neglected in West Bengal. Much like the reformists' campaigns in Kerala, therefore, in spite of the potential, the programmes did not build wide enough support among people who could defend and further develop them.

Resisting abuse of public resources – Reclaiming public services

Probably, however, the victory of the conservative Hindu nationalists in the 2014 parliamentary elections was less due to the insufficiently grounded rights policies than the corruption and crony capitalism associated with the Congress-led government. The graft was especially conspicuous in the constructions for the Commonwealth Games, real-estate speculation and the distribution of mining concessions and telecom licences. Increasing numbers of people were attracted to the India against Corruption (IAC) movement with renowned social reformer Anna Hazare, and senior taxation bureaucrat Arvind Kejriwal, in the forefront. Participants included sympathizers of the social rights and welfare programmes but also, of course, cynical anti-Congress groups, even the semi-fascist *Rashtriya Swayamsevak Sangh* (RSS) and other *Sangh Parivar* Hindu-nationalist organizations. IAC's major demand was the introduction of a politically independent ombudsman (*Lokpal*) with powers to arrest and charge government officials accused of corruption – much like the Indonesian Eradication of Corruption Commission (KPK) from 2002 (Chapter 10 and 14). Huge numbers of people rallied in the streets and Hazare went on indefinite hunger strike to put pressure on the parliament and government. Thus far, the dynamics were similar to the loosely organized popular protests against crooked politicians and crony capitalists in many other countries, including those against the corrupt Brazilian left of centre politicians organizing the football World Cup a few years later and, at the time of writing (late 2020), the protests in Chile and Lebanon. In the end, Congress lost the 2014 elections – as did, subsequently, the left of centre governments in the Philippines (Chapter 13) and Brazil.

A party of their own

Some of the IAC activists had second thoughts, however. They accepted the argument that the anti-corruption agency they asked for would bestow immense powers on a few supposedly unimpeachable individuals and that, in any case, it was for democratically elected leaders in parliament, rather than activists in the street, to decide about such an institution. In late summer 2012, in a New Delhi workshop on Scandinavian and

Indian experiments in Social Democracy, political pundit and non-party activist, Yogendra Yadav, excused himself to me, saying he had to leave: because the IAC is cracking and, believe it or not, some of us are preparing a party of our own to fight corrupt politics more democratically.

The *Aam Aadmi* 'Common Man's Party' (AAP) was established in early October that year to participate in the local elections in New Delhi in 2013. In addition to Yadav and Kejriwal, the pioneers included sociologist, Anand Kumar, Supreme Court lawyer Prashant Bhushan and his father, the former Law Minister Shanti Bhushan. The main focus was simple: to curb corruption and put an end to Congress's as well as BJP's dirty politics through more democracy.

Compared to other anti-corruption movements, AAP was remarkable by not just focusing on big-scale political and business corruption but also on how ordinary people were ripped off and suffered from poor public services. Unfortunately, from a social democratic point of view, AAP neglected the building of democratic collective movements, turning directly to populist mobilization against corruption. But positively, it did not limit itself to slogans for 'good governance'. There was also a focus on the second foundation of Social Democracy – democratic links between active citizens and the state. The aim was to combine direct and representative democracy and really try to win elections.

Corruption is certainly not the root of the problems in India, and AAP did not even have a policy regarding employment conditions and inclusive development or many other issues that cannot be handled on the local level and through participation in neighbourhood and town hall meetings. Yet, as several scholars have shown, the party convinced people in the slums that poor provisioning of water and electricity, for example, was due to corruption. Moreover, the activists approached people directly and engaged in immediate voluntary assistance showing citizens how to claim their rights. They also enrolled them in selecting AAP's candidates for the elections and in drawing up the party's main action programme.

Thus, at least the committed activists bypassed vote banks based on party favours, clientelism and ethnic and religious networks. Equally important, shop owners and merchants, as well as professionals in better areas, were also interested in 'a non-corrupt force' to handle their daily frustrations with public services. Finally, the claims for more democracy were related to the growing concerns, among the younger generation in particular, over gender rights and even problems of rape. Thus there was an impressive new wave of mostly younger people involved with these and other human rights issues.

Much to everybody's surprise, AAP emerged victorious from the Delhi State Assembly elections in December 2013. Still, BJP remained the largest party and in command of the central government, which retains control of law and order in the capital. So even though AAP finally formed a local government with the support of a heavily depleted Congress, it was hard to get much done. Chief Minister Kejriwal resigned after only forty-nine days in office, devoid of an agenda for how to really implement many of AAP's promises.

AAP's subsequent effort at also reaching out all around India in the 2014 national elections was a total failure. The positive 'take home' to come from this was that its success was not just down to media hype about corruption that might carry the party anywhere, but was grounded in a movement in Delhi that was lacking elsewhere. In fact, AAP made an amazing comeback in the 2015 Delhi State Assembly elections, winning sixty-seven of seventy seats. How was that possible?

Proven potential but populist downturn

One explanation for the landslide was that people recalled the previous achievements with regard to livelihood issues; another that anti-corruption and local democracy remained on top of the agenda. AAP had no doubt proved that anti-corruption need not be limited to a technocratic middle-class agenda but can be combined with ordinary people's problems and the ability to make a difference through more democracy. But there were also two other factors. One, as exposed in the media, was that APP had engaged in listing well-fixed and 'electable' legislative assembly candidates (MLAs). Another, as suggested by political scientist Niraja Gopal Jayal, was that it had turned populist. Indeed, AAP was a good illustration of our definition of populism (Chapter 2) in terms of a thin ideology about the 'common people' and its 'general will' – identified by 'strong leaders' like Kejriwal – in contrast to democratic constitutionalism and against 'the establishment' (in this case BJP and Congress leaders) – all in combination with a rather vague commitment to 'direct democracy'.

The claim was that AAP practised internal party democracy and had no high command like the other major parties in India. But immediately after the victory in 2015 it was clear that no genuinely democratic organization existed that could handle the party's own problems. While Kejriwal celebrated the victory and blamed the failure in the national election on co-founders Yadav, Bhushan and Kumar, they in turn disclosed severe problems of internal democracy, including in the appointment of MLA candidates, and, as a result, the troika was thrown out of the party. Said Bhushan: unfortunately we allowed for Kejriwal to be given too much power (…) we should have taken greater care to ensure that there would be robust systems built in to prevent this kind of autocratic takeover of the party, which he did by getting his minions in place and thereafter using them to effectively and unilaterally take over the party and remove all dissenting voices.

According to anthropologist Stéphanie Tawa Lama-Rewal, it should also be acknowledged, however, that AAP's populism comes with an element of inclusive mediation. Elected representatives and their assistants attend neighbourhood assemblies (*mohalla sabhas*) and parents take part in school management committees. This brings to mind aspects of the reformists' campaigns in Kerala (Chapter 11). But just as in Kerala, one needs to ask questions of participation, priorities and transparency. So it remains an open question to what extent it is possible to mobilize popular support for transformative politics and build broader alliances.

When AAP lost the battle against Prime Minister Modi for an ombudsman against corruption and more local powers, focus was shifted to other matters. The party's own reputation in terms of good governance was also soiled by conflicts with the bureaucracy; Delhi's chief secretary was even harassed by AAP MLAs. Afraid of being branded pro-Muslim, the Kejriwal has also steered clear of the struggle for equal citizenship rights – even to the extent of being praised by the Mumbai-based Hindu chauvinist *Shiv Sena* party. Top priority is given instead to essential public services, especially cheap electricity, free water, improved schools and local health (*mohalla*) clinics in addition to mitigating Delhi's severe problems of traffic and air pollution. These are crucial issues that are vital in building a broad progressive alliance. In the 2020 Assembly elections, the AAP's track record in terms of 'delivering' on them was sufficient to withstand BJP's massive right nationalist campaign as well as to humiliate Congress in the 2020. The party won sixty-two of seventy seats, but one should not forget that the margin over the BJP in terms of votes was 'only' 15 per cent.

In conclusion, from a social democratic point of view, the bottom line is, thus, that AAP's transformative capacity has eroded. Populist mobilization has become a substitute for democratic principles and organization, there are better public services but little attention to development based on social rights, and the ideological compass has been mislaid.

Modi's triumph

The outcome in Delhi was nevertheless another sign that while counter-movements might make a difference on the state level, India as a whole is another matter. In 2018, BJP had also not done well in a number of other state assembly elections, but nationally the 2019 parliamentary elections were a disaster for progressives. Prime Minister Modi's Hindu-chauvinist *Sangh Parivar* machine and the even broader nationalist sentiments generated by his military campaign against Muslim Pakistan were overwhelming. AAP gained only one seat. The Left lost out in its strongholds. Congress leader Rahul Gandhi's accusations of corruption against the BJP government was easy to counter with reference to the poor record of his party's previous administrations, including under his own father Rajiv. The party's new social reform programme to create jobs and a minimum income was launched much too late and poorly anchored in progressive movements and organizations, just like the previous rights-reforms. Fundamental civil and social rights are now under threat, democracy is being undermined and repression is building. In the 2020 Bihar Assembly elections, the democratic opposition tried to unite against the onslaught. Soon after, some 250 million people came out in a general strike around the country against anti-worker policies. And farmers staged massive rallies against market deregulations. The plight of the agricultural workers was not on the agenda, but both manifestations testified to the fundamental importance of popular interests in confronting right-wing populism. Meanwhile Kerala remains the only bastion for progressives. Is it up for grabs or a possible beacon?

Opening in Kerala?

History matters. Kerala's social and political rights, the importance given to education in development and personal life, as well as the state's record of respect for religious pluralism stood tall against the attempt by Modi's central government and the *Sangh Parivar* to gain a foothold in the 2019 elections to the national parliament by reviving Hindu and caste loyalties in a dispute over fertile women's access to a temple. And in spite of opponents adding administrative and economic means, allied with allegations of corruption, the Leftist roots proved solid enough in the late 2020 local council elections: and, remarkably, the 2021 State Assembly elections too.

The Kerala Left will also not fall into the trap of West Bengal. Having clamped down on the reformist campaigns (Chapter 11), most leaders came to their senses. There was nothing like the drastic West Bengal shift from social rights as a basis for growth to foreign investments in manufacturing for markets elsewhere, and the belief that benefits might trickle down to common people. The UDF government that returned to office in 2001 clung to such ideas, but it was soon infected by the same abuse of power that gave rise to the India against Corruption campaign in Mumbai and Delhi, and the debacle in Kolkata. So almost as West Bengal's old land reform leader, Benoy Choudhury, had fallen out with his own government in 1995 because of their collusion with contractors, Kerala's similarly senior agricultural labour leader V. S. Achuthanandan criticized political and business corruption and promised to crackdown on it if he was elected. Importantly, Achuthanandan was more successful than Choudhury, giving the Left a new lease of life in the 2006 Assembly elections and for some time after.

Neoliberal dynamics and vague alternative

However, defence is one thing and progress another. By 2006, the reformists' effort at renewal by popular participation had fallen away. So aside from unity on defending vulnerable sections of the population, the LDF leaders lacked an alternative to neoliberal development and suffered from internal competition for powerful positions, which opened the way for the UDF in the 2011 elections.

The reformist campaigns to bring about change had been impressive (Chapter 11). There is now more space for local democratic action and a few pioneering schemes remain and thrive, such as the women's labour *Kudumbashree* groups, a democratic combination of production-oriented self-help and employment guarantee. But the campaigners did not succeed in building a mass movement and institutionalizing the efforts at more democratic links between citizens and state. Perhaps worst of all, they tried, but did not manage, to generate a new democratic formula for the combination of equity and growth. Already from the 1990s, the increasing rate of economic growth in Kerala was related instead to the liberalization of the Indian economy. Moreover, Kerala's 'wealth' was increasingly dependent on remittances from the more than 2.5 million migrant labourers, primarily in the Gulf countries, who were thus also at the mercy of unstable oil economies and contributing to climate change. The common estimate is that the migrants sent back about US$ 13 billion per year, equivalent to more than a third of Kerala's GDP – before many migrants returned home due to Covid-19.

The competitive power of Keralites in international markets rests on previous struggles for civil and social rights and public investment in education, but it is certainly not the underprivileged and poorly educated people who are successful in these job markets. Moreover, in spite of the inflow of cash, the growth rate (of at best 8 per cent, before Covid-19) is only on a par with other high-performing Indian states. The remittances are difficult to tax and the money has generally not been used to underpin Kerala's development. Typically, they keep being diverted for consumption, house construction and investments in property and the service sector, often generating more imports, speculation, environmental destruction and greater inequality. So, although the unemployment problem has been reduced (the reasonably reliable pre-Corona figure was about 9 per cent), almost the same number of low-paid north Indian labourers have moved south to take the construction and service sector jobs in Kerala, as Keralites have become well-paid emigrants to other countries.

There is a growing opinion within the Left of the need to combine programmes to defend the least well-off and the provisioning of social housing, with modern industrial and infrastructural development that appeal to the aspirations of the middle classes. Efforts were made during the 2016 state election campaign to discuss an alternative view of how to secure equity and growth under the new neoliberal conditions, but, until recently, the contours have been blurred.

Scattered counter-movements

Growing inequality and retrenchment of earlier efforts at building a welfare state are not the only problems. Business leaders are influential but factionalized and the rapidly expanding new middle classes have few expectations of the state, finding it inefficient and corrupt. Hence, they mainly opt for individual solutions to precarity, in addition to family and community solidarities. Sections of the old middle classes that were crucial partners in the historical achievements may still be interested in defending the remnants of the welfare state. But the most vulnerable people – between a quarter and one-third of the population, including the *adivasis* (tribal populations), Dalits and workers in the old informal sectors, agriculture and industries – are badly affected and have little bargaining power. We shall return to the changes that occurred during the pandemic.

The previously dynamic trade unions are mainly defensive and rarely present in the new dynamic sectors of the economy such as tourism and technology, which typically have informal employment relations. By now it may only be the Self Employed Women's Association (SEWA) that engages in innovative organizing. While the state government provide some welfare, Kerala unions make almost no effort to work among the large numbers of poorly paid migrant labourers from other parts of India, although there are some reports of scattered efforts by unions from outside Kerala.

This does not mean there are no protests on the part of hard-hit people in Kerala. Many *adivasis* agitate for land, some fisher folk claim basic rights and numerous people resist dispossession and environmental degradation of their land and neighbourhoods. But these actions tend to be scattered and localized. Some support is coming from various political parties and civil society, but the outcome is rarely positive. There is certainly new activism in civil society, including campaigns by KSSP against the high prices paid for medicines by ordinary people, popular attempts at organic cultivation and support for pioneering local government efforts to clean up cities. There are also protests against corruption and the moral policing by conservative Hindu and Muslim communities. Women are increasingly active. But most actions are local, scaling up is difficult and coordination beyond what is possible through commercial and new social media has been poor. The main exception is the *Kudumbashree* groups. In short, the mainstay of social democratic advances in Kerala – broad democratic organization and movements – has been weakened.

Undermined state–society links

The critical factors involved in the recent transformations and efforts at change in Kerala often relate to the linkages between state and society. The main connections remain personal, via lobbying of mistrusted parties and leaders. Confidence in public governance has been low for many years, and the Congress-led government that entered office in 2011 in Kerala was particularly ridden with corruption. Criticism against this mismanagement and abuse of power was the major factor behind the return to power of the Left in the 2015 elections of local councils and the 2016 State Assembly elections. The CPI-M in particular is far better organized than the UDF-affiliated parties, which mainly rely on personal networks and clientelism. But the Left parties are centralized and trapped by a culture of loyalty and obligation in return for favours. In short, while people can now take their problems to quite powerful local governments, and while spontaneous protests, civil society organizing and social movements remain common, their room for manoeuvre is constricted. So in spite of some rethinking of the problems of combining representative and participatory governance, not much has changed with regard to the persistent dominance of parties and politicians. This applies even to self-help and residential groups and town hall meetings. While local government institutions are now in place, they remain weak and little has happened without the intervention of members of the legislative assembly (MLAs) and state-level ministers. Since 2016, the new Planning Board has been addressing this. Said member K. N. Harilal: one of our top priorities is to make up for the slow institutionalization of democratic decentralization.

Positively, the local governments have been crucial during the flood and the pandemic. And while it is true that much of the popular participation that was introduced during the previous People's Planning Campaign through ward-level assemblies (*grama sabhas*) and development seminars (Chapter 11) has withered away, there are signs of renewal here too.

New focus on local public action

For many years, the mounting problem of insecure employment relations and the need to institute social security protections did not generate the renewed interest in public welfare systems in Kerala that has come about in, for example, Indonesia and East Asia. The various parts of the Left certainly wanted to remedy this situation, but the priorities remained unclear. Meanwhile some from the vulnerable sections of the population are abandoning the Left and returning to communal solidarities – hence, the BJP is making inroads, including among *Ezhavas* who have often voted Left.

However, as already indicated, the severe floods of 2018 and 2019, the arrival of Covid-19 in early 2020, and the return of huge numbers of migrant labourers have all altered the situation. The decentralized governance and public action that progressives had fought for since the 1980s (Chapter 11) now proved indispensable. It is true, for example, that the landslides in particular might have been prevented had the resource mapping of the 1990s been consistently implemented, but the local public action was unquestionably vital in the rescue and relief operations and containment of the virus. The pandemic, moreover, was fought extremely well from January until May 2020, proving to the world what was possible with decentralization and popular participation. Left Front Health Minister Mrs K. K. Shailaja, a well-read former secondary school teacher, even gained international rock star fame along with her medically trained team for containing community spread of the virus.

Crisis calls for coordination

By late May, however, the situation changed again. The local governance and popular engagement were insufficient to handle problems that called for wider action. This was when conflicts arose with the central government and local opposition over how to check the medical status of returning migrants and handle massive data; when popular trust was crumbling and the state government felt it had to deploy the police to enforce instructions; and when wider community infection called for testing and tracing beyond local clusters. Equally important, growing numbers of people lacked jobs and livelihoods, adding to the already high rate of unemployment, especially among educated youth.

In other words, the dilemmas of inadequate links between central and local government, as well as between the local and wider economy, and popular organizations, returned to the foreground, not having been fully addressed during the democratic decentralization and People's Planning Campaign of the 1990s and early 2000s (Chapter 11). As is Scandinavia during the region's rapid industrialization – when the local space proved inadequate in the provisioning of relief to the increasing numbers of impoverished labourers, and when popular self-help was also insufficient – there is a need for universal welfare state-programmes. The same applies to comprehensive planning, locally as well as on the state level. It cannot just encompass local public resources, but must also consider wider markets and private undertakings.

These were tasks that we could not solve during the People's Campaign, said B. Ekbal, now back on the Planning Board: the board is in charge of public investments (...) the enrolment of other actors is up to the ministers, and to public bodies, such as hospitals, which can mobilize funds from other sources too (...) it should be better coordinated.

Comparative challenges of coordination, and of combining welfare and growth

The unresolved question was how to facilitate better coordination. It is incredibly difficult to strengthen the weak ties between local and state government, and the local and wider economy and the popular organizations. As discussed earlier, not even the authoritarian Chinese Communist Party was able to connect the dispersed people's communes (Chapter 11). A social democratic orientation calls for good organization of the most crucial actors, from capital to labour, and democratic channels to counterbalance overly dominant political parties and politicians. Political organization and leadership are certainly not a problem as such, as long as the vested interests of the parties and leaders are kept at bay. But in view of social democratic experiences, it is also necessary to institutionalize democratic channels of autonomous representation in public governance of significant interest and issue organizations. This includes labour organizations but also investors and employers and a number of associations focusing on vital issues such gender inequality and environmental degradation. The problem in Kerala is, of course, that many of them are close to assorted political parties.

In terms of combining welfare and growth, moreover, Kerala has essentially bypassed the stage of industrial development (that never really was achieved in the 1950s and afterwards) in favour of post-industrial activities. The state has little of the Global North's broad labour movement and production-oriented class of employers that demonstrated themselves to be capable of negotiating social pacts allowing for the combination of growth and welfare, facilitated by the government. As a result, Kerala needs to negotiate and regulate the current phase of rapid uneven development that, if left unchecked, threatens to dispossess the weakest sections of the population of their land, livelihood and housing without substituting decent alternatives. Many workers and members of the middle class may also benefit from a new pattern of development.

The Left Front government from 2016 has been comparatively unified behind efforts at appealing to different constituencies – with reinvigorating, on the one hand, public health, education and small-scale local development initiatives in the interests of, primarily, less well-off people, and, on the other, backing industrial and other modern development projects which acknowledge the aspirations of the educated middle classes. However, in view of similar ambitions elsewhere – such as during the United Progressive Alliance in central Indian politics, the centre-left government in the Philippines before Duterte (Chapter 13), the related efforts in Indonesia and the more politically fraternal regimes in South Africa and Brazil – there are obvious challenges involved in combining liberal economic growth that accedes to global demands and welfare measures in its backyards.

These common obstacles are not confined to insufficient productive investment and impartial administration of revenues during a commodity boom, such as in Brazil (and even worse, of course, in Venezuela), or for that matter the way remittances are dealt with in Kerala. The welfare measures that have been implemented have often been limited to handouts for the poor. There is a good case for a universal basic income – not least to address the socio-economic problems due to the pandemic. But only to complement, not substitute for, collective action in favour of social democratic transformative reforms, which can generate good jobs (including in welfare sectors) and enhance ordinary people's wellbeing and bargaining power, as well as their health, skills and other aspects that are crucial for inclusive and more competitive production.

Some synergies between welfare reforms and growth can certainly be designed by states with centralized apparatuses and undisputed authority, as recently demonstrated in East Asia during the struggle against Covid-19. But social democrats prefer liberties and democratic governance. Historically, the necessary agreements between capital and labour and other involved parties, such as in Scandinavia, presupposed powerful democratic interest organizations, and, of course, a supportive government. Despite an otherwise unusually broad labour movement, South Africa suffers from poor organization and representation of informal labour, the absolute majority of the population. In countries where organization has been even weaker, a common shortcut has been the mobilization of counter-movements behind reformist populist leaders who oppose various strands of neoliberalism, followed by their supposedly direct-democratic governance in co-operation with 'friendly' movements and associations. Jokowi's rise to power in Indonesia is an example of this process in action (Chapter 14). Typically, however, there have been more populist mobilizations against neoliberalism than broad campaigns in favour of well-designed and anchored strategic reforms. This, in addition to insufficient interest organization and representation, has opened the space for right-wing nationalists to employ similar populist methods in order to hijack sections of the counter-movements. Duterte in the Philippines, Bolsonaro in Brazil and the undermining of President Jokowi's reform agenda in Indonesia (Chapter 14) all testify to the strength of this reactionary co-option of mass hostility to neoliberalism.

Potentials for renewal in Kerala

Contexts differ, but several of the challenges are similar in Kerala. It was a mighty effort to give life to the People's Planning Campaign, but this time the tasks may be even tougher. Moreover, the central government is unfriendly, revenues are insufficient and taxation is difficult. Cooperative banks have been merged but, all the same, more funding is needed. And private resources among investors, as well as migrants' remittances – severely depleted during the pandemic – must be mobilized in comparatively risky ways to sustain welfare during the pandemic and win elections. What should be done?

The participatory local planning did not manage to connect to private actors with the wider economy and politics. The Planning Board (or for that matter a party or chief minister) cannot mimic the efficacy of heavy-handed developmental states in designing and enforcing comprehensive plans inclusive of both state and private priorities. The professional associations and interest-based organizations among labourers, as well as those encompassing employers/investors, are too narrowly based and not coherent enough to negotiate the combination of productive welfare reforms and investment.

In a November 2018 public discussion in Thiruvananthapuram when I tried to outline the potential for social democratic-oriented development, several participants thought the arguments overly optimistic. My contention was that Kerala, in comparative perspective, might have the capacity to handle the roadblocks which like-minded partners elsewhere have stumbled over. Firstly, Kerala can benefit from the historical legacy of two periods of pioneering and successful formation of broad democratic alliances by combining citizen rights and interest-based politics. There will be no repetition of the Left's disaster in West Bengal. Secondly, Kerala is blessed by a quite widely accepted emphasis on equal citizen rights (at least beyond the broad private-family sphere that is harmful for women in particular). This includes principles of active and independent citizens as well as democratic direct links between state and society via parties and interest and citizen organizations – in contrast to mediation through communal organizations and their strongmen. Thirdly, Kerala's recent efforts at equity and growth have not been dependent on an unreliable commodity boom, which elsewhere has kick-started primitive accumulation and corruption, along with landlords and oligarchs. Kerala in fact may rather benefit from having uprooted landlordism some time ago. It can also reap the rewards from having fostered public health, with its positive impact on a productive economy, education, which is more difficult to monopolize, and tourism, which may be regulated. And thanks to democratic decentralization, local health services have also proved crucial in helping people cope with recent environmental disasters and the coronavirus. Thus, Kerala initially stood out as a model case in India and elsewhere for how to combat the floods (and later the pandemic) in both a fair and efficient way. But there is an urgent need for better links between local and central governance, the local and wider economy, as well as between public and private plans and investments.

My conclusion was, therefore, that the prime potential in Kerala is the capacity to take advantage of the historical experiences and lessons in promoting sustainable and inclusive development based on knowledge. Inclusiveness, however, calls for welfare reforms and investment in education and training. Kerala has relatively more children in private schools than any other Indian state. The educational investments need to be attractive for both middle classes and, by now, increasing numbers of less-privileged Keralites. The latter must also be brought into education-based production and services, within the state as well as in consultancies outside it. Thus social rights and welfare – the third foundation of Social Democracy – can both unify people and spur production. Admittedly, the necessary revenues and investment are particularly hard to mobilize when an unfriendly central government tries to starve dissident state governments, Kerala in particular. Current interest rates may be low, but loans and other ways of mobilizing resources come with the need to cooperate with many private actors, from migrant workers to entrepreneurs, as well as requiring coordination between local level investments and wider markets.

A year later, Finance Minister Isaac's 2020 budget was a promising step in this direction. But then came the pandemic. Initially the Left was strikingly successful in combatting many of the new challenges by way of local public action, but by May 2020, as noted above, it seemed daunted by the overwhelming problems. So maybe those who were sceptical about the chances for social democratic-oriented development were right, after all?

New roadmap?

Indeed, from the mid-2020 onwards, there were good reasons to be concerned about the problems of improving on the initially successful local public action to contain Covid-19, provide relief and foster development. The problem was not only administrative and organizational coordination of selected lockdowns, and large-scale testing and tracing to fight the rising community transmission of the virus, which had further intensified during the extensive travel in advance of the *Onam* harvest festival.

Equally important, many more people were suffering from precarious conditions with insecure livelihoods and fewer jobs, which added to the already high rate of unemployment, especially among educated young people.

Meanwhile the hostile right-wing nationalist government in New Delhi made every effort to reduce the capacity of the Kerala government. The means included questioning the legal basis for entering the international investment market to raise funds, suggesting mismanagement of local banking and Covid-19 health data, and exposing a gold smuggling scam that undermined confidence in Chief Minister Pinarayi Vijayan's principal and private secretaries. These accusations seemed to harm the Left's chances in the run-up to the elections in December 2020 for around 2,000 local councils.

The blessing in disguise was, however, that the political challenges were best handled with intensified state-wide measures to fight the pandemic and, especially, to launch social and economic reforms to guarantee people's livelihoods.

The welfare and development programmes in themselves were certainly not enough to fight Covid-19 as such. With the elections on the horizon, it was even hard for politicians to insist on strict discipline, and party political priorities and a lack of unifying overall policy consensuses disrupted local action against the pandemic. But the focus in the electoral manifesto on reforms which combined state financed and coordinated welfare, with job-generating production reforms, and dependent on local contributions and implementation, was no doubt a major factor behind the compelling victory. Another factor was the inclusion of liberal allies and the trust in candidates with good records from joint social and development work. For example, 70 per cent of the seats reserved for women in the local bodies are reported to have been won by *Kudumbashree* members. The Left sustained its remarkable results from 2015 (with a clear majority of the village and block *panchayats*, even winning eleven of the fourteen district *panchayats*, and although triumphing in less than half the number of municipalities making crucial advances in the major cities).

Just as important, the politically successful combination of, on the one hand, welfare and inclusive development policies, and, on the other, state-level direction and local contributions, paved the way for the drafting of an even more visionary long-term budget. This was backed up by the State Planning Board and vigorously presented to the parliament by Finance Minister T. M. Thomas Isaac, highlighting the major points in his three-hour long speech by reciting schoolchildren's poems about a better Kerala. In contrast with the 1990s' efforts at local priorities, self-help and resource mobilization, the new focus was on supplementing local public action with, for example, electronic platforms for regulated gig jobs, combined with major state-driven investments in infrastructure, education and training, along with private investments in value-added production. The nub of the new policy was the potential of educated youth and the promotion of internationally competitive and environmentally sustainable 'knowledge-based development'. This was an economic strategy beyond reliance on remittances from migrant labourers in unsustainable oil economies in the Gulf countries.

This served as a basis for the manifesto for the April 2021 State Assembly Elections in terms of what Isaac calls 'a new edition of the Kerala model'. Remarkably, the momentum was sustained, in-spite of the pandemic, and the progressives did more than well in the State Assembly Elections, enabling the Left Front a second historical term and thus the chance to further develop and implement its long term plan, at best setting an example for the rest of India and the world.

Comparative encouragements and worries

Promisingly, the Kerala opening is reminiscent of those in other contexts. Even in parts of the Global South such as in Indonesia, with weaker and more fragmented civic and popular organizations, it proved possible for a decade to build broad local and national alliances of unions, informal labour groups as well as CSOs and politicians behind comprehensive welfare and development reforms. The best example is probably the successful campaign for the national public health reform in the early 2010s (Chapter 14).

Yet, there are also worrying lessons from the Indonesian and international developments. One is that there need to be a chain of transformative reform programmes. In Indonesia, the leading actors and related think tanks did not prepare a follow-up reform. So the broad alliance and transformative process came to a halt (Chapter 14). Another obstacle is that paradigmatic models call for adaptation in other settings. Among premises, the social democratic growth strategy from Scandinavia, also adopted by the International Labour Organization, presupposes good capacity to create new jobs when old ones disappear as a result of social pacts to combine improved productivity with better conditions for the employees who keep their jobs. Consequently, the model is less fruitful in countries with huge numbers of informal labour and unemployment, tragically illustrated by South Africa. In these contexts there must also be forceful supplementary policies to generate more – decent and important – jobs (Chapters 2 and 16). Encouragingly, this seems be a priority in the new Kerala plans.

The other major worry, however, applies to Kerala too. This is that there must be inclusive negotiations with all concerned major partners, to design, finance and implement welfare-based development reforms. This includes employers as well as unions plus organizations among informal labour and professionals. In addition, the policies need to be comprehensive rather than separate. Talks about minimum wages, for example, are harder if one cannot also consider employment conditions, job creation and welfare programmes.

This did not happen in Indonesia (Chapter 14). There was no framework to negotiate general agreements on wage levels, employment conditions and welfare measures. And there was poor representation of the parties concerned, especially of unions and organizations representing informal labourers. The unfortunate substitute was leftist and rightist populism, and transactional deals, followed by confrontations and losses for the progressives in particular (Chapter14).

Kerala might

In Kerala, the struggle in the 1990s for decentralized public action and development was guided by the State Planning Board, which provided instructions about consultations and broad agreements on local priorities. There was less focus on comprehensive policies and planning. Beyond public investments, it was difficult to also consider private assets and resources, as well as the economy outside the local settings and coordination of local popular action in wider arenas.

Fortunately, some of this may now be addressed in the context of the state-wide welfare and economic reforms that are indicated in the five-year budget plan. In other words, the crucial links between local and wider government, economy and popular actions may be built in the very process of designing and implementing the reform programmes. These are policy-driven advances.

The remaining challenge is to also create a format for partnership governance of the comprehensive reform programmes. How shall all concerned partners participate and contribute. There is no forceful developmental state at hand, as South Korea once was. Are there democratic alternatives?

One dilemma, then, is the scattered and party-partisan character of interest and issue organizations on the labour, as well as capital, side. The feasibility of the Scandinavian model of social partner representation and public commissions is thus partly diminished (in any case now undermined in Scandinavia itself by neoliberal governance). Another challenge is how to improve the welfare and education system, so that they become more supportive of production, as well as transformative. Yet another hurdle is represented by the unavoidable negotiations on finance and investments. This is particularly sensitive in view of the West Bengali Left's concessions to big capital and subsequent demise, analysed earlier in this chapter. In addition, Kerala has no currency of its own, limited rights to tax and borrow, and is, as we know, constrained by an unfriendly central government.

Innovative solutions are necessary in these respects, involving partnerships between public and private actors. As widely admitted by governments of different complexions around the world, the pandemic has made it necessary to stimulate crisis-ridden economies by different means, even by debt-financing, as long as it does not cause high inflation and is for 'self-liquidating' social and economic investments only. But the deals and social pacts need to be democratically anchored – among people in general as well as entrepreneurs. In the case of Kerala, this democratic ballast needs to be particularly weighty in order to weather the predictable storms from New Delhi. In my understanding, these issues of governance have been given little attention as compared to the economic and educational priorities, including in early 2021 at the State Planning Board's otherwise comprehensive congress 'Kerala looks ahead'. Given the progressives' previous emphasis on democratic participation, it would be a contradiction of sorts, and a possible source of instability, if the necessary negotiations and agreements were to rest solely with individuals within the government, leading party and expert committees.

Inconclusive left-of-centre politics
in the Philippines

It is time to return to the Philippines, now in the late 1990s. After the elite had captured the 'people power revolution' in 1986, the democratic Left tried to reinvent from the bottom-up the first foundation of Social Democracy of democratic popular-interest collectivities, but faltered (Chapter 8). One obstacle was the dearth of common class interests and ideology among the common people. Another was the fragmentation of issues and civil society groups. Yet another was the difficulty in combining community organizing with political aspirations and struggles based on diverse interests in production and workplaces, such as among workers and small farmers. Indonesia records similar experiences (Chapters 9 and 10).

Judging by the similarities, it seemed unworkable to build new broad democratic organizations from the bottom-up – at least when there was no convincing and unifying alternative to the mainstream concepts of elite democratization and market-driven development.

Even the herculean efforts in Kerala by way of popular campaigns and decentralization of public resources and governance stumbled over related problems (Chapter 11). In this context, as well as during the experiences during the national Indian left-of-centre government 2004–14 (Chapter 12), it was also clear that targeted social rights and welfare schemes did not foster broad movements.

Equally problematic, the public schemes tended to complement, rather than transform, market-driven development, which thus became increasingly exploitative and corrupt. The New Delhi-based Common Man's Party (AAP) was remarkably successful in substituting populist mobilization against the corruption of public services for more challenging collective organizing. But the populist fast track was at the expense of democratic governance and principles, as well as an agenda for transformative social and economic reforms (Chapter 12).

As we return to the Philippines, the challenges of new Social Democracy thus began to converge over time and space and seemed to be mounting. Before moving on, however, we may also recall the promising news from the Philippines in Chapter 8.

The scattered leftists in trade unionists and in civil society outside the Maoist movement had managed in 1998 to establish a coalition party, *Akbayan*, which stood out as *the* left-democratic alternative. Immediately it won a seat in the parliament through the new party-list election of 20 per cent of the House of Representatives –

the lower house in the Filipino system. The question for this chapter is thus whether these advances opened up for new ways of realizing the difficult reinvention of Social Democracy.

Timeline the Philippines 2000–2019

2000
- Populist President Estrada accused of serious corruption.

2001–2004
- Estrada ousted in 2nd 'People Power' revolution.
- No-progressive transition government. Vice President Gloria M. Arroyo takes over.
- Maoists 'tactically' supports Arroyo, thus gaining favours.
- Maoist harassments (including assassinations) of leftist critics intensify.
- Pro-Estrada groups fail with a 3rd 'People Power' uprising.
- Years of protests, street battles and conspiracies follow.

2004
- Democratic left does well in elections.
- Arroyo accused of cheating in elections.
- Widespread protests follow, now inclusive of Maoists too.
- Radical protests not supported, as previously, by liberals and many in middle classes.
- Arroyo consolidates conservative regime.

2007→
- Democratic left's efforts to build local base suffers from focus on protests in Manila.
- Setbacks in mid-term elections.
- New *Akbayan* strategy of cooperation with liberals to get into government and senate.

2010
- 'Noynoy' Aquino III wins presidential elections. *Akbayan* joins coalition government.
- *Akbayan* leaders gain strategic positions in government.
- Focus on non-corrupt market driven development plus land-reform and welfare.

2013–2016
- Reforms delayed.
- Some liberal and social democrat losses in mid-term elections.
- Outside criticism and conflicts in *Akbayan* over slow reform politics – defections.

2016
- Liberals and left lose elections.
- *Akbayan's* Risa Hontiveros gets into senate.
- Strongman Duterte wins presidential elections, initially with Maoist support.

2019
- Duterte encourages extra-legal killings against victims of drugs.
- Further losses for liberals and leftists in mid-term elections.
- Duterte's candidates and he himself retains popular support.
- Democratic left contemplates new priorities.

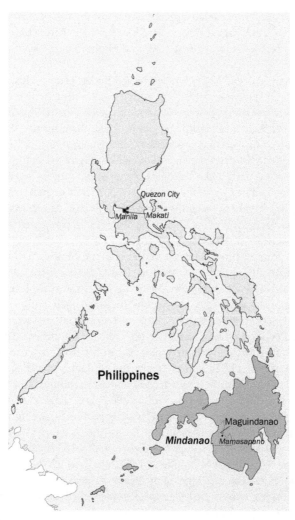

Map 14 Philippines.

Failing insurgencies

It did not start well. The friends of *Akbayan* who were less patient made a parallel attempt in 1998 at fast track populism when they lined up behind nationalist senator Joseph Estrada's bid for the presidency. Initially they were successful. Several progressives gained important positions in the new administration. Soon enough, however, the populist project deteriorated and capsized in October 2000 when Estrada was accused of an illegal gambling racket.

As the impeachment trial against Estrada derailed, rival traditional politicians, along with moderate social democratic technocrats and civil society organization (CSO) leaders (Chapter 8), as well as leftist *Akbayan*, agreed to oust him in a second 'people power' demonstration in early 2001. This time the above-ground Maoists joined too. My radical friends said a progressive transitional government was in sight. But the police and army helped conservative Vice President Gloria Macapagal-Arroyo to take office, while Estrada was first convicted of plunder and later pardoned – by Arroyo.

Unsurprisingly, the abuse of power continued under Arroyo. This paved the way for the military to return to politics. In addition, President Arroyo also honoured Maoist support in her rise to power. Maoists were invited to take important positions and she endorsed their new legal party, *Bayan Muna*. Its chairman, Satur Ocampo, told me the party was a serious proposition, but remained 'tactical', indicating that the underground Maoist party was in command. With Arroyo's endorsement and the backing of the Maoist party and combatants, *Bayan Muna* gained good numbers in the party-list elections, while opponents were harassed. There was even a series of killings of defected Maoist members, including union leader Popoy Lagman in February 2001. The purge lasted for several years. Dissenting leaders who had joined left-democratic rival *Akbayan* were on the hit list too.

There were years of protests, street battles and conspiracies. Pro-Estrada forces tried an unsuccessful uprising as early as March 2001. Then, in 2003, officers launched a mutiny against corruption, including inside the army. Principled liberals and social democrats of various convictions sustained their critique and protests. Some progressives tried to resist from inside the administration, such as civil society activist and senior administrator Karina Constantino-David, chair of the Civil Service Commission. But increasingly many critics had to act from outside. They exposed new fraudulent activities by President Arroyo and her family and friends. Meanwhile *Akbayan* stood tall against the Maoist harassment and continued to expand its local bases and number of affiliated mayors. In the 2004 party-list elections it did well by stressing the primacy of democracy and 'good governance', gaining the maximum three seats in the House of Representatives.

Less than a year after the elections there were credible revelations suggesting that Arroyo had even rigged the 2004 presidential elections in which she claimed victory. A broad mass movement labelled 'Fight of the People' (*Laban ng Masa*) was launched to impeach and oust her too. As the legal process was blocked, the mass movement had to take to the streets, yet again.

Unfortunately, however, as former revolutionary-turned-senior-scholar Nathan Quimpo argues, the focus on building municipal strongholds between 1998 and 2004 was now overrun by the urgent demonstrations and insurgency plans in Manila. In that process, moreover, some of the democratic principles that progressives had fought so hard for were lost. While liberals and moderate social democrats in the cabinet failed to muster a majority to replace President Arroyo, the new aim of the mass movement was expressed in terms of a 'revolutionary government', and the means included cooperation with coup plotters as well as Maoist activists. A wider alliance against corruption but *for* democratic governance was thus unfeasible. Sections of the democratic Left were at loggerheads, again. Two attempts were made at combining military mutinies and mass demonstrations (February 2006 and November 2007). Both failed. Instead, conservative rule was consolidated under Arroyo, who not only dominated traditional electoral politics but also corrupted the party-list elections by forming proxy organizations and ensuring they were eligible to run. *Akbayan* itself had focused on the protests in Manila at the expense of local mobilization. The result was a setback in the 2007 elections.

Losing ground

Akbayan's idea of combining a national presence with breakthroughs in a number of local strongholds – akin to the Workers' Party under Lula in Brazil – had thus failed to make headway. In addition to the prioritizing of the protests in Manila, another reason was that to make a difference in the party-list elections with a single national constituency, the party had to mobilize and negotiate votes around the country.

In addition, progressive CSOs were weak outside the large cities. There were certainly sustained efforts at training activists for 'good local governance' on the *barangay* (village) level (Chapter 8). But there were problems there too – how to relate this internationally funded civil society vision with organized politics and broader union and farmer action, plus how to scale it up to the municipality level? Especially as foreign funding began to dry up. In lieu of alternative reform-proposals for various activists and movements to unite behind in what could have been *Akbayan* strongholds, groups and communities remained divided in their affiliations to various political candidates and parties. The dilemma applied generally – from the supposedly non-political *barangay* administrations to the municipalities and the local development councils (stipulated in the Code for Local Government). All of them were thoroughly embedded in the local political economy of symbiotic political bosses and oligarchs.

Another roadmap

Those were the years when I could not follow the developments closely, being committed to democratization in Indonesia. More than a decade later, therefore, it was enjoyable indeed to rejoin with former *Akbayan* President, Ronald Llamas (Chapter 8), for a discussion of what had really happened. This was in late 2017 and given Duterte's anger over criticism of his mass killings of poor drug addicts, the arrangements for our reunion had again to be secretive. We met in a grand hotel lobby in the Makati business district, in front of a certain Christmas tree, proceeding through backdoors to a huge shopping mall and a privileged empty upstairs terrace. 'Here we can talk', smiled Llamas: you remember how *Akbayan* was cornered in the 2000s (…) We handled the Maoist harassments, but could not finance our work by collecting their kind of 'revolutionary taxes'. Moreover, the party-list was undermined by the regime plus limited to a maximum number of three seats per party. So we had to develop another roadmap.

Like the Maoists, *Akbayan* might of course have nourished several parties for special sectors such as women, labour, teachers and so on – so that they could all engage in the party-list elections and get seats in the House of Representatives – and then run a secret politburo to direct them all. But the ambition was a mass-based open party and electoral reforms to improve representation. So the only option was a coalition with the Liberal Party to advance in local elections and get more seats nationally, including a representative in the Senate.

Added Llamas: How did we manage to do this? You know the strategy from the 1990s. The liberals and the moderate social democrat technocrats wanted a progressive touch to their bid, plus our good activists – since they did not have any – while we wanted resources and access. (…) No, this was different from the populists' jumping on Estrada's bandwagon and the Maoists' horse-trading with Arroyo. We were based on a democratic party of our own. And there was a transparent agreement with the progressive liberals to fight corruption and poverty by improving democracy.

Bright start

Given the abuse of power and poor development under Arroyo, it was widely expected that the Liberals, along with *Akbayan*, would win the 2010 presidential and parliamentary elections. Especially as charismatic Benigno 'Noynoy' Aquino III, 'PNoy' to his friends, was made presidential candidate when Corazon Aquino, his esteemed and sacred mother, passed away in 2009. Young Aquino promised to take a 'straight path' to renewing democracy and fighting corruption. This, he claimed, would boost the economy as well as reduce poverty. For some years, he seemed to pull it off. Economic growth accelerated while corruption decelerated.

Akbayan did well too, doubling its number of votes in the party-list elections, almost carrying its shining candidate Risa Hontiveros, with roots in civil society-oriented *Pandayan* (Chapter 8), into the Senate, and getting several other leaders appointed to crucial positions in the administration. Pro-democracy stalwart Loretta 'Etta' Rosales became chair of the Commission on Human Rights. Other leaders were well represented in the National Youth Commission, and some worked with the Commission for the Urban Poor. Potentially most crucial of all, Llamas was made presidential adviser for Political Affairs, with a staff of his own, and Joel Rocamora, party-founding member and senior researcher, was appointed head of the National Anti-Poverty Commission (NAPC). Thus, both were also members of the cabinet.

The liberals and moderate social democrats certainly dominated the government, and *Akbayan*-related union and farmer leaders felt the party was too lenient on neoliberal economic priorities. But the terms of engagement included stern action on Marcos's stolen wealth and new corrupt officials such as Mrs Arroyo, compensation to the victims of Marcos's Martial Law, continuity of the agrarian reform programme, measures against the subcontracting of jobs, laws on reproductive and universal health care and improvements to the political system. And initially, a fair amount of these issues were addressed, thanks to extra-parliamentary pressure. Hontiveros, for one, mobilized support for the bill on reproductive health that she had drafted during her previous stint in the House of Representatives, and 'Noynoy' Aquino, as president, saw to its enactment. Congressman Walden Bello pushed again for effective implementation of the agrarian reform, recalling a massive campaign among small farmers in 2009 to this end. And Joel Rocamora initiated the world's only nationwide system of participatory budgeting, which, in combination with direct support for families with children, had the potential to reduce the rule of local bosses as well as poverty, as in Lula's Brazil.

Good times past

'Noynoy' Aquino was generally considered honest, *Akbayan* was deemed progressive and expectations remained high in face of the 2013 mid-term elections. The pro-administration candidates did well, or reasonably well. But the good times were over.

Just after the elections, new abuse was revealed of the already infamous 'pork barrel fund' for projects in the congress-representatives' constituencies. Typically, presidents of all shades since Marcos had employed the funds to gain support in the Congress, while the representatives used them to please their local voters and business associates. In mid-2013, *The Philippine Daily Inquirer* revealed that the funds were even used fraudulently by way of 'ghost projects', fake foundations and 'non-existent NGOs'. To bypass the embarrassing problem, Budget Secretary Florencio 'Butch' Abad, a moderate social democrat and 'friend of civil society', tried a so-called disbursement acceleration programme, but only made things worse, upsetting the Congress as well as the Constitutional Court.

Meanwhile, the government's ineffectual attempts to improve public services and infrastructure were also subject to criticism. This intensified with the indecisive actions in support of the victims of the super typhoon Yolanda (elsewhere named Haiyan) in late 2013. There was also slow law enforcement. This was well-illustrated by the delayed trial of those responsible for massacring thirty-four journalists, among others, in Maguindanao (Mindanao) in 2009, and the media exposure of rich criminals enjoying life in secret luxury prisons cells replete with strip bars, drugs and Jacuzzis.

Most serious, the positive economic growth was obviously non-inclusive, due, primarily, to remittances from the many migrant workers, outsourcing practices (such as to call centres) and the new tycoons' investments in service sectors and speculative real estate. Similarly, the old landed oligarchy continued to hold back implementation of the land reform, including, initially, in the Aquino-clan's own hacienda, Luisita. The minister in charge – de los Reyes – was ineffective and big business groups turned to the countryside for large-scale industrial agriculture and real-estate development. The result of their economic growth was not less but more social inequality unemployment and poverty.

What could the progressives do to alter these tendencies and counter the increasingly common depiction of *Akbayan* as adjusting to the unconvincing liberal combination of economic growth, 'good governance' and welfare?

Breakup

Akbayan voiced concern and critique but lacked the power to alter the bad omens. As Rocamora ironically reflected: every time we win the arguments but lose in practice.

Congressman Walden Bello reasoned that the coalition had been helpful on social issues such as the law on reproductive health. But matters concerning fundamental relations of power such as agrarian reform were delayed and even 'good governance' was set aside. Hence, the party must put its foot down.

According to Bello, however, the party was not acting firmly enough, so he bypassed it and wrote publicly to the president, urging him to fire Budget Secretary Abad and Agrarian Reform Secretary de los Reyes, so as to show that the government remained committed to 'good governance'. *Akbayan* distanced itself from the demands in order not to ruin the cooperation with the president, and urged Bello to acknowledge that he was not elected as a district congressman but as a party representative who must follow its collective decisions.

Bello conceded, but already in early 2015 there was another instance of 'bad governance'. This time the president did not account for having sent the Special Armed Forces to arrest a US wanted terrorist in the territory of the Moro Islamic Liberation Front in Mamasapano (southern Mindanao), thus endangering ongoing peace negotiations and getting forty-four men from the Special Forces massacred. Bello asked *Akbayan* to urge the president to accept responsibility for the operation, in return for sustained support, and dismiss his commander as well as the other main 'bad governance' figures, Secretaries Abad and de los Reyes. But while the *Akbayan* leaders could agree on some of the demands, they did not want to abandon the president, the coalition and the chance to make a difference in other respects. So when the president insisted in putting all the blame for the disastrous operation on his ground commander, Bello resigned from the House of Representatives, and many frustrated *Akbayan* leaders and activists distanced themselves too. Was the breakup inevitable and did it illustrate that an effective centre–left coalition is impossible?

During a lunchbreak in late 2017 at the Human Rights Commission, where senior and ever-active Etta Rosales, its former director and veteran *Akbayan*-representative in Congress, was now busy training volunteers to resist Duterte's killing squads, she put her words to me quite carefully: Walden had valid critique, but we must defend our precious and vulnerable democratic institutions. He should not have played extra-parliamentary politics from inside parliament but used his position as Congress representative to ask questions and criticize, with support from outside.

Even so, how does one galvanize cooperation and when does one call time on it? Josua Mata, general secretary of the party-related national labour centre *Sentro*, which was critical of the coalition from the outset, said the compromise among the *Akbayan* leaders, when the decision was taken to join the government, had been to review performance continuously, but that this was of little avail as there was no bottom line to measure against.

A 'breaking-point' might certainly be difficult to specify. But Mata and I agreed it should anyway be possible to evaluate *strategies* which combine parliamentary and extra-parliamentary work.

Unsettled strategy

So what was the strategy? I asked those who should know. Jennifer Albano, among the critics and director of the *Akbayan*–related labour education network *Learn,* replied curtly, 'no, there was not anything like that'. And Etta Rosales, among the endorsers, said: no, sorry, I am not aware of any comprehensive strategy for the coalition work (…) the focus was on certain leaders and what they could do.

One of them, Ronald Llamas – *Akbayan* president until appointed President Aquino's adviser – answered by discussing the immediate problems and options. But current Chair, Senator Hontiveros, agreed that the party 'was not able to maximise the opportunities'. And others concurred, though General Secretary Mariquit 'Kit' Melgar concluded, with a smile: at least, by now we are not a male-dominated but women-led party.

More fundamentally, former farmers' leader and *Akbayan* Chairman Ric Reyes, who was upset with the coalition, seemed to suggest that maybe it was even futile, in the Philippines, to combine participation in a government and activism outside. In a parliamentary system like in Europe or India, he argued, a progressive party can be loyal to a government platform but still put forward proposals that are not covered by the agreement and propagate its own programme. In Philippines, however, he reflected, *Akbayan* was ensnared in a presidential system where one is either for or against personal leaders and especially the president.

Does that mean that progressives must abstain from participation in government? Discussing wider experiences with trade unionist Orlando 'Marlon' Quesada, having worked with Scandinavian as well as Indonesian, Philippine and other South East Asian unions, we agreed that *strategies* to combine coalition work and activism outside government *are* possible. So what were the experiences in this regard? Was not this exactly what pioneering *Akbayan* leader Joel Rocamora tried to do as head of the NAPC, the Anti-Poverty Commission?

In the belly of the beast

NAPC was crucial, among other reasons, for including representatives from organizations drawn from fisher folk, farmers, unions, informal labour and the urban poor as well as organizations addressing them. The commission did not have much of a budget on its own, but there was a great potential, if agreements could be negotiated –

with major ministries such as Budget, Social Welfare and Development (DSWD) and Interior and Local Government (DILG) – to de facto direct large tracts of government spending.

Joel Rocamora acknowledged that he was thus working 'in the belly of the beast', but said he thought it would still be possible to make a difference. Crucial in this respect was the 'Hyatt 10' group of liberals and moderate social democrats who had crossed over from President Arroyo's increasingly corrupt administration to 'Noynoy' Aquino's campaign and cabinet. Public policy scholar Björn Dressel characterizes them as technocrats focused on linking public finance and development-oriented civil society groups. The supremo was Liberal Party member and moderate social democrat Budget Secretary 'Butch' Abad. He wanted to promote 'good governance' in conjunction with CSOs and to support private sector-led economic growth. Also vital was like-minded DSWD Secretary Corazon 'Dinky' Soliman, who favoured World Bank-driven community development and conditional cash transfers. Equally fundamental but an outsider was DILG Secretary Jesse Robredo, who as former celebrated Mayor of Naga City had worked closely and admirably with civil society and popular organizations.

Rocamora, a skilled arbiter, managed to combine these actors' priorities with those of his own. These were, firstly, to support civil society and popular organizations of the poor as well as progressive local politicians and, secondly, to replace the clientelistic 'pork-barrel fund' and other links between the central and local–level traditional politicians ('trapos') with impartially regulated Bottom up Budgeting (BuB) and a selection of central programmes through his Commission (NAPC). Initially it seemed to work. Extensive funds were allotted for the first nationwide expression of participatory budgeting in the world.

However, the turning point came in late 2012 when Jesse Robredo died in a plane crash. Up to that point, NAPC's policy had been impartiality. Rocamora was not in favour of special treatment to *Akbayan* associates. But now liberals and moderate social democrats manoeuvred in favour of their own friends and CSOs. DSWD Secretary Soliman and Budget Secretary Abad were instrumental in this respect. Liberal Senator Mar Roxas was made head of the DILG, which reclaimed operational responsibilities from the NAPC.

As shown by political scientist Garry Rodan, the door then opened for the return of the traditional politicians and their associated CSOs. Budget secretary Abad may also have been in search of other resources for local allies to replace the disputed 'pork barrel funds'. The liberals tried to mobilize support as comprehensive elections in 2016 neared, when Roxas was bound to be the Liberal Party's presidential candidate. Subsequently, moreover, there was more emphasis on the DSWD's community-oriented approach and the conditional cash transfers, which reached out quickly to more voters and relieved politicians of troublesome civil society groups and popular movements.

Rocamora and his team did not give up, still resisting the traditional politicians' control and providing impartial support for civil society and popular organizations that had been initiated after the fall of Marcos (Chapter 8). The main problem was not that conditional cash transfers to families with children 'only' improved people's individual power, but that the greater emphasis on community support and the 'elite capturing' of the BuB programme reduced the opportunities to improve their collective power. As Rocamora points out, in an evaluation of the NAPC, people's organizations such as unions and farmer's organizations cannot be confined to *barangay* communities but must work on larger scales, linking up with activists in different workplaces and contexts. Moreover, as we know from Chapter 8, progressive CSOs are weak outside the major cities and, like popular organizations, must be backed up in order to gain access and influence. This applies especially to those groups that do not just spend time in seminar rooms trying to 'solve problems' but also attempt to mobilize pressure.

Likewise, Rocamora and his colleagues said, it must be acknowledged that CSOs themselves were 'not able to keep pace despite a whole series of steps to push participation'. And some years' later *Akbayan* Chair Hontiveros, as well as President Marie Chris 'Machris' Cabreros, confirmed: yes, Joel did his best, but the party should have mobilized in support of the reforms and taken advantage.

In comparative perspective

Akbayan's attempt through the NAPC at combining work inside and outside government was grand and perhaps unrealistic, yet imaginative. Rocamora smiled but did not comment when I later on mentioned that friends in Kerala were up against major problems with their Planning Campaign, in spite of benefitting from stronger civil society groups and weaker opponents because of land reform (Chapter 11). Similarly, the NAPC's attempt to involve popular interest organizations, which could promote collective strength by scaling up projects beyond the communities, was even more ambitious than Brazil's more localized participatory budgeting. The Kerala campaigners tried that too, but encountered similar problems as those in the Philippines – headaches to do with reconciling the agendas of combative interest organizations and local civil society groups.

More generally, *Akbayan's* problems of cooperating within a centre-left government dominated by proponents of a combination of handouts for the poor and liberal economic growth were also not unique. The challenges in the Philippines resembled the main flaw in the Indian Congress government's rights and welfare programmes in the early 2000s in terms of weak roots in grounded civil society groups and popular organizations (Chapter 12). Similarly, the Philippine as well as the Indian rights and welfare programmes benefitted the poor but were not really designed to also facilitate a more inclusive growth strategy, as is the case with public health and unemployment insurance and production-oriented education and training. In part, this applied in Kerala too (Chapters 11 and 12).

Finally, in India as well as in the Philippines, corruption remained a major challenge – tragically as much as under Lula da Silva and Dilma Rousseff in Brazil and Jacob Zuma in South Africa. Positively, the Common Man's Party (AAP) in New Delhi managed to fuse anti-corruption with ground-level issues of public services and welfare (electricity, water, health and education). But populist mobilization substituted for democratic organization, the democratic compass has been lost and issues of working life and rights-based growth have been set aside (Chapter 12).

In the next chapter, we shall discuss how these insights relate to the Indonesian efforts at populist reformism under the rise and governance of President Jokowi (Chapter 14) – before considering them in wider comparative context in the conclusion of the book.

The rise of Duterte and what left democrats can do

Philippine presidents are only eligible to serve one term. In 2016, *Akbayan* supported Mar Roxas, the Liberal Party's presidential candidate to succeed 'Noynoy' Aquino. Yet, he was part of the undermining of NAPC's Bottom up Budgeting, was notoriously 'unable to connect' and ended up with only 23.5 per cent of the vote. Had there been only one liberal candidate, Rodrigo Duterte might have lost (the other liberal-oriented candidate Grace Poe got 21.4 per cent). But in any case there was a momentum for the violent local strongman from Davao (Mindanao) who promised to protect 'ordinary people' and received 39 per cent – so the crucial question is why.

The most convincing argument, by political scientist Mark Thompson among others, is that although 'Noynoy' Aquino was deemed a charming 'good guy', the liberal-reformist idea of combatting corruption and favouring productivity to promote growth and thus fight poverty had not worked – just as in India, Indonesia, Brazil and elsewhere. The rule of law remained weak and even liberals were mired in corruption. Economic growth was there, but there were fewer new jobs than expected, the poor remained poor and many in the elite and middle classes feared for their personal security. So instead of a 'kind man', many of them looked for a 'strong man'. And as usual, the Maoists provided 'tactical support', embracing Duterte in search of benefits.

The national-level senatorial elections are much about individuals. *Akbayan* Chair Risa Hontiveros was able to swim against the tide, finally making it to the Senate with an impressive 16 million votes (while Walden Bello got 1 million and lost). In addition to benefitting from the support of the Liberal Party as well as skilled *Akbayan* activists, Hontiveros communicated well and was increasingly popular for her engagement in welfare and women's issues.

In the party-list election, however, *Akbayan's* performance was disastrous. While traditional politicians supported friendly party-list groups based on their local strongholds, *Akbayan* had lost local strength by focusing on national politics. Within the tattered coalition, moreover, the party had become its own best enemy by being unable to demonstrate how the positive aspects of the liberal reformist project could be employed to foster Social Democracy. *Akbayan* President 'Machris' Cabreros summed it up: there were fourteen landmark advances but who remembers when there isn't a convincing general policy? Now the party must be 'refounded'.

How would that be possible? Ideology was taboo in 1998, when Joel Rocamora and others managed to unite scattered left-democrats from different 'political blocs' and numerous civil society and 'sectoral' interest organizations and form *Akbayan*. Instead, the common ground was 'active citizenship' and 'participatory democracy'.

Now, Rocamora and many others argue, the 'political blocs' with varying ideologies have lost steam, so *Akbayan* itself must resurrect a clear-cut leftist agenda. Human rights and democracy, they say, shall certainly be defended against Duterte's killings and authoritarianism, but the violent strongman came to power because people had lost faith in the liberal reformist project. So, the real alternative must be phrased in terms of what decent democracy and popular participation shall be used for – fighting poverty and inequality, promoting welfare and public health, including against the pandemic, and fair taxation, plus a deal for inclusive and sustainable development based on these tenets.

Would a leftist turn be feasible for Risa Hontiveros, who needs a huge number of votes to be re-elected senator? Would she rather hold on to a liberal-oriented coalition? 'No', she says. 'They are losing out. We must return to the youth, the movements and the communities.' Thus, she envisions a broad alliance behind crucial questions, such as was possible, until recently, in Malaysia against the corrupt regime.

General-Secretary Kit Melgar cautions: yes, but the bottom line is to develop a coherent reform agenda (…) I travel a lot (…) we need an umbrella so that crucial issues and actors around the country can come together.

This seems particularly important in view of veteran activist-scholar Nathan Quimpo's core argument in a long-distance call that *Akbayan* must finally overcome its preoccupation with high politics and central-level conflicts in Manila, in favour of inspiring and coordinating the building of 'progressive local bailiwicks' based on broad alliances in districts, municipalities and cities. Rocamora concurs and adds: in such contexts we shall not build on famous figures but on leaders who depend on our organization.

14

Whither 'reformist populism'?
The Indonesian experience

By the late 2000s in Indonesia, both elitist democratization and pro-democrats' efforts to reform the system were exhausted. To recall developments after Suharto (Chapter 10), the elites had adjusted to the new democratic institutions by dominating them, so the rule of law remained poor, the reign of corruption prevailed and the system of representation excluded potential actors of change. For organized interests such as unions and other pro-democrats in civil society, there were limited chances to nurture active citizenship and policy as well as membership-based organizations and parties. In short, the most essential foundations for democratization were lacking. Pro-democrats tried numerous ways to get inside the secluded system and reform it, but by 2009, the only remaining options seemed to be to horse-trade with powerful politicians ('contracts') or get into mainstream parties ('diaspora politics'). The former yielded some benefits, but in the end, both proved disastrous.

Meanwhile, however, the third round of the participatory democracy assessments – this time with the politics department at the University of Gadjah Mada – identified a series of populist openings for progressives. Might they be an alternative route to new Social Democracy?

A small team of concerned scholars and reflective activists monitored the efforts to make use of the new opportunities and analyse problems and options.[1] During several years of exciting and joyful work, we combined insights and sources from crucial frontlines – inside government, unions and CSOs as well as from other contexts – India and the Philippines for example – and with reference to the history of Social Democracy. In addition to the democracy assessments, we were standing on the shoulders of other engaged scholars (some advising the PDI-P and President 'Jokowi'). And we added joint interviews and arranged group discussions with leading actors. As the Indonesians in the team were always on the move, deeply ensconced in efforts to give tangible form to our ideas, we tended to exchange results and impressions in coffee shops. Hence, there was little time for comprehensive reports, so I turned secretary and now benefit extensively from my notes at the time.

---

[1] Aside from myself, they were Dr Luky Djani who combined insights from local politics around the country, the anti-corruption movement and 'Jokowi's' advisers; Dr Surya Tjandra, student of labour law and propelling actor in the campaign with unions for the social security reform, later leading member of the Solidarity Party (PSI), and currently deputy Agrarian and Spatial Planning Minister; and lastly, Osmar Tanjung, who, having coordinated civil society work in Sumatra, thereafter did the same in *Seknas 'Jokowi'*, which aims to provide expertise for progressives in government.

Timeline Indonesia 2005–2020

2005
- Joko 'Jokowi' Widodo elected Mayor of Solo.

2006
- Social pact in Solo between 'Jokowi' and urban poor/informal labourers.
- Reformist combatants and CSO activists win Aceh elections but do not build party.

2009
- Aceh CSO activists lose elections but Governor Irwandi Jusuf remains in power.

2011–12
- Solo-like mayor–CSO alliance in Aceh Selatan stumbles over ignorant Swedish donor.
- Rightist Aceh combatants and Jakarta allies delay governor elections to counter Irwandi Jusuf.
- Rightist combatants' party wins Aceh governor elections.
- Reformists and CSO activists form new party, but have lost steam.

2010–13
- Reformist mayor elected in Surabaya, in cooperation with CSOs.
- Successful alliance (unions, informal labour, politicians) for public health reform.
- Hard to scale up 'Solo-model', but 'Jokowi' and Basuki T. 'Ahok' Purnama elected Jakarta governors.
- 'Jokowi' tries Solo-like social pacts with urban poor; 'Ahok' reforms governance.
- Public health reform alliance not sustained in favour of further reforms.
- No format for state-business-labour negotiation of wages, welfare and development.

2013
- Rieke Pitaloka and Teten Masduki almost win West Java governor elections.
- Reformist mayor elected in Bandung, in cooperation with CSOs.
- Unions and allies try engaging in politics via various parties.
- Best-organized unions strike deal with presidential candidate strongman Prabowo.

2014
- 'Jokowi' elected president based on elitist coalition rather than broad popular alliance.
- CSOs and popular groups having supported 'Jokowi' ignored in new government.
- Progressives in Aceh humiliated in local elections.

2015
- Teten Masduki is head of 'Jokowi's staff, but fails to initiate major alternative reforms.
- 'Ahok' dishonour 'Jokowi's' pact with urban poor and opts for Singaporean governance.

2016–17
- Opponents of 'Ahok' and 'Jokowi', including Prabowo, for Muslim identity politics.
- Favourite candidate in governor elections, 'Ahok', accused of blasphemy.
- Massive 'Muslim demonstrations' in Jakarta against 'Ahok'.
- 'Ahok' loses elections and is imprisoned.
- Comprehensive welfare and work-rights reforms suggested to counter identity politics.

2018–19
- 'Jokowi' opts instead for accommodation with Muslim leaders, business and military.
- Masduki replaced by General Moeldoko as head of president's staff.
- 'Jokowi' opts for Ulama Ma'ruf Amin as vice-presidential candidate.
- 'Jokowi' wins presidential elections. Focus on power-sharing, incl. with Prabowo.

2020
- 'Jokowi' stresses economic development at expense of democracy and rights.
- Pro-business 'Job Creation Law', without consultation with labour and rights and issue organizations.

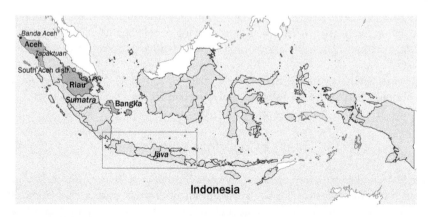

Map 15 Indonesia.

Map 16 Java.

Contextual variants

Current populism is often associated with nationalist mobilization of the 'people' against liberal internationalism, such as by Donald Trump or European chauvinists. However, while this may be one outcome of populism, it does not equal populism. As discussed in Chapter 2, populism may generally be understood as a thin ideology – of which there may be leftist, rightist and other versions – about the 'common people' and its 'general will', defined by common identity and with direct relations between leaders and people.

The best historical illustration of left-populism in Indonesia is President Sukarno. He claimed to be the mouthpiece of the 'common people' and their will – bypassing intermediary organizations and parties by turning directly to the people and forging a common identity in resisting neo-colonial imperialism. Generally, social democrats too tend to promote unity among the 'common people' and emancipatory popular movements, beyond a narrowly defined working class (Chapter 2). But they prefer modern knowledge and expertise to the idea of a 'popular will'. They favour representative democracy via citizens' own organizations to direct democracy (except on micro levels). They believe in rallying people behind reform proposals based on equal citizenship rights rather than identity politics pitted against an enemy.

Consequently, as populism comes in many shades, one needs to analyse it contextually. What were the potentials and sequels of Indonesia's new populism?

Roots of 'reformist populism'

The first foundation for the populist opening was institutional. The new direct elections from 2004 of political executives (mayors/heads of districts, governors, presidents) certainly favoured moneyed candidates but called also for wider support than before.

Previously the executives had been appointed by parliaments, and, thus, de facto by the elections to them based on proportional representation, so the rival parties tended to rely on clientelism and their particular socio-religious and ethnic followers. In the new direct elections, however, successful contenders had to go beyond this pattern by popular appeals to more voters.

The other foundations were structural and ideological. One was that increasing social mobility and urbanization made it difficult to win elections only by patron–client relations involving an element of trust. Another was that politicians had to counter an increasing critique of elitist politics and corruption by new attractive ideas and non-establishment candidates. Yet another was strong support for universal and public welfare programmes – in preference to insufficient patronage and self-help. This was after the Asian economic crisis, which brought in its train more 'flexible' employment conditions. Mayors and heads of districts were able to launch social reform programmes and increasing wages, thanks to the sweeping decentralization of decisions and resources after Suharto.

The new conditions paved the way for what I call 'reformist populism'. This was certainly characterized by the usual ideas of the 'common people' and their 'general will', to be given a voice by leaders outside the established elites and political parties. However, to unify the people, the new leaders emphasized professional leadership and pluralism rather than 'strongmanship' and identity politics against elites, and more focus on inclusive and universal social and economic reforms based on equal citizenship rights, as opposed to targeted support for favoured groups.

The politics of 'reformist populism' opened up several windows for pro-democrats, from unions to urban poor and CSOs. One was that the powerful candidates were eager to gain supplementary support from organizations and campaigners in civil society with good reputations and substantial followings. Another was that direct elections with fewer contenders than in proportional elections made it easier for the notoriously divided pro-democrats to agree on what candidate to strike deals with and support. Similarly, many pro-democrats were attracted by the new focus on welfare and anti-elitism as well as by direct links between the leader and the people, which promised to reduce the powers of parties and patrons. Interestingly, the conditions and openings are reminiscent in many ways of those that enabled the Workers' Party and popular movements in Brazil to make huge advances in local direct elections and foster participatory politics from the mid-1980s. We shall return to wider comparisons in the concluding chapter.

In short, 'reformist populism' gave life to democratization and the idea of inclusive development. Even the world's most reputed liberal magazine, *The Economist*, was positive. Yet, there was also cause for concern. In the 2014 elections, a rightist counter-movement began to rise, two years later almost eclipsing the reformists. How did this happen? As we shall see, the reformists countered the threats in such a way that they succeeded in getting re-elected in 2019 – in contrast to left of centre governments in India, the Philippines and Brazil. But, in the process, they also undermined liberties, equal citizenship, democracy and the efforts at inclusive development. How was this possible?

Informal social pact in Solo

East of Jogjakarta, the royal city of Solo and its dynamic surrounding districts are part of the largest educational, commercial and manufactural hubs in Central Java. It is also an old stronghold for radical politics (Chapters 4, 9 and 10). Solo in particular had been hit hard by conflicts during the fall of Suharto's regime and the Asian economic crisis. In my logbooks from early visits, the city is portrayed as chaotic, run down, dusty, dirty, smelling of poverty. Increasingly many poor people tried to find a living on the pavements and in other public places, as well as on the riverbanks.

The first populist opening after Suharto is best illustrated by Solo. Unsurprisingly, Megawati's PDI-P won the 1999 local elections, but *Golkar* and Muslim parties were also strong. The prospective Mayor, Slamet Suryanto from the PDI-P, therefore had to compromise in the city council and develop good relations with the bureaucracy and popular organizations among the poor themselves, often facilitated by progressive CSOs. Hence the popular groups and CSOs gained some strength.

In the run-up to the first direct election of Mayor in 2005, Suryanto, the incumbent, was denounced within the PDI-P and accused of corruption. As an alternative, the party was convinced to launch fresh outsider as the main candidate. He was Joko 'Jokowi' Widodo, with a background as an engineer from the Forestry Faculty, a modest furniture supplier and the leader of a local association in this sector. A manager and technocrat, not a strongman.

'Jokowi' promised 'change' by fighting corruption and fostering inclusive development. He got most votes but not a majority. So to get anything done – without too many transactions in the city council – he had to expand the already-minted extra-parliamentary cooperation with business as well as CSOs and popular groups. When necessary, this could be backed up by the Deputy Mayor and party boss Hadi 'Rudy' Rudyatomo and the PDI-P's muscular task force, *satgas*. Putatively participatory planning from below (*musrembang*) had been initiated by the former mayor in local areas with selected citizens and with support from foreign donors such as Ford Foundation. But the participants were accountable to the politicians and administrators, not to ordinary people. To really boost urban development, the no-nonsense alternative was direct discussions with sectoral organizations among informal labourers and other urban poor people, with support from CSO activists.

As the story goes, the urban poor flatly refused to evacuate public spaces and demanded fair compensation and alternatives when 'Jokowi' suggested business-friendly and middle-class-driven modernization of the city centre. The turning point was just before Independence Day celebrations in 2006, due to take place in one of these public places. So 'Jokowi' had to concede. Equally important, he then talked directly with the urban poor groups and activists, not to them, and not via parties, bosses and bureaucrats. Thus agreements acceptable to all involved were sealed and 'Jokowi', as well as the activists, delivered. The city flourished and became renowned. 'Jokowi' was awarded an international prize for being one of the best mayors in the world. And in 2010 he was re-elected with 90 per cent of the votes. Unsurprisingly, 'Jokowi' was then suggested as the PDI-P's candidate for the gubernatorial elections in Jakarta, to which we shall return.

Most important at this point, however, is that as he left for Jakarta, the promising informal social pact between the mayor, business partners and the urban poor supported by CSO activists deteriorated. When I revisited the activists in late 2013, their 'Consortium of NGOs' (*Kompip*) – which facilitated much of the urban poor's negotiations with the city government, and housed numerous organizers from among informal labourers, petty traders and even sex workers – remained active, but the coordinators lacked the necessary resources and donors had lost interest. Meanwhile, in a joint article, close advisers of the PDI-P and 'Jokowi', Professors Cornelis Lay and Pratikno (later the president's closest aide and state secretary), emphasized the importance of institutionalizing and thus sustaining the informal negotiations in Solo. But that was of no avail.

Middle-class and union-driven pacts

The openings for reformist populism were not confined to Solo but varied with context and social bases. In commercial and industrial Surabaya, for example, city planner Tri Rismaharini was widely acclaimed as an efficient and non-corrupt Mayor. In Bandung, the country's major city for technology and advanced industry, another architect and urban planner but also supporter of knowledge-based economic activities, Ridwan Kamil, was elected mayor in 2013, he did remarkably well in cleaning up the city and then promoting technology-driven economic development. However, the industrial areas and labouring classes are outside the prosperous city proper, within which the urban poor were not strong enough to matter and therefore possible to get rid of. Thus Kamil's rise to fame and power was instead middle-class driven. In a smart downtown restaurant, where I could get wine for a change, leading anti-corruption activist, Sely Martini, described the campaigning: Kamil's association with Prabowo's *Gerindra* party was only a formality, though some deals may have been done. Actually, the campaign was very social media-driven and participatory. Educated individuals appreciated taking part in specific actions and dropping into coffee shops for deliberative discussions. Concluded Martini: they expanded the public space in a 'Habermasian sense', not by building old-fashioned democratic organizations.

Meanwhile, unions in industrialized districts and provinces realized that the decentralization – including tripartite negotiations of minimum wages – opened up the field for horse-trading (Chapter 10). To gain influence in the wage councils, with limited numbers of seats, the otherwise fragmented unions networked, agreed on basic positions and staged demonstrations. In this way they could negotiate contracts with the politicians likely to take up seats in the councils. The unions delivered votes to successful candidates in return for better conditions. To some extent, informal labourers also benefitted, but the major unions did not prioritize social movement unionism and populist campaigns. The intensively industrialized Batam municipality in Riau Islands Province, close to Singapore, served as a testing ground, pointing to the importance of union networks in overcoming leaders' rivalries. Later, in 2012, the most successful agreement between unions and the gubernatorial candidate, in Jakarta, resulted in a 45 per cent wage hike.

That candidate was 'Jokowi', having been so successful in Solo that he had advanced to the capital. We shall return to his ascension, but first let us turn to Aceh. Because after the peace treaty it was possible for progressives to build local parties and participate in elections. Did it help?

Disgraced local politics in Aceh

In Aceh populism was driven by the previous struggle against Jakarta's economic and political suppression and human rights abuses, followed by a peace accord that generated a unique chance to build local democratic politics. In 2006, as we know from Chapter 10, reformists in GAM and allies in civil society honoured the peace accord by running as independents in elections for political executives while the conservative leaders were left behind for a while. The reformists made it to the offices of the governor as well as those of many heads of districts. But they did not build a joint party, hoping that it would be possible to reconcile with the conservatives in GAM. Consequently, their allies in civil society who built parties of their own were devoid of patronage and suffered humiliation in the 2009 legislative elections. Additional reasons were harassment by the conservative GAM-leaders as well as CSO activists' own inability to develop significant new democratic policies. This was in the context of donors' and Jakarta's separation between post-tsunami reconstruction and democratization. So what else could progressives with social democratic inclinations do then?

Three compatible openings were put to the test, all drawing on the strength of popular-oriented Governor Irwandi Yusuf, commonly known as Irwandi, in office from 2007 to 2012, and re-elected in 2017. One option was cooperation between civil society and local governments in building new democratic institutions, endorsed by the governor. Another possibility was forming a new party behind the same governor, based on reformists in GAM and CSOs. The third opening was to develop a popular-oriented platform to get Irwandi re-elected in 2017. Remarkably, all three options proved possible, but once achieved, they fell to pieces. Why?

Rise and demise of local democratization

In view of the setbacks so far (Chapter 10), scholars supportive of the reformists in GAM and their partners in civil society concluded that it was unrealistic to build new Social Democracy in Aceh from the bottom up – without somehow managing to first develop complementary public institutions and policy agendas. Donors had separated post-tsunami and post-conflict development from local governance, by either setting up separate agencies or bypassing the district governments with support to civil society at lower levels. That meant avoiding the problems of democratic governance and marginalizing the progressives who tried to overcome them. So what could be done?

Inspired by the rise of 'reformist populism' in Solo and social democracy in Scandinavia, the concerned scholars and activists pursued another idea, with the blessing of the governor. They would select a district far away from political conspiracies in Banda Aceh (the capital) that could serve as a test case for an alternative. South Aceh was chosen. In this test case they would offer the head of district (*bupati*), his deputy and their administrators a complementary review of the problems and options of local development. The review would be carried out in cooperation with actors in fledgling civil society – from farmer and fisher groups to teachers and business associations, as well as activists for human rights and good governance. Having agreed on what should be done, the team would inaugurate projects in continuous cooperation between the administration and the actors in society. This should strengthen implementation as well as popular organization and participation. The researchers would monitor and assist. The *bupati* and other politicians could decide whether they wanted to promote or reject the implementation. But irrespective of their decision, the plans would be made public. Meanwhile the participants and local leaders would benefit from an exchange programme with a Swedish municipality. A beautiful plan, but would it work in messy post-conflict Aceh?

Strangely, it did work, until disrupted by even messier Swedish donors. For about a year, there were numerous studies, discussions and conclusions about what could be done in South Aceh. Finally we could even draw on Governor Irwandi's enthusiastic support, reported in the media. In February 2011, our team – this time along with Swedish donor representatives – once again slowly made its way along the scenic but tsunami-affected Western highway, still short of bridges but not potholes and macadam, between the capital and South Aceh.

During a full day in a packed seminar room in South Aceh's administrative building, the team presented its results and proposals, and major administrators and other actors made additions. In the afternoon, everybody happily agreed on the framework and directions. Thereafter the critical issue was to get the blessing of the *bupati*. Some said he was a bit of a warlord, and there was hesitation in the air when the senior researchers and donor representatives were invited to take a seat in his pompous official residence. Beyond the niceties, the agenda was clear enough: what would be in it for him?

Team leader Dr Leena Avonius carried some respect, with long experience from promoting the peace accord as well as overseeing the decommissioning of tough combatants. She mobilized all her Finnish diplomatic skills – kind but crisp. The *bupati* nodded, interested. I added that the programme might be useful in the forthcoming election campaign and that the *bupati* would, of course, take the final decision to approve it or not. The *bupati* smiled. I finished, saying that we would only have the right to publish the studies and recommendations, approved or not. Then he got the point, but remained interested and asked the donor representatives about visiting colleagues in Sweden. Everybody understood this would boost his tarnished reputation, but that was the price for building transformative democratic politics. Hence, the donor representatives said a visit was quite possible, as soon as a Swedish counterpart-municipality had been identified.

Back in our lodge, we were jubilant. The field seemed wide open. The partners on the ground had agreed on an innovative programme. The governor was supportive and the *bupati* was happy. The only detail left – which should not be a problem – was for the donor directors in Sweden to identify a partner municipality, which would get funds to proceed and backing from Aceh. But the donor directors never really bothered to identify such a partner. So the opening, and all the investments, came to nothing.

A vigorous progressive party?

As we know, the reformist GAM leaders and CSO activists who had won the 2006 elections combined remnants of their old command structures in GAM with governmental positions and hoped for reconciliation with the conservative GAM leaders' Aceh Party (PA) rather than putting their energies into building a new party or supporting CSO activists. As the 2011 gubernatorial elections approached, it was obvious that Irwandi, the incumbent reformist commander, had failed to be accepted by the conservatives in PA. Lacking a party, he had therefore to place his trust in his own network of loyal combatants, businessmen and CSO leaders, as well as burnishing his own popularity. Having launched some popular welfare and education programmes, there was a momentum in his favour.

PA, however, undermined this by delaying and boycotting the elections, arguing against independent candidates. This was in spite of both a clause in the peace accord that independent candidates were eligible to participate and a national regulation to the same effect. So the Constitutional Court ruled that PA was wrong, of course, and reopened registration, but this took quite some time. Meanwhile the local government was dysfunctional and Irwandi lost his momentum. Equally important, PA stoked the fear that peace was at stake if it did not win. So eventually, it did win.

By then the battle lines were clear enough, however. Irwandi and his allies simply had to build a party of their own, which was baptized the *Aceh Nanggroe Party* (PNA). There were some promising dynamics, including among women activists, but also disorder. Former commanders and CSO activists had different ideas and styles of governance. And Irwandi remained the supremo whom everyone related to. Most importantly, as Thamrin Ananda, PNA spokesperson and former leader of the most radical civil society party, PRP put it: Aceh remains devoid of progressive popular movements and citizen organizations, which we, who are not part of the combatants' old command structure, can relate to. That is why we are weak.

Other CSO activists were simply fed up. Explained former SIRA leader Faisal Ridha: I can't stand the quarrels among the former combatants anymore. And I do not want to be subordinated to their instructions.

Hence, he and many others joined various national parties instead, just as their fellow pro-democrats in other parts of the country who opted for 'diaspora politics' had.

While PA lost ground in the 2014 legislative elections, it was less to the benefit of PNA than the national parties. According to the former negotiator in Helsinki, Nur Djuli, PNA seemed to have the right mix of freedom fighters and CSO activists. But now it was humiliated and in despair, without a clear programme and with many activists feeling they had been pushed aside by 'the big leaders'. The only woman who made it to the local parliament was Irwandi's wife, Darwati A. Gani who checked with her husband on what to say before we met.

Technocratic populism out of hand

Irwandi himself, however, was eager to take revenge and return to the governor's office in the 2017 elections. While arranging his own contacts and funding, the party was made his electoral machine. To get sufficient number of votes, however, he had also to put on his populist hat. The obvious enemy was PA's poor performance and corrupt practices while in government. But how would Irwandi reach out to people and frame their 'popular will'? Obviously, he was in need of a little help from former friends.

Several of the senior GAM and SIRA leaders who engineered the victory in the 2006 elections were called upon as a success team. They polished Irwandi's style and designed an attractive programme that acknowledged Muslim values but mainly emphasized public welfare and education, inclusive development, good public service and impartial governance. Even most respected GAM ideologue and old spokesperson, Bachtiar Abdullah, flew in from Sweden to lend his support. If victory was achieved, the core team would continue to serve as an 'inner cabinet' to help design and implement specific policies.

Irwandi got his electoral revenge – not with a landslide but comfortable enough. So how would he govern? Given the positive role of the success team, which had put the reformists on the right track, I was astonished to find out a few months later – from one of the graduate students who received scholarships during Irwandi's first period as governor – that a core group of the students had become his special staff. They would 'protect him from being abused by supporters asking favours'. Upset senior leaders Nur Djuli, Shadia Marhaban and Munawar Liza confirmed that they and others in the team who had carried Irwandi to victory had been dumped. Their conclusion was that Irwandi had betrayed GAM/SIRA and the ethos of the freedom struggle. Obviously, I must get to talk to Irwandi himself and his new staff.

The governors' office displayed power, of course. But it looked more Indonesian than Hendri Yuzal, the considerate adjutant and leader of the new special staff, whose perfect suite and American English made me think of a stock broker in Wall Street or senior World Bank official. While waiting for Irwandi for a good number of hours, Yuzal told me of his background as a master's student in urban planning from Hawaii, followed by work for Jakarta and donors' joint reconstruction agency, BRR, the local UN development programme and then as a consultant. He and his student friends had been upset by PA's rule, and Irwandi had asked them to reactivate his old projects, coordinate his policies with national programmes and help him build professional and impartial governance. Added Yuzal: we are not politicians, only professionals (...) neither we nor others shall govern the governor (...) I only follow his directions (...) we prepare the agenda and help him focus.

Finally I ended up in Irwandi's residence instead. Relaxed and self-confident as ever, he asserted: I know they [the success team members] say I am betraying GAM, but GAM is history. Only the spirit is there. There is no structure. KPA [the commanders' transitional committee] was intact until 2012, but thereafter I am not responsible to any of the others. (...) At this point I need technocratic professionals to govern well and impartially (...) No, I am not excluding anyone, neither old friends nor PA (...) but nobody shall get special favours, there shall be equal chances for all.

So how will you, I asked, decide on politics and gain votes if you abandon your senior political advisors? He smiled, but did not answer. As for votes, he said he had 'a good enough name' and that he only did what most people wanted – confident as always about his popularity. A charismatic populist, I thought, with loyal technocrats relived of any democratic control, even his senior political advisers.

A few months after our discussion, Irwandi's charm in other respects led him to earmark 'special funds' for projects spearheaded by his entrepreneurial new second, younger wife. Yuzal and another member of his 'impartial staff' stood by. In early July 2018, they were arrested by KPK (the Indonesian Corruption Eradication Commission). Irwandi was sentenced to ten years in prison, the others to five and six years, respectively.

Consequently, PNA did less well than expected in the 2019 legislative elections, being disgraced and divided for or against Irwandi, who tried to govern from prison via his first wife Darwati Gani, a member of the provincial parliament. PA suffered losses too, while the national parties increased their votes even more.

Lost opportunities

The reformists who negotiated democratic peace in Aceh, and many others who fought during decades against suppression and for fair chances to develop their own potential, feel, now, that they might have to revive the old struggle as their ideals have been lost in a process which they thought would be democratic but which turned out not to be. The openings for 'reformist populism' rested with the progressives in GAM, their allies in civil society and the international community in favour of peace and reconstruction by democratization. However, most reformist leaders opted for reconciliation with the conservative GAM leaders. This was at the expense of building a representative political movement and government for social and economic reforms along with the CSO activists. Meanwhile, the international community also neglected such efforts, while pro-democrats in civil society, left alone, were too scattered and weak to make a difference. A showcase of lost opportunities for social democrats.

Scaling up to Jakarta

Back to Solo, Central Java, in 2010, 'Jokowi' had received more than 90 per cent of the votes when he was re-elected mayor. Consequently, he was an attractive figure for the political elites in Jakarta, searching for an electable candidate in the 2012 gubernatorial elections.

The Indonesian establishment likes order and hates anarchy but has nonetheless, due to its vested interests, produced one of the most disordered and anarchic cities in the world. Jakarta is not just, like many mega cities in the Global South, extremely polluted and devoid of reasonable public transportation and housing for the poor majority of its inhabitants. It is also virtually sinking – in some parts by as much as 25 cm per year. Actually, it is about to be submerged, not just morally but also physically. Partly because the well to do pump up the ground water and have covered the surface of the city with concrete and asphalt and heavy constructions – from way up on the rainy hillside behind Bogor, now littered with fancy villas and hotels, down to the swamp, upon which the old Jakarta was erected by the Dutch. So something must be done. Huge walls against the ocean are needed, and public transportation must be constructed, and canals cleaned, and green areas created and much more. But it is more feasible to bulldoze the poor than the rich.

'Jokowi' ran in Jakarta's 2012 gubernatorial elections. His deputy candidate was Basuki Tjahaja 'Ahok' Purnama, a Christian engineer of ethnic Chinese background, who first served as *bupati* of the Bangka Islands outside Sumatra, did well and was then elected to the national parliament on a *Golkar* ticket. Initially Ahok contemplated running as an independent in Jakarta but realized he would not make it, thus accepting support of the *Gerindra* party under infamous General (ret.) Prabowo who a few years later would stab 'Ahok' in the back but at this point in time wanted to prove he was not against ethnic Chinese. In any case, 'Jokowi's' patrons were keen to complement his success story from Solo with Ahok's reputation as an efficient manager.

It was difficult, however, to scale up the Solo model. This was not because, initially, several CSO activists supported middle-class-oriented economist Faisal Basri instead. Basri had social democratic inclinations but few labour and welfare proposals, and he himself kept telling me he did not have a popular base; others would have to fix that. So unions and many radicals opted out or switched sides when 'Jokowi' and 'Ahok' gained the upper hand and began to campaign with more resources and a more effective message based on good track records of promoting social welfare related to education, health and protection of the poor. Moreover, 'Jokowi' was particularly successful in selling his populist programmes, especially in the media. Journalists covered his frequent unannounced visits, *blusukan*, to troubled neighbourhoods, where he wore chequered common man shirts, used simple means of transport, and rarely made speeches, instead humbly listening to stories of local people's problems.

The more serious problem of scaling up the Solo model was that the negotiation and cooperation with CSOs and the urban poor could not be duplicated. In Jakarta, CSOs were less strong and focused on general advocacy and on lobbying the national government and parliament, thus keeping gubernatorial elections at arm's length. By contrast, some union leaders indicated their support, including, at that point in time, Said Iqbal of the well-organized Federation of Metalworkers Unions (FSPMI). Moreover, several young people were fascinated by the idea of backing clean candidates with good track records in the same vein as Barack Obama's campaign for 'change'. They made use of social media in particular. And on the grassroots level in East Jakarta the organization 'Volunteers for a New Jakarta' mobilized crucial support, spearheaded by noted scholarly activist, Hilmar Farid. Said Farid: this was not about civil society projects with the poor but politics and votes, so we worked with hamlet and neighbourhood groups and leaders.

Generally, however, there were few equivalents of the CSOs and sectoral groups in Solo which had gained some real clout and catered to the needs of political elites to muster extra-parliamentary support. 'Jokowi's' main adviser in this regard, Eko Sulistyo, the former director of the local CSO in Solo that coordinated 'Jokowi's' social pact, was brought over to Jakarta. But he had to apply quick fixes in unchartered waters, with the support of scattered CSO activists and community facilitators. Local fixers gained ground too. In a conversation about the challenges,

Sulistyo appeared stoic. Consequently, 'Jokowi' and 'Ahok' had to rely quite extensively on the elite-driven political machines of PDI-P and *Gerindra* to win the elections, which they did.

Aside from the differences, there were also similar problems in Solo and Jakarta. The new cooperation between popular and civic groups and reformist politicians was not institutionalized. One example was the agreements with the urban poor on acceptable compensation and alternative housing when urban development demanded their relocation. The popular groups were not strong enough to enforce them. And just as in Solo, the deputy governor stepping in for 'Jokowi' when he left for other priorities – in this case 'Ahok' when 'Jokowi' took aim at the presidential elections in 2014 – did not really honour the promises. 'Ahok' gave top priority instead to quick Singaporean-like urban development. This in turn paved the way for the political and social reaction in 2016 that undermined the reformist political opening. But first to its most promising dynamics – the broad alliance for universal public health.

Broad alliance for universal welfare

The 'reformist populist' opening was more than social pacts between political executives and the urban poor (as in Solo and partly Jakarta), the middle class (as in Bandung) and the unions (as in Batam and partly greater Jakarta). The most promising element of 'reformist populism' was the successful campaign for Indonesia's universal social security programme in 2010–11. The campaign was based on a policy proposal drafted by progressive parliamentarians and CSO activists, with the support in particular of the vibrant metalworkers' union and soon of other unions too, as well as human rights and urban poor organizations.

Charisma is rarely negative in politics, but Rieke D. Pitaloka looked sharply into my eyes, assuring me that when entering party politics, she benefitted less from her fame as the beautiful flimsy young wife of an auto rickshaw driver in a popular old soap opera than from her master's thesis about philosopher Hannah Arendt. Arendt's argument that bureaucracies may routinize evil reminded me, Rieke said, of how important it was to sustain some of the activism from her student years in order to invigorate parliamentary procedures. Combining extra-parliamentary and parliamentary engagement was the only chance to improve and make operational the public health reform that had been introduced during Megawati Sukarnoputri's presidency, but then ignored and, by 2009, was on the verge of being annulled. So Rieke involved fellow parliamentarians and cooperated with union and CSO activists to improve and get the public health bill accepted.

In March 2010, numerous unions, CSOs and individuals formed a joint action Committee for Social Security Reforms (KAJS). They were facilitated in particular by the FSPMI with vigorous Chairman Said Iqbal and the Trade Union Rights Centre (TURC), with dynamic director Surya Tjandra, plus the Friedrich Ebert Stiftung (FES). This was a historic shift. Several union leaders came together with many other groups, including from informal labourers such as domestic workers (possibly a quarter of the workforce) and the urban poor, poorly organized but outnumbering, of course, the proportionally few permanent workers. Sympathetic academics, reform-oriented bureaucrats and progressive politicians took part too.

Initially, unions had responded negatively to the idea of a universal health scheme, to be financed by employers and contributions from the self-employed and state-subsidized poor people. Unions represented a minority of the workforce and wanted instead to defend and expand their previous special benefits for formal-sector permanent employees and leaders. During discussions with allies, however, most bosses realized that they needed wider support and therefore had to include others too. The most realistic proposals were worked out and numbers of actions, inside as well as outside parliament, made possible the enactment of the law on the Social Security Executing Agency, BPJS.

BPJS was activated in early 2014. By international standards it is a major achievement and success. At the time of writing, some 80 per cent of the population are covered and crucial in fighting the Covid-19. This is good, although much remains to be done and premium payment remains a major problem, especially under the pandemic – not just from the poor without fixed employment and with limited access to social security, but also from the better-off and some private employers.

Alliance discontinued – Renewed electoral attempts

The main problems, however, were how to scale up and follow up. In this case, the campaign remained on the national level, rarely involving unions and other groups around the country. Most crucially, the broad alliance of progressive politicians, unions and CSOs, aside from its role in overseeing implementation, was not sustained. Having celebrated the victory, union leaders returned to their main task of fighting for better wages and employment conditions.

Struggles for higher minimum wages and restrictions on social dumping by subcontracting work certainly benefitted many casual workers too. And unions were eager to gain broader support in a series of national strikes during 2012 and 2013 as well as when putting pressure on local politicians to increase minimum standards. But according to senior urban poor campaigner, Wardah Hafidz, informal labourers were soon marginalized. And Lita Anggraini, remarkable initiator of domestic workers' own organizations, said that she, too, found little understanding of their cause among unionists and parliamentarians.

Meanwhile Iqbal and other labour activists also tried to participate in politics directly, not merely to build a broad alliance for alternative policies. Their grand attempt came together in slate of genuinely labour and CSO-based candidates in the 2013 elections of governor and vice governor positions in West Java, the most populous province close to Jakarta. The PDI-P, bravely, nominated two major pro-democrats with roots in the province. Rieke Pitaloka – the young charismatic parliamentarian who focused on labour relations and co-directed the successful struggle for the universal public health reform – was selected to run for the position of governor. Teten Masduki – the politically independent pioneer of labour rights, thereafter the country's prime anti-corruption campaigner – was chosen for deputy governor.

In a Muslim-dominated province, Pitaloka and Masduki did better than many other candidates including those endorsed by former President Yudhoyono and retired General and Oligarch Prabowo. The progressives lost by only 4 per cent to the incumbent governor and his running mate, who were supported by a Muslim-driven coalition. This was a remarkable achievement, given that neither Pitaloka nor Masduki was strong in rural areas, that a young woman who rarely wore the veil was running for the highest position in a Muslim-dominated province and that neither of them could refer to previous successful local governance, as 'Jokowi' could by pointing to Solo. However, they might have done better and won. Aside from being poor at social media, the prime problem, according to Pitaloka, was that she was not supported by all the unions, some of which would have preferred a deputy candidate of their own. Actually, Pitaloka and Masduki were not even supported by the union leader in the former alliance for the public health reform, Said Iqbal, who retained links to the brotherhood Prosperous Justice Party (PKS). Masduki, moreover, the 'NGO candidate', was disappointed by the poor support from the CSOs. They were much weaker and unwilling to engage in political battles than he had expected. A typical comment from when I asked CSO leaders about the insufficient support for the progressive team was: the candidates were a bit arrogant (…) and not so close to our own organizations (…) and we were busy with our own business, beyond partisan politics.

The second major union attempt to engage on its own in politics related to legislative elections. Building union parties had failed (Chapter 10), so competitive union leaders had to relate to existing parties, which subordinated them to party priorities and put them at the tail end of their lists of candidates. In 2009, however, a new system of open lists of party candidates in each constituency enabled individual candidates to compete. This benefitted politicians with lots of money, thus increasing vote buying, but also unions who could mobilize support for their nominees. In the early 2014 legislative elections, a heroic attempt was therefore feasible in the industrial city of Bekasi east of Jakarta to coordinate union leader candidates in different party lists.

Internal political training was in the union's impressive new office building as well as in Handoko's *Omah Tani*, the meeting place for small farmers and their friends in Batang (Chapter 10). Thus inspired, sympathetic union leader Obon Tabroni and his followers (who had stood by Pitaloka and Masduki) opened a similar meeting place for workers and their friends in Bekasi, *Omah Buruh*. This was under colourful shelters on an abandoned 'white elephant' bridge. The happy message was that the candidates would mobilize votes from the rank and file of labour, and then 'go from factory to the public sphere', addressing citizens' general problems. There were numerous challenges of specifying a convincing programme beyond labourers' special preoccupations, as well as of trying to coordinate and backseat drive candidates in different parties. Still, for the first time ever, a union obtained at least two parliamentary seats, even though the margins were small and the candidates got even fewer votes than the number of resident union members.

Union and political rivalries unions remained a problem. Obon Traboni, for example, did not give up and built up a momentum beyond the factory gates during the collection of signatures in support of his independent candidacy in the 2017 head of district (*bupati*) elections in industrial city of Bekasi. Yet he still lost out – lacking the full backing of other unions and workers affiliated to conventional parties.

Return to horse-trading

Given the bleak results in the electoral experiments, most union leaders returned to the tactics of gaining better minimum wages by striking the best-possible deals with the most powerful politicians who would be able to deliver tangible results. In 2012, 'Jokowi' and 'Ahok' had been positive, but once in power they wanted to discuss not only higher wages but also other matters such as welfare. This did not work. Why?

As Said Iqbal, the forceful leader of the metalworkers and one of the propelling forces in the KAJS alliance, told me in an intense conversation it made less sense to sustain and expand a broad alliance for better labour conditions and social welfare than to fight for higher wages and secure employment. Why? His answer, along with that of several other leaders in a late 2013 workshop, boiled down to the message that there was no way to negotiate agreements on both wages and welfare, not to mention principles for economic development. Even if there were such discussions, unionists could not trust soft promises that would not mean anything concrete for their members.

This was the beginning of the end for 'reformist populism'. As the 2014 presidential elections neared, Iqbal himself, without a convincingly anchored mandate, responded by opting instead for an agreement on behalf of the metalworkers and their confederation with infamous former general and business oligarch, Prabowo Subianto. Support was given in return for favours and a promise Iqbal would become minister of labour. Subsequently other unions turned to Prabowo's rival, 'Jokowi', for rival 'contracts' or tried to survive as principled lone riders. Similarly, numerous CSOs abandoned the approach of the joint KAJS campaign and returned to lobbying for special access and favours for their organizations and the vulnerable people they served.

However, several concerned scholars and activists rejected this dissidents' version of 'transactional politics'. The alternative, they reasoned, was to foster change within or in alignment with 'Jokowi's' team. How did they fare?

Floating president

Dissidents' setbacks in electoral politics and the resumption by many of them of divisive horse-trading with various politicians weakened the progressive movements. But 'Jokowi's' momentum was sufficient enough for the advisers of PDI-P matriarch Megawati Sukarnoputri to convince her that she was a less electable presidential candidate than he was. Thus, 'Jokowi' retained some autonomy and was not a party-man' who Sukarnoputri could dictate to. Still, he remained a technocrat without a consolidated movement or a distinct policy agenda. So instead of picking a pro-democratic candidate for the vice presidency, it was necessary to garner support among powerful politicians, entrepreneurs, clerics and generals.

In these transactions, it was possible to combine 'Jokowi's' personal popularity as a non-elitist and non-corrupt pragmatic leader in favour of inclusive politics and development, with the worries of sections of the elite about his opponent – Prabowo, the oligarch, former general and son-in-law of Suharto. Prabowo was an authoritarian nationalist, and, while not being religious himself, associated with Muslim radicals and politically exclusionary politics. Thus, 'Jokowi's' sponsors in the elite told him to ask the previous Vice President, Jusuf Kalla – widely respected *Golkar* and business leader from the 'outer islands' – to be available for another period.

Tuning down 'reformist populism' to gain wider support among the elite was, however, not as successful as expected in the opinion polls. There were general statements about inclusive development, anti-corruption and human rights but no concept and strategy that could catch people's imagination. In the end, 'Jokowi' was only saved by his opponents' mistakes and an intensive campaign, especially on social media, by a genuine movement of volunteers from all walks of life. Thanks to them, moreover, the campaign concluded with a mass festivity in Jakarta's major stadium featuring several of the country's popular artists – in vivid contrast to Prabowo's previous mass meeting when he paraded in uniform on a horse and inspected ceremonial troops, bringing to mind a certain Italian leader of the 1930s.

Lost in transition, again

'Jokowi' and Kalla won with a rather thin margin of about 6 per cent, and it took time for Prabowo to concede. Most importantly, however, key players from the parties and powerful organizations that had backed 'Jokowi" and Kalla's campaign immediately established a 'transition office' to divide the spoils and share the top-level positions in state and government. The inexperienced and uncoordinated progressives lost out entirely in the distribution of influential positions. 'Jokowi' tried to put up some resistance by recalling a promise that the main criteria for selecting ministers and other crucial positions would be professionalism rather than political affiliation, and that there would be zero tolerance for corruption. The Commission to Eradicate Corruption (KPK) would screen the candidates. Immediately, however, the new president had to concede to pressures from the powerful actors in his coalition. The CSO groups and the media, having asked for the screening and supported 'Jokowi' to fight corruption, were not able to generate enough popular pressure to make a difference. The progressives were not even granted leadership of 'Jokowi's' own staff (KSP), being pushed aside by his trusted business friend in *Golkar*, General (ret.) Luhut Pandjaitan.

In my minutes from interviews and conversations at the time with pro-democrats who supported 'Jokowi', there were frequent notes of distrust, resignation and cynicism. One could not but recall the reactions in 1998 among the pro-democrats who had ousted Suharto but lacked a programme and strategy, and were thus abandoned within a few months when the main political players and their international sponsors opted for elitist democracy (Chapter 9). By 2014, though, there was more criticism in influential circles. So a year later, the progressives were granted a major concession. Teten Masduki –

previously labour rights and anti-corruption campaigner, vice governor candidate in West Java and decisive co-leader in 'Jokowi's' presidential campaign – was appointed head of the president's staff of advisers.

Masduki never really managed, however, to develop new universal welfare and development programmes, nor to build effective cooperation with interest and citizen action groups. Some said he was not strong enough. When meeting in the palace for a conversation two years later, he himself joked about occupying the dictator Suharto's old office but, in stark contrast, not being able to do much of what he wanted to do. Some advances were made with regard to community forestry and redistribution of unused land. But whatever one might conclude about Masduki's strategizing and coordination of his staff and the programmes of various departments, his basic powers rested with the popular movements and CSOs which were weak. Even like-minded expert CSOs that were asked by Masduki's office to contribute proposals and comments demanded horrendous honorariums or claimed to be busy with other matters. Otherwise, CSOs themselves came with diffused proposals that were not part of anything resembling a comprehensive and transformative reform agenda. Similarly, very few popular organizations and CSO groups were really able to monitor and push for progressive use of government schemes, such as the huge sums of money that the government vested with the heads of the villages.

Masduki's major concern by late 2017, however, was that everyone in the palace had become afraid of the radical Muslims and their supporters. A year before, they had been able to mobilize hundreds of thousands of people in the streets of Jakarta and win the local elections. So naturally, I asked what Masduki could do, given that the progressives were, at best, able to rally a few thousand people? He did not have an answer, and a few months later, he lost his key position, degraded to special assistant of the president. How was it possible for the conservative opposition to alter the situation so drastically? To answer, we must first turn back in time.

Rise and containment of religious right-wing populism

During the 1950s, the radical nationalist and reformist communist movement attracted many underprivileged not very devoted Muslims by stressing pro-poor policies and struggles for equal citizenship. By contrast, Suharto relied extensively on extreme Muslim groups during the annihilation of the popular movement in 1965. In consolidating his rule afterwards, he reverted to central military and bureaucratic control and technocratic developmentalism (Chapter 4). Towards the end of his reign, however, when losing ground and becoming more patrimonial, he sought to win legitimacy by once again reaching out to the Muslims – this time by nurturing cooperation with the major Muslim organizations (Chapter 9). The institution for this was the state-sponsored, yet autonomous, Indonesian Ulama Council, MUI, which amassed increasing importance over time. Suharto also supported Vice President B. J. Habibie's Association of Muslim Intellectuals (ICMI), many members of which were, in addition, associated with the major socio-religious modernist organization,

Muhammadiyah. The next President, Abdurrahman Wahid (1999–2001), was the leader of the rival traditionalist Muslim association, *Nahdlatul Ulama* (NU), and of a more pluralistic persuasion, but he nevertheless nourished, for example, the practice of sharia law in Aceh. President Megawati Sukarnoputri (2001–4), by contrast, tried to contain Muslim privileges, but she soon lost out to General (ret.) Yudhoyono. His victories in the presidential elections in 2004 and 2009 were much thanks to Muslim support, which he honoured with favourable legislation, institutional support to the MUI and handouts to related groups and leaders, while the pro-democrats lost ground (Chapter 10).

The rise of 'Jokowi's' 'reformist populism', then, was a game changer. He sought to find a middle course between Megawati's hard-line defence of nationalism and Yudhoyono's accommodation of hard-line Muslims. 'Jokowi' reduced their economic favours and treated liberals, Christians and ethnic Chinese like 'Ahok' as equal citizens. This was the background for why Muslim social movement leaders and establishment political adversaries of 'Jokowi's' reformism came together in 2016 in an effort to regain their privileges. Why were they successful?

Muslim street power

A year ahead of the early 2017 gubernatorial elections in Jakarta, it was widely expected that acting Governor 'Ahok' would be elected, given his high approval ratings. In November and December 2016, however, masses of people – possibly even more people than in the demonstrations against Suharto – came out in the streets in protest against 'Ahok'. The ethnic Chinese and Christian acting governor had made an ill-advised statement about his opponent's attempt to use a verse in the Koran to get people to vote for him and reject 'Ahok'. Thus, the floodgates were opened. MUI issued a *fatwa* and militant Muslim groups, supported by 'Ahok's' opponents, including Prabowo, accused him of being against Islam in general and poor Muslims in particular. Actually, when 'Jokowi' was elected president, 'Ahok's Singaporean-style management was accentuated. He dishonoured, for example, promises to the urban poor. So many of them were now prepared to abandon him in return for protection against eviction. Finally, 'Ahok' lost the election (to a previous Jokowi loyalist, Anies Baswedan, now supported by Prabowo) and was then convicted of blasphemy and imprisoned.

Indirectly the campaign was directed at 'Jokowi' too. He was accused, for example, of not being a true Muslim but of having liberal inclinations and a communist past (even though he was born as late as 1961). His chances of being re-elected in 2019 were obviously in jeopardy. What could he do?

Reformist alternative abandoned

In late 2017, a proposal by concerned scholars to counter the rightist identity politics by launching a major participatory welfare programme was discussed with close advisers of the PDI-P and 'Jokowi' in a Jogjakarta dinner. The idea was to follow up the universal social security scheme, which had gained wide popular support and strengthened the pro-'Jokowi' groups. The participants nodded and we discussed a possible quick start. Yet, the advisers worried about what the other parties in the president's coalition – apart from the PDI-P – would say. By January 2018 the answer was clear enough. Popular and civil society-oriented Teten Masduki was dismissed as head of the president's advisory staff and replaced by the former Commander of the Armed Forces, General Moeldoko.

'Jokowi' was up against a similar kind of right-wing populism to the one that opposed centre-left governments in other parts of the world. For example, in India in 2014 propelled by Hindu fundamentalists and in the Philippines 2016 and Brazil 2018 led by strongmen Duterte and Bolsonaro, respectively, or for that matter in the United States in 2016 personified by Trump and in much of Europe by conservative chauvinism. As we shall see, 'Jokowi' was more successful in that he held onto power, but at the cost of democracy and welfare based on equal citizenship. How did this happen?

Belt-and-braces

Having abandoned a transformative social democratic alternative, 'Jokowi' and his team opted for a defensive belt-and-braces approach. They combined the common reactions around the world in terms of enhanced state authority, accommodation of populist leaders and favours for their voters. The Indonesian package came in four interrelated parts. The first step was to accommodate military leaders in favour of central rule and national unity with equal, though not necessarily democratic, citizenship and religious pluralism. This was symbolized by the five state principles, *Pancasila*[2] – in contrast to Muslim values and communities. Hence, loyal military leaders were brought into the government and civil administration and the police were strengthened. Laws and regulations were revised to constrain hate speech and disinformation including in social media, which could be used to muzzle opposition against the government and *Pancasila* – partially at the expense of human rights and democratic principles.

Secondly, however, leading Muslims who were prepared to accept pluralism and *Pancasila* more generally were also accommodated, along with their organizations and pietistic values. The same applied to their followers' concerns. Muslim communities and areas benefitted from targeted welfare measures. In 2018, 'Jokowi' even selected the traditionalist Ulama Ma'ruf Amin as his vice presidential running mate. Tactically this was of course brilliant, dividing the Muslim camp and reducing Prabowo's ability to resume the contentious populist identity politics of 2016–17 that had brought down 'Ahok' and cornered 'Jokowi'. But the price was high and the long-term effects uncertain. Amin was the supreme leader of NU and chairperson of the MUI, which issues *fatwas* such as the one against 'Ahok'. He was also instrumental in waging campaigns for a so-called anti-pornography law and against the supposedly deviant Muslim *Ahmadiya* movement and the LGBT community.

---

[2] Currently framed as 'Belief in the One and Only God; a just and civilized humanity; a unified Indonesia; democracy, democracy led by the wisdom of the representatives of the people; social justice for all Indonesians'.

Even though political and social liberties were curtailed, the third priority was to enhance liberal economic development, prioritizing state-led infrastructural investments and world market-oriented manufacturing and services. The assumption was that people would benefit from more jobs and better pay. There was no mention, however, of negotiations with employers and unions on these matters. But there was still hope that there would be steps towards universal welfare programmes, based on equal citizen rights and with participatory governance. They did not materialize. Rather – as indicated – there was targeted support, often via Muslim groups, to contain opposition and win crucial votes.

Finally, the three manoeuvres were brought together. This had less to do with the old Javanese rulers' habit of increasing their powers by absorbing their rivals – as suggested by culturally oriented pundits – than with the quite universal 'politics of triangulation', pioneered by Bill Clinton in the United States and by Tony Blair and others in Europe. That is, to blend the most attractive parts of the major contenders' views while also trying to transcend them in a third direction. Blair, for one, brought neoliberal politics into the British Labour government and claimed to combine them with a politics of equality and opportunity, thus offering a 'third way'.

In Indonesia, 'Jokowi' and his team seem to have tried to revive President Sukarno's way of boosting his agenda by bringing together nationalist generals and Muslim leaders who agreed to *Pancasila*. Sukarno, however, was able to add his own popular base and vision, along with the following of the world's then third largest reformist communist party while 'Jokowi' nurtured neither a captivating vision nor the popular movements prepared to support him. In spite of being the stronger of the two, Sukarno felt he had no choice but to opt for 'guided democracy', but then Suharto annihilated the popular movements (Chapter 4). As for 'Jokowi', his triangulation seemed to reduce both the essentials of democracy and the popular opportunities to promote inclusive development. Was this apprehension confirmed by the outcome of the 2019 elections and the subsequent transactions?

From democracy to power-sharing

'Jokowi' and his coalition of parties won the elections by a comfortable margin. The results suggested stability, but that was fictitious. There were many votes but few alternative voices. The politics of triangulation revived the political geography of socio-religious pillars and patronage politics, which had dominated Indonesia before Suharto's 'new order'. 'Jokowi'-Ma'ruf secured their heartlands in Hindu-dominated Bali, and among the ethnic Javanese in East and Central Java. They triumphed too in other provinces with significant numbers of Javanese migrants, and among the non-Muslim voters for whom tolerance and pluralism is crucial. Vice presidential candidate Ma'ruf Amin's Nahdlatul Ulama (NU) is particularly strong in vote-rich East and Central Java. 'Jokowi's' core followers of pluralist Muslims – many of whom belong to the less privileged classes – were combined with non-Muslim voters as well as traditionalist NU sympathizers, the latter often from among landowners and the petit bourgeoisie.

Meanwhile Prabowo and his vice president candidate Sandiaga Uno, the deputy governor of Jakarta after 'Ahok', gained overwhelming support from the typically well-to-do and well-educated members of Muslim organizations with theologically modern orientations, including *Muhammadiyah*, in addition to the brotherhood PKS party. They won in the Muslim strongholds in the western parts of Java and Sumatra and elsewhere.

The positive aspect of 'Jokowi's' politics of triangulation was the momentum for tolerance and pluralism. But elitist power sharing became the main game in town at the expense of liberal democracy with checks and balances and effective parliamentary opposition. And in contrast to previous 'reformist populism', there was the identity politics of moderates against a 'fundamentalist Muslim enemy' as opposed to the introduction of welfare reforms based on equal and democratic–oriented citizenship.

Predictably, Prabowo and his Muslim devotees did not acknowledge defeat, claiming there had been massive and systematic fraud and calling for 'people power' demonstrations. The accusations never gained credibility. The major Muslim organizations were reluctant to support militant protests, and some political allies signalled they might jump ship in parliament. Yet, street riots for two days were a clear enough indication that Prabowo would cause trouble if he was not accommodated with honour. So he was. As Prabowo distanced himself from the most militant Muslims, 'Jokowi' appointed him minister of defence.

Already in his inaugural address, moreover 'Jokowi' stated that the main point was not the process – obviously referring to democracy with equal and human rights – but stability and results in terms of economic development. Meanwhile, the parliament hastened to weaken the anti-corruption agency and the regulations on mining and land acquisition, as well as to revise the criminal code to reduce critical freedoms.

Liberal media such as the major magazine *Tempo* reacted strongly. And remarkably, for some weeks, many students reclaimed the streets around the country in protests – showing that not just militant Muslims but also progressives could mobilize people. But 'Jokowi' made minor adjustments, postponed the laws and brought in a few critics as junior ministers. Unintentionally, moreover, an extremist Muslim served as a symbol of 'the main enemy' by stabbing the outgoing Coordinating Minister of Politics, Law and Security, Wiranto. So the protests amounted to little more than an indication that were still some limits to what politicians could do.

From social contracts for inclusive development to market-driven growth

In early 2020 'Jokowi' returned to what he meant by 'development first' in his inaugural address. He proposed a comprehensive 'Job Creation Law' – extensive but swiftly drafted and accepted by the parliament before the end of the year. The main components include streamlined business regulations, reduced rules against investments with negative effects for the environment and popular neighbourhoods, promotion of foreign investments and employment of overseas workers, relaxed rules against outsourcing, reduced severance pay, liberalized rules on minimum wages and more flexible employment conditions generally. In return, formally employed labour get a symbolic 'sweetener bonus'. Informal labour get next to nothing, aside from some support for small and micro-businesses and, at best, more but unsecure jobs. The sole positive step in the right direction is an unemployment insurance but it is insufficient and does not alter the basic character of the law.

There is no doubt that Indonesia needs more clear-cut rules and regulations as well as investments in manufacturing and production-oriented services after years of relying on the extraction of natural resources and the consumption of the upper classes. And there must be more jobs, certainly. But to foster growth by exploiting nature and reducing the cost of hiring labour in general – rather than by increasing productivity, facilitating productive public works and services for basic pay, supporting labour-intensive production for local markets and increasing demand – is neither sustainable nor just. Equally worrying, the bill suggested that more powers on related matters would be vested with the president. And the proposal was drafted without any democratic consultation with workers' and informal labourers' organizations and related experts. Only business and its specialists were asked for opinions. Those complaining were asked to lobby the parliament – most members and parties of which had already committed themselves to supporting the president and his cabinet. In fact, there is not even one single little party in parliament to represent the views of employees and sufferers of environmental degradation.

Predictably, the employers' association was jubilant, while the unions in particular put their foot down. Within weeks, an increasing number of them refused to talk to the administration and set aside differences over what politicians they might otherwise make deals with. Meanwhile, organizations for democracy, human rights and the environment raised their voices too, as did students. But there was no broad organized alliance and no firm alternative policy proposal. So by the end of 2020, momentum was lost, and 'Jokowi', his staff and business allies proceed, politely conceding that they might consider some polishing in the process of implementation.

Causes for setbacks

With the 'Job Creation Law', in one fell swoop the president undermined the social democratic potential of the wide consultations and negotiations with 'ordinary people' on socially acceptable development that had once brought him to power, preferring instead market-driven growth, along with some handouts, which might, in time, he argued, generate jobs and welfare. Retracing the processes, what were the root causes for the regression and what can progressives do?

From irony of success to tragedy of failure

During a decade and a half after democrats made Soeharto step down and rulers put on new cloths, mainstream scholars like Donald Horowitz and Larry Diamond dubbed Indonesia a showcase of liberal democratization. Edward Aspinall certainly cautioned that what he called 'the irony of success' was that the elites had adjusted to new freedoms and democratic institutions in return for the containment of popular movements. But the expectation remained that, since the elites adjusted to the new rules of the game, they would also, gradually, build better parties, reduce corruption and respect the rule of law and human rights. Actually, it was clear already since 2004 that this expectation did not materialize and that the main reason (according to the nationwide surveys of how grounded experts assessed the dynamics) was that pro-democrats were not given fair chances to get into politics and propel progress. Still, this fundamental problem of representation was brushed aside, while most experts focused on institutional flaws, and the political economists stressed the dominance of the oligarchs (Chapter 10).

It was not until Prabowo gained vast support for his strongman agenda in the 2014 elections, and populist identity politics undermined then-governor 'Ahok', followed by 'Jokowi's' dubious countermeasures, that most scholars agreed (in several international assessments and in Australian National University's 2019 Indonesia update) that democracy is indeed regressing. Yet, the focus remains on the institutional decay along with the manoeuvres of the political elite, the oligarchs and their followers in uncivil society. This is of course important, but although it should be clear by now that democratization is not a technical matter that the elite will fix on its own, nothing is there of the processes and actors that might have resisted the perpetrators and nurtured positive change. Ironically, this bias is now unmasked by reality itself through the 'Job Creation Law', exposing how the 'irony of success' for elitist democratization has turned into a tragedy of failure.

Anatomy of populist setbacks

The effort to deepen 'reformist populism' was a step forward, so why did it fail? Over the years, most notes in the taskforce that traced the processes pointed to the way progressives handled two troublesome aspects of left-populism – neglect of democratic representation and a shortage of alternative reform proposals. We shall return to the details, but first it is essential to recall the longer history of similar challenges, which goes a long way to explaining why there is still no notable leftist dimension in Indonesia's social and political life.

Most progressives have still not revisited the developments in the late 1950s when radical nationalists and reform-oriented communists abandoned the successful efforts at equal citizen rights, which had proven even more fruitful in Kerala, by adjusting to Sukarno's 'guided democracy', in tandem with nationalist generals and traditionalist Ulamas (Chapters 4 and 5). In the mid-1960s, it was not even possible to resume the primacy of equal citizen rights to resist the political genocide, directed by generals who combined central despotism with colonial-like indirect rule and repression through religious leaders and communities (Chapter 4). In the 1970s, the earlier positive experiences had faded away, and the Left was in a mess – both those who subordinated themselves to Sukarno and those who turned to Maoism had failed bitterly. Liberal-socialist critics of Suharto even deemed the social democratic lynchpins of interest-based collectivities and democracy premature (Chapter 9).

The pioneering activists who from the late 1980s reinvented the struggle for democracy tried to build these foundations from the bottom-up, among the victims of Suharto's reign. But they were constrained by the diverse interests of subjugated people in the context of a very unevenly developing economy, as well as by their own divisive practices and priorities. They were also not able to develop alternative concepts for democratization and inclusive development. Rather, they congregated against Suharto. This unity and identity of standing up against a common enemy, however, were of no avail when the dictator departed and the powerful actors retained their businesses and adjusted to elitist democracy, with international support (Chapter 9).

The obvious alternative, then, was promoting unity and democracy by building alternative new parties and participating in elections. But this was also not possible due to the extremely demanding and costly party entry and nomination thresholds (Chapter 10). During the 2000s, similar challenges to the 1990s – of building broad popular-interest collectivities and fostering democracy from the bottom-up – returned to the fore, when activists failed to build non-party political blocs by politicizing the many different popular protests, unions and activist groups. Adding ideological slogans as a way of uniting the factions did not help much either. Finally many leaders rather turned to agreements with least worst influential political executives and the 'politics of diaspora' by entering various mainstream parties, but this merely multiplied divisions and transactions (Chapter 10).

Meanwhile, aside from bashing neoliberalism and corruption, the pro-democrats have never really worked out a programme of inclusive development based on equity, as an alternative to the liberal growth-first dogma. In addition, Suharto's state corporatism was not replaced by a framework for social democratic negotiations between interest organizations and the state, but only by liberal lobbying and horse-trading. In retrospect, the only dynamic openings in several decades for building the social democratic foundations – of democratic popular-interest collectivities in spite of diverging interests under uneven development, and democratic links between state and citizens based on equal rights – have been associated with 'reformist populism' since the mid-2000s. Within this framework, it was even possible to lay the ground for the other two foundations – universal welfare policies and social pacts towards fairer development.

This time, however, in a similar pattern, the progressives were lost in two negative aspects of left-populism – (i) unmediated relations between citizens and rulers instead of democratic representation and negotiation and (ii) identity politics against an enemy instead of unifying behind alternative reforms based on equal citizen-rights.

Direct democracy instead of representation and negotiation

The social pacts in Solo and Jakarta unified many people behind a common idea of bypassing bosses and patrons, thus agreeing on better urban development. This pointed to the potential of deepening democracy. Unfortunately, there were no institutionalized representation of the parties involved in the negotiations and no formalization of the agreements. The populist leaders discussed and agreed informally and individually with various groups and leaders, but did not build democratic institutions. The discussions and agreements rested with individuals and informal trust and chemistry. Elsewhere, similarly, unions and popular organizations negotiated temporary deals with influential political figures.

In contrast, the broad alliance for the public health reform largely took the form of representation of various unions, CSO groups and politicians in a joint action group. This was a showcase of what was possible. But the cooperation could not be sustained and expanded into new areas of social and economic policies. One pivotal reason was the lack of a format to negotiate with local and central government, and business representatives, about how to develop welfare measures, employment relations and dynamic inclusive development. The issues remained separate. The progressives did not even fight for more democratic representation and comprehensive negotiations. Instead, the unions returned to specific deals with employers and politicians. The latter used the same practices to negotiate special interests with union leaders – dividing and ruling. Informally employed labour was marginalized, again. CSOs continued to lobby for special access and favours for their organizations and beneficiaries.

By implication, it was also difficult to use participation in governance to build stronger popular movements that could, in turn, provide more support for progressives working 'within' government. If that had worked out, the progressives would have felt more able to resist concessions to political elites and big business as well as to religious mass organizations.

Identity politics against an enemy instead of reforms based on equal citizen-rights

The second major reason for advances and setbacks related to the tendency of populist politics to mobilize people by way of a common identity against somebody or something bad rather than build unity behind alternative reforms based on equal rights for all citizens. Pro-democrats certainly put forward various demands, but they were usually particular and not aggregated under any other umbrella than slogans, such as against elites and neoliberalism.

The positive exceptions of unity for alternatives included the vision of social pacts, from Solo to South Aceh, towards fairer development, and, of course, the remarkable universal public health reform. This pointed to what could be achieved. But the vision and reform were not followed up. There were few genuine pacts on alternative development. And there was no strategy of transformative reforms to increase people's capacity with one reform, so that they can fight for a more advanced reform, for example, by expanding welfare reforms, and connect them with employment conditions and economic development. As for the unions and CSOs themselves, the predominant strategy was to procure favours for their own organizations and followers, not to forge collective action behind comprehensive public reforms for all.

Even though the progressives had access to public offices for some time and directed the president's staff, they were not able to successively draft and negotiate new comprehensive welfare and development reforms based on equal citizenship, which various movements and groups could unite behind and gain strength. Thus emboldened they might also have been able to back up the government against rightist identity politics. Further welfare measures were often targeted and mediated by Muslim groups, to counter discontent, instead of being based on equal citizen rights and facilitated by public agencies for all.

Similarly, the struggle for welfare reforms was rarely combined with campaigns for better public administration. The anti-corruption agency and anti-graft groups focused on the important middle-class preoccupation with impartial governance and large-scale corruption among the political elite, but ignored the corruption of public services and welfare, which affects ordinary people and may generate broader counter-movements. The experiences from New Delhi in this regard are instructive (Chapter 12).

Democratic representation and transformative reforms

What are the major conclusions? The first is that, in contrast to liberal assumptions, 'reformist populism' may indeed be an opening for social democratic-oriented development and international cooperation to that end. The second conclusion, however, is that the supposedly direct links between ruler and people, and identity politics against an enemy are destructive. Thirdly, the positive experiences from the efforts at pacts and the public health reform show that it is possible to alter these priorities. This can be done by better democratic representation of popular-rooted organizations for crucial issues and interests in public governance, combined with transformative reforms based on equal rights that movements and groups can agree on and support. Thus, movements can get stronger, and both back up leaders and keep them accountable. But are progressives able to fight for it, now?

Out of the box

The contemporary challenges are thus historically rooted in the abandoning (in the late 1950s) of the most successful way so far of building Social Democracy in the South – that is, by equal citizen rights-based democratization as a framework for broad alliances for socio-economic reforms – and thereafter disremembering what had been achieved. The best case was Kerala, but Indonesia was also en route before 'guided democracy'. Hence, it remains crucial to fight for better democratic representation and transformative universal reforms. But how can this be done now when 'reformist populism' has been overtaken by the politics of triangulation, power sharing and neoliberal and environmentally destructive policies? We need to think outside the box.

Not everything is bleak. Firstly, it is true that some unions only cater to their own members, who now suffer from less secure employment conditions. But others realize that political change calls for broader alliances. The argument from the Presidential Palace, then, that 'there are so many unions' is like saying that CSOs should not also be listened to because they are so many and do not represent society at large. Most importantly, not just unionized employees but also the urban poor and numerous rights and environmental organizations, as well as independent media, have come out against the exclusionary policies. As have many students – increasingly worried about limited democratic freedoms and their own future as professionals in precarious labour markets.

Secondly, while the 2019 resistance against the legislation to weaken the anti-corruption agency and revise the criminal code focused on the undermining of liberal democracy, the 2020 protests against the 'Job Creation Law' have taken a step ahead by also criticizing the absence of democratic participation in the preparation of the law by unions, informal labourers' organizations and environmental groups. 'Jokowi' and the Palace had – like the Bonapartists in Paris and the supposedly enlightened regimes in East Asia – relied on top-down policy development, in close contact with business, party bosses and selected labour and religious players exclusively.

Thirdly, the need to fight Covid-19 has made it clear for many actors, business included, that universal public health policies, as well as social security and economic stimulation, are indispensable. Just like 'Jokowi' and his business friends in Solo in the mid-2000s, the dynamic employers who have to survive by way of higher productivity and increasing domestic demand may realize that it is more profitable to negotiate social and other rights than to fight frustrated labourers and professionals facing precarious work conditions.

Maybe it is therefore not impossible to campaign for alternative reforms based on equal citizen rights, in the same tradition as the public health reform. Given that the 'Job Creation Law' is comprehensive, it cannot be fought by exclusively defending the right to 'decent work' and fixed employment. The priority of the new law is business investment based on more exploitation of people and nature, along with handouts for the victims, and prevention of democratic participation in public policymaking. This calls for a comprehensive alternative that stresses the participation of unions and informal labourers' organizations and their experts, as well as environmental organizations, on an equal basis with state and capital in working out a model for inclusive and sustainable development. Development, that is, which is built on social contracts delivering increased productivity and more decent jobs through training and socio-economic and environmental equity, plus production-oriented programmes for the underemployed.

How might this be initiated? The draft public health reform was worked out during President Megawati's administration, and further developed by progressive parliamentarians and the Committee for Social Security Reforms (KAJS). The hope was that follow-up reforms would be drafted under President 'Jokowi', but this did not happen. Hence, while not giving up on joint efforts with progressives 'working from within', it is now necessary to proceed from the outside, such as by way of think tanks that are rooted in popular and citizen action movements.

Ironically, Muslim leaders of various inclinations have managed to secure the support of the government and international bodies to build up an immensely influential Ulama Council (MUI) as a means of perpetuating the indirect rule of 'their people', the *ummah*. But the democracy-oriented issue and interest movements, progressive politicians and experts, and the pro-democratic international community have not yet tried to establish a similar forum for the deliberation of public policies between the state and citizens.

15

Implications and options in the North: The Swedish stalemate

The weakness of partners in the South was a crucial factor in the failure of Palme, Brandt and others in the 1970s to build a New International Economic Order, alongside a 'North-South Programme for Survival', which would have enabled social democratic rights and welfare-based development to take place on a global level. Instead the floodgates were opened for market-driven globalization and the bifurcation, in countries like Sweden, of providing aid and promoting exports to and investments in the South. Chapter 7 discussed the case of the Swedish social democrats' adjustment to these realities while trying, not really successfully, to defend welfare and employment at home and tailor support for others in the liberal wave of democracy. Chapters 8–14 addressed the challenges in the South of building new Social Democracy under these conditions. Before we conclude, it is time to consider again the implications and options in the North. Sweden remains a good case in point, given its deep dependence on global developments and the faltering of social democrats' long-standing capacity to promote alternatives.

Northern impasse

In 2014, a think tank within the Swedish Ministry for Foreign Affairs summarized the global trends and issues at stake for the next ten years. Its main argument was that the relocation of industry to the South, as well as rapid technological development, was likely to exacerbate Swedish challenges in terms of rising unemployment, structural adjustment, increasing class differences and pressure on the public welfare system. Additional issues were climate change and the inflow of migrants and refugees. Taken together, the dynamics were rooted in market-driven globalization and extractive and uneven development in the South. Related conflicts might generate xenophobia and extremism in the North as well.

Ironically, many social democrats played down the troublesome scenario. One reason was the primacy of exports and free trade. Another was to resist the claims by employers, bourgeois parties and rightists within their own ranks that the international challenges called for further reduction of taxes and wages for less qualified jobs, the downgrading of public spending and services, and the deregulation of business and employment conditions, in order to defend Sweden's competitiveness. The counter-proposal was to improve the remnants of the Swedish model and bolster similar thinking in the European Union. This would, hopefully, enable Swedish adjustment to globalization in more socially responsible ways. One could foster competitiveness and exports based on efficient and innovative Swedish production and services, as well as education and decent relocation and protection of labour. Thus by reducing the dependence on weak partners in the South, one could save as much of Social Democracy as was possible in one's own country.

Timeline Sweden 1980s–2020

1980s→
- New International Economic Order (NIEO) failed with weak partners in the South.
- Gates opened for neoliberalism and market-driven globalization.
- Swedish growth and welfare model thus undermined and adjusted.

1990s→
- Disciplining of finance and market-driven globalization via EU, UN cooperation and third wave of democracy unviable with weak local partners and elitist democracy.
- Further adjustment to globalization and domestic neoliberalism.

2012–2015
- Stefan Löfven becomes leader of weakened social democratic party; coalition with the Greens.
- Löfven reclaims 'Swedish model' and rights-based foreign policy.
- Suggests ILO-inspired 'Global Deal' to fight ills of globalization.
- Fails to combine these priorities with export and investment priorities in the South.

2015–2020
- Entry of large numbers of refugees. Wide support for nationalist right-wing populists.
- Social democrats adjust – short of internationalist alternative – but remain weak.
- Rights-based foreign policy and 'Global Deal' efforts in shambles. Quests for renewal.

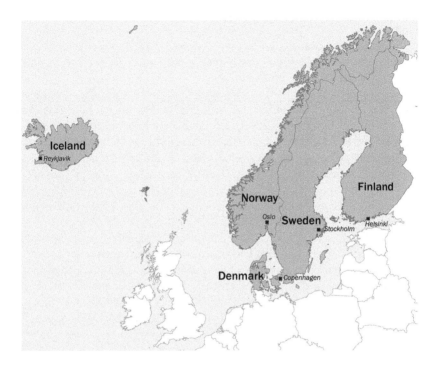

Map 17 Scandinavia-Nordic.

These ideas faced several obstacles. They may be summarized in terms of the four foundations of social democratic development (Chapter 2). First, there was more 'southern-like' uneven development and inequalities in the North too. They made it more difficult to organize democratic political collectivities based on common popular interests and ideas. Second, privatization and neoliberal governance shrunk the number of vital issues that could be handled democratically and undermined the efficiency of the public administration and services (this is a major explanation for the high numbers of victims of Covid-19 in Sweden). In addition, international economic concentration of power increased dramatically, reducing competition and investment in Sweden too. Third, the links between state and civil society were weakened, especially the participation of issue- and interest groups in public governance. Fourth, as compared to wage taxation, it was much more difficult to levy the increasing incomes from capital and speculation, which cause most of the spiralling inequalities and thus also to finance a universal public welfare system. The same applied to the difficulties of restructuring the economy and addressing the mounting inequalities and unemployment among migrants and refugees. Fifth, several of the conditions for the social pact between capital and labour were undermined. Its basis within industry had been hollowed out. It is much more difficult to increase productivity in the new low-wage sectors of private and public services and welfare than previously in trade and production, and the services and welfare cannot be closed down, but who shall pay? The major task was no longer just to handle a shortage of skilled labour but also unemployment. And much of the growth strategy could no longer be controlled due to the international mobility of capital and labour.

Unsurprisingly, Swedish Social Democracy was thus in a crisis, partly reflected in toothless policy development, internal conflicts and reduced membership. In particular, support plummeted among those negatively affected by structural adjustment and financial speculation. Most of these lost voters linked up instead with the chauvinist right-wing party. Meanwhile numerous intellectuals and young people lost interest and trust in politics. Worst, while the root causes for the problems relate to neoliberalism and market-driven globalization and weak partners in the South, the Social Democratic leadership – as well as its leftist critics – has failed to address these obstacles with viable international policies.

In trying to regain direction and strength, the Social Democrats opted in 2012 for their first trade union leader, Stefan Löfven, a former welder. After the 2014 elections, Löfven formed a new government with the Greens and called for the reinvention of the old Scandinavian model with tripartite negotiations between state, unions and employers. But Löfven was not just any trade union leader. He was the chair, and formerly international secretary, of the Industrial and Metal Workers Union (IF-Metall) who had suffered most from deindustrialization. Hence, Löfven wanted to reinvent the Scandinavian model in a global framework.

Restart

Löfven's union-driven vision was a so-called 'Global Deal'. The Scandinavian model could not be exported but its ethos could be added to the principles of the International Labour Organization (ILO) in terms of an international 'handshake' between labour, employers and governments 'so that the benefits of the global market can be shared by everyone'. The same idea of dialogues between 'social partners' and government was projected as the major means to fulfil the UN's 2030 agenda[1] and particularly its eighth goal: 'to promote sustained, inclusive and sustainable economic growth, full and productive employment and decent work for all'.

Löfven was not alone. The party and related unions were supportive, and even though responsibility for international development cooperation was ceded to the Green coalition partner, social democrats with long experience from the UN, the EU, development cooperation and civil society gained new ground for their ideas. A special minister would direct strategic studies to help coordinate ministerial work and efforts by unions and other progressive organizations.

[1] No poverty; Zero hunger; Good health and wellbeing; Quality education; Gender equality; Clean water and sanitation; Affordable and clean energy; Decent work and sustainable economic growth; Industry innovation and infrastructure; Reduced inequalities; Sustainable cities and communities; Responsible consumption and production; Climate action; Life below water; Life on land; Peace, justice and strong institutions; Partnerships.

Promising but stumbling

Löfven gained international reputation for his idea of a Global Deal. Unions, employers and state representatives in some regions were invited to promotional workshops. Unions could complement work in the ILO with engagement in multilateral institutions such as the Organization for Economic Co-operation and Development (OECD), now in charge of fleshing out the concept. In spite of advances in international cooperation, however, local implementation was up against the same challenges that Palme and Brandt faced in the 1970s – a shortage of strong enough progressive partners in governments, unions and CSOs on the ground. The remaining task was thus to shape preconditions so that they came to resemble those when the iconic social pacts in Scandinavia were first forged in the 1930s.

Meanwhile the new Minister for Foreign Affairs (2014–19), Margot Wallström, initiated a bold feminist-oriented policy for democracy and human rights in favour of Agenda 2030, bilaterally and within international organizations. This was one platform for Sweden's successful candidacy for the Security Council. These policies met with immediate resistance, however, in particular from Israel when Sweden became the first EU member to recognize the state of Palestine, but also from a number of rulers in the Arab world. Consequently, Swedish businesses and unions with interests in exports to these and similar countries became worried too.

The export dilemma

Social democrats are eager to promote export and 'free trade on equal terms', to quote the former Minister of Trade and now Minister for Foreign Affairs, Ann Linde. But what if the terms are not equal? While paying due respect to democracy and human rights, business and some unions prefer codes of conducts for the concerned companies, in return for freedom to trade and invest in all countries that are not affected by international boycotts. As the social democratic chairman of the Swedish parliament's Committee on Foreign Affairs, Kenneth G. Forslund, put it: 'I do not think that the politicians shall decide on each and every Swedish business deal to export arms.' Subsequently, Sweden even maintained its commitments to sell arms to Saudi Arabia and the United Arab Emirates in spite of their contribution to the conflicts in the Middle East that people had to flee from – including to Sweden itself.

Potentially, however, there is also a progressive dimension to the interest in exports. In 2014, the blue-collar workers confederation (LO) published a major report arguing that it was necessary to increase wages and investments to foster full employment. This was in stark contrast to the dominant austerity measures and efforts to compete by neglecting work conditions. The analysis focused on Sweden, but the authors, Carl-Mikael Jonsson and Ingemar Lindberg, told me that the original argument was expanded to the rest of Europe and the Global South too, given that weak economic demand outside Sweden was not just bad for the other countries but also for Swedish exports. The case of southern Europe was obvious. In the South, moreover, it is insufficient to rely on uneven and environmentally disastrous development and the buying power of the nouveau riche. However, Jonsson explained somewhat sheepishly: the top LO leaders who thereafter negotiated the general report felt that the sole focus had to be on Sweden, because improvements in other contexts were too far away.

Beyond provincial minds, however, the fact remains that Sweden's economy is internationally oriented and the demand for its products must be considered beyond Europe and North America. So far Swedish exports to the South have mainly consisted of (i) machines and services for mining and drilling companies, and for factories relocated to the South to benefit from exploitation of labour and nature and (ii) luxury Volvo cars and other 'necessities' for the rich and upper middle classes only. One challenge is that many of these products are now provided locally, even if there is still demand for inputs from Sweden. Another is that the uneven development in the South implies negative effects for people on the ground as well as for countries like Sweden. One effect is environmental destruction, causing global climate change; another the political crises triggering forced migration; yet another the growing inequalities, reducing the potential of increasing demand from ordinary people, including for environmentally friendly solutions and products.

From this point of view, Sweden should take steps to raise demand in the South by way of more equitable and sustainable development while also increasing its own imports of products from the South that are produced in an environmentally friendly way and by decently paid labour. It should also abstain from those aspects of the international trade and investment agreements that generate uneven development and reduce the space for progressive politics. If not, like-minded partners in the South will have less chance to foster social democratic development and increase demand in their own countries. And they would have good reason to suspect that the well-wishers in the North were primarily protecting their own short-term interests. But would mainstream social democratic leaders agree to this?

Strengthening partners?

As we know from previous chapters of the book, the expansion of markets by means of more equitable and sustainable development in the South calls for altered power relations and the representation of ordinary people and progressives. So how could the positive vision of Agenda 2030, the ILO, the OECD and the Global Deal be implemented on the ground? It is true that when local regimes sign international conventions without applying them this may anyway legitimate external support for unions and CSOs that try to enforce implementation. But the fundamental factor is whether these progressives are strong enough in their own right.

An early attempt to strengthen partners was made by the Ministry for Enterprise and Innovation (and later the Ministry of Trade). It agreed with business and unions to combine a campaign for exports to unevenly developing and often authoritarian countries[2] with corporate social responsibilities that the unions, and not just the companies themselves, would oversee. One dilemma, however, is that unions and managers tend to prioritize what is good for their own companies and employees.

---

[2] The countries included Algeria, Angola, Brazil, China, Egypt, India, Indonesia, Kazakhstan, Malaysia, Nigeria, the Philippines, Saudi Arabia, South Africa and Thailand.

Another is that well-implemented codes only apply to individual Swedish companies and, at best, a local union, not collective action among other workers. Similar problems may beset unions' international cooperation. As we know from previous chapters, only a minority of workers in the South have formal employment and are unionized, and many of them do not value the importance of broad alliances with other labourers. Sofia Östmark, until recently leading the Swedish non-political union-to-union organization, claims: this is why we support demands for formal employment of many more labourers, efforts at wider and stronger organization, plus that unions link up with others to, for example, improve employment conditions and minimum wages.

A supplementary approach is contained in the international framework agreements such as between IF-Metall, the IndustriALL Global Union and the retail-clothing company H&M, ideally affecting some 1.6 million workers. The idea is to strengthen the right to organize and the bargaining power of workers in subcontracted H&M units. However, senior union researcher Mats Wingborg says the reality does not live up to the hype: while H&M benefits from good media attention and the leading unions enjoy the benefits of a profitable 'mother company', the local unions are weak and informal labourers not contracted by H&M's partners remain unaffected.

Similar challenges apply to the Swedish backing for the ILO to promote the Global Deal concept by negotiations between unions, employers and government (to reduce conflicts, increase productivity and improve workers' rights), such as in Bangladesh. Opportunities to include and strengthen weak unions, promote democratic principles, enrol temporary workers and labourers in sweatshops vary with the initial strength of the established unions and the decency of the regime. The problems in Bangladesh in these respects would thus be even more serious in, say, China.

In some contrast, the priority of the explicitly social democratic Olof Palme International Center (Palme Center) is to surmount the insufficient capacity of unions and like-minded popular organizations by building cooperation between them. This route is supported by the results in this book. They point to the potential of broad alliances of progressive politicians, unions, other popular groups and CSO activists – including the media – for welfare and other reforms that are based on equal rights and include representation of the social partners in implementation and further policy development. None of these actors are strong enough to make it on their own. Actually, Swedish social democrats realized already in the early 1930s that it was impossible to make democratic advances on the basis of the working class and the unions alone – they had to build broader alliances. Broad alliances are obviously even more crucial in the South where industrialization is less comprehensive and unions are weaker.

Coordination in despair

Löfven also assigned a special minister, Kristina Persson, to identify the strategic challenges and synchronize policies in favour of Agenda 2030. She appointed experts from unions, business, think tanks and the like to three advisory groups. These were tasked to suggest ideas, respectively, about working life, the environment and global cooperation. But the groups consisted of volunteers in the special minister's network and lacked representatives from some crucial ministries and vital organizations such as the Palme Center, as well as some of the best qualified scholars to review previous insights and experiences. In short, the groups differed from the practice of the old public commissions that – in addition to tripartite negotiations – are crucial elements of participatory governance in the Scandinavian model worshiped by Löfven. This saved time and money, but the outcome was a list of ideas to be followed up – in contrast to a well-anchored and knowledge-based platform for the coordination and implementation of social democratic vision. Instead of correcting this and supporting the special minister, in May 2016 she was sacked and coordination withered.

The new policy for international development cooperation, for example, was as incoherent as ever. In the policy guideline, the Green Party minister in charge produced an extended list of poorly connected priorities, including her own special concern for environmental issues, the foreign minister's feminism and the prime minister's Global Deal. These priorities, moreover, did not stress how to fight poverty by way of fostering human and social rights, plus democratization, but rather emphasized market-driven uneven development, which was credited with having reduced poverty in spite of generating spiralling inequality. Support for poor countries remained a priority but at the expense of the many impoverished people in rapidly growing, though thoroughly unequal, economies. Analyses of progressive actors of change and what reforms they may promote and unite behind were next to absent, and support for progressive unions, CSOs and parties remained marginal. Agenda 2030 for inclusive democratic development and the treaties to reduce global warming was celebrated, but implementation remained technocratic, skating over power relations and the politics of change.

Collapse

When I stepped off the train in Stockholm in mid-November 2015 to make early interviews for this chapter, the central station was full of tired refugee families comforting their children – but also numerous social service workers and volunteers helping them out. At the time Sweden received the most refugees in Europe in proportion to population. There were good reasons to be proud and hopeful despite the challenges. If well attended to, most of our asylum seekers would not forget but strengthen joint international work.

Only two weeks later, however, the government imposed restrictions, to give the authorities 'some breathing space', but not the refugees. Most other European countries did not share the responsibility for human rights, and there were few safe havens elsewhere. Most remarkably: when nationalist right-wing populists gained votes by xenophobic propaganda against the immigrants, many social democratic and union leaders adjusted. Some added proposals to prohibit begging, similar to those deemed shameful and unconstitutional even by the High Court in a country with somewhat tougher challenges, India.

Social democrats certainly try to subordinate the international mobility of both capital and labour to democratic decisions for inclusive development, especially to the benefit of Sweden, but also to honour human rights for refugees (Chapters 2 and 7).

However, since the 1990s in particular there have been inconsistencies. As highlighted in Chapter 7, there has been limited support for a comprehensive and far-reaching refugee policy, such as advocated by, among others, the leading Norwegian social democrat, Thorvald Stoltenberg, during his stint as UN High Commissioner for Refugees. Most importantly, Swedish social democrats have not matched pushes for regulation of labour migration with prioritizing the struggle they had committed themselves to, especially under Olof Palme, to address the root causes of forced migration – from apartheid to imperial policies and undemocratic rule. Later on, this neglect in turn made it possible for right-wing nationalists to develop and monopolize for their own xenophobic purposes the argument that refugees 'should be supported in their own countries'. In late 2015, the Social Democrat/Green Party coalition government even debited much of the cost for attending to the refugees in Sweden to the budget for international development cooperation, rather than using it to, again, confront the fundamental reasons for why the refugees had to flee in the first place. In short, the mainstream social democrats' turnaround since the 1990s has demonstrated a total inability to develop an alternative international strategy to that of right-wing nationalism.

To numerous social democrats, this was a moral and political tragedy. The unions were silent but several social democratic associations and individuals objected. In my own village, for one, many devoted party members refused to campaign for the leaders' national policies in the 2018 elections. Meanwhile former sympathizers around the country, afraid that their welfare and jobs would diminish because of the refugees, rarely returned to the fold, despite the party leaders' concessions to the right-wing populists. The top leadership avoided a full-scale electoral disaster only by promising, at the eleventh hour, a new welfare scheme – after which they stayed in office by negotiating liberal support in return for marginalizing the former communist but now increasingly social democratic-oriented Left Party, reducing tax for the better off and committing to 'more flexible' labour market regulations.

The admirable aim for these retreats was to hold back the right-wing national-populists, but there was no firm alternative to their xenophobic priorities. Leftist critics (with the think tanks *Arena* and *Katalys*, green leftist daily *ETC*, social democratic party association *Reformisterna* and the Left Party in the forefront) suggested sustainable Keynesian and more radical welfare policies – partially inspired by Bernie Sanders in the United States, Jeremy Corbyn in Britain, *Podemos* in Spain and António Costa in Portugal – but primarily turned inward. The global root causes, the need to internationalize Keynesian policies beyond the EU, and the importance and potential of Social Democracy in the South remained non-issues.

The attempt at an internationalist restart collapsed in Sweden, and Corbyn suffered a humiliating electoral defeat in 2019 for want of an international alternative to Brexit.

Another go?

Not everyone gave up. Committed and typically younger social democratic cadres try to reinvent the links between, on the one hand, the 'domestic' problems of welfare, climate, employment and integration of migrants, and, on the other, their root causes in global dynamics. Says the party's new international secretary Johan Hassel: the challenge is to communicate these links and suggest feasible policies. International development cooperation, for one, is disconnected from other policy areas. There is not even a social democratic policy for this. We hope to build a team of committed people in the party, ministries, unions and popular organizations.

Anna Sundström, directing the Palme Center, concurs. It remains to be seen if these efforts will succeed. At least, the Center proved its capacity in late 2019 by co-arranging, in conjunction with its annual 'Palme Days', a dynamic convention, hosted by the party, of the Progressive Alliance (PA), aimed as a substitute for the degenerated Socialist International. The vibrant North American social democrats were missing but the many attending leaders and local activists expressed relief that somebody was able to push for a restart, to share insights and initiate common work. Löfven, for one, was impressed by António Costa's achievements in Portugal. North Macedonian Prime Minister Zoran Zaev asserted the conflict resolution with Greece was because socialist leaders had a common understanding. Israeli parliamentarian Tamar Zandberg, of the recently successful Meretz party, stressed mutual values too – echoed by Palestine Prime Minister Mohammad Shtayyeh, who added the importance of support for economic development to limit conflicts and forced migration. Philippine senator Risa Hontiveros asked for advice from her (until recently) successful Malaysian colleague to build a united front against Duterte. Norwegian labour party leader Jonas Gahr Støre suggested PA support for local initiatives that other members approved of too. Outgoing Swedish LO leader Karl-Petter Thorwaldsson asserted he would focus on international unionism, and Frans Timmermans of the European Commission promised to stand tall. All agreed to counter climate change by embracing smart technology and favouring social equality to share the burden.

But when European leaders also asserted that nobody would be left out by technological advances thanks to social democratic welfare and further education, Indian social activist Ruth Manorama spoke up, asking if they might also, perhaps, consider that most oppressed people in the world are offline and exempted from social security. In a dinner conversation later, young Swedish activists stressed the importance of their direct links across the borders with counterparts and realities on the ground. Veterans told me this is increasingly rare: full-timers dominate more than they facilitate.

And intriguingly, the media did not bother about these discussions, not even the leftist media. There were hardly any reports. The contrast with the interest during the late 1960s and 1970s in linking up with kindred movements for change could not have been plainer. According to Oscar Ernerot, international secretary with the blue-collar workers confederation LO: it is uphill now (…) right-wing populists are eating into the unions, there is lack of alternative policies and it is difficult to reach out (…) we must even remind people of the history.

The new Minister for Foreign Affairs, Ann Linde, previously in charge of Trade and EU relations, wishes to heal the friction with business and unions caused by predecessor Wallström's rights-based priorities. In the 'Palme Days', Linde stressed cooperation and dialogue with adversaries too, and pointed to the limits of what can be done to defend democracy and equal rights in official state and multilateral cooperation, even in the EU, against recalcitrant member-states. But her conclusion was essential: this is why there must be strong local opposition. While sustaining contacts, we must also, increasingly, support CSOs critical journalists, unions, social dialogue and feminism.

This resonates with the conclusion in previous chapters of the importance of strengthening sympathetic local partners, which calls for synergies between priorities and groups. But will it be given emphasis to? An organization like the Palme Center, which is entrusted to oversee the international engagement of various parts of the social democratic movement, is best set to address this task. According to Mikael Leyi, former head of its international department, support for alliances in the South needs to be negotiated in light of the natural attraction among unions of working with their own counterparts, as well as the need to support parties. In view of this book, there are several options, but they must adhere to Olof Palme's dictum against the temptation to export favourite solutions – that cooperation with partners in the South must be based on an understanding of the conditions they face in their own contexts. The open question is if this will be fundamental in the social democratic party's new international programme, expected in 2021. There are worrying signs. For instance, most social democratic critics of growing inequalities continue to be inward and EU oriented, setting aside the global dimensions. The new editor of the party's ideological magazine *Tiden* says international issues will be given less attention in its pages. And much like 'Blue Labour' in Britain, the party's think tank, with strong backing, suggests protection of refugees should be subordinated to the capacity to integrate immigrants and defend the welfare system for 'ordinary citizens'.

Picture 12 (private) When Suharto banned investigative journals in 1994, senior editor and author Goenawan Mohamad concluded that freedom of speech and the media obviously called for democracy too. Hence, journalists became crucial in fighting for change. But when the regime started crumbling in early 1998, he sighed: we have still no organization and common programme, and we are short of time, so we need a figure, a symbol, to rally behind. But there are no Indonesian equivalents to the Philippines' 'Cory' Aquino and Cardinal Sin.

Picture 13 (private) As the elite dominated the dismantling of Suharto's dictatorship, progressives decided to analyse the problems and options of real democratization. Investigative journalists and scholarly activists like Stanley Adi Prasetyo (left) and A. E. Priyono (right) were crucial, since academics were hard to enrol for the pennies at hand.

Picture 14 (private) Aceh was hard hit by both conflict and the tsunami. Pro-democrats in the freedom movement such as M. Nur Djuli and Shadia Marhaban gained prominence during the peace negotiations, in cooperation with civil society groups, but were marginalized when Jakarta and the international community separated democratization from peace and reconstruction.

Picture 15 (private) Former Congress-socialist and then communist patriarch E.M.S. Namboodiripad was a vital supporter of the Kerala reformists. In early 1996, in what turned out to be our last conversation, he stated: if we win the State Assembly elections, we shall overcome bureaucratic rule with democratic decentralization and encourage not just the followers of my party but also many others to engage in the panchayats and cooperatives.

Picture 16 (private) Kerala's democratic decentralization and planning campaign was probably the world's boldest attempt at social democratic development from below. In the midst of the debates about the hurdles, it was hard to know the situation in the villages. During a fact-finding tour in early 1999 to a sample of them, the discussions with leaders and experts were as open as in an academic seminar – but often better informed.

Picture 17 (private) Kerala's land reform was the best in India, but many rural poor people did not benefit and those who did rarely increased production. 'Group farming' among the new landowners was unconvincing, but teams of typically women workers were prepared to till land efficiently.

Picture 18 (courtesy *Akbayan* party) In the mid-2000s, the democratic Philippine Left made great advances by deprioritizing street protests in favour of cooperation with progressive liberals, to thus advance in elections and get into government. Radical reforms were delayed, however, and the liberals' market-driven growth did not generate inclusive development. So even though shining *Akbayan* leader Risa Hontiveros (middle) made it to the Senate in the comprehensive 2016 elections with a firm social rights agenda, the liberals as well as her party lost out – and strongman Duterte rose to power.

Picture 19 (private) In Solo, Central Java, in the mid-2000s, directly elected Mayor 'Jokowi' wanted to 'clean up' the city for which he needed, however, a deal with the many urban poor organizations that were facilitated by civil society activists. This was successful, scaled up to Jakarta too and (albeit with problems) even made Jokowi president in 2014. However, the good practices and popular representation were never institutionalized. Among others, popular women leaders in Solo concluded: we were abandoned.

Picture 20 (private) From the mid-2000s, Indonesian unions engaged in politics for better employment regulations and higher minimum wages. This called for cooperation with casual and informal labour too. The process culminated in the early 2010s with an even broader successful alliance for a universal public health reform – this time also including urban poor groups, progressive politicians and civil society activists.

Picture 21 (private) Progressive parliamentarian and former soap opera star Rieke Pitaloka was decisive in mobilizing political support for labour and the public health reform. Rieke and anti-corruption crusader Teten Masduki (poster) might even have won the 2013 governor elections in the Muslim stronghold of West Java – had unions and CSOs provided full support. Later, Masduki briefly headed President 'Jokowi's' staff, but lacked organized popular support to nurture progressive policies as a counter to right-wing populism.

Picture 22 (private) How should labour 'go politics'? In a late 2013 workshop with crucial actors, Said Iqbal of the strongest union (in between critics Jamaludin and Surya Tjandra) rejected broad alliances and negotiations with government and employers on socio-economic development, 'since there is no reliable format'. Unions, he concluded, must rather hold on to their core issues of wages and employment conditions, and strike deals with the 'highest bidding' politicians. Hence, he supported Ret. General Prabowo against 'Jokowi' the 2014 elections – paving the way for right-wing religious populism.

Picture 23 (private) After the peace accord in Aceh, the head of intelligence in the freedom movement, Irwandi Yusuf, was elected governor, along with loyal commanders and civil society groups. Conservatives sabotaged his re-election, but in 2017 old reformist friends helped him to come back. They expected to start anew, but were deposed in favour of young technocrats like Hendri Yuzal. Yuzal (at the desk) briefed me for hours in Irwandi's office until the boss received me at home (inserted picture) instead, self-confidently explaining his priorities. A few months later, they were both arrested for corruption.

Part Four

Reinventing Social Democracy

Lessons for a new Social Democracy

Even though broad Social Democracy in terms of sustainable development based on socio-economic justice by democratic means is more important than ever, it is losing ground. This book has been about why that is, and whether it can be reinvented.

The crisis is global: first, because the original northern model became undermined by neoliberalism and market-driven globalization, and their signature features of unfettered finance, rising inequality, forced migration, natural exploitation and excessive use of fossil energy; second, because the deepest roots of that debilitation lie in the setbacks experienced by southern progressives fighting the heedless exploitation of people and resources. Hence, the key to renewal is in the South. But even the promising efforts during the third wave of democracy, to meld global markets and welfare, have run aground. So we need to find out why, and if there are any signs of new social democratic roadmap on the horizon.

The challenges in the South are often studied in view of the conditions that enabled social democracy's rise during industrialization in the North. From that angle, the conclusion is self-evident. Nothing like the historical circumstances which obtained in the North – especially a broad and relatively unified working class movement for inclusive democracy, welfare and growth – are feasible in the South. This is due to uneven industrialization, huge numbers in informal sectors, ineffective and often corrupt administration, dictatorships or shallow democracies, fragmented civil societies and the politicization of religious identities.

But this perspective is as biased as the assumption of modernization theory that development must copy what happened in the North. This book has instead defined Social Democracy in accordance with its broader classical meaning of development based on social (and now also environmental) justice, and the democratic politics it takes to get there. Supported by historical evidence from various contexts, this essence has been specified in terms of four common cornerstones of (i) democratic popular-interest collectivities, (ii) democratic links between the state and equal citizens, (iii) social rights and welfare (R&W) and (iv) economic growth pacts between the state, primary producers, labour and employers – and related strategies. We have used these dimensions to analyse the mysteries of setbacks and advances in the critical cases of Indonesia, India (mainly Kerala) and the Philippines under the second and third generations of Social Democracy. Along the way, we have also asked about implications for the first-generation social democrats in the North as reflected in the paradigmatic case of Sweden. The contrasting contexts of social democratic efforts have provided commentaries on each other. In this concluding chapter, it is time to gather the general insights and consider their validity in broader comparative perspective.

Dilemmas of second-generation Social Democracy

The second generation's enduring lessons – that unity and democracy may after all be feasible, despite being undermined, and that politics was seminal in the rise of capitalism – have been ignored.

Broad unity and democratic routes possible

The thesis that social democratic politics is doomed in the South because of divisive identities and uneven economic development and the absence of unifying class interests was contradicted in Kerala as early as the 1930s and in Indonesia from the early until the late 1950s. In both contexts, the demands for equal citizenship and democracy against colonialism, and representation through ethnic, religious and other forms of communal representation, served as a unifying frame for interest-based struggles among scattered classes and groups. The leftists in Kerala and Indonesia built huge democratic movements for progressive reforms and were on the verge of political hegemony.

Democracy suspended

In the Philippines, however, the issues of citizenship and democracy were not top priorities among progressives. The Americans had long ago introduced elements of democracy and citizen rights. The problem was that the United States, along with local oligarchs, entirely dominated the system. The common conclusion was thus that these enemies must be fought before democracy might be viable. By the late 1950s, something similar happened in Indonesia. The progressives advanced in elections but were threatened by anti-communists and subordinated themselves to President Sukarno's left-populism. Massive campaigns against imperialism for 'genuine national independence' and land reforms within 'guided democracy' were deemed more important than democracy based on equal citizens and their own mediating organizations.

Liberals and related social democrats claimed their political losses in Indonesia and elsewhere were due to the weakness of the middle classes and communist abuse of popular discontent. The modernization theory that liberal social and economic progress would spawn middle-class-driven democracy was supplemented with the thesis that, paradoxically, the attainment of liberal democracy also called for firmer political and legal institutions by way of a 'politics of order' – in the worst cases through 'middle class coups' supported by 'the only modern institution', the army, backed by the United States.

Over the years, the 'politics of order' approach, theorized by Samuel Huntington, spread all around the South, but the pioneering case was the overthrow of Sukarno in Indonesia in 1965-6. Here, the middle-class 'politics of order', far from being shaped by liberalism, was characterized by the revival of the colonial form of despotic indirect rule through communal leaders in the form of army-led massacres of leftists in cooperation with religious and other militia groups. The progressives were left helpless, having abandoned the unifying focus on equal citizenship and democracy by subordinating themselves to Sukarno's left-populism and 'guided democracy'.

Developments in Kerala were less drastic but had similar effects. In 1957, the state elected reform communists to lead its first government. Soon enough, however, this government was destabilized by rightist activists with US support, and unseated by New Delhi in 1959.

Similarly, Eastern bloc modernization-theorists were for their part worried that workers and nationally oriented capitalists remained weak. The suggestion was therefore that progressive leaders and army officers might try to overcome their frailty, and promote 'non-capitalist development'. This approach, which also spread around the South, legitimized Indonesian 'guided democracy' and the cooperation between the pro-Moscow Indian communists and Indira Gandhi's Congress party, including during her emergency rule.

In Kerala, over the years, the dissident Indian communists (in the CPI-M) regained electoral dominance, and the others (in the CPI) returned to the fold. But after years of competition and efforts to use government positions to strengthen party-related organizations, politics continued to be based less on unifying popular demands than on dividing the spoils. The coalition partners used perks to grow memberships and separate interest organizations, CSOs and to attract business support. In short, party-clientelism replaced the previous unity under the umbrella of equal citizenship, social rights and democracy. Later in West Bengal, the CPI-M even formed something close to a party-state.

Political pathway to capitalism neglected

The Indonesian developments from the late 1950s, followed by those in the Philippines, were even worse. Increasingly Maoist-oriented leaders referred to Marx, but abandoned his historical analysis of the rise of capital by 'primitive' coercive and political means, which was particularly crucial in the South. Thus the leftists did not effectively fight the real source of power of the 'bureaucratic capitalists' (the generals, top bureaucrats and political bosses) – which was their control of public assets, resources and the means of coercion. 'That is not a real class base in production', the leftists protested. Hence, they concluded, political control rested instead with landlordism and US imperialism. But fighting imperialists and landlords did not help much. In Indonesia, most generals, for example, even supported the nationalization of foreign companies and then gained control of them. Instead, progressives needed to give priority to the struggle for democratic control of public assets and resources. But the struggle for democracy had been set aside, deprioritized. The same characterization applied to the Philippine oligarchs (including Marcos). For many years, they had typically used the US-exported electoral system to gain office in local and state governments and bureaucracies in order to accumulate power and wealth for private investments. But not even the non-Maoist Left focused on containing this political accumulation of capital by fighting for democratic control of public office, assets and resources until the 'primitive accumulation' and Marcos himself were overturned by the traditional liberal elite, which thus gained the initiative in the struggle for democracy and reaped the benefits of the 'people power revolution' in 1986.

Internationalization of Northern Social Democracy stalled

Nationally confined Social Democracy in the North was first undermined by the breakdown of the Bretton Woods agreement on fixed currency exchange rates in 1971, followed by the oil crisis. Palme, Brandt and others tried to overcome the impasse with global Keynesianism through a 'New International Economic Order' and a 'North-South Programme for Survival'. But they failed. A major reason was the poor support from the South, where the second-generation social democrats were on the retreat, while the oil-exporting states increased prices and speculated rather than investing, and new industrializers in East Asia coupled firm governance with low wages in order to boost exports. Thus the field lay open instead for neoliberal globalization. And innovative technologies for global transportation and communication facilitated the new dispensation.

There was a positive side, however. Except where dictatorial regimes were supported by hegemonic parties, as in China, or competing global powers, as in the Middle East, rulers could rely more on expanding markets. So the importance of imperial force was reduced, especially after the ebbing of the Cold War. One implication was more space for progressives to resist the 'politics of order' and 'statist regimes'. Another was the rise of the third wave of democracy. The new political environment served as a breeding ground for a third generation of Social Democracy. Things looked bright to begin with, but over the years the outcomes have been disappointing.

The major questions in this book have been why the third-generation social democrats in the South did not do better, and if there are new options. But first, what were the implications in the North?

Just as the efforts at global Keynesianism were hamstrung not least by the setbacks for the progressives in the South, the new problems for the third-generation social democrats also narrowed the field for their siblings in the North. Palme was assassinated in 1986. Even in the Swedish stronghold, increasingly unambitious social democrats found no alternative to 'Social Democracy in one country' – that is, prioritizing Sweden's own short-term interests in fostering growth, and at best welfare, by adjusting to market-driven globalization of trade and production, hoping that some of the negative effects could be ameliorated within the EU and the UN. Several activists, along with concerned professionals, educators and scholars, sustained their solidarity and work with partners in the South, but these efforts were no longer integral aspects of social democratic priorities and politics.

Stumbling third-generation Social Democracy

The third wave of democracy was as potent as the fall of the wall in Berlin, but also as protracted in realizing hopes for a better future. In both the Philippines and Indonesia, the pro-democrats lost out in the transition from authoritarian rule. They ended up as subordinated partners in elite-dominated democracies, with few chances to participate in elections and make a difference through participatory governance. Most activities were confined to lobbying, civil society work, and doing deals with politicians in need of support.

There were similar dynamics in India. Mrs Gandhi's state of emergency in the mid-1970s was fought but political and administrative institutions were undermined. Clientelism became increasingly important. Still, the rudiments of political democracy stood firm. From the mid-1980s, these were sustained through a new emphasis on active citizenship and R&W. In spite of impressive initiatives – especially in Kerala in the 1990s and ten years later by the Left-supported Congress government – progressives lost ground.

Keeping the contextual factors in mind, what were the major stumbling blocks and potentials? Brought together in view of the foundations for Social Democracy and wider comparison, six arguments stand out.

Dearth of common class interests

There is no doubt about this. The first premise for Social Democracy of democratic popular-interest collectivities cannot be based on the working class – as it was in the North – to anything like the same degree in the South. Labour and democracy activists rarely combined their priorities even in the struggle against Suharto. Workers themselves are too few, too scattered and often divided by specific interests and demands. Some 90 per cent of India's workforce, for example, is in the informal sector. Unity is difficult on the workplace level and between them, and higher up the system, union leaders tend to develop their own preferences, such as striking deals with dubious politicians like Indonesian ex-general Prabowo. Informal sector labourers tend to be neglected. This happened even during leftist rule in West Bengal. Efforts at overarching demands for decent jobs and universal minimum wage, as suggested by international labour organizations, may be fine for casual and informal sector labour too – in principle. But there must also be policies to compensate for the lack of similar conditions to those in Scandinavia during the peak of Social Democracy – low levels of underemployment and the steady growth of new jobs. Even South Africa, with its strong unions, tragically presents an example of a country where, in common with many others in the South, these components do not exist.

Kerala, however, showed informal labour may well organize successfully through time-honoured methods such as closed shops. Professional associations in the gig-economy might try too. Specific informal sector unions are growing and 'old' unions are trying to enrol casual labourers. But since many lack a fixed employer, demands for rights to work and welfare must be put to politicians. And negotiations should involve all partners. Positively, the Indonesian struggle for universal health care reform – 2010–12 – suggests broad unity is possible.

In short, democratic popular-interest collectivities can hardly be built at the level of production, but this reality calls for common interests in comprehensive reforms – to which we shall return shortly.

The same applies to primary producers. When the remarkable land reform in Kerala was implemented, people did not join hands and develop production. Tribal populations and fisher folks got nothing, while plantations were exempted and former tenants gained more than their workers who asked for better pay. Hence, the beneficiaries invested elsewhere. Similarly, the collapse of former guerrilla leader Buscayno's huge cooperative in Tarlac in the Philippines was not primarily because Mt Pinatubo erupted but because of scattered interests among the small farmer member households who had to find multiple livelihoods. A joint democratic-political project would have helped but proved difficult for other reasons. Handoko, the human rights activist and adviser of small farmers fighting against dispossession of their land in Batang, Central Java, confronted analogous problems.

Bottom-up polycentrism difficult to connect to wider public action

A major hallmark of the radical third-generation social democrats was democratization and reformist policies from the bottom-up. But while necessary, bottom-up reforms proved insufficient. One reason was that previous emphasis on citizenship and democracy was neglected. In Kerala, the successful focus from the 1930s until the late 1950s on equal citizenship and democracy as an umbrella for class-related priorities was undermined from the 1960s by leftist party-clientelism, and was not reinvented until the mid-1980s when reformists tried popular campaigns from below. The Philippines did not even have an analogous history to revive, and in Indonesia the old Kerala-like formula was abandoned with 'guided democracy'. Hence, Indonesian progressives could not even draw on the imperative of citizen rights and democracy to resist the killings in the mid-1960s. And from the 1970s, the new dissenting CSO activists certainly pitied the victims but forgot about the history of why equal citizenship and democracy had been overlooked in the first place.

Consequently, there were few exceptions in the Philippines – and even fewer in Indonesia – to the liberal view of civil society, fostered by donors, that it was little more than a corrective supplement to the increasingly dominant formula for elite-negotiated democracy. This may be a cause for regret, but the main challenge for progressives was how to maximize the available space and advance in a social democratic direction.

Pro-democracy spearheads among investigative journalists and students were immensely important but at times ran ahead of themselves – neglecting organization and protection of the people they spoke up for. Local organizers trying to do just that were often disowned, including when pro-democracy activists made separate deals with influential actors and politicians. Scaling up and forming broader movements, regionally and nationally, were particularly difficult.

Cause-oriented groups – watchdogs as well as those aiding resistance among farmers, labourers and urban poor – were typically issue driven, dependent on donors' priorities and mutually competitive. Building broader alliances and wide membership was not a priority. Quick, visible results were easier to achieve by actions, media coverage, lobbying and 'good connections'. An additional effect was that the CSOs were weak outside the major cities, and that the local associations were dependent on well-connected patrons in the metropolises. In Indonesia, for example, civil society leader

Teten Masduki, during his 2013 campaign for the deputy governorship in West Java, found the province – with the exception of Bandung – 'quite empty of CSOs'. The same applied to the reformists in Aceh when they tried to build progressive local parties outside Banda Aceh. In the Philippines, leftist *Akbayan* leader Joel Rocamora, who served as a cabinet member during the first part of the 2010s in his capacity as head of its National Anti-Poverty Commission (NAPC), found that progressive local CSOs and popular organizations were so weak that they could rarely take advantage of the opportunities NAPC provided.

A major problem was – and is – for CSOs to engage politically. This is mainly because of their fragmented and, at times, narrow priorities, but also due to the hesitancy of their donors to be associated with politics. Unions also remain focused on special issues and concerns. The attempts to build new parties based on CSOs and unions were ultimately failures. This is in sharp contrast to how unions and other popular organizations built social democratic parties in the North. The only partial exception in our cases is the *Akbayan* party in the Philippines, inspired by the Workers' Party in Brazil. *Akbayan* was formed as a coalition between political organizations, with related unions and CSOs, but without a strict ideological profile. This made it easier for CSO activists to join in.

Kerala was different. In contrast to the common problem in Indonesia and the Philippines, as in most other parts of the Global South – that civil society and popular groups are scattered and focus on specific issues and 'community organising' – Kerala's particular dilemma is top-down party-politicization of special interest organizations and dominance in civil society. Fortunately, CPI-M, the main left party in Kerala, was not as dominant as its sister party in West Bengal (which thus dwindled) and the ANC in South Africa (which is losing ground). Kerala CSO activists who also engaged politically could, thus, initiate impressive campaigns for total literacy and popular education, village-level resource mapping and participatory development. They could also launch supportive decentralized planning. Not that there were not numerous obstacles, most of which are reminiscent of those in the Philippines and Indonesia. The prime ones were the difficulty of combining representative and direct democracy as well as participatory and professional governance – in addition to providing space for not just CSO activists but also party and interest organizations. There were also problems of combining the development of production and welfare, to which we shall return. But the Kerala campaigns did prove it was possible for civil society and government institutions to work in tandem. Moreover, the activists themselves managed to unite numerous scattered local projects towards a sketchy but still alternative development route for Kerala at large. This was a major factor behind the Left Democratic Front's victory in the 1996 elections. And a reason why the party leaders had no choice but to allow politically concerned CSO activists and scholars to launch the People's Planning Campaign. It is true that bottom-up politics was brought to an end in 2001. But the inbuilt challenges could have been dealt with and were not the major causes for its defeat – top-down political hijacking was.

In short, bottom-up activism is crucial but remains fragmented and difficult to scale up and link to broader organizations and central institutions without a unifying framework. We shall return to insights on how this may be achieved.

Decentralization in need of linkages

Third-generation Social Democracy was also about decentralization, in order to counter authoritarian and top-down rule, and foster local democracy. The advancements for the democratic Left in the context of Brazil's decentralization caught worldwide attention. Its participatory budgeting attracted liberals too. Less notice was paid to the preconditions – that the Workers' Party (PT) won mayoral elections and thereafter introduced the popular deliberations from the top-down, along with trusted rules and regulations. Similarly, it took a long time before attention was drawn to the fact the local participants had not been able to keep an eye on the central-level political corruption that generated so much distrust in the 2010s and lit the flame of right-wing populism.

Our case studies support the general lessons from Brazil. Decentralization in Indonesia and the Philippines was no panacea for local democracy as long as progressives in CSO and popular organizations were not strong enough to make a difference. When they were, results were tangible – such as in the mid-2000s when activists in the Central Java city of Solo managed to put pressure on then Mayor 'Jokowi' to agree a deal for more inclusive urban development. Or the progressives in the Moluccas who pared down the elitist elements in customary governance of local communities, and their local fishing and forestry, while also negotiating similar changes in citizenship and democratic governance in other sectors and administrative levels.

Equally instructive, the admirable social democratic introduction in the Philippines of bottom-up budgeting in the early 2010s was soon undermined by competing political elites, municipal and provincial bosses and the weakness of local progressives. Only in Kerala where local oligarchic rule had been uprooted through land reform and decades of struggle for citizen civil and social rights could progressives in civil society and government cooperate and introduce both democratic decentralization and participatory planning.

Yet, as we know, there were major problems in Kerala too, and some of them related to the very localization of politics. One was that since the villages are now open economies, everyone cannot be expected to share the responsibility for all residents' welfare, including those who are active outside the villages and might have lost their jobs. Hence, there must also be welfare *state* programmes. Moreover, effective local development planning should consider both public and private investments, as well as outside links, including the villagers working in the Gulf countries and sending money back home. Rarely did this happen, so as in China when the regime was unable to connect the people's communes, the matter was left to the market. These unresolved challenges were again apparent during the struggle against Covid-19. Local public action was initially very effective and the Kerala achievements gained worldwide fame, but they proved insufficient when numerous problems arose, such as to fight community transmission of the virus and provide sufficient socio-economic relief and investments that could not be handled locally only.

Similarly, local communities are difficult places in which to combine the preoccupations of CSO activists and unions and other organizations that are not confined to the local territories but related to production and workplaces. This was equally important in our Indonesian and Philippine cases. In Solo, Indonesia, for example, the social contracts were not feasible in the framework of territorial and community development planning (*musrembang*). Rather, they called for discussions with people's own organizations in various sectors – from casual labourers and petty traders to sex workers – in different locales around the city.

The insight that the participation of sectoral organizations based on interests in work and production is crucial to establishing 'trans-territorial' linkages is verified by Scandinavian history where these organizations served to negotiate and institutionalize many of the failing connections. This takes us to the next conclusion about representation.

Neglected representation in democratization calls for alternative approach

For all its promise, the third wave of democratization turned out to involve the accommodation of elites who adjusted to – and then dominated – elementary democratic rules of the game. Scattered pro-democrats in CSOs and popular movements rarely gained access to the playground, except as individual subordinates in the elite-teams. This nourished populist reactions that turned increasingly rightist, even in 'old democracies' like India. Dedicated liberals and social democrats worry but lack alternatives. In recent years, some of them have even returned to the old idea from the late 1950s that weak states with poorly enacted rule of law and rampant corruption must be fixed before democratic deficiencies are attended to – an updated version, courtesy of Francis Fukuyama, of Huntington's 1960s' recommendation of a 'politics of order'.

This book has arrived at another conclusion. There are weak states and corruption, but nothing suggests that returning to authoritarian rule would be better today than in the late 1950s, the 1960s or early 1970s. The alternative is equal citizen rights and better democratic representation of the collective actors with a genuine interest in change. State capacity rests on trust in institutions which must therefore be impartial. But this cannot be fixed by top-down administrative reforms alone (unless combined with repressive measures to enforce consent). Rather, such reforms must be allied with equal citizenship rights and partnership governance, according to democratic representative principles. This is the main lesson of how Sweden transformed its public administration, which by the middle of the nineteenth century was thoroughly corrupt.

From this point of view, the problems are not just that elites have captured the democratic systems and the new drives for a 'politics of order'. An equally important obstacle is that social democrats of various persuasions have not been very good at improving citizen rights and representation. What general explanations for this failure emerge from our case studies?

Firstly, it took a long time to recall a lesson never learnt by the second-generation social democrats – that substantive democratization of the state and governance is not just something to aim at but the best defence against government suppression, and also the best way to overcome clientelism and the primitive accumulation of capital by coercive means, cronyism and even state capture.

Secondly, the Kerala progressives had fought for centuries to gain equal citizenship rights, including within public governance, and could thus combine civil society initiatives with reformist politics in order to bring about democratic decentralization of public governance. But the weaker attempts to this end in the Philippines and Indonesia were lost in the transitions from Marcos and Suharto to elitist democracy.

Thirdly, generally, the frustrated progressives were therefore mainly confined to building alternatives within their own ranks, from the bottom-up. While doing this, the Kerala CSOs certainly claimed to represent many more people's views and aspirations than those of their own members. But their number of their members was still huge and their voluntary work and internal democracy was deemed much more crucial than in the Philippines and especially Indonesia. Still, not so many of the civil society activists in Kerala were also active in organized politics.

In all our cases, CSO activists typically deemed electoral participation ineffective, except individually through mainstream parties. Local organizers of communities, workers and farmers cared more about numbers and representative leaders. But internal democracy in their own organizations and movements was limited, and the attempts, if any, to engage in elections were often abortive. In Indonesia, genuine leaders without 'proper formal education' were not allowed even to run for office locally. Kerala progressives rejected alternative party-building in favour of trying to reform, affect and cooperate with the actually existing leftist parties. In Indonesia, by contrast, many progressives avoided 'dirty politics' but failed to build broad enough parties of their own to make a difference, often resorting instead to transactions with mainstream leaders.

Akbayan in the Philippines is the shining exception of how leftist groups, CSO activists, unions and other movements *can* join hands, but so far it has failed to make much progress. Remarkably, anti-corruption activists in New Delhi also managed to build a party of their own. This was partly due to India's liberal electoral legislation as compared to Indonesia where it is impossible for local parties to participate in elections. But the main factor for success was that the activists' focus on anti-corruption regulations and popular participation in matters of livelihood and welfare were crucial for both the urban poor and the middle classes, and stood out as a convincing way to do something to improve miserable public services. However, populist politics soon overshadowed solid democratic practices and the development of broader agendas on inclusive development.

Meanwhile, reform-oriented populist leaders such as Estrada in Philippines and 'Jokowi' in Indonesia agreed to deals with CSOs and popular movements. This was an opening for progressives – especially in Indonesia – as long as the agreements were unambiguous and based on comprehensive reforms. But soon enough it was clear they were not. A major reason for failure was informal individual negotiations and transactions, in tandem with populist ideas of direct relations between leaders and 'the people' instead of democratic representation in institutionalized collective negotiations. Some of this kind of representation took shape within the Philippine Anti-Poverty Commission, but it came to little in the absence of solid backing from sufficiently strong CSOs and popular movements.

The most promising achievement was instead the successful democratic alliance in Indonesia in the early 2010s between CSOs, urban poor associations, unions and progressive politicians and media in favour of a universal public health reform. The alliance could not be sustained, however. There was no forum with democratic representation of the vital partners involved which could assume the role of negotiating follow-up reforms with the government. Sadly, none of the progressives suggested such a format, rather returning to their own special issues, and transactions with individual politicians.

To make matters worse, international democracy-donors also failed to provide CSOs and popular movement activists with support to encourage representative democracy. Locally, pro-democrats were often used and cracked down on, even by otherwise progressive leaders and parties. For example, Indonesian students were let down by elitist reformists in the final struggle against Suharto. Aceh reformist democrats were sidelined by the autocratic leaders of the independence movement, GAM. Philippine democracy activists were harassed and assassinated by Maoists. The Left in West Bengal built a party-dominated state, much like the ANC in South Africa. And their comrades in Kerala clamped down on the leaders of the People's Planning Campaign, but fortunately came to their senses. Top-down politics is certainly not the answer to the problems of democratic representation.

The unresolved issue is, however, what dynamics and actors might generate and promote better representation? We shall return to this question.

From challenged ideas of welfare-based growth to new openings

The conclusions so far are, thus, that the social democratic foundations of collective actors and democracy are hard, though not impossible, to build in the South. But what about the third and fourth pillars of rights and welfare (R&W) and economic growth pacts. They have been considered almost inconceivable outside the comprehensive industrialization in the North.

The solution of second-generation social democrats like Nehru to prioritize state-led industrialization and import-substitution – plus at best moderate land reforms – ahead of equal rights and welfare, was inconclusive. Even the farmers who benefitted from Kerala's most consistent land reform rarely increased production, rather cherry-picking more profitable but less productive off-farm investments. The farmers in former guerrilla leader 'Dante' Buscayno's cooperative were hesitant too, and his politics towards a more comprehensive development framework foundered.

In that regard, the Kerala reformists were much more successful with their decentralized people's planning. In short, they aimed at local R&W-based growth pacts. Group farming was crucial and meant to fit into the local plans. But the farmers were reluctant, the local plans did not extend beyond public investment, there were limited links and coordination beyond the villages, and the middle classes disengaged, as most welfare and other measures were targeted. Although there were exceptions, the *Kudumbashree* labour groups did well. Yet, support for local development remains crucial for all those who do not benefit from the thriving market-driven development in construction, technology, service, education, etc. Compared to elsewhere in India and the Global South, Kerala's participatory government-facilitated solidarity and the coordination of resources and public health have proved remarkably adept at handling environmental disasters, such as the recent flooding and, initially, the coronavirus.

In contrast, in the 1990s the leftist leaders in West Bengal entirely gave up on efforts at rural development and welfare-driven development, in favour of East Asian-inspired industrialization by outside investors and production for markets elsewhere. India had enough democracy to allow citizens to resist and vote the communists out of power when this was at the expense of small farmers and informal labourers.

Unfortunately, the immensely important democracy and human rights activists themselves, who in all our cases stood up for the victims of this common kind of exclusionary development, had little to say in terms of viable development alternatives. The same applied to union leaders. In Indonesia for example, activists concentrated on fighting oppression, corruption and reckless exploitation, leaving economic issues to reformist liberals, who favoured adjustment to globalization along with some welfare reforms.

Social democrats in the North, such as in Sweden, acted similarly, adjusting to market-driven globalization while trying to protect labour regulations and the welfare state. The fashionable expression was climbing the 'value added ladder'. Production should be subcontracted to 'low cost countries', exports to 'emerging markets' expanded, and low-wage products, such as garments, imported. This was in order to make good money and ensure enough taxes for welfare. Quite a few benefitted, but others did not and some fell by the wayside. Short of an international alternative to adjustment, many of the unfortunate have asked for nationalist protection, be it from migrants or viruses.

Equally problematic, while unions commendably tried to internationalize their work, the demands remained based on the first social democratic generation growth models. Within these models, decent jobs and good, collectively negotiated or regulated minimum pay (to 'compress the wage level') would stimulate productivity and generate more jobs in expanding economies. In the South, this was expected to be facilitated by new more democratic 'developmental states'. And that might indeed be valid in sectors with good markets. But it remains insufficient where there is huge underemployment and poorly developed production for nearby markets, such as within agriculture, food and clothing where many people must eke out a living. In such sectors, producers and retailers cannot survive immediate global competition. One example is social democratically oriented South Africa. Likeminded Swedes, among others, did not 'export' all their foundational experiences since the 1930s to South Africa. These 'non-exports' included additional pacts (to those between capital and labour) with farmers and others in rural areas to protect them against the onslaught of free markets so they do not lose their land and livelihood. They also comprised the enrolling of farmers, not just workers, in universal welfare schemes, and general support to create new jobs. A narrow focus on the pact between capital and organized labour is one reason why the Northern social democratic 'road-map' is insufficient.

Raising the resources for such additional policies is not easy. Short-sighted business and middle classes rarely contribute. In some contexts, the commodity boom was helpful. Social democratic-oriented 'developmental state' governments in Brazil, for example, combined global market-friendly economic growth with welfare programmes. In India too, during the centre-left Congress governments of 2004–14, adjustment to market-driven development was blended with technological advances and impressive

R&W reforms. But the market-based growth generated more inequality than new jobs. The R&W measures were typically supplementary; they were not designed to transform the growth model. The middle classes said there was little in the programmes for them. And mismanagement, corruption and crony capitalism were ubiquitous side effects.

In New Delhi, progressives have certainly won elections by connecting anti-corruption to demands for decent public services, but not to inclusive development. And populism has elbowed out democratic government.

Meanwhile, the centre-left Philippine government of 2010–16, in which social democrats participated, also could not renew its mandate. 'Good governance', improved productivity and some welfare measures failed to make much of a dent in the negative effects of market-driven growth, making increasing numbers of people more interested in a 'strong man' than a decent one.

The Indonesian dynamics are similarly troubling but also point to escape routes. 'Reformist populism' was based on local negotiations between politicians and unions, with CSO activists facilitating popular movements among informal labourers for improved wages, welfare measures and liveable urban development plans. Divisions certainly arose, including between unions and informal labourers, and scaling up was hard, but a broad alliance proved possible for a universal public health reform.

In other words, after decades of experiments of how to build democratic popular-interest collectivities that might negotiate welfare-based development, this was obviously the way forward: unity behind comprehensive R&W reforms.

Most recently, the new openings in Kerala also verify this. When local public action had demonstrated its limitations in combatting the pandemic and providing relief and further economic development, the progressives drafted programmes to combine state and local efforts towards welfare-based development. The result was shining victories in the late 2020 local elections. This was followed up by a five-year budget and preparations at the State Planning Board, aimed at sustainable knowledge-based development. Thus, many of the crucial missing linkages between central and local, public and private, and the concerned actors may forge in the designing and implementation of the comprehensive programme. This vision helped sustain the momentum and garnered broad popular support in the April 2021 State Assembly elections.

Yet, there were also tough lessons in Indonesia. In contrast to Kerala, there was no strategy to continue work for more reforms. And there was no way to sustain negotiations between all the concerned parties. This applies to Kerala as well.

In Indonesia, no one even tried to develop this. And populist ideas of direct supposedly democratic relations between leaders and their people only made things worse. So unions returned to their regular priorities and transactions with politicians while informal labourers, as well as 'freelancers', were scattered and marginalized. When challenged by conservatives, President 'Jokowi' toned down his 'reformist populism' in favour of compromises with political elites. In 2020 he even suggested a 'Job Creation Law' – only negotiated with business, not labour – to create new jobs by less burdensome environmental and employment regulations but without substantive compensation in terms of R&W.

Kerala, in the context of right-wing central governance, has few chances to mobilize public resources but can use other means. This is thanks to the history of public health and education, as a result of decades of popular struggles. Education can be further enhanced, benefitting a wider pool of citizens than skilled individuals and well-paid émigré labourers in the Gulf countries and elsewhere, thus serving as a renewed basis for R&W-based development. But it calls for negotiations with the parties concerned – democratic partnership governance – in order not to fall into the quagmire of a top-down 'developmental state' as in Indonesia.

Transformative strategy overlooked

It is often stated, such as by progressive political economist Daron Acemoglu, that the Social Democracy which developed in Europe and especially the Nordic countries differs from 'Democratic Socialism'. Nobel laureate Joseph Stiglitz even calls his social democratic-oriented policy proposals 'progressive capitalism'. If 'Democratic Socialism' is associated with dogmatic struggle against markets and private ownership, they are right – but if it is about the character of society aimed at, they are wrong. Because Social Democracy and 'Democratic Socialism' can be combined. It might be useful to recall how quintessential social democrat Olof Palme linked the two concepts in his declamation 'why I am a democratic socialist' in a televised debate during the 1982 Swedish election campaign (it is available with English subtitles on YouTube). This book argues, much like Palme, that while Social Democracy is certainly not about either smashing capitalism by revolution or dogmatically rejecting markets in favour of public ownership and planning, it is about employing democratic means to nourish development that is both based on, and supportive of, *the aims* of 'Democratic Socialism' in terms of as much social, political and environmental equity and welfare as possible. When private ownership and markets can be governed to foster this, fine; when they cannot, there is a need for alternatives by democratic means.

Further, this book argues that from a historical point of view there are four cornerstones to get there – democratic popular-interest collectivities, democratic citizen–state relations and R&W-based growth pacts. Erik Olin Wright's last book (on *How to Be an Anticapitalist*) helpfully summarizes some of the major strategies to construct the cornerstones: (i) getting into office and then dismantling vital elements of capitalism; while also (ii) taming it with various reforms; (iii) resisting it by protests and alternatives in civil society; and (iv) escaping it by non-capitalist ideas and ways of living. But he forgot the fifth and probably the most important social democratic method of (v) combining these roadmaps and unifying and strengthening agents by way of transformative politics and policies. This is often overlooked.

Similarly, Social Democracy is not only a Polanyian counter-movement to make capitalism liveable by regulations and taxation to finance better welfare, as Acemoglu and Stiglitz suggest. There is a difference between taming a wolf and breeding it into a working dog. As just alluded to, Social Democracy is also about transformative strategies of striving for and orchestrating public reforms and civil society agreements that strengthen the capacity of broad collectivities to fight for more advanced reforms, and then even better reforms after that – towards a system where equity, equality and welfare are both investments and outcomes.

Insufficiently transformative politics and reforms stand out as the final major factor behind the decline of many of the admirable openings that I have tried to bring alive and analyse in this book. One example is the post-tsunami reconstruction and 'democratic' peace accord in Aceh. Both were facilitated by the international community, which was hopeful. But the same community (including Sweden and Norway) neglected a strategy to combine these processes and support the pro-democrats, who could have done the job but thus lost ground, after which Aceh lost out too. Another is the remarkable broad alliance in favour of the Indonesian public health reform which not only fell apart, as already explained, because of insufficient organization for negotiating further reforms towards sustainable development. There was also an absence of ideas about what other comprehensive reforms the progressives could rally behind to thus embolden gradual change. It was a similar story with the centre-left coalitions in Brazil, India, Indonesia and the Philippines in the early 2000s. They aimed at combining market-oriented development and R&W reforms but were typically devoid of a strategy for what reforms might transform the growth model and unify progressives to fight for it. At the time of writing, the Kerala progressives are making more promising attempts to combine welfare, education and sustainable growth.

Towards a roadmap

There have been many obstacles, but what are the insights that point to openings for Social Democracy, and what do they suggest should be done?

Broad alliances behind unifying policies

Kerala of the 1930s, and later Indonesia until the late 1950s, proved it was possible to overcome the dearth of broad class-based collective actors with campaigns for equal citizenship and democracy. They served as a unifying frame for diverse interests among classes and social movements to fight indirect post-colonial governance. Such an approach remains vital, including as an alternative to ethnic, religious and other forms of communal identity politics.

More recently, it has also been possible to build broad alliances for mutually acceptable urban development, non-corrupt public service delivery and universal public health. This has unified formal as well as informal labour, professionals, progressive politicians and others. And progressive movements have been strengthened. In fact, alliances beyond the core labour organizations for universal welfare and inclusive economic growth were also how social democrats came to prominence in the 1930s in comprehensively industrializing Scandinavia.

Democratic partnership governance

Reforms such as for better welfare, services and urban development call for state and government involvement, and coordination with business. Aside from weak unions and employers' associations, a major reason why alliances for such reforms have been difficult to sustain is popular distrust in state and business. But how does one achieve such trust? This is not a new dilemma. As already indicated, trust in Scandinavian governance, for one, is no doubt due to impartial institutions. Such equitable institutions were not just the results of top-down bureaucratic reforms but also because of the development of equal citizenship and representative partners in local governments as well as in business, labour and CSOs. In the early 1930s, Scandinavian labour movements only toned down their own self-help programmes in favour of universal welfare-state programmes when allowed to participate in and influence public governance, along with business and other social partners. Partnership governance is thus in the interests of the actors who want R&W reforms. They may come to realize that partnership governance is necessary to design and implement their reforms. In other words, social democrats need partnership governance in order to work effectively with states and governments and further social democratic aims, and governments need it to gain legitimacy and capacity.

In Indonesia, however, the impressive alliances withered when agreements and negotiations were not democratically institutionalized and inclusive of all concerned partners. They also disintegrated in the absence of negotiated links between public health, employment conditions, wages and economic policies. Populist ideas of direct links between leaders and people did not help, quite the contrary. As a result, actors returned to special priorities, transactions and confrontations. Later, the 'Jokowi' administration even sought refuge by linking up with conservative political and business elites as well as with religious leaders.

Democratic partnership governance is a challenge in Kerala too, but some of its components may be fostered – along with coordination of public action at different levels, and joint ventures with private actors – in the very process of shaping and implementing comprehensive programmes.

With regard to typically elite-dominated democracies, partnership governance is probably also the best way to deepen democracy – provided representatives are appointed by, and accountable to, their own organizations rather than by political leaders and bureaucrats. It is certainly not a substitute for direct citizen participation when issues really can be handled in town hall meetings. It is needed only to address the increasingly numerous matters that cannot be solved locally but call for outside coordination. Partnership governance is also not a substitute for political parties and democratic parliaments and executive offices; its purpose is only to fight elitist democracy by widening and deepening democratic governance – and to strengthen the ability of interest and cause-oriented organizations to also build their own strong parties.

Rights and welfare (R&W)-based growth pacts

Northern social growth pacts were based on comprehensive industrialization, unified unions and employers' organizations, effective and impartial governance, favourable markets and limited unemployment. Thus, there were also resources and business interest in productivity-oriented welfare. This has not been realistic in the South. The second-generation social democrats tried state-led industrialization and land reforms ahead of welfare, but were not very successful. The East Asian Tigers added production for global markets, but were authoritarian. Moderate third-generation social democrats aimed at an improved 'developmental state' that adjusted to global market-driven growth combined with anti-corruption, democracy and welfare measures, but lost their way. Growth generated more inequality than jobs, the use of fossil energy spiralled, corruption endured, democracy stagnated and the welfare measures did not transform the dynamics. Coalition governments in Brazil, India and the Philippines fell, and those in Indonesia and South Africa beat a retreat. Meanwhile the first-generation growth pacts and welfare states in the North were undermined by neoliberalism and market-driven globalization. In the process social democrats lost support from liberal winners, environmentalists and the people left behind.

Insights analysed in this book suggest the impasse in the South may be overcome by resequencing social democratic development. The already-mentioned broad alliances for transformative R&W reforms, along with partnership governance, might serve as precursors to social growth pacts: firstly, by generating the necessary collective actors among labour and capital, and better governance; secondly, by calling for selected reforms that contribute to inclusive growth; and thirdly, by demanding more public redistribution than in the original model (like the supplementary Scandinavian pacts with farmers) to support survival along with balanced development and decent jobs in sectors that otherwise lose out in globalized markets.

Minimum programme coalitions

In others words, R&W-based growth is difficult but may be possible with broad alliances, democratic partnership governance and comprehensive reform proposals. Centre-left coalitions might stand a better chance than before with minimum programmes based on these principles. Thus, economic development and R&W may not bifurcate but converge. And social democrats can fight for these transformative dynamics without walking away from liberal-led coalitions, as some of them did during the 2010–16 Aquino government.

Social democratic development cooperation

International social democratic cooperation has lost steam. Early 'national internationalism' was based on support for every nation's capacity to develop its own transformative policy. This was undermined by the failure to introduce a 'New International Economic Order' along with a 'North-South Programme for Survival' and the expansion, instead, of market-driven globalization. Social democrats felt they had to adjust and try to benefit, while providing some assistance to the worst affected. The Socialist International degenerated and a new 'Progressive Alliance' is still in search of a forceful agenda. The efforts to tame the negative dynamics under the third wave of democracy have petered out. The centre-left combinations of global market-driven growth and R&W did not work well even in initially celebrated cases like Brazil. International agreements, including Agenda 2030, sound impressive but ignore how local progressives will be able to enforce them on the ground. Union-driven efforts to export the old social democratic growth and labour market model ignore seminal differences between the North and the South, neglecting contradictions between formal and informal labour, the need for broad alliances in favour of not just decent but also more jobs and associated R&W.

The book suggests this record of failure can be altered by international agreement on prioritizing support for those CSOs, unions and coalitions that relate their priorities to broad alliances for democratic R&W reforms and partnership governance towards sustainable growth.

This is not about altruism but actual development cooperation. The revival of Social Democracy calls for the internationalization of its cornerstones – popular-interest collectivities, democracy and R&W-based sustainable development.

This applies in the North too. Demands for more radical social democratic R&W policies at home, along with taxation of incomes from capital, not just wages, such as advocated by dissident followers in Britain and Sweden, are necessary. But as alternatives to populist and xenophobic 'defence' against globalization they are insufficient. There must also be an alternative internationalism.

This presupposes support for progressives in the South who can overcome the enticing conditions for the super exploitation of nature and people in their countries as this propels destructive globalization and undermines Social Democracy in the North too. Without stronger partners in the South who will struggle for inclusive and sustainable development, how will northern social democrats be able to implement ideas like as the 'global deal for decent jobs' and support a 'global green deal'? How can they resume efforts to alter unequal international trade regulations and the dominance of finance capital? How can they support and benefit from social and economic policies in the South that generate increasing demand in the South for non-destructive products and services from the North? How will they hold back climate change and reduce forced migration and the numbers of refugees, or contain pandemics? How will they develop viable alternatives to chauvinist policies in their own countries?

The way ahead

The prime challenge, then, is to model gradual reforms in the South that implement democratic R&W in such a way as to also promote sustainable growth and to identify the broad alliances of actors in politics and society that can come together in pressing for government support and democratic partnership governance. In cooperation with like-minded partners in the North. However, the insights collected and analysed in this book are insufficient for making further advances in thinking about what is possible and should be done. There is a need for more, from others. Many scholarly studies and activists' experiences in different contexts relate to this challenge. Our common results and insights should be brought together and deliberated. This calls for a joint forum, facilitated with social democratic-oriented practitioners. Efforts are ongoing. Interested readers are welcome to visit my homepage www.olle-tornquist.com for updates and follow-up analyses.

References

Introduction

The analyses and conclusions in this book are substantiated in my previous publications on the problems and options of social democratic-oriented development. For the details on sources *and* further references, one should thus consult these publications first hand. This appendix is meant as a guide to the publications that are relevant for each chapter. Readers who want to consult a specific source but cannot access the text may visit my homepage www.olle-tornquist.com. This is also where updates and follow-up analyses will be made available.

The guide also includes (i) notes about the interviews I made that are drawn upon and cited in this book and (ii) references to literature explicitly mentioned and new information and results by other scholars that I have benefitted from while writing this book but that are not referred to, or insufficiently referred to, in my previous work.

Chapter 1: The mystery and how to solve it

Anderson, B. (1991) *Imagined Communities*. London and New York: Verso (2nd revised and extended edition).
Anderson, B. (2016) *A Life beyond Boundaries*. London and New York: Verso.
Olin Wright, E. (2019) *How to Be an Anti-capitalist in the 21st Century*. London and New York. Verso.
See also Chapters 2 and 16.

Chapter 2: What is Social Democracy

The main sources *and* further references are in these works (in order of publication):

Rudebeck, L. and Törnquist, O. with Rojas, V. (Eds) (1998) *Democratization in the Third World: Concrete Cases in Comparative and Theoretical Perspective*. London and New York: Macmillan (1st edition 1996, Uppsala University: The Seminar for Development Studies).
Törnquist, O. (1999) *Politics and Development: A Critical Introduction*. London, Thousand Oaks and New Delhi: Sage Publications.
Harriss, J., Stokke, K. and Törnquist, O. (2004a) *Politicising Democracy: The New Local Politics of Democratisation*. Houndmills, Basingstoke: Palgrave.
Stokke, K. and Törnquist, O. (Eds) (2013a) *Democratization in the Global South. The Importance of Transformative Politics*. London and New York: Palgrave (Chapters 1, 2 and 14 by Stokke and Törnquist; Chapter 3 by Heller).
Törnquist, O., and Webster, N. and Stokke, K. (2009a) *Rethinking Popular Representation*. New York: Palgrave.

Törnquist, O. (2013d) *Assessing Dynamics of Democratisation. Transformative Politics, New Institutions and the Case of Indonesia.* New York: Palgrave.

Törnquist, O. and Harriss, J. with Chandhoke, N. and Engelstad, F. (Eds) (2016a) *Reinventing Social Democratic Development – Insights from Indian and Scandinavian Comparisons.* Copenhagen: NIAS books; New Delhi: Manohar (Chapters 1 and 2, by Törnquist and J. Harriss; Chapters 4, 7, 9 and 10 by H. Sandvik, T. Svensson, F. Engelstad and K. Moene about basic elements in northern Social Democracy, in addition to J. Harriss Chapter 5 and P. Bardhan's Chapter 12, on the challenges in the South).

Törnquist, O. (2018a) 'New Social Democracy in the South? Reflections from India, Indonesia and Scandinavia in Comparative Perspective'. In C. Tapscott, T. Halvorsen, and T. Cruz-Del Rosario (Eds) *The Democratic Development State. North-South Perspectives.* Stuttgart: Ibidem.

Törnquist, O. (2018b) 'Problems and Options of Renewing Social Democracy'. *CROP Poverty Briefs,* no. 46 (Special Issue on the democratic developmental state). https://www.crop.org/CROPNewsEvents/problems-and-options-of-renewing-social-democracy.aspx (last accessed 09.04.20).

Törnquist, O. (2020a) 'Dilemmas of Reformist Populism'. Forthcoming In C. Derichs, A. Andrea Fleschenberg, S. Sumrin Kalia and L. Knorr (Eds) *Local Responses to Global Challenges in Southeast Asia – A Trans-regional Studies Reader.* Based in Singapore: World Scientific Press.

Törnquist, O. (2020b) 'Challenges for Social Democracy in the South'. Forthcoming In Ø Bratberg, N. Brandal and D. E. Thorsen (Eds) 'Social Democracy in the 21st Century' *Comparative Social Research* 35.

Törnquist, O. (2020c) 'Contribution to the Critique of "Social Democracy in one country"'. Forthcoming In S. Nygård et al. *North and South: Rethinking the History of Post-War European Social Democracy.* Helsinki: Renew.

Additional references (in alphabetical order):

Anderson, B. (1991) *Imagined Communities ...* op. cit.

Augustin, O. G. (2020) *Left Wing Populism. The Politics of the People.* Bingley: Emerald.

Bengtsson, E. (2020) *Världens Jämlikaste Land?* Lund: Arkiv.

Hägglund, M. (2019) *This Life – Secular Faith and Spiritual Freedom.* New York: Pantheon.

Karleby, N. (2018 [1926]) *Socialism inför Verkligheten* (Socialism in the Face of Reality), most recent edition. Furusund: Greycat Publication House.

Mouffe, C. (2018) *For a Left-Populism.* London: Verso.

Mudde, C. and Kaltwasser, C. R. (2017) *Populism-A Very Short Introduction.* Oxford and New York: Oxford University Press.

Olin Wright, E. (2019) *How to Be an Anti-capitalist ...* op. cit.

Rudebeck, L. (1992) *When Democracy Makes Sense: Studies in the Democratic Potential of Third World Popular Movements.* AKUT: Uppsala University.

Sandbrook, R., Edelman, M., Heller, P., and Teichman, J. (2007) *Social Democracy in the Global Periphery: Origins, Challenges, Prospects.* Cambridge: Cambridge University Press.

Sandbrook, R. (2014) *Reinventing the Left in the Global South. The Politics of the Possible.* Cambridge: Cambridge University Press.

Wacquant, L. (Ed.) (2005) *Pierre Bourdieu and Democratic Politics.* Cambridge and Malden: Polity Press.

Chapter 3: Cases and contextual puzzles

Nil

Chapter 4: Progress and demise of the world's largest popular reform movement in Indonesia

The main sources *and* further references are in these works (in order of publication):

Törnquist, O. (1984a) *Dilemmas of Third World Communism: The Destruction of the PKI in Indonesia*. London: Zed Books (Indonesian translation 2011. Depok: Komunitas Bambu).

Törnquist, O. (1984b) *Struggle for Democracy – A New Option in Indonesia?* The Akut-series No. 33. Uppsala: Uppsala University.

Törnquist, O. (2019b) 'How Long Is Now? Of Indonesian Reformasi and Its Belated Reclaiming of the Cold War History'. *Kyoto Review* 26.

Törnquist, O. (2019c) 'The Legacies of the Indonesian Counter-revolution: New Insights and Remaining Issues'. *Journal of Contemporary Asia* (18 June), pp. 635-52, https://doi.org/10.1080/00472336.2019.1616105

Törnquist, O. (2021) 'The Missing New Indonesian Left', in 'New Mandala' and in Indonesian in 'Forum 100 Ilmuwan Sosial Politik LP3ES'. https://www.newmandala.org/part-1-the-missing-new-indonesian-left/https://www.newmandala.org/part-2-the-missing-new-indonesian-left/(last accessed 01.05.21)

Additional references (in alphabetical order):

Green, G. (1955) *The Quiet American*. London: Heinemann.

Melvin, J. (2018) *The Army and the Indonesian Genocide. Mechanics of Mass Murder.* Oxon: Routledge.

Robinson, G. B. (2018) *The Killing Season. A History of the Indonesian Massacres, 1965–66.* Princeton: Princeton University Press.

Roosa, J. (2006) *Pretext for Mass Murder. The September 30th Movement & Suharto's Coup D'état in Indonesia.* Madison: The University of Wisconsin Press.

Roosa, J. (2020) *Buried Histories. The Anticommunist Massacres of 1965–1966 in Indonesia.* Madison: The University of Wisconsin Press.

Interviews referred to (in first name alphabetical order):

Abdul Haris Nasution, Jakarta, 22/11/80. Djadi Wirosebroto, Jakarta, 26/11/80. Ina Slamet, Jakarta, 19/10/80. James C. Scott, Oslo, Spring 2002. Joesoef Isak, Jakarta 14/10/80, 25/2/91, 2/11/94. Mentioned in the text as 'typical statements': interviews in Indonesia late 1980 and in the Netherlands and Indonesia 1984. Sitor Situmorang Jakarta mid-1979. Suparna Sastra Diredja the Netherlands, 3/10/80.

Chapter 5: The rise and stagnation of Kerala's emancipatory Left

The main sources *and* further references are in these works (in order of publication):

Törnquist, O. (1989) *What's Wrong with Marxism? Volume I: On Capitalists and State in India and Indonesia.* New Delhi: Manohar.

Törnquist, O. (1991a) 'Communists and Democracy: Two Indian Cases and One Debate'. *Bulletin of Concerned Asian Scholars* 23:2, pp. 63–76. (Also Rudebeck, L. (Ed.) *When Democracy Makes Sense: Studies in the Democratic Potential of Third World Popular Movements.* AKUT, Uppsala: Uppsala University).

Törnquist, O. (1991c) *What's Wrong with Marxism? Volume II: On Peasants and Workers in India and Indonesia.* New Delhi: Manohar.

Törnquist, O. and Harriss, J. (2016b) 'Comparative Notes on Indian Experiments in Social Democracy: Kerala and West Bengal'. In O. Törnquist and J. Harriss, et al. (Eds) (2016a) *Reinventing Social Democratic Development ...* op. cit.

Interviews and discussions drawn upon referred to (in first name alphabetical order):

Ashok Mitra, Kolkata, 5/3/85. E.M.S. Namboodiripad, New Delhi, 14/3 85. Female extension officer, Ulloor, December 1990. Nalini Nayak, Thiruvananthapuram, 8/2/85. P. K. Michael Tharakan, Thiruvananthapuram, 4/2/85. T. M. Thomas Isaac, Thiruvananthapuram, 1/2/85.

Chapter 6: The 'people power' mystery in the Philippines

The main sources *and* further references are in this work (in order of publication):

Törnquist, O. (1991b) 'Communists and Democracy in the Philippines'. *Economic and Political Weekly* 26:27–8, pp 1683-91 and 29, pp. 1757-63. (Also with the title 'Democracy and the Philippine Left'. *Kasarinlan* 6:1–2, 1990.)

Additional references (in alphabetical order):

Quimpo, N. (2016) '"People Power" 1986 in Retrospect: A Conjunctural Analysis'. In J. Paul, S. Manzanilla and C. Hau (Eds) *Remembering/Rethinking EDSA.* Mandaluyong City: Anvil Publishing.

Sidel, John (2004) 'Bossism and Democracy in the Philippines, Thailand and Indonesia: Towards an Alternative Framework for the Study of "Local Strongman"'. In J. Harriss, K. Stokke and O. Törnquist (2004a) *Politicising Democracy: The New Local Politics of Democratisation,* op. cit.

Interviews, discussions and document referred to (in first name alphabetical order):

Bernabe 'Dante' Buscayno, Tarlac, Tarlac 25–26/03/90. Edicio 'Ed' De La Torre, the Netherlands, 03/05/90. Edicio 'Ed' De La Torre cited from Alex Magno 'CPP: Rethinking the Revolutionary Process', in *Diliman Review,* 34:4, p. 18. Etta Rosales, Quezon City 23/03/90. Francisco 'Dodong' and Anna Maria 'Princess' Nemenzo, Canberra, 01/05/84. Francisco 'Dodong' Nemenzo, Quezon City, 23/03/90. Horacio 'Boy' Morales, Quezon City, 27/03/90, Jesus Lava Quezon City, 19/01/90. Joma Sison, Utrecht, 03/05/90. Document: Plaridel Papers No 2, p. 2, August 1984.

Chapter 7: Effects in the North: From Swedish internationalism to 'Social Democracy in one country'

The main sources *and* further references are in these works (in order of publication):

Törnquist, O. (2016c) 'Implications for Scandinavian Social Democracy and International Cooperation'. In O. Törnquist and J. Harriss et al. (Eds) (2016a) *Reinventing Social Democratic Development* … op. cit.

Törnquist, O. (2020b) 'Challenges for Social Democracy in the South', op. cit.

Törnquist, O. (2020c) 'Contribution to the Critique of "Social Democracy in one country"', op.cit.

Additional reference (summarizing much research published in Swedish):

Therborn, G. (2018) 'Twilight of Swedish Social Democracy'. *New Left Review* 113, pp. 5–26.

Statements:

Göran Persson on China. https://www.svd.se/citat-svenska-ministrarna-om-kina (last accessed 14.04.2019).

Gro Harlem Bruntland on Indonesia. https://www.klassekampen.no/50623/article/item/null/slakteren-fra-jakarta (last accessed 14.04.19).

UN Special Rapporteur on extreme poverty and human rights. https://chrgj.org/2020/07/05/philip-alston-condemns-failed-global-poverty-eradication-efforts/ (last accessed 12.07.20).

Chapter 8: Philippine experiments for a democratic Left

The main sources *and* further references are in these works (in order of publication):

Törnquist, O. (1991b) 'Communists and Democracy in the Philippines', op. cit.

Törnquist, O. (1993) 'Democratic "Empowerment" and Democratisation of Politics: Radical Popular Movements and the May 1992 Philippine Elections', *Kasarinlan* 8:3. (Also *Third World Quarterly* 14:3, pp. 486–515.)

Törnquist, O. (1998a) 'Popular Movements and Politics of Democratisation. The Philippine Experience in Comparative Perspective'. In M. Mohanty and P. Mukherji with O. Törnquist (Eds) *People's Rights: Social Movements and the State in the Third World*. New Delhi, Thousand Oaks and London: Sage.

Törnquist, O. (1998c) 'Making Democratisation Work: From Civil Society and Social Capital to Political Inclusion and Politicisation – Theoretical Reflections on Concrete Cases in Indonesia, Kerala, and the Philippines'. In L. Rudebeck and O. Törnquist with V. Rojas (Eds) *Democratization in the Third World: Concrete Cases in Comparative and Theoretical Perspective*, op. cit.

Törnquist, O. (2002) *Popular Development and Democracy: Case Studies with Rural Dimensions in the Philippines, Indonesia and Kerala*. Geneva and Oslo: UNRISD and SUM.

Additional references (in alphabetical order):

Quimpo, N. (2008) *Contested Democracy and the Left in the Philippines after Marcos.* Quezon City: Ateneo de Manila University Press.

Rocamora, J. (2004), 'More than Difficult, Short of Impossible: Party Building and Local Governance in the Philippines'. In J. Harriss and K. Stokke and O. Törnquist (Eds) (2004a) *Politicising Democracy ...* op. cit.

Törnquist, O., Tharakan, P. K. M., and Quimpo, N. (2009) 'Popular Politics of Representation: New Lessons from the Pioneering Projects in Indonesia, Kerala and the Philippines'. In O. Törnquist, N. Webster, and K. Stokke (Eds) (2009a) *Rethinking Popular Representation*, op. cit.

Tolosa, B. T. Jr (Ed.) (2011) *Sosdem: Filipino Social Democracy in a Time of Turmoil and Transition, 1965–1995.* Manila: FES and Ateneo de Manila University Press.

Interviews and discussions drawn upon and referred to (first name alphabetical order):

Akbayan activists in General Santos, 5–6/05/98, Cebu City, 6–7/05/98, and in Bacolod, 29–30/4/98. Antoinette 'Toinette' Raquiza, Quezon City 07/05/98. Antoinette 'Toinette' Raquiza, Isagani 'Gani' Serrano and Lisa Dacanay, Quezon City, 02/02/98. Arman Alforque Cebu City 6–7/5/92 and 9/05/95. Bernabe 'Dante' Buscayno in Tarlac-Tarlac 29/04/95, 30/04/95 and with 'Dante' and Fatima Penilla 21/01/90, 24–26/03/90. Edicio 'Ed' De La Torre, Quezon City, 27/04/92, 02/02/98 and 03/12/02. Eduardo 'Ed' Tadem, Quezon City 01/02/98. Fatima Penilla, Quezon City, 24/03/95. Francisco 'Dodong' Nemenzo and Anna Maria 'Princess' Nemenzo, Quezon City 08/05/98. Francisco 'Dodong' Nemenzo Quezon City 04/12/02; Gerry Bulatao, Quezon City, 04/05/92. Gwen Ngo Laban and Timmy Tejedor, Cebu City, 06/05/92. Horacio 'Boy' Morales, Quezon City, 27/04/90 and 04/05/95. Isagani 'Gani' Serrano, Quezon City, 19/01/90, 20/03/90, 12/05/92 and 20/05/92. Joel Rocamora, Carmel Abao and Ronald Llamas, Quezon City 31/01/98 and 28/04/98. Karina Constantino-David, Quezon City 27/04/95, 02/05/95, 03/02/98. Lisa Dacanay, Bataan 13–16/05/92. Rosalita 'Lita' Nunez, General Santos, 05/05/98. Pandanon fishing cooperative members 7–9/05/92 and 6–7/05/95. *Pandayan*'s leading members D. Macasaet, A. Alegre, T. Salvador and R. Tuano, Quezon City 30/01/98; PRRM's male community organizers in Bataan, 15/05/92; Randolf 'Randy' David, Quezon City, 28/04/92; Ronald Llamas, Quezon City, 11/05/92. Ronald Llamas and Joel Rocamora Quezon City, 5–6/12/02. Satur Ocampo, Quezon City, December 05/12/02; Soliman 'Sol' Santos, Quezon City, 28/02/98.

Chapter 9: Rise and demotion of the Indonesian democracy movement

The main sources *and* further references are in these works (in order of publication):

Budiman, A., Törnquist, O., et al. (2001) *Aktor Demokrasi: Catatan Tentang Gerakan Perlawanan di Indonesia.* Jakarta: ISAI.

Stokke, K. and Törnquist, O. (2013e) 'Paradigmatic Failures of Transformative Democratic Politics: Indonesia and Sri Lanka in Comparative Perspective'. In K. Stokke and O.

Törnquist (Eds) *Democratization in the Global South. The Importance of Transformative Politics*. London and New York: Palgrave.

Törnquist, O. (1984b) *Struggle for Democracy – A New Option* ... op. cit.

Törnquist, O. (1989) *What's Wrong with Marxism*. Volume I ... op. cit.

Törnquist, O. (1990a) 'Notes on the State and Rural Change in Java and India'. In A. Budiman (Ed.) *State and Civil Society in Indonesia*, Centre of South East Asian Studies. Melbourne: Monash University.

Törnquist, O. (1990b) 'Rent Capitalism, State and Democracy'. In A. Budiman (Ed.) *State and Civil Society* ... op. cit.

Törnquist, O. (1991c) *What's Wrong with Marxism. Volume II* ... op. cit.

Törnquist, O. (1996) 'From New to Human Order in Indonesia?' *NIAS nytt*, No. 3, October. (Also *Economic and Political Weekly*, 31:40, pp. 2726–7.)

Törnquist, O. (1996) 'Old Communism Irrelevant'. *Jakarta Post*, 23 August.

Törnquist, O. (1997) 'Civil Society and Divisive Politicisation. Experiences from Popular Efforts at Democratisation in Indonesia'. In E. Özdalga and S. Persson (Eds) *Civil Society, Democracy and the Muslim World*. Istanbul and London: Swedish Research Institute & Curzon Press.

Törnquist, O. (1998d) 'The Indonesian Lesson'. *Bulletin of Concerned Asian Scholars* 30:3, pp. 79-81 (Also *Jakarta Post* August 1998, *Conjuncture* 10:3, and (with altered title) in Liddle, B. (Ed.) *Crafting Indonesian Democracy*. Jakarta: PPW-LIPI, Ford Foundation and Mizan Pustaka, 2001).

Törnquist, O. (1998b) 'Sizing up an Appropriate Electoral System'. *Jakarta Post*, 9 December.

Törnquist, O. (1999b) 'Birth of the World's Third Largest Democracy'. *Jakarta Post*, 2–3 July. (Also *Economic and Political Weekly*, 36:26, pp. 1666–67.)

Törnquist, O. (1999b) 'No Shortcut to Democracy: Olle Törnquist with Gerry van Klinken'. *Inside Indonesia* 57.

Törnquist, O. (1999c) 'Reconciliation a Must in East Timor'. *Jakarta Post*, 27–28 September. (Also *Economic and Political Weekly* 36:39, pp. 2784–85.)

Törnquist, O. (1998c) 'Making Democratisation Work ... ' op. cit.

Törnquist, O. (2000b) 'Dynamics of the Indonesian Democratisation'. *Third World Quarterly* 21:3, pp. 383–423. (Also *Economic and Political Weekly* 35:18, pp. 1559–75.)

Törnquist, O. (Ed.) (2000c) *Political Violence: Indonesia and India in Comparative Perspective*, SUM Report No. 9. Oslo: University of Oslo.

Budiman, A., Törnquist, O., et al. (2001) *Aktor Demokrasi: Catatan Tentang Gerakan Perlawanan di Indonesia*. Jakarta: ISAI.

Törnquist, O. (2004b) 'Labour and Democracy: Reflections on the Indonesian Impasse'. *Journal of Contemporary Asia* 34:3, pp. 377–399.

Stokke, K. and Törnquist, O. (2013e) 'Paradigmatic Failures of Transformative Democratic Politics: Indonesia and Sri Lanka in Comparative Perspective'. In K. Stokke and O. Törnquist (Eds) *Democratization in the Global South. The Importance of Transformative Politics*. London and New York: Palgrave.

Additional References (in alphabetical order):

Aspinall, E. (2005) *Opposing Suharto. Compromise, Resistance, and Regime Change in Indonesia*, Stanford: Stanford University Press.

Crouch, H. (1994) 'Democratic Prospects in Indonesia'. In D. Bourchier and J. Legge (Eds) *Democracy in Indonesia: 1950s and 1990s*. Clayton: Monash Asia Institute.

Lane, M. (2008) *Unfinished Nation. Indonesia before and after Suharto*. London and New York: Verso.

Mahsun, M. (2017) 'Peasants and Politics: Achievements and Limits of Popular Agency in Batang, Central Java'. *Contemporary Southeast Asia* 3, pp. 470–90.

Robison, R. (1986) *Indonesia, The Rise of Capital*. Sydney: Allen & Unwin.

Interviews and discussions drawn upon and referred to (first name alphabetical order):

Abdurrahman Wahid, Jakarta-Semarang, 15/11/94. Adi Sasono, Jakarta, 10/5/84, 24/5/84, 4/11/94, 13/8/96. AJI Independent Journalists' Association, Jakarta 18/12/98, Alfred Stepan: OT personal archives, LIPI conference August 12–13/98. Ali Sadikin, Jakarta, 8/11/94, 20/8/96, Ariel Heryanto, Salatiga 01/03/91. Arief Budiman, various places, 18–19/5/84 and (and regularly until 1999) of special importance for the text: 28/2/91, 01/3/91, 02/03/91, 22–24/4/92, 23/10/94, 15–16/11/94, 24/7/96, 31/5/99, Arief Djati, Surabaya (?), 28/7/96, Asmara Nababan, Jakarta, 11/11/94. Buyung Nasution, 03/11/94, 21/11/94, 18/8/96, 07/2/98, 08/12/98, 06/3/03. Chris Siner, Jakarta, 04/11/194, 28/8/96. Daniel Indrakusuma, Jakarta, 27/02/91. Dita Sari, Tangerang prison, 19/12/98. Fauzi Abdullah, 02/05/84, 17/7/96, 16/8/96, 04/02/99, 03/06/99, 30/11/02. *Gang Rode*, Jogjakarta, 04/03/91; 24/10/94. Gebjok interviews June 1999 and November 1999. George Aditjondro, Jogjakarta 24/10/94, Goenawan Mohamad, Jakarta, 12–13/8/96, 19/7/96, 05/02/98, 11/03/98, 25/11/02. Hariman Siregar, Jakarta, 14/5/84, 7/3/91. Johny Simanjuntak: various places, 03/03/91, 23/4/92, 28/10/94, 07/08/96; 04/06/99; June & November 1999 (Gebjok), 22/10/00, 26/10/17. Kartjono, Jakarta, 9/5/84, 14/11/94, 8/8/96, 5/2/98, 14/3/98. Kedung Ombo, conversations with villagers while touring the area: 03/03/91. Kwik Kian Gie 07/11/94. LBH internal seminar, Jakarta, 11/11/94. Liem Soei Long, the Netherlands, 11/4/84. Marsillam Simanjuntak, Jakarta, 03/11/94, 18/7/96. Marzuki Darusman, Jakarta,10/11/94, Matori Abdul Jallie, Jakarta, 09/11/94, 15/8/96. Muchtar Pakpahan, Jakarta, 4/12/98, 3/3/07. Mulyana Kusumah, Jakarta, 06/02/98. Munir, 08/12/98, 03/06/99, 31/10/00. Poncke Princen, Jakarta, 02/02/91, 05/03/91, 01/11/94. 'PKI-leaders', see Törnquist (1994a), (1994b) and Pak Bur et al. Jakarta, 06/03/91. PRD activists, Solo, 06/06/99, Rewang, Solo, 30/10/94. Stanley Adi Prasetyo 07/11/94, 06/3/91. 'Students, Jakarta', 13/08/98; 3–5/12/98. Teten Masduki, Jakarta, 11/11/94; 3/12/98. Teten Masduki & Mulyana Kusumah: 19/7/96, 21/8/96, 06/02/98, 02/06/99. Tigor 'Coki' Naipospos, Jakarta, 07/11/94. Todung Mulya Lubis, Jakarta, 07/11/94. Xanana Gusmão, Jakarta, 14/06/99.

Chapter 10: Dilemmas of deepening democracy after Suharto

The main sources *and* further references are in these works (in order of publication):

Törnquist, O. (1999b) *Birth of the World's Third Largest Democracy* ... op. cit.

Törnquist, O. (2000b) *Dynamics of the Indonesian Democratisation* ... op. cit.

Törnquist, O. (2000c) *An Open Letter to Indonesian Reformists, Jakarta Post*, 17 April.

Prasetyo, S. A., Priyono, A. E. and Törnquist, O. (Eds) (2003a) *Indonesia's Post-Soeharto Democracy Movement*. Jakarta and Copenhagen: Demos and NIAS Press.

Törnquist, O. with Prasetyo, S. A. and Priyono A. E. (2003b) 'Floating Democrats'. In S. A. Prasetyo, A. E. Priyono and O. Törnquist (Eds) (2003a) *Indonesia's Post-Soeharto's Democracy Movement* ... op. cit.

Harriss, J., Stokke, K., and Törnquist, O. (Eds) (2004a) *Politicising Democracy.* op. cit.

Törnquist, O. (2004b) *Labour and Democracy* ... op. cit.

Törnquist, O. (2004c) 'The Political Deficit of Substantial Democratisation'. In J. Harriss, K. Stokke and O. Törnquist (Eds) (2004a) *Politicising Democracy* ... op. cit.

Törnquist, O. (2004d) 'The Death of a Human Rights Campaigner'. *Jakarta Post,* 26 November.

Törnquist, O. (2005) 'The Mulyana Soap Opera'. *Tempo,* No 4.

Törnquist, O. (2006a) 'Assessing Democracy from below: A Framework and Indonesian Pilot Study', *Democratization* 13:2, pp. 227–55.

Törnquist, O. (2006b) 'The Political System Needs to be Opened'. Not Closed, *Jakarta Post,* 27 December.

Priyono, A. E, Samadhi, W. P. and Törnquist, O. (2007a) *Making Democracy Meaningful. Problems and Options in Indonesia.* Jogjakarta and Singapore: Demos, PCD Press, ISEAS.

Törnquist, O. (2007b) 'Muslim Politics and Democracy. The Case of Indonesia'. *Journal of Indonesian Islam* 1:1.

Törnquist, O., Tharakan, P. K. M. and Quimpo, N. (2009) 'Popular Politics of Representation: New Lessons from the Pioneering Projects in Indonesia, Kerala and the Philippines'. In O. Törnquist and N. Webster and K. Stokke (2009a) *Rethinking Popular Representation* ... op. cit.

Törnquist, O. (2009a), 'The Problem is Representation'. In O. Törnquist, and N. Webster and K. Stokke, *Rethinking Popular Representation,* op. cit.

Samadhi, W. P. and Warouw, N. (Eds) (2009c) *Building Democracy on the Sand. Advances and Setbacks in Indonesia.* Jogjakarta and Jakarta: PCD and Demos.

Törnquist, O. (2011) 'Dynamics of Peace and Democratisation: The Aceh Lessons'. *Democratization* 18:3, pp. 823–846.

Törnquist, O., Prasetyo, S. A. and Birks, T. (Eds) (2011) *Aceh: The Role of Democracy for Peace and Reconstruction.* Jogjakarta and Singapore: PCD and ISEAS.

Stokke, K. and Törnquist, O. (2013e) 'Paradigmatic Failures of Transformative Democratic Politics: Indonesia and Sri Lanka in Comparative Perspective'. In K. Stokke and O. Törnquist (Eds) (2013a) *Democratization in the Global South* ... op. cit.

Törnquist, O., Prasetyo, S. A., and Birks, T. (2014b) 'The Indonesian Marginalisation of Class Interests and Democracy'. In Indonesian in A. E. Priyono and Usman Hamid (Eds) *Merancang Arah Baru Demokrasi: Indonesia Pasca Reformasi.* Jakarta: KPG.

Törnquist, O. (2013d) *Assessing Dynamics of Democratisation* ... op. cit.

Additional references (in alphabetical order):

Beetham, D. (1999) *Democracy and Human Rights.* Oxford: Polity Press.

Caraway, T. L. and Ford, M. (2020) *Labor and Politics in Indonesia.* Cambridge: Cambridge University Press.

Interviews and discussions drawn upon and referred to (first name alphabetical order):

Abdon Nababan, Jakarta, 24/11/09, 21/11/10. Abrianto Amin, Samarinda, 28/11/13, Abu Muiyadi, Banjarbaru, 11/12/13. Alo Jamlean, *Kei Kecil,* 20/04/07, 21/10/17. Arbani et. al. in Insan, Kotabaru, 9–10/2/07. Arief Djati, Surabaya (?), 28/7/96. Azas Tigor Nainggolan, Jakarta, 21/09/07. Asmara Nababan 2006–7 (OT's archives from work with Demos). Bambang Widjojanto, Jakarta, 26/12/02 and frequent other discussions incl. with H. S Dillon. Bantul Citizen Forum: 15/02/07, Bengkulu PPR activists (incl. Usin and Muspani), Bengkulu, 8–13/12/07. Berry Nahdian Forqan, Jakarta, 9/12/13. Bjørn Blokhus, Jakarta, January 2004. Dahlan Jamaluddin, Banda Aceh, 22/11/09. Dita Sari, various places, January 2002, 5/12/06, 6/12/06, 11/11/09, 18/11/13. Discussions about Demos' work in Aceh (2007–8) and cooperation with the Olof Palme Center/Jan Hodann: OT's archives. Elyza Kissya, Pulau Haruku, 21–22/04/07. Erwin Schweisshelm, Jakarta, 06/05/08. Handoko, Batang and other places, 20–21/11/2006, 29–30/09/07, 05/05/08, 08/11/09; 5–6/11/13, 24/10/17. Hemma Sari, 25/10/01, 24/11/02, 29/10/13. Henci Petrus 'Fes' Efraim, *Kei Kecil*, 21/10/17. Hendardi 19/07/96, 3/12/98, 4/6/99. Irwandi Yusuf (via Aceh research team 2008–11). Juliana 'Uli' Jamlean, *Kei Kecil*, 21/10/17. KKJD-Demos' reference group among activists (OT's archives from work with Demos). Lerry Mboeik, Kupang and Jakarta, 1/4/07/09, 4/11/09. M. Nur Djuli, Banda Aceh and elsewhere, 25/09/07, 12/03/08, 21/11/09, 11/12/07, 17/03/08. Maria Ngamelumbun and Pieter Elmas, *Kei Kecil*, 20/04/07, 13/01/14. Muchtar Pakpahan, Jakarta, 04/12/98, 03/03/07, Muhammad Nazar, Banda Aceh, 26/04/07. Munawar Liza, Banda Aceh, 11/01/07, 22/11/09. Munir, Jakarta, January 2004. Muspani, Bengkulu, 05/10/07. Noorhalis Majid, Banjarmasin, 6–9/02/07; Papernas and PPR activists, Palu, 22/01/07, 25/01/07. Pieter Elmas, Jakarta, 31/07/19 (via Nusya Kuswantin). Poengky Indarty, Jakarta, 25/10/01. Putu Wirata Dwikora et al. of *KORdEM*, Bali, 10/02/17, 21/02/07, 12–13/11/09; 15/01/14; Ridha, 'Edhang' Saleh, Jakarta, 02/03/07, 05/12/07, 10/11/09. Roem Topatimasang, Kaliurang, 09/11/13. Sahat Lumbanraja, Medan and other places, 16–17/07/07, 27/09/07, 4/12/09, 03/12/13. Seram *Adat* leaders, 18/03/07. Shadia Marhaban, Banda Aceh and elsewhere, 25/09/07, 11/12/07, 12/03/08; participatory research team with book 2008–11. Syaiful Bahari, Jakarta, 05/12/06, 21/12/06, 05/10/07, 09/09/09. Taufiq Abda, Banda Aceh, 12/01/07, 16/03/08. Teten Masduki, Jakarta, 02/03/07, 30/10/07. Wardah Hafidz, Jakarta and elsewhere, 26/10/2000, 22/11/02, 26/10/02, 22/11/02, 17/11/06, 04/10/07, 12/11/13.

Chapter 11: Kerala renewal of Social Democracy

The main sources *and* further references are in these works (in order of publication):

Törnquist, O. (1995) (with P. K. M. Tharakan) *The Next Left? Democratisation and Attempts to Renew the Radical Political Development Project – The Case of Kerala* (with P. K. Michael Tharakan), NIAS, Copenhagen. (Also *Economic and Political Weekly* 31:28, 29, 30; 1996.)

Tharakan, P. K. Michael (1998) 'Socio-religious Reform Movements, Process of Democratization and Human Development: The Case of Kerala, South West India'. In L. Rudebeck and O. Törnquist with V. Rojas (Eds) *Democratisation in the Third World. Concrete Cases in Comparative and Theoretical Perspective.* London: Macmillan and St Martin's Press.

Tharakan, P. K. Michael (2000a) 'Of New Popular Politics of Development: The Kerala Experience'. In G. Parayil (Ed.) *Kerala: The Development Experience. Reflections on Sustainability and Replicability.* London: Zed Books.

Tharakan, P. K. Michael (2001) 'Movement, Politics and Development. The Case of Kerala'. *Social Scientist* 29:11–12.

Tharakan, P. K. Michael (2002) '*Popular Development and Democracy. Case Studies …* ' op. cit.

Tharakan, P. K. M. (2004) 'Historical Hurdles in the Course of the People's Planning Campaign in Kerala, India'. In J. Harriss, K. Stokke and O. Törnquist (Eds) (2004a) *Politicising Democracy …* op.cit.

Törnquist, O. (2004c) 'The Political Deficit of Substantial Democratisation'. In J. Harriss, K. Stokke and O. Törnquist (Eds) (2004a) *Politicising Democracy* ... op. cit.

Törnquist, O. (2007) 'The Politics of Democratic Decentralisation'. In M. A. Oommen (Ed.) *Decentralisation in Kerala: Experiences and Lessons.* New Delhi: Institute of Social Sciences & Har-Andand Publications.

Törnquist, O. with Tharakan, P. K. M. and Quimpo, N. (2009b), 'Popular Politics of Representation ... ' op. cit.

Törnquist, O. (2010b) 'Decentralisation and New Popular Politics of Representation: Recent Experiences and old Lessons', *Journal of Parliamentary Studies* 1:1.

Törnquist, O. and Harriss, J. (2016b) 'Comparative Notes on Indian Experiments: Kerala and West Bengal'. In O. Törnquist and J. Harriss et al. (Eds) (2016a) *Reinventing Social Democratic Development* ... op. cit.

Törnquist, O. (2019d) *Kerala Efforts at Inclusive Development in View of the Global Crisis of Social Democracy.* Thiruvananthapuram: the Kerala Council for Historical Research.

Additional references (in alphabetical order):

CPI-M (2001) Election review of the May 2001 Assembly Elections Adopted in the 11–12 August 2001 Meeting of the Central Committee Vol. 18:11.

Heller, P. (2013) 'Participation and Democratic Transformation: Building Effective Citizenship in Brazil, India and South Africa'. In K. Stokke and O. Törnquist (Eds) (2013a) *Democratization in the Global South* ... op. cit.

Heller, P., Harilal, K. N., Chaudhuri, S. (2007) 'Building Local Democracy: Evaluating the of Decentralization in Kerala, India'. *World Development* 35, no. 4.

Isaac, T. M. T. (2014) 'Politics of Democratic Decentralization in the Developmental State: A Study of the Kerala Experience'. In M. Williams (Ed.) *The End of the Developmental State?* New York: Routledge.

Isaac, T. M. T. and Franke, R. W. (2000) *Local Democracy and Development. People's Campaign for Decentralised Planning in Kerala.* Delhi: LeftWord (Updated edition 2002, Lanham and Oxford: Rowman & Littlefield).

Krishnakumar, R. (2000) 'Kerala Elections'. *Frontline* 17:21.

Rajesh., K. (2013) *Institutions and Practices: A Study of the People's Planning Campaign and the Kerala Development Programme.* PhD thesis, Institute for Social and Economic Change, Bangalore.

Shue, Vivienne (1994) 'State Power and Social Organisation in China'. In J. Migdal, A. Kohli and V. Shue (Eds) *State Power and Social Forces.* Cambridge: Cambridge University Press.

Williams, M. (2008) *The Roots of Participatory Democracy: Democratic Communists in South Africa and Kerala, India.* New York and Houndmills: Palgrave.

Interviews and discussions drawn upon and referred to (first name alphabetical order):

A. K. Balan, Thiruvananthapuram, 26/02/93. Binoy Viswam, Thiruvananthapuram, 06/01/02, DC (district collector; anonymous), 18/02/99, E.M.S. Namboodiripad, New Delhi, 14/03/85, Thiruvananthapuram, 18/02/96 (plus statement in *Deshabhmani,* 1 March 1991), E. M. Sreedaharan, 16/12/01. Govindan Nair, Thiruvananthapuram, 16/02/99. Harkishan Singh Surjeet, New Delhi, 14/03/85, 18/03/85. International Conference on Kerala Studies, Thiruvananthapuram, August 1994 (OT archives).

International Conference Planning Campaign, Thiruvananthapuram, 23–8 May 2000 (OT archives). K. K. George, Ernakulam, 05/01/02. Kalliasseri interviews, incl. with T. Gangadharan, 28/02/96. M. A. Oommen, Thiruvananthapuram, 11/03/93, 21/12/01. Mar Paulose, Thrissur, 26/02/93. M. K. Prasad, various, incl. 05/03/93, 23/02/96. M. P. Parameswaran, various places, 08/12/90, 21/02/93, 23/02/96, 10/12/96, 05/01/02. Mrs Gowri, Alappuzha, 06/03/93. P. K. Michael, various, 14/02/99 and continuous. R. Krishnakumar, 16/02/99; Srikumar Chattopadhyay, Thiruvananthapuram, 16/02/93, 13/2/96, 15/12/96. Subrata Sinha and Srikumar Chattopadhyay, Palakkad. IRTC, 06/12/90 at IRTC. T. M. Thomas Isaac, various places, incl. 14/02/99, 15/02/99, 17/02/99, 9–10/01/99. T. N. Seema, Thiruvananthapuram, 27/12/01. Veliyam Bharghavan, Thiruvananthapuram, 16/02/99, Interviews and discussions re. Resource Mapping in Vellore, 27/02/93. Interviews and discussions on the Planning Campaign during visits to villages 18(?)–2/02/99. V. S. Achutanandan, Thiruvananthapuram, 23/12/01, V. V. Raghavan, Thrissur, 22/02/93.
* Frequently consulted 'leading KSSP activists' (in addition to those mentioned in the text) included P. V. Unnikrishnan, T. Gangadharan and N. Jagajeevan.
* Frequently consulted 'intellectuals in the party' (in addition to those mentioned in the text) included E. M. Sreedaran, Govinda Pillai, M. A. Baby, C. P. Narayanan, T. N. Seena.
* IRTC seniors mentioned in text included Professors Subrata Sinha, Chandan Ray, M. K. Prasad IRTC 24–25/02/93.

Chapter 12: Counter-movements in India?

Parts of this chapter were insufficiently covered in my previous research. I have therefore made follow-up studies and consulted colleagues. With regard to the sections on new movements, activism and AAP, I am particularly thankful for comments and continuous discussions with John Harriss, as well as to conversations with Neera Chandhoke, Niraja Gopal Jayal, Reetika Khera, Sanjay Ruparelia, and inputs and assistance from Radhika Chatterjee.

***

The sources *and* further references regarding **West Bengal** are (in alphabetical order) in:
Bag, Kheya (2011) 'Red Bengal's Rise and Fall'. *New Left Review* 70, July–August, pp. 69–98.
Bardhan, P., Mitra, S., Mookherjee, D. and Nath, A. (2009) 'Local Democracy and Clientelism: Implications for Political Stability in Rural West Bengal'. *Economic and Political Weekly* 44:9, pp. 46–58.
Bardhan, P., Mitra, S., Mookherjee, D. and Nath, A. (2014) 'Changing Voting Patterns in Rural West Bengal: Role of Clientelism and Local Public Goods'. *Economic and Political Weekly* 49:11, pp. 54–62.
Bhattacharya, D. (2009) 'Of Control and Factions: The Changing "Party-Society" in Rural West Bengal'. *Economic and Political Weekly* 44:9, pp. 59–69.
Bhattacharya, D. (2010), 'Left in the Lurch: The Demise of the World's Longest Elected Regime?' *Economic and Political Weekly* 45:3, pp. 51–9.
Kohli, A. (1987) *The State and Poverty in India: The Politics of Reform*. Cambridge: Cambridge University Press.

Mukherji, R., Jha, H., and Roy, M. N. (2019) 'Ideas and Policy Paradigms: Explaining the Fall of Welfare Politics in West Bengal'. *Indian Politics & Policy* 2:2, pp. 53–80.

Nielsen, B. K. (2018) *Land Dispossession and Everyday Politics in Rural Eastern India.* London and New York: Anthem.

Törnquist, O. (1991a) 'Communists and Democracy: Two Indian Cases' op. cit.

Törnquist, O. and Harriss, J. (2016b) 'Comparative Notes on Indian Experiments: Kerala and West Bengal'. In O. Törnquist and J. Harriss et al. (Eds) (2016a) *Reinventing Social Democratic Development* ... op. cit.

The statement by Benoy Choudhury is quoted from *Mainstream* Vol. LIII, No. 40, 2015.

Logbook: Törnquist, O. Observations and conversations in West Bengal, 1992.

***

The sources *and* further references on **new activism and AAP** are (in alphabetical order) in:

Agarwala, R. (2013) *Informal Labor, Formal Politics, and Dignified Discontent in India.* Cambridge: Cambridge University Press.

Chandhoke, N. (2016) 'The Chequered History of Social Rights in India'. In O. Törnquist and J. Harriss et.al. (Eds) (2016a) *Reinventing Social Democratic Development* ... op. cit.

Chatterjee, R. (2017) *The Politics of the Aam Aadmi Party: Promise and Performance,* Paper to workshop on Governing Urbanizing India: Citizenship, Policy and Politics, Oslo, 8th–9th June 2017.

Harriss, J. (2016) 'What Are the Prospects for a Social Democratic Alliance in India Today?' In O. Törnquist and J. Harriss et al. (Eds) (2016a) *Reinventing Social Democratic Development* ... op. cit.

Harriss, J., Jeffrey, C. and Brown, T. (2020) *India: Continuity and Change in the 21st Century.* Cambridge: Polity.

Jenkins, R. (2019) 'India 2019: A Transformative Election?' *Pacific Affairs* 92:3, pp. 475–97.

Jenkins, R. and Manor, J. (2017) *Politics and the Right to Work: India's National Rural Employment Guarantee Act.* New York: Oxford University Press.

Karat, P. (1984) 'Action Groups/Voluntary Organisations: A Factor in Imperialist Strategy'. *The Marxist*, April–June.

Naqvi, S. (2015) *Capital Conquest: How the AAP's Incredible Victory Has Redefined Indian Elections.* Gurgaon: Hatchette.

Outlook (2018) March thematic issue on AAP. https://www.outlookindia.com/magazine/issue/11558 (last accessed 07.04.20).

Palshikar, S. (2013) 'Of Radical Democracy and Anti-Partyism', *Economic and Political Weekly* 48:10, pp. 10–13.

Palshikar, S. (2016) 'Who Is Delhi's Common Man?' *New Left Review* 98, March–April, pp. 113–28.

Ramani, S. (2013a) 'For a Minimum Living Wage: Workers' March to Parliament', *Economic and Political Weekly* 48:52, pp. 12–14.

Ramani, S. (2013b) 'The Aam Aadmi Party's Win in Delhi: Dissecting It through Geographical Information Systems'. *Economic and Political Weekly*, Web Exclusive http://www.epw.in/journal/2013/52/web-exclusives/aam-aadmi-partys-win-delhidissecting-it-through-geographical.m (last accessed 07.04.20).

Roy, S. (2014) 'Being the Change: The Aam Aadmi Party and the Politics of the Extraordinary in Indian Democracy'. *Economic and Political Weekly* 49:15, pp. 45–54.

Ruparelia, S. (2013) 'India's New Rights Agenda: Genesis, Promises, Risks'. *Pacific Affairs* 86:3, pp. 569–90.

Saxena, N. C. (2016) 'Governance Reforms in India'. In O. Törnquist and J. Harriss et al. (Eds) (2016a) *Reinventing Social Democratic Development* ... op. cit.

Shukla, S. (2013) 'Myopia, Distortions and Blind Spots in the Vision Document of AAP'. *Economic and Political Weekly* 48:7, pp. 16–18.

Shyam Sundar, K. R. (2019) 'Dynamics of General Strikes in India'. *Economic and Political Weekly* 54:3, pp. 22–4.

Tawa Lama-Rewal, S. (2019) 'Political Representation in the Discourse and Practices of the "Party of the Common Man" in India'. *Politics and Governance* 7:3, DOI:10.17645/pag.v7i3.2122

The Hindu, 14/02/16, Review of APP's governance performance.

The Hindu's and *Frontline's* 2020 review of the Delhi Assembly election.

Notes:

*The references in the text to Supriya Roy Chowdhury and M. Vijayabaskar are from Harriss (2016).

*The note on applicants to India's rail service is from Jenkins (2019) and https://www.reuters.com/article/us-india-unemployment-railways/more-than-25-million-people-apply-for-indian-railway-vacancies-idUSKBN1H524C (last accessed 07.04.20).

Interviews and discussions drawn upon and referred to:

Prakash Karat, New Delhi March 1985. Yogendra Yadav, New Delhi, August 2012. Prashant Bhushan 15/11/18 (via Radhika Chatterjee).

***

The main sources and further references on **Kerala** are (in order of publication) in:

Törnquist, O. and Harriss, J. (2016b) 'Comparative Notes on Indian Experiments: Kerala and West Bengal'. In O. Törnquist and J. Harriss, et al. (Eds) (2016a) *Reinventing Social Democratic Development* ... op. cit.

Törnquist, O. (2019d) *The Kerala Efforts at Inclusive Development* ... op. cit.

Törnquist, O. (2021) 'Comparative Swedish and Kerala Notes on the Pros and Cons of Decentralisation in Fighting the Corona'. In Joseph Tharamangalam and Jos Chathukulam, *Cooperativism, Self-management and Decentralised Development* (forthcoming. Routledge).

Törnquist, O. (2021) *Linking Public Action,* Essay to publication based on the International Webinar on 'Rethinking the Role of Local Governments in a post Covid-19 World'. 10–14 December 2020, Central University of Kerala and CRM, Kottayam, Kerala.

Additional references (in alphabetical order):

Harilal, K. N. (2014) 'Confronting Bureaucratic Capture. Rethinking Participatory Planning Methodology in Kerala'. *Economic and Political Weekly* 48:36, pp. 52–60

The Hindu, The Wire and *Frontline – continuous reports.*

Interviews and discussions drawn upon:

I am particularly thankful for comments and continuous discussions with P. K. Michael Tharakan in addition to J. Chathukulam, J. Devika, B. Ekbal, M. Eapen, K. K. George, K. N. Harilal, T. M. T. Isaac, M. S. John, N. Nayak, M. A. Oommen, J. Prabash and K. Rajesh.

Chapter 13: Inconclusive left-of-centre politics in the Philippines

Like Chapter 12, parts of this chapter were insufficiently covered in my previous research, which prompted follow-up-studies, with kind support from colleagues. Special thanks to T. Encarnacion-Tadem, E. Tadem, N. Quimpo, J. Rocamora, R. Llamas, M. Cabreros, R. David and the late K. Constantino-David; plus F. Pecson, kindly dispatching books when neither of us could travel in corona times.

***

The sources *and* further references are in these works (in alphabetical order):

Abinales, P. N. (Ed.) *The Revolution Falters: The Left in Philippine Politics after 1986.* Ithaca, NY: Southeast Asia Programme Publications, Cornell University.

Bello, W. (2015) 'Why I resigned as *Akbayan's* rep in Congress', https://news.abs-cbn. com/blogs/opinions/06/12/15/why-i-resigned-*akbayans*-rep-congress (last accessed 11/04/2021).

Bello, W. (2014) 'Agrarian Reform: Powerful Law, Ineffectual Bureaucracy'. In *Philippine Daily Inquirer*, 10 June.

Bello, W. (2019) *Counter-revolution: The Global Rise of the Far Right.* Rugby, Warwickshire: Practical Action.

Carvajal, N. C. (2013), 'NBI probes P10-B scam'. In *Philippine Daily Inquirer*, 12 July.

Cay, G. D. and Nonat V. (2014) '*Akbayan* Gives in to LP Framework'. In *Philippine Daily Inquirer*, 13 July.

Cayadong, P. M. Esguerra, J., Labajo, M. and Rocamora, J. (2017) *Rearranging Local-Central Government Relations: The 'Bottom Up Budgeting (BUB) Program.* Draft manuscript 09.26.17.

Curato, N. (Ed.) (2017) *A Duterte Reader.* Quezon City: Buhhaw, Ateneo de Manila University Press.

Dressel, B. (2012) 'Targeting the Public Purse: Advocacy Coalitions and Public Finance in the Philippines'. *Administration and Society* 44 (6 supplementary) https://news.abs-cbn. com/blogs/opinions/06/12/15/why-i-resigned-*akbayans*-rep-congress (last accessed 08.04.20).

Nathan G. Quimpo (2008) *Contested Democracy and the Left in the Philippines after Marcos.* Quezon City: Ateneo de Manila University Press.

Rodan, G. (2018) *Participation without Democracy: Containing Conflict in Southeast Asia.* Ithaca and London: Cornell University Press.

Thompson, M. (2016) 'Bloodied Democracy: Duterte and the Death of Liberal Reformism in the Philippines'. *Journal of Current Southeast Asian Affairs* 35:3, pp. 39–68.

Törnquist, O., Tharakan, P. K. M., and Quimpo, N. (2009) 'Popular Politics of Representation: New Lessons from the Pioneering Projects in Indonesia, Kerala and the Philippines'. In O. Törnquist, N. Webster and K. Stokke (Eds) (2009a) *Rethinking Popular Representation* ... op. cit.

Interviews and discussions drawn upon and referred to (first name alphabetical order):

Anna Maria 'Princess' Nemenzo, Quezon City, 02/12/02. Carmel Abao, Quezon City, 03/12/02. Ed Tadem 12/11/17. Edicio 'Ed' De La Torre, Quezon City, 03/12/02. Etta Rosales, Quezon City, 02/12/02, 18/11/17; Francisco 'Dodong' Nemenzo, Quezon City, 04/12/02, 13/11/17. Gerry Bulatao, Quezon City, 04/12/02. Jennifer Albano, Quezon City, 17/11/17. Joel Rocamora Quezon City, 05/06/12, 11/11/17, Oslo, 29–30/11/17. Josua Mata, Quezon City, 19/11/17. Karina Constantino-David, Quezon City, 05/12/02. Lisa Dacanay and Isagani 'Gani' Serrano, Quezon City, 3/12/02, 15/11/17. Marie Chris 'Machris' Cabreros, Quezon City, 17/11/17, Stockholm. 13/11/19. Mariquit 'Kit' Melgar, Quezon City, 12/11/17. Orlando 'Marlon' Quesada and Josua Mata 02/12/02, Nathan Quimpo, Skype, 05/06/19. Orlando 'Marlon' Quesada 17/11/17. Randy David & Karina Constantino-David, Quezon City, 12/11/17, Ric Reyes, Quezon City, 5/12/02, 16/11/17. Risa Hontiveros, Stockholm, 13/11/19. Ronald Llamas and Joel Rocamora, Quezon City, 5–6/12/02. Ronald Llamas, Makati, 05/12/02, 19/11/17. Satur Ocampo, Quezon City, 05/12/02.

Chapter 14: Whither 'reformist populism'? The Indonesian experience

The main sources *and* further references are (in order of publication) in these works:

Works on earlier history, see references for Chapter 4.

Törnquist, O., Prasetyo, S. A., and Birks, T. (Eds) (2011) *Aceh: The Role of Democracy for Peace and Reconstruction* ... op. cit.

Mahadi, S., Nurdin, M. R. with Avonius, L. and Törnquist, O. (Eds) (2013) *Local Democracy in Post-Conflict Society: The Case of Aceh Selatan, Indonesia.* Denpasar: Pustaka Larasan.

Törnquist, O. (2013) 'Popular Aspirations, Decentralization and Local Democracy'. In Öjendal, J. and A. Dellnäs (Eds) *Imperative of Good Local Governance: Challenges for the Next Decade of Decentralization.* Tokyo: United Nations University Press.

Savirani, A. and Törnquist, O. (Eds) (2015) *Reclaiming the State. Overcoming Problems of Democracy in Post-Soeharto Indonesia.* Jogjakarta: PolGov and PCD.

Djani, L. and Törnquist, O. with Tanjung, O. and Tjandra, S. (2017b) *Dilemmas of Populist Transactionalism. What Are the Prospects Now for Popular Politics in Indonesia?* Jogjakarta: PolGov and PWD.

Hiariej, E. and Stokke, K. (Eds) (2017a) *Politics of Citizenship in Indonesia.* Jogjakarta: Pustaka Obor and Polgov.

Törnquist, O. (2017c) 'The Downside of Indonesia's Successful Liberal Democratisation and the Way Ahead. Notes from the Participatory Surveys and Case Studies 2000–2016'. *Journal of Current Southeast Asian Affairs* 36:1, pp. 123–138.

Törnquist, O. (2019a) 'Lots of Votes – Little Voice: Indonesia's 2019 Presidential and Parliamentary Elections'. *Pacific Affairs* 92:3, pp. 459–474.

Bourchier, D. M. (2019) 'Two Decades of Ideological Contestation in Indonesia: From Democratic Cosmopolitanism to Religious Nationalism'. *Journal of Contemporary Asia* 49:5, pp. 713–733.

Diprose, R., McRae, D. and Hadiz, V. R. (2019) 'Two Decades of Reformasi in Indonesia: Its Illiberal Turn'. *Journal of Contemporary Asia* 49:5, pp. 691–712.

Törnquist, O. (2020a) 'Dilemmas of Reformist Populism' ... op. cit.

Additional references (in alphabetical order):

Augustin, O. G. (2020) *Left Wing Populism* ... op. cit.

Caraway, T. L. and Ford, M. (2020) *Labor and Politics in Indonesia,* op. cit.

Ford, M. and Pepinsky, T. (Eds) (2014) *Beyond Oligarchy: Wealth, Power and Contemporary Indonesian Politics.* Ithaca, NY: Cornell Southeast Asia Program.

Hadiz, V. R. (2014) *Islamic Populism in Indonesia and the Middle East.* Cambridge: Cambridge University Press.

Lane, M. (2019) *An Introduction to Politics of the Indonesian Union Movement.* Singapore: ISEAS.

Manor, J. (2013) 'Post-clientelist Initiatives'. In K. Stokke and O. Törnquist (Eds) (2013a) *Democratization in the Global South ...,* op. cit.

Mietzner, M. (2018) 'Fighting Illiberalism with Illiberalism: Islamist Populism and Democratic Deconsolidation in Indonesia'. *Pacific Affairs* 91:2, pp. 261–82.

Power, T. and Warburton, E. (Eds) (2020) *Democracy in Indonesia: From Stagnation to Regression?* Singapore: ISEAS.

Pratikno and C. Lay (2013) 'From Populism to Democratic Polity: Problems and Challenges in Solo, Indonesia'. In K. Stokke and O. Törnquist (Eds) (2013a) *Democratization in the Global South,* op. cit.

Seekings, J. (2013) 'Is the South "Brazilian"? The Public Realm in Urban Brazil through a Comparative Lens'. *Policy & Politics* 43:3, pp. 351–70.

Van Klinken, G. and W. Berenschot (Eds) (2014) *In Search of Middle Indonesia: Middle Classes in Provincial Towns.* Leiden: Brill.

Interviews and discussions drawn upon and referred to:

Logbooks: Törnquist, O. Observations and conversations Indonesia 2005–19. Including meetings and briefing with co-researchers Luky Djani, Osmar Tanjung, Surya Tjandra and M. Didit Saleh.

Informal workshops organized by the author and co-researchers with reflective activists:

Closed workshops with Bandung activists CSOs, 30/03/13–01/04/13.

Closed workshop with Kompip-related activists, Solo, 4/11/13.

Closed workshop with labour organizers (including Iqbal), Jakarta, 21/12/13.

Closed workshop with PDI-P and Jokowi advisors, Jogjakarta, 02/11/17.

Closed workshop with pro-Jokowi activists cum experts, Jakarta, 21/11/13.

Closed workshop with Surabaya activists, Surabaya, 02/11/13.

Closed workshop with women activists related to PNA, Banda Aceh, 22/01/14, 27/10/17.

Workshop and conversations in Tapaktuan (South Aceh) late September–early October 2010 and February 2011.

Interviews (specifically drawn on in the chapter; first name alphabetical order):

Akbaroedin Arief, Solo, 04/11/13, 06/10/17. Akhmad Ramdon, Solo, 06/10/17. Carolinie Paskarina, Bandung, 01/11/13. Faisal Basri, Jakarta, 13/03/07, 20/11/13.

Dhalan Jamaluddin, Banda Aceh, 22/11/09. Darwati Gani, Banda Aceh, 21/01/14. Eko Sulistyo, Jakarta, 27/11/12. Faisal Ridha, Banda Aceh, 21/01/14. Hendri Yuzal, Banda Aceh, 31/10/17. Irwandi Yusuf, 27(?)02/11, 31/10/17. Lita Anggraini, Jakarta, 07/12/13. Munawar Liza, Banda Aceh, 22/11/09, 21/01/14. M. Nur Djuli, Banda Aceh to Lhokseumawe, 7–8/06/13. Nezar Patria, Jakarta, 31/10/18. Obon Tabroni, Bekasi, 09/12/14, 06/11/17. Otto Samsjuddin, Banda Aceh, 28/10/17. Rieke Pitaloka, Jakarta, 20/11/13, 11/12/13, 17/10/17. Said Iqbal, Bekasi, 06/12/13. Sely Martini, Bandung, 30/10/13. Shadia Marhaban and M. Nur Djuli, Banda Aceh, 12/03/08, 17/03/08, 21/11/09, 18/01/14, 21–22/01/14, 27–28/10/17, and via phone 31/10/17. Shaivannur M. Yusuf, Jakarta, 16/10/17. Taufiq Abda, Banda Aceh, 20/01/14, 30/10/17. Teten Masduki, Jakarta, 25/10/17. Thamrin Ananda, Banda Aceh, 19/01/14, 31/10/17.

Chapter 15: Implications and options in the North: the Swedish stalemate

The main sources *and* further references are in these works:

Törnquist, O. (2016c) 'Implications for Scandinavian Social Democracy and International Cooperation' ... op. cit.
Törnquist, O. (2020b) 'Challenges for Social Democracy in the South' ... op. cit.
Törnquist, O. (2020c) 'Contribution to the critique of "Social Democracy in one country"' ... op. cit.

Additional references (in alphabetical order):

Brochmann, G. *'From Bounded Universalism to the Trial of Internationalization: Migration and Social Democracy in Scandinavia'*. Forthcoming in Bratberg, Ø, Brandal, N., and Thorsen D. E. (Eds) 'Social Democracy in the 21st Century'. *Comparative Social Research* 35.
Färm, D. A.-M. Lindgren, Rynoson. M. and Stjernkvist, L. (2020) *Ordning och reda i vandringstid. En mer hållbar, rättvis och integrationsdriven asyl och migrationspolitik.* Stockholm: Tankesmedjan Tiden.
Kansliet för strategisk analys (2014) *Strategiska trender i globalt perspektiv 2025: en helt annan värld?* Stockholm: Utrikesdepartementet.
Linde, A. (2019) 'Murarna reser sig'. *Tiden* 2, pp. 58–60.
Moula, P. (2019) 'En förnyad inriktning för Tiden'. *Tiden* 2, p. 7.
Therborn, G. (2018) 'Twilight of Swedish Social Democracy', op. cit.

Interviews and discussions drawn upon and referred to:

Logbook
Törnquist, O.: Observations and conversations during the Progressive Alliance Convention and 'Palme Days', Stockholm, 15–17/11/19.

Interviews and statements (drawn on in the chapter; first name alphabetical order):

Carl-Mikael Jonsson (Swedish LO), Stockholm, 10/11/15. Ingemar Lindberg (former LO researcher), e-mail 03/11/15 and 05/11/15. Oscar Ernerot (Swedish LO) 21/11/19, Johan Hassel (International secretary Swedish Social Democratic Party)

16/11/19, Stockholm, 16/11/19. Mikael Leyi (head international unit Olof Palme Center), Stockholm, 17/11/19. Anna Sundström (general secretary, Olof Palme Center), Stockholm, 17/11/19. Mats Wingborg (independent trade unions researcher), via telephone, 19/11/19. Sofia Östmark (head of the Swedish 'Union-to-Union' association), via telephone, 26/11/19.
- Statement by Ann Linde (Swedish Minister for Foreign Affairs) in panel discussion 'Palme Days', Stockholm, 16.11.19.
- Statement by Kenneth G. Forslund Member of Swedish Parliament and Chairperson of its Foreign Affairs Committee (in Swedish: 'Jag tycker inte att politiken ska sitta och besluta affär för affär om svensk vapenexport'). https://www.svt.se/nyheter/inrikes/sverige-saljer-krigsmateriel-som-kan-anvandas-i-jemenkriget; (accessed 14.04.2019).

Chapter 16: Lessons for a new Social Democracy

References for wider comparisons (in alphabetical order):

Acemoglu, D. (2020) 'Social Democracy Beats Democratic Socialism', *Project Syndicate*, 20 February. https://www.project-syndicate.org/commentary/social-democracy-beats-democratic-socialism-by-daron-acemoglu-2020-02?utm_source=Project±Syndicate ±Newsletter&utm_campaign=2173367897-sunday_newsletter_23_02_2020&utm_medium=email&utm_term=0_73bad5b7d8-2173367897-104764633&mc_cid=2173367897&mc_eid=e2cc4949c3

Alvarez, S. E., Rubin, J. W., Thayer, M., Baiocchi, G. and Laó-Monten, A. (Eds) (2017) *Beyond Civil Society. Activism, Participation, and Protests in Latin America*. Durham: Duke.

Baiocchi, G., Braathen, E. and Teixeira, A. C. (2013) 'Transformation Institutionalised? Making Sense of Participatory Democracy in the Lula Era'. In K. Stokke and O. Törnquist (Eds) (2013a) *Democratization in the Global South ...* op. cit.

Bull, B. 'Social Movements and the "Pink Tide" Governments in Latin America: Transformation, Inclusion and Rejection'. In K. Stokke and O. Törnquist (Eds) (2013a) *Democratization in the Global South ...* op. cit.

Heller, P. (2013) 'Participation and Democratic Transformation: Building Effective Citizenship in Brazil, India and South Africa'. In K. Stokke and O. Törnquist (Eds) (2013a) *Democratization in the Global South ...* op. cit.

Nattrass, N. and Seekings, J. (2019) *Inclusive Dualism. Labour-intensive Development, Decent Work, and Surplus Labour in Southern Africa*. Oxford: Oxford University Press.

Olin Wright, E. (2019) *How to Be an Anti-capitalist ...* op. cit.

Palme, O. *Why I am a Democratic Socialist* https://www.youtube.com/watch?v= 7i2Ws1X5DSA (most recently accessed 08.05.20). Palme was inspired in particular by Nils Karleby's ideas of 'functional socialism', see his *Socialism inför Verkligheten* (Socialism in the Face of Reality), op. cit.

Sandbrook, R. (2014) *Reinventing the Left in the Global South. The Politics of the Possible*, op. cit.

Seekings, J. and Nattrass, N. (2015) *Policy, Politics and Poverty in South Africa*. Houndmills, Basingstoke: Palgrave.

Stiglitz, J. (2019), *People, Power, and Profits – Progressive Capitalism for an Age of Discontent*. New York: W. W. Norton & Company.

Svensson, T. (2016) 'Strengthened Control of Fostering Trust? Indian Politics and Scandinavian Experiences'. In O. Törnquist and J. Harriss et al. (Eds) (2016a) *Reinventing Social Democratic Development* ... op. cit.

Therborn, G. (2012) 'Class in the 21st Century'. *New Left Review* 78, pp. 5–29.

Therborn, G. (2014) 'New Masses?' *New Left Review* 85, pp. 7–11.

Chapter 17: Towards a roadmap

Nil

Consolidated Index